Latin American Education

Latin American Education

Comparative Perspectives

EDITED BY

Carlos Alberto Torres
Adriana Puiggrós

WestviewPress

A Division of HarperCollins*Publishers*

For Carlos and Nicole (CAT)
Para los chicos (AP)

Copyright © 1997 by Westview Press, A Division of HarperCollins Publishers, Inc.

Published in 1997 in the United States of America by Westview Press, 5500 Central Avenue, Boulder, Colorado 80301-2877, and in the United Kingdom by Westview Press, 12 Hid's Copse Road, Cumnor Hill, Oxford OX2 9JJ

Library of Congress Cataloging-in-Publication Data
Latin American education : comparative perspectives / edited by Carlos
    Alberto Torres and Adriana Puiggrós.
      p. cm.
    Includes bibliographical references.
    ISBN 0-8133-8978-X (hc)
    1. Education and state—Latin America—Cross-cultural studies.
2. Basic education—Latin America—Cross-cultural studies.
3. Education, Higher—Latin America—Cross-cultural studies.
4. Popular education—Latin America—Cross-cultural studies.
5. Educational change—Latin America—Cross-cultural studies.
I. Torres, Carlos Alberto.   II. Puiggrós, Adriana.
LC92.A2L38   1997
379.8—dc21   96-49253
                                                                      CIP

The paper used in this publication meets the requirements of the American National Standard for Permanence of Paper for Printed Library Materials Z39.48-1984.

10   9   8   7   6   5   4   3   2   1

Contents

Acknowledgments   *vii*

Introduction: The State and Public Education in Latin America
Carlos Alberto Torres and Adriana Puiggrós   1

PART ONE
THE POLITICAL ECONOMY OF
EDUCATIONAL REFORM IN LATIN AMERICA

1   **Financing Education for Democracy in Latin America**
    Ernesto Schiefelbein   31

2   **Education Policy and Human Development in the
    Latin American City**
    José Luis Coraggio   65

3   **Neoliberal Education Policies in Latin America:
    Arguments in Favor and Against**
    Robert F. Arnove   79

PART TWO
BASIC EDUCATION IN LATIN AMERICA

4   **Dewey Under South American Skies:
    Some Readings from Argentina**
    Inés Dussel and Marcelo Caruso   103

5   **Contemporary Brazilian Education:
    Challenges of Basic Education**
    Moacir Gadotti   123

6   The Problems of the Decentralization of
    Education: A View from Mexico
    Sylvia Schmelkes   149

7   Teacher Education Reform Initiatives:
    The Case of Mexico
    Maria Teresa Tatto and Eduardo Velez   165

PART THREE
HIGHER EDUCATION IN LATIN AMERICA:
ARGENTINA IN COMPARATIVE PERSPECTIVE

8   The Paradox of the Autonomy of Argentine
    Universities: From Liberalism to Regulation
    Marcela Mollis   219

9   University Restructuring in Argentina:
    The Political Debate
    Daniel Schugurensky   237

10 Women, Education, and the State in Cuba
    Sheryl L. Lutjens   289

PART FOUR
POPULAR EDUCATION IN LATIN AMERICA:
OLD AND NEW DREAMS

11 Freire, Frei, and Literacy Texts in Chile, 1964–1970
    Robert Austin   323

12 Popular Education and the Reconstruction of
    El Salvador
    John L. Hammond   349

    About the Editors and Contributors   373
    About the Book   375

Acknowledgments

The editors want to thank Xochitl Perez, Erwin Epstein, Nina Moss, Sarah Kincaid, the UCLA Graduate School of Education & Information Studies, and the UCLA Latin American Center for their support on this project.

Introduction: The State and Public Education in Latin America[1]

Carlos Alberto Torres
Adriana Puiggrós

Introduction

Past efforts and available resources have made possible basic education for all children, helped to extend the years of schooling, provided early and preschool education, facilitated the access of disabled children to education, and improved the chances of the poor, migrants, girls, and indigenous children to attend public schools in Latin America. In addition to improving the equality of educational opportunities, schools have improved their overall capacity to retain students and even to promote them to higher education. However, equality, quality (including effectiveness, equity and efficiency) and relevance of educational provision in the region continue to be critical issues especially now that Latin American states are financially pressed. Elementary and secondary schooling in the region continue to be segregated by class, with the poor attending public schools and middle and upper classes attending private institutions. With few exceptions preschooling, decisive in shaping the cognitive structure of children, is not widely available for the children of the poor in the region. Illiteracy continues to plague educational planners, with the gender gap to the disadvantage of women ever widening. Illiteracy and the educational condition of the rural populations, particularly those of indigenous origin, continue to be pressing issues, with adult education remaining at the top of the agenda for policy making. *Popular education*, an indigenous paradigm of nonformal education developed in the region, is facing serious challenges in the context of post-modernism and post-Marxism in Latin America. Teachers' training, their political views and technical skills, continue to be central for educational reform in the region. Tatto and Velez's chapter documents a process of reform in teacher education that shows the complexities of teacher

1

education in Latin America. Current social, political and economic changes in Latin America underscore the pace, texture and scope of educational development, educational quality and the relevance of education. In this context, educational planners, children, youth, parents and communities deal with the implications of the lack of economic growth in the eighties, the growing external debt, increasing fiscal constraints, and intended and unintended impacts of structural adjustment of economies and neoliberal states. Alas, the relationships between education and social change continue to be revisited by those seeking educational reform, but the challenges of poverty remain seemingly intractable for public policies—especially education—and democracy.

This book offers a relevant sample of the current research on Latin American education in comparative perspective. Throughout the different chapters, the most relevant topics, research agendas, and some of the key theoretical and political problems of Latin American education are presented, discussed and analyzed. While the different chapters offer theoretical and analytical insights which are extremely useful to the study of the educational problematic in the region, it is important to offer a general theoretical framework to situate the discussion. This introduction thus provides a historical and theoretical context for a systematic discussion of education in Latin America. It draws from political sociology of education, theories of the state, and deconstructionist theories, with a focus on changes in state formation and its implications for the constitution of the pedagogical subject in public schools.

The State in Latin America:
From the Oligarchical State to Neoliberalism

During the second half of the nineteenth century and the first three decades of this century, the predominant state model in Latin America was a liberal state which has been defined as an oligarchical state.[2] The oligarchical state consolidated the nation and generated relative political stability. In this political model, the oligarchy maintained tight control over the political process, at times by means of direct control over the state, and at other times through control of the parliament and important political parties. In order to implement this control on occasion electoral fraud or simply open repression was employed.[3]

Systems of public education were developed as part of the project of liberal states that controlled by a landowning oligarchy sought to establish the foundations of the nation and the citizenship. When the oligarchical state collapsed in the early thirties it was replaced by several forms of the state sharing fundamentally a corporatist orientation. In some cases, the state models followed a Keynesian or welfare state-like style. Despite these changes, the role and function of public education remained by and large unchanged. However, since public education systems attempt to create a citizen as a "disciplined pedagogical subject," the role, mission, ideology, and training of teachers, including the prevailing notions of curriculum and school knowledge are all marked by the prevailing philosophy of the state.[4] The chapter by Dussell and Caruso offers an interesting analysis of Argentinean education at the turn and early part of the twentieth century.

After the experience of the oligarchical state, a reorganization of the state took place in Latin America. New state models varied including experiences as diverse as the Mexican post-revolutionary state, the democratic state that emerged in Costa Rica after the 1948 revolution, the liberal-democratic states that were implemented by democratic pacts between liberal and conservatives parties in Venezuela and Colombia, or developmentalist regimes implementing modernization policies in the Chilean, Uruguayan, Brazilian, and Argentinean State after the fifties. A key element in the debate about state-society relationships was the experience of populism, and the new presence of trade unions in the public sphere. In addition to populism, a central element of the Latin American state has been the implementation of public policies with a welfare orientation. State interventionism in the modernization of societies followed similar although not identical paths than the welfare state.

The welfare state is considered a particular form of the democratic liberal state in industrialized societies. Its origins have been associated with the industrial and financial reconstitution of the post-depression era in the United States, based on a "social pact" (New Deal) and concertation policies between employers and labor. A striking feature of the Welfare State is its interventionist role in the economy, including enlarged public spending in both productive and non-productive sectors of the economy. Welfare polices are defined as government protection of minimum standards of income, nutrition, health, housing and education. As Wilensky argued, these welfare benefits were assured to every citizen as a political right rather than as charity.[5]

Several elements, some intrinsic to the structure and political culture of Latin America, some the result of external pressures, conspired against the full implementation of the Welfare state model in Latin America. These include the extreme unequal distribution of income, in part due to the resiliency and power of landowners elites and the new bourgeoisie that emerged after the process of industrialization. Second, the economic vulnerability of the states and economies in facing the pressure from multinational corporations and even foreign governments—well-captured in the notion of dependency developed by diverse theoretical currents in the region. Third, the lack of unemployment insurance and welfare benefits. Finally, populist experiences disorganized the bureaucratic control of the state creating diverse constraints but also inducements for specific public policies. In short, the state that propels the modernization of the economy and politics is still a dependent-development capitalist state.[6]

The decade of the seventies was marked by state authoritarianism, perhaps by what Guillermo O'Donnell defined as the Bureaucratic-Authoritarian state. This new authoritarianism had clear expressions in the military dictatorship that took over the state in Brazil (1964-85) and Argentina (1966-73).[7] The decade of the eighties was marked by a return to liberal-democratic governments, with the demise of authoritarian military dictatorships and the implementation of new democratic forms of government. However, in the political-economic arena, a grave crisis of capital accumulation and income distribution coupled with a fiscal crisis of the state and the growing external debt threatened the return to democracy in the region. Hence, not surprisingly, the 1980s has been labeled as the "lost decade." for development. It was during this decade that the region witnessed a cycle of high inflation, even hyper-inflation, and recession never before experienced. The oil crises of 1973 and 1982, coupled with the debt crisis left the region in a state of economic disarray. Faced with rising international interest rates, Latin American countries found it increasingly difficult to meet their debt repayment schedules. International agencies (specifically the International Monetary Fund and the World Bank) exhorted governments in the region to adopt structural adjustment policies to address balance of payment difficulties and fiscal deficits. The attempt to return to economic stability through restructuring of the economy and of the relationships between state and society prompted several scholars, politicians, and informed observers to notice the formation of a new social pact controlling the capitalist states in Latin America. This new pact of domination has been termed the neoliberal state.[8]

Neoliberalism—or the neoliberal state—are terms employed to designate a new type of state which emerged in the region in the last two decades. The first example of economic neoliberalism is usually associated with the policies implemented in Chile after 1973. In many respects, neoliberal policies are for free trade and small public sectors, and against excessive state interventionism and tight regulation of markets. Lomnitz and Melnick argue that historically and philosophically neoliberalism has been associated with structural adjustment programs. Structural adjustment, in turn, is usually described as a broad range of policies recommended by the World Bank, the International Monetary Fund and other financial organizations. Although the World Bank differentiates among stabilization, structural adjustment, and adjustment policies, it acknowledges that the general use of these terms "is often imprecise and inconsistent." [9]

This model of stabilization and adjustment has resulted in a number of policy recommendations, including the reduction of government expenditures, currency devaluations to promote exports, reduction in import tariffs, and an increase in public and private savings. Key aims of this model are a drastic reduction in the state sector, the liberalization of salaries and prices, and the reorientation of industrial and agricultural production toward exports. The overall purpose of this policy package is, in the short-run, to reduce the size of fiscal deficits and of public expenditures, to drastically reduce inflation, and to reduce exchange rates and tariffs. In the medium-term, structural adjustment relies on exports as the engine of growth. To that extent, structural adjustment and subsequent policies of economic stabilization seek to liberalize trade, to reduce any distortion in the price structures, to end any "protectionist" policies, and therefore to facilitate the rule of the market in the Latin American economies.[10] There are variations in the implementation of these models of economic liberalization and structural adjustments. Some countries benefit from their economic endowments or aggressive policies and successful performance of their exports commodities (e.g., Chile) others benefit from specific free trade deals within larger regional markets (e.g., Mexico with the NAFTA agreement and Chile most recently; Brazil, Argentina, Paraguay and Uruguay with Mercosur), and others such as Argentina capital markets benefit from the political instability of Eastern Europe. Arnove's chapter offer a fascinating balance of the implications of neo-liberalism in education.

The Socio-Political Background

Latin American societies have a long tradition of political authoritarianism which has, to some extent, permeated many different policy arenas, including education. The historical irony is that the return to democracy in the eighties and nineties, and the overall project of redemocratization is being marked by unusual economic constraints. The political debacle of the region's left, the failure of a socialist revolution in Central America in the 1980s (i.e., Nicaragua, El Salvador, Guatemala), and the collapse of the socialist economies, created the "right conditions" for structural adjustment policies to be fully implemented region wide. Thus the deadlock which had existed between the programs of the lower class sectors (particularly trade unions) and the economic and political preferences of elites was finally broken with the onset of this period of adjustment.[11]

While the extent of the social consequences of the crisis and stabilization policies are still a matter of debate, it is evident that for a number of international agencies, the overall welfare of the people in the region is worse, in many respects, than it was 20 years ago.[12] For instance, according to the Economic Commission of Latin America (ECLA), approximately forty-four percent of the continent's population (183 million) in 1990 were living below the poverty line—an increase of 112 million over 1970. ECLA attributed this growing impoverishment to "the dramatic fall in average income, which marked a tremendous step backwards in the material standard of living of the Latin American and Caribbean population."[13] Similar analyses and forecasts are presented in a recent report by the Inter-American Dialogue.[14]

To address the economic and fiscal crisis and its social and political consequences, stabilization and structural adjustment programs have been carried out under different names—by regimes with diverse ideological orientations—within the context of a general and deep crisis. Economic stabilization came about in Latin America as a response to debt crisis, fiscal crisis, industrial recession, and inflation (in some contexts hyper-inflation). This happened, however, only after key social actors in the distributional conflict (the working class, campesinos, and even sectors of the middle classes) relinquished, by default or purpose, their ability to challenge cuts in public expenditures. The state's reform reduced its interventionist role in welfare policies but facilitated, through privatization and diminishing expenditures in welfare policies, the rule of market forces in Latin American societies. This, of course, has implications for state legitimacy and for the role of public education in the region.

The State and Public Education

The 19th century liberal state, and the diverse state models that emerged in the wake of the struggles of the 1920s and depression of the 1930s, granted to public education systems a major role in the integration and legitimation of the political systems and the modernization of Latin American countries.[15] As part of its development policies the state extended social benefits to vast sectors of the population, particularly in Argentina, Costa Rica, and Mexico. Education played a key role in these social programs, because mass schooling was viewed as a means of building a responsible citizen, skilled labor, and increasing social mobility. In the early sixties, human capital theories and educational planning justified educational expansion not only as a good investment in skill training but also as a prerequisite for liberal democracy.

The Latin American educational expansion during the early phase of industrialization in the 1960s accounts for the highest rates of educational growth in the world.[16] Between 1960 and 1970, the indices of growth for higher education and secondary education were 247.9 percent and 258.3 percent, respectively; however, the enrollment in primary basic education grew only 167.6 percent, while the illiteracy rate remained more or less constant in most countries of the area.[17] One study of the late 1970s shows a fundamental continuity in this pattern of educational development.[18] Ernesto Schiefelbein argues that in the last four decades Latin America made significant progress toward democracy by "(i) expanding access to education for most the children reaching school age; (ii) extending the years of schooling; (iii) improving timely entrance to school, (iv) providing early care to an increasing number of deprived children, and (v) increasing the provision of minimum inputs and eliminating tracks for social levels."[19] Schiefelbein's chapters offers a systematic analysis of financing education in Latin America and its implications for democracy.

Enrollment in elementary education has grown steadily in Latin America. While enrollments continue to grow, the rate of growth of educational expenditures adjusted by inflation diminished in the 1980s. Fernando Reimers shows that between 1975 and 1980, total expenditure in education increased in all countries in the region. However, between 1980-1985, the total expenditure in real terms diminished in 12 of the 18 countries he studied.[20] In contrast to previous achievements in the expansion of public education, the past two decades have witnessed a decline in quantity and quality of schooling in the region.[21] Reimers argues that ministries of education in the region have been forced to sacrifice equity and efficiency in order to reduce their educational expenditures under the constraints of structural adjustment policies. These cuts have disproportionately affected primary education and are reflected in the limited resources available for teaching materials, school facilities and in falling school enrollments rates.[22] These cuts have alienated teachers' organizations, forcing them to develop defensive actions, and occasionally, conflicting with the state in the formulation of educational policies.[23]

As Reimers and Tiburcio argue: "An analysis of the changes in public government financing of education in Latin America between 1970 and 1985 concludes that the adjustment led to disproportionate cuts in expenditures on education as a percentage of government expenditure or of GNP. Within education, capital expenditure suffered disproportionately as did expenditure on non-salary items, while increasingly more countries reduced expenditures at the level of primary education disproportionately. A study of the financing crisis in Central America between 1979-1989 concludes that most of the countries (except Honduras) show a tendency to spend a smaller percentage of GDP on education, that teachers salaries have depreciated in real terms with losses of about two-thirds and that at the end of the decade most of the budget in primary education goes to salaries."[24] A similar analysis is made of Brazil and Mexico where decline in educational expenditures took place "against the background of a growing government sector relative to GDP."[25]

These changes take place against this background, and are perhaps the result of a new global economy which is emerging and operates in very different ways from the former industrial economy. The old economy was based on high volume and highly standardized production with a few managers controlling the production process from above and a great number of workers following orders. This economy of mass production was stable as long as it could reduce its costs of production (including the price of labor) and retool quickly enough to stay competitive. Because of advancements in transportation and communications technology and the growth of service industry, production has become fragmented around the world. Production now moves to locations where there is either cheaper or more highly trained productive labor, favorable political conditions, access to better infrastructure and national resources, larger markets and/or tax incentives.[26]

The new global economy is more fluid and flexible, with multiple lines of power and decision-making analogous to a spider web, as opposed to the static pyramidal organization of the traditionalist capitalist system.[27] While the public education system in the old capitalist order was oriented toward the production of a disciplined and reliable work force, the new global economy seems to have redefined the goals of public education in development. The new roles for public education—and for many, the future of public education—is at stake in the current debates about educational policy.

From a political economy of education, the performance of the economy is a major issue underpinning educational policies. The question is to what extent the prescribed recipes of structural adjustment as a cure to the economic malaise will help or hinder educational expansion, quality of education and equality of educational opportunity in the region. This is the bedrock underscoring the political behavior of the main actors concerned with educational services in Latin America today, particularly teachers organizations, the neoliberal state and their agencies, and the role of international organizations, particularly the World Bank.

It is imperative to situate the national and regional educational policies of Latin America within the context of global economic, political and social changes of the past years. The current regional context is affected by innumerable changes including the rise of the newly industrialized countries in Asia and the Pacific rim, and its impact on the models of economic development in Latin America; the promise of consolidation of regional economic markets (European Economic Commission, NAFTA and MERCOSUR); the intensification of competition among the major industrial powers of Germany, Japan and the United States; the opening of Eastern Europe; and the resurgence of regional ethnic and religious conflicts.[28]

These changes and contradictions are increasingly related to the process of globalization of economies, cultures and societies, showing how very powerful are structural forces involved in education at times of severe crisis and re-structuring of policy priorities and systems.

State Corporatism and Dependency

Public education also plays a major role in the legitimation of the political systems and the integration and modernization of countries in Latin America in the context of corporatism and dependency.[29] The "dependency perspective" should be placed in the context of broad schools of development which include Modernization, Dependency, Bureaucratic-Authoritarianism, Post-Imperialism, and Interactive Local Political Economy perspectives. Modernization focuses on the nature and characteristics of the social structure of less developed countries as causes of underdevelopment. Dependency theories instead focus on the structure of international capitalism and the lack of availability of capital for autonomous expansion of a less developed economy. Bureaucratic-authoritarianism explains dependent-development as a result of problems in the model of import-substitution industrialization implemented by several Latin American countries. A key factor of instability are the growing demands of the working class undermining both the legitimacy of the overall model of development, and its ability for capital accumulation. The answer to this development crisis is the emergence of an Authoritarian state. Dependent-development theories spring from dependency theories and are compatible with world system analysis.[30] Dependent-development point to the centrality of the state for the accumulation in the periphery of the capitalist world system. Post-Imperialism theories attempt to explain underdevelopment as part of a process of transnational class formation in the developing world. Finally, the perspective that focuses on the interaction of social domestic forces using a modern political economy emphasizes that the complex interaction of domestic socioeconomic and political trends determine policy outcomes, insisting on the centrality of economic pressures by domestic socioeconomic actors in the determination of policy options and outcomes.[31]

Political economists of education and political sociologists from a dependency perspective have helped to identify the institutional identity of the state as crucial in understanding the role education has played in development and social change.[32] The theory of the "conditioned states" in the Third World, expanding upon and clarifying the notion of the dependent state,[33] argues that the state is conditioned: "by the nature of the peripheral role that its economy plays in the world system and the corresponding enormous influence that the dynamic of metropolitan capitalism has on its development process. The Third World state is also conditioned by the significant noncapitalist (postfeudal) elements in its own political system."[34] Coraggio offers in his chapter an analysis of educational policies in the urban environments of Latin America.

Using historical and theoretical analysis, it has been argued that in Latin America 'conditioned states' have not been able to carry out their public functions properly for a number of reasons. On the one hand, the fragility of the local economies made local dominant groups unwilling to allow the pluralist participation of the masses in the selection of the state bureaucracy. On the other hand, since the state historically has been identified by the popular sectors more as a pact of domination by the dominant classes, or a surrogate state, it has not been seen as an independent state working on behalf of the citizenry.[35]

Similarly, the vast social gap between the dominated and the dominant classes, both in material and in cultural terms, prevented the state from performing its function as a lawmaker, ruling on behalf of the entire citizenry. Whereas the state is not subjected continuously to the law of the political market where everybody agrees or disagrees by conventional institutional means (i.e., regular voting) on the performance of the state's personnel, the state ends up overruling the law by increasing their degree of repression of the civil society instead of improving its own legitimation through consensus.[36]

Another question is the ability of the state to consolidate the nation and the market. Since the boundaries of the market are externally defined by the presence of external powers and multinational corporations, the definition of the nation is continually and historically respecified by a complex matrix of exogenous-endogenous processes. More often than not the conditioned state has little control over its own political economy dynamics.

Finally, the position of the state in the periphery of technological creation and the use of science and technology for improving capital accumulation makes the state impotent to link the capitalist division of labor with science and technology. The brain drain of the nation's intellectuals is a typical example.

While the notion of dependency, dependent-development, and the conditioned state set the tone for a discussion on the nature of the state in Latin America, drawing from the tradition of political corporatism, the notion of state corporatism and political sociology of education has been employed to study the peculiar characteristics of political regimes in the region, and particularly educational policy formation in Mexico. Corporatism has been defined by Phillips C. Schmitter as: "A system of interest representation in which the constituent units are organized into a limited number of singular, compulsory, noncompetitive, hierarchically ordered and functionally differentiated categories, recognized or licensed (if not created) by the state and granted a deliberated representational monopoly within their respective categories in exchange for observing certain controls on their selection of leaders and articulation of demands and supports" [37]

Corporatism, particularly the constitution of teachers unions in intimate relationship to the state, and the ideology of "normalism" in some countries, help to explain the nature of educational policy formation in the region. For instance, the development of the educational system in Mexico has been dependent on the consolidation of the corporatist state as a mode of governance and political legitimation.[38] Corporatism in Mexico refers to a form of State that, being the result of a popular revolution, has a broad mass-base of popular support. The concept of corporatism is also used to refer to the incorporation of peasants, workers, and middle-class sectors into the political party apparatus—the Revolutionary Institutional Party, or PRI—and into a system of distribution of power and influence in the State. Thus, corporatism in Mexico refers specifically to the organizational characteristics of the state structure, party, and political control that depends to a certain degree on popular participation and mobilization, both being carefully controlled and manipulated for nondemocratic ends. The basic premises of the post-revolutionary state were redistribution of land, strengthening of labor unions, massive education, and the principle of nonreelection.[39]

Education has played a fundamental role in the legitimation of the post-revolutionary state, and has contributed to state hegemony. It has been argued that the corporatist nature of the post-revolutionary state has deeply conditioned the way educational policy has been organized, implemented and evaluated, and that education (particularly adult education) in Mexico is part of a comprehensive project of compensatory legitimation. While the Mexican case is perhaps too specific—and this in part explains, until now, the political stability of the Mexican system in the midst of the turmoil of Latin American recent history—it could be argued that historical changes in the patterns of relationships between state and society during this century created the conditions for the widespread implementation of corporatist arrangements, and the development of corporatist states. Schmelkes' chapter discusses the recent attempt at educational reform in Mexico and its implications for the educational system. Similarly, educational expansion, and the premise—if not the actual—social mobility of lower classes through education was an important component of the democratic pact in Latin America. This is exactly the preocupation of Hammond in his chapter analyzing popular education and its democratic promise in the region.

Yet research has shown that educational systems, and particularly adult education have been usually co-opted by the State and employed as an instrument of social legitimation and the extension of state authority rather than as a tool for self-reliance of individuals and poor communities. This has serious implications for policy, planning, and quality of education. Educational policies, planning, and programs become an arena for struggle of competing political agendas, therefore deeply undermining the potential pedagogical contribution of these policies and programs, because "the various set of actors are shown to be pursuing their own educational agenda in the face of conflicts and contradictions in the national political economy."[40] Education as compensatory legitimation, and corporatism as the framework for the operation of educational systems in Latin American "conditioned states," contributed to the constitution of the social and pedagogical subjects. The Cuban experience, discussed by Lutjens in her chapter, shows the different orientation of the socialist system and particularly the implications for women's education.

The Pedagogical Subject

The region's school systems were founded during the second half of the XIX century under the guidance of the educational philosophy of cultural liberalism. The State is considered the main agent in charge of educating the people. Educational systems should prepare modern citizens, integrating the nation, and homogenizing the population in cultural terms. Hence a desirable goal was the achievement of some degree of uniformity in pupil's behavior, customs, ways of thinking, and political and cultural language. This pedagogy was imposed on those to the older generations who faced an inflexible school life, full of fear, where voices could not be raised, students could not move out of line, nor have a creased or ink-stained school overall—either in the primary or secondary school. Students wrote with pen and ink in inkwells and did not dare to speak to primary or secondary teachers without permission.[41]

School enrollment reached significant levels in Latin America, but in each country in the region the success of the liberal project was linked to the degree and type of development of each society as a whole. Therefore, there were different pedagogical subjects in each country, and also different from those students imagined as citizens by the XIX century liberals. In fact, cultural homogenization did not take place. Rather the partial, unequal participation of each sector in public culture stimulated the growth of subjects characterized by different structures.

In the sixties, the Alliance for the Progress in Latin America borrowing from the experience of the war against poverty in the Unites States, promised a social engineering solution to poverty, inequality, and equality of educational opportunity. However, despite these social programs, social inequalities continue to increase between developed and developing countries. In 1968, the developed countries (with almost 1/3 of the inhabitants and 1/4 of the youth population in the world) invested 120,000 million dollars, while the developing countries invested less than 12,000 million dollars. Differences increased and educational expenditures declined in the underdeveloped world. In 1980, total public spending on education in relation to GNP was 3.6 percent in Argentina; 4.4 percent in Bolivia; 4.4 percent in Mexico, and 7.8 percent in Costa Rica; in 1985 Argentina had dropped to 2.2 percent; Bolivia to 0.5 percent, Mexico to 2.6 percent, and Costa Rica to 4.7 percent.[42]

Concern over the crisis in education acquired an international dimension in the late sixties with the publication of the classic works of Philip Coombs and Edgar Faure.[43] They reflected the concern over the increasing quantitative and qualitative deficits in education, caused by the urgent educational needs of the Third World countries, particularly the population which remained outside the school system. Such systems led to dropping out, repeating, inappropriateness of contents to scientific and technological progress, and were inefficient in technical and political training. But the crisis those authors reported did not question the existence of the school system, nor did the solutions they proposed reduce education to the needs of the market. On the other hand, they supported State obligations with regards to public education and proposed that both the state and international organizations should increase their investment in education.

In the late sixties, educational systems faced an explosion of demand at all levels, a serious lag in curricular content in relation to the cultural, scientific and technological advances that were occurring worldwide, and a lack of training for work and in the political preparation of citizens. With the exception of Mexico and to a lesser extent Venezuela and Brazil, countries did not carry out the reforms necessary to respond to such a demand. Most of the systems accentuated their problems and in the late eighties it was public knowledge that quality of education was not appropriate to meet the social demands.[44]

Indeed, there was talk of an unprecedented crisis in the region.[45] A real dislocation between the discourse of teachers and pupils; between the adult and younger generation, and between leaders and followers was reflecting something more than the already endemic crisis of operation of the system.[46] This crisis was different from the one perceived in the late sixties. It was not a question of a mere repetition of the problems that had affected schooling systems for a century, such as dropping out or repetition, but others that reflected a profound "ineffectiveness" of the agents of education (teachers, parents, public and private educational institutions) and a break of cultural links between generations. The gravity of this crisis suggest the hypothesis that Latin American education is going through an organic crisis. This crisis is affecting the educational system as a whole, showing a breaking in the linkages between teachers and pupils. This generational gap makes inter-generational cultural transmission more difficult, creating also new cultural fractures in the population.

The process of globalization, that is, "the intensification of worldwide social relations which link distant localities in such a way that local happenings are shaped by events occurring many miles away and vice versa,"[47] has expanded modern culture among the high, middle and working urban sectors in Latin America. However, through the mass media and through political, cultural and educational programs, the process of globalization began to reach the most economically backward and culturally most remote groups in Latin America such as the villages in the Andean cordillera, pockets of Argentine's Patagonia, and the alienated urban populations in the shanty towns in Rio de Janeiro, Caracas, or Bogota. The global culture is reaching places where the school has not arrived in full force.[48] Globalization also explains the heterogeneity of production, which in turn, increases income distribution inequalities[49] Consequently, there are new combinations between traditional popular cultures, the cultural makeup of the states in the region and a transnationalized mass culture. The result is the establishment of new subjects who are the product of multiple ethnic, linguistic, social, and ideological combinations. This situation can be illustrated by a tour around the numerous cafes and bars in the city of Buenos Aires. In recent years they have been filled by a population of children begging, the so-called "street children." Although they cannot read since they have either dropped out or never attended school, they understand the rules of city life and can look after themselves perhaps better than middle class children. An analysis of their discourse shows that they have articulated statements from their peasant and working class language with others originating in city violence. Adult reasoning with profoundly childish images. They love and hate schools, that privileged place they have been excluded from. Their imagination is full of television images and characters from their neighborhood. They have not learnt geography and have no idea that their country is located in Latin America, but they refer confidently to situations that they have seen on television, happening in faraway countries.[50]

These changes are also reflected in the appearance of new school rituals. In 1991, the Argentina rock singer Charly García made a respectful musical arrangement of the National Anthem. This musical arrangement scandalized Argentine society. Few schools decided to play the national Anthem with its arrangement in rock music, and the youngsters, who previously had refused to learn the traditional hymn, began to enthusiastically sing the Anthem. An important ritual for reproducing the collective conscience had been rescued for a new generation by articulating it with musical statements that resonate and give an identity to the Argentine youth of today.

School boundaries have been broken, the walls of educational establishments are unable to protect the children from external influences, and perhaps many teaching and learning processes have ceased to be fulfilled in schools. There is a fracture between teachers and pupils, and among adults, children and youth. The concept of organic crisis developed by Antonio Gramsci,[51] suggests that the discourses of traditional teachers no longer articulate the discourses of the new pupils. Thus, teachers complain that: "Nobody listens"; "Children are on another wavelength"; "They don't read, they don't learn anything."[52]

During the last 15 years, the distance between adults and young people has widened, to the point where this gap seems in the eyes of the older generation to be nothing but a vacuum because its contents are unrecognizable: "Children today have got empty minds"; "They don't read"; "They are not interested in culture"; "They are not interested in politics"; "They don't feel like responsible citizens"; "There are no bridges between their language and ours." These are common complaints by parents and teachers.[53]

These are not sudden cultural changes but the product of long simmering processes. These cultural processes are the product of numerous ruptures of words, of myths, of painful changes in values. Many earlier processes converged, condensed, and produced a break with the previous situation. But this is not readily available to the understanding of the (adult) public opinion and teachers. Trained in the typical logic of modernity, adults seek coherence, continuity, similarity between cultures. Influenced by functionalist thought and being the inheritors of evolutionism and positivism, many intellectuals and pedagogues in particular, have difficulties in understanding the "border" situations, i.e., those where the limits of modern culture appear in their broadest meanings. The inadequacy of customs, rituals, and organizational forms that affects traditional knowledge is disruptive, altering the transmission chain of culture from adult to younger generations. In short, the Latin American school system is going through an organic crisis.

The diagnosis of this organic crisis in education requires a thorough analysis of the categories involved, including a cross-disciplinary and multi-disciplinary analysis from a political sociology of education, educational policies, and historiography.[54] Among other features, this organic crisis relates to increasing difficulties in the teaching and learning of reading and writing, in the alienation of students regarding to reading books; in the secondary place that adolescent give to writing as a means of expression and communication at schools and elsewhere; in the obstacles in the use of reading and writing in the learning of the scientific and technical disciplines by university students despite the fact that they have become proficient in the new technologies through self-taught of informatics. In addition, there is a gap between the basic languages taught at schools (e.g., alphabetic, graphic) and the new languages of modern culture (e.g., mass media images, music, etc.). New languages that the students learn and appropriate with unusual speed. Compatible with this situation is the growing ignorance of students regarding the history of their nations and the world history, showing profound gaps in the transmission of culture (and official knowledge) between generations. While younger generations accept fundamentalist explanations of the beginning of life and fundamental values, they are totally indifferent regarding collective values or notions of solidarity. Most of them are apolitical in their attitudes—a feature highly contrasting with the situation of Latin American youth in the sixties and seventies—but they reject the ideological and cultural essentialism, logocentrism, and authoritarianism of the older generation.

Despite this organic crisis, the school continues to be the designated institution reserved for the socialization of children into the official knowledge of the nation and the culture of the older generations. Social differences now have symbolic values in the contrasting experiences of nighttime musical entertainment, attendance to soccer matches, or the middle and upper class pastime of gathering in the paddle and tennis courts. Traditional clubs, neighborhoods streets and even political parties activities do not attract young people, nor do they have appealing cultural offerings for them.

This organic crisis is quite different from the endemic crisis of quality of education that was perceived worldwide by the educational reformers in the sixties and seventies. The key questions of children and youth's perceptions of reading and writing as obsolete, are indications of an organic crisis rather than mere symptoms of systemic dysfunction. How does this crisis affect the same definition of the term "education"? In other words, can we proceed to expand the educational system when the elements that make up the educational landscape in the traditional and modern pedagogical imagination are disappearing, or have little if any meanings to the new generations? In answering these questions, it should be borne in mind that the organic crisis affects not only modernist educational discourses but also pedagogy per se. The concepts that constitute the training of pedagogues and scientists, responded to the laws of standardized grammar and modernist expressions of schooling, either reflected in the New School movement or in the different strains of pedagogical liberalism, socialism, and popular education approaches. If pedagogues are not able to question their own premises and concepts, they will only be able to receive the mirror image of their (our) own decadence as teachers, while lamenting the decadence of the school system or the poor quality of education. In so doing, educators and policymakers will not be able to understand the complexity of phenomena that cause this crisis, nor develop new theoretical and programmatic strategies. Retaining old discourses without deconstructing them prevents social transformation, even though the concept that pedagogues and policymakes employ may have been the most progressive of their time.

In this context, teachers are questioned in two fronts by the cultural changes. They are questions as social subjects[55] in general (i.e., as citizens, heads of family, workers, or consumers) and as citizens responsible for the professional transmission of the basic cultural norms and values to the younger generations. They are overwhelmed for their responsibility in the modern times. For over a century, they were responsible to transmitting the legal and legitimate modern cultural capital, i.e., the transmission of culture. The same definition of the "subject" of the educational process, and the articulation between teachers, students and knowledge seems to be disintegrating. The "pupils" imagined by modern education are deeply fractured and new combination of identities arise with different perspectives. Instead of being unified by the same pedagogical discourse in the school classroom, school rituals connect teachers, students and knowledge combining bits of different cultural origins, and statements from dissimilar discourses. This is perhaps best exemplified by the school Latino population in the border between the United States and Mexico, the "pachuco" culture which is the product of complex political, cultural and pedagogical subjects, and by implications, diverse identities.[56]

In the context of countries in the Southern Cone like Chile, Uruguay and Argentina that had developed some of the earlier modern educational systems in the region, the experience of authoritarian governments in the seventies coupled with the economic collapse of the eighties and early nineties, brought about the collapse of pedagogical circuits that connected with school knowledge. The discourse of the public school that educated so many generations of immigrants and native Argentinians, Chileans and Uruguayans was the product of a pedagogical consensus constructed by the state—hence the ideology of normalism and their implications for pedagogical practices.[57] This discourse has become less comprehensible for the new impoverished social classes—the son and daughters of immigrants from neighboring countries who speak indigenous languages—and for vast sectors of the urban youth.

While the organic crisis is a profound fracture in the operation of educational systems, it is not so different from the cultural gap that prevailed in the foundations of the school system in countries with large indigenous populations including Guatemala, Bolivia, Peru, Ecuador, and to a lesser extent Mexico. In many of these countries, the educational system has been unable to cross the linguistic and cultural barriers, and the culture of society has been fractured for more than a century.

Dissimilar pedagogical discourses deeply wounded Sarmiento's notion of public, compulsory, and massive schooling as the answer to the opposition of civilization or barbarism.[58] The notion of public education as a political mandate of the state is now under siege by the neoliberal drive when proposing that the logic of the market, and market exchanges should regulate educational investment. Previous inequalities, and the growing distinctions between schooling for the poor and schooling for the rich mark the educational landscape of Latin America. This dualization of school systems is the result of many political decisions, including relinquishing the responsibility of the state to educate all its citizens. Today, some Latin American states aim at just providing basic education to the majority of the population, and in some countries such as in Peru, this is not even the case. Drastic reduction in public schools funding, and growing out-of-pocket costs for parents increase inequalities. New fees are charged for services that previously were free, including access to libraries, exams, salaries for teachers in special subjects. Thus, leaving the main school expenditures to the ability of parents cooperatives and associations (in some countries they are termed *cooperativas escolares*, in others school foundations) to raise revenues to supplement dwindling state subsidies. Decentralization, including transferring schools from the federal to the municipal system, leaves many poor provinces and local municipal authorities in charge of a system of education where they lack the appropriate material, financial, and even human resources. Some even claim that this transference of schools from federal to municipal authority condemn many educational systems to poverty.[59] In some cases, funds are released only after an assessment of the efficiency of the establishments, or when mechanisms for nationally centralized systems of control of the teaching profession are established, paradoxically, in the context of increasingly decentralized public education systems.[60]

Private education may not be the ultimate solution for the educational crisis. Many parents and students are unable to meet the cost of their own education and the investment of private education (either in their religious, business or professional corporation orientation) may not be sufficient to meet the social demand. Increasing unemployment, growing numbers of children living in the streets, and/or alienated from the cultural foundations of their societies, and the phenomena of poverty place educational development at risk. For example, in Venezuela, a recent study shows that 43.7 percent of the population living in poverty, and malnutrition affects sixteen percent of children under 15 years of age.[61] Thus, not surprisingly, and despite the lack of reliable statistics, in countries like Argentina and Uruguay educators suspect that illiteracy, an educational problem that was considered virtually solved in the past, is growing. In this context, some researchers argue evaluating the neoliberal experiment applied in Chile, that the strategy implied in the reduction of economic, political and technical investment of the state in public education, attempts to eliminate the public school as a privileged space for the preparation of political and cultural subjects. The outcome is the segmentation of the population with different and unequal cultural configurations and educational levels.[62]

Conclusion: Rethinking/Unthinking Latin American Education in Comparative Perspective

Understanding the theoretical and political problems of Latin American education needs greater conceptual sophistication than traditional theories and methodologies in comparative education. Recent scholarship in the region incorporates concepts that may be employed in understanding the complexities of education, including the notions of unequal and combined development of Latin American educational systems, the notion of an organic crisis, the presence of new subjects of education, the role of the democratic state, and the presence of fractures and "borders" in modern education.

The notion of unequal and combined development suggests the intersection of pockets of modern, highly educated populations, including postmodernist expressions in art, humanities, and science, side by side with pre-modern, peripheral, marginal, and even pre-Columbian cultures and populations. These cultures are marked by deep cultural and linguistic discontinuities with the dominant cultural capital prevailing in schools and societies. Public schools were conceived by the state as central tools and tenets of a modernist discourse. Their goals were to produce an homogeneous citizenry and highly trained workers in the framework of an unequal and combined development of Latin America. Thus, the Marxist concept of unequal and combined development popularized in the sixties and seventies, the emblematic notion of dependency utilized to assess the interconnections between external and domestic factors as a leit motif of underdevelopment, and the notion of hybrid cultures—a cultural melange of mestizos, indigenous, and Spanish and/or Portuguese people that García Canclini so aptly has discussed in his anthropological studies[63] —all point to the intersection of modern and traditional cultures. These modern and traditional cultures through constant cultural border crossings,[64] produce and reproduce new identities and the "asynchronic development of Latin American educational models."[65] Theoretically, the notion of multiple identities also relates to Derrida's notion of "diférénce"[66] and the feminist notion of "otherness," essential concepts to capture the magnitude of this unequal and combined cultural development in the region.

Perhaps it was Paulo Freire who very early in his *Pedagogy of the Oppressed* addressed the meanings of border crossings, otherness, hybrid cultures, and asynchronic development in Latin America. In so doing, he showed the political implications of pedagogical work. Freire argues that notions of oppression and domination are part and parcel of the pedagogical relationships between teachers and pupils in traditional classrooms. Thus the notion of "extensionism" (i.e., the provision of the dominant educational discourse to peasants in the context of agrarian reforms) was expressed not only as part and parcel of a pedagogical discourse but also as part and parcel of a political discourse.

The chapter by Houston offers an insightful analysis of Freire's early work in Chile, one of the founding moments of popular education in Latin America. A fundamental insight of Freire is that the social and pedagogical subjects of education are not fixed, essential, or inflexible—i.e., the teacher is a student and the student a teacher. The cultural and pedagogical implications are that the place and role of a teacher is not always and necessarily the extension of the role of the adult white men, or conversely a role performed by a female teacher subsumed under the discourse of hegemonic masculinity.[67] Similarly as a product of European logocentric thought, school knowledge is not always reproduced in schools, but it is also subject to contestation and resistance. While Freire criticized the western school in Latin America as banking education and as an authoritarian device (that is, as a device transmitting official knowledge and, at the same time, eliminating the pupil as subject of their own education), his pedagogy of liberation invites to dialogue in the context of multiple political and social struggles for liberation. Dialogue appears not only as a pedagogical tool, but also as a method of deconstruction of the way pedagogical and political discourses are constructed.[68] More than thirty years after Freire's main books were published,[69] the concept of dialogical education still appear as a democratic tool for dealing with complex cultural conflicts in the context of unequal and combined development of Latin American education.

The notion of crisis of hegemony implies also finding new concepts to take stock of the "new subjects"—teachers and pupils—in the new political and cultural formations emerging in Latin America.[70] Similarly, it is important to understand how the crisis of hegemony relates to the problem of national identity; what role that state attributes to the school system and teachers professional work; how the public/private cleavage in education is changing in the context of neoliberalism; and how the new social problems drastically depart from the social problems school systems faced in the past. These new social problems in Latin American education include, but are not limited to, the educational needs and the educational alternatives for street children, how the culture of drug trafficking is affecting educational establishments, and how private networks of communication and informatics are changing the status, reliability, and accessibility of school knowledge in the region.[71] The chapters by Mollis and Schugurensky analyze in detail the problematic of higher education in Argentina which exemplify many of the pressing issues in the region's higher education system.

The concept of subjects refers to the notion of social and pedagogical subjects, and their relationships with knowledge and structures. In Latin America, the notion of a pedagogical and social subject,[72] involves an analysis of a complex cultural and social milieu which are the result of multiple parallel determinations, including class, gender, race, ethnicity, religion, and regionalisms.[73] At the same time, by placing the notion of the pedagogical subject at the center of competing educational discourses, it is possible to find a heuristic device to understand the complex determinations—actions and reactions—resulting from the decadence of the old political order (and their social agents). It also helps to understand the progressive breakdown of national identities while at the same time, local and regional identities emerge as relevant in decision-making and political and social struggles. Finally, the concept of subject is useful to explore the disappearance of cultural and educational traditions in schools and societies.

The role of the conditioned state continue to be problematic for democracy and public education in the region. While we have argued that the institutional identity of the state is crucial in understanding the role education has played in development and social change, the notion of the dependent or "conditioned" state help to understand not only the contradictions in public policy formation, but also the disparate roles and functions that the Latin American states play in the context of peripheral capitalism. Conditioned by the dynamic of metropolitan capitalism, the significant noncapitalist (although perhaps postfeudal) elements in its own political system, and the political alliance in power, the nature of the democratic state in the region continues to pose serious constraints to the political and economic democratization of civil societies. More so when, despite the political shortcomings of the Latin American democracies and their limitations in endowments and resources, the liberal state in the region attempted to develop a system of public education that provided access and permanence to the system to vast sectors of the population, including the poor. The policy rational was clearly synthesized by Sarmiento's premise that the state should "educate the sovereign." A critical extension but also de-construction of this premise emerged in the sixties with the notion of a pedagogy of the oppressed, conscientization, and popular education. The current debate in the region is, on the one hand, whether the systematic withdraw of resources from public education under the political economy of neoliberalism has deeply affected the traditional educational role of the states, the performance of the systems vis a vis equality of educational opportunity and quality of education, and by implication the nature of the democratic pact. On the other hand, the prevailing theories and methodologies and the political-technical rationale for educational planning, are seen as subsidiary to the main goals of neoliberalism. These goals are currently expressed by international institutions like the IMF and World Bank with their political economy of conditionalities and policy preferences, but also are accepted and graciously implemented by neo-liberal states in the region. In this context, many scholars, teachers, policy activist, and communities wonder whether the dynamics and dominant institutions of metropolitan capitalism are shaping the discourse and praxis of education in the region. The question is whether, given the process of globalization, these internationally-induced policies are compatible to fundamental notions of democratic accountability, national sovereignty, and community empowerment. The question about the nature of the state and public policy is also a question about the future of public education in Latin America.

Fractures and "borders" in education refers to the way education is produced, and the way official knowledge is selected, organized, and hierarchically ranked in the curricula as well as to the nature of the prevailing pedagogical practices. Fractures and borders in education refer to conflicts between means of production, distribution, and use of knowledge originated (and validated) in different cultures, and across hybrid cultures as well. Old and new political and cultural struggles resulting from the confrontation of new subjects will continue to besiege the public school in Latin America. Different ways of imaging, understanding, and theoretically analyzing (and seeing) reality will clash in the schools. Thus, a discussion is just beginning in educational settings, addressing the rights of the various social subjects to participate in decision-making, and in the production, development, and evaluation of the process of teaching and learning. Most likely, this discussion will remain central in the pedagogical and political thought of the region.

The risk of further fragmentation of the school system, and given the withdrawal of the state from the pedagogical utopia of public education in Latin America, the exacerbation of cultural diférénce and otherness, will become critical in the unequal and combined development of schooling and societies. Therefore, the possibility of establishing a basic democratic consensus, and the articulation of diférénce in the constitution of identities will become even more remote and certainly more costly.

Notes

1. This is an expanded and updated version of Torres, C. A. and Adriana Puiggrós, "The State and Public Education in Latin America." Introduction to the special number on education in Latin America published by *Comparative Education Review* (Vol. 39, N° 1, February 1995). Published with permission.

2. Atilio A. Boron. *The Formation and Crisis of the Oligarchical State in Argentina*, 1880-1930. Ph. D. dissertation, Harvard University, 1976.

3. Ruth Berins Collier and David Collier, *Shaping the Political Arena. Critical Junctures, the Labor Movement, and Regime Dynamics in Latin America* (Princeton, New Jersey: Princeton University Press, 1991).

4. Adriana Puiggrós, *Democracia y autoritarismo en la pedagogía argentina y latinoamericana.* (Buenos Aires: Galerna, 1986); Adriana Puiggrós, *Sujetos, disciplina y curriculum en los orígenes del sistema educativo argentino.* (Buenos Aires: Galerna, 1990); Adriana Puiggrós, et.al., *Escuela, democracia y orden (1916-1943).* (Buenos Aires: Galerna, 1992).

5. See Harold L. Wilensky, *The Welfare State and Equality.Structural and Ideological Roots of Public Expenditures* (Berkeley and Los Angeles: University of California Press, 1975); Harold L. Wilensky *The New Corporatism: Centralization and the Welfare State* (Beverly Hills: SAGE, 1976); Thomas Popkewitz, *A Political Sociology of Educational Reform. Power/Knowledge in Teaching, Teachers Education, and Research* (New York and London: Teachers College, Columbia University, 1991).

6. Martin Carnoy, *The State and Political Theory.* (Princeton, New Jersey: Princeton University Press, 1984, chapter 8); Martin Carnoy and Joel Samoff, with A. M. Burris, A. Jonhston & C. A. Torres *Education and the Social Transition in the Third World: China, Cuba, Tanzania, Mozambique and Nicaragua.* (New Jersey. NJ: Princeton, Princeton University Press, 1990); Heinz Rudolf Sonntag and Héctor Valecillos, *El estado en el capitalismo contemporáneo* (México, Siglo XXI editores, 1977).

7. Guillermo O'Donnell, *Bureacratic Authoritarianism: Argentina 1966-1973 in Comparative Perspective* (Berkeley and Los Angeles: University of California Press, 1987).

8. Larissa Lomnitz and Ana Melnick, *Chile's Middle Class. A Struggle for Survival in the Face of Neoliberalism* (Boulder and London: Lynne Rienner Publishers, 1991), pp. 9-47.

9. Quoted in Joel Samoff, *More, Less, None? Human Resource Development: Responses to Economic Constraint* (Palo Alto, June 1990), mimeographed, p. 21.

10. Sergio Bitar, "Neo-Conservatism versus Neo-Structuralism in Latin America," in *CEPAL Review*, No. 34, 1988, p. 45.

11. Raúl Laban and Federico Sturzenegger, *Fiscal Conservatism as a Response to the Debt Crisis* (Los Angeles and Santiago de Chile, manuscript, 1992).

12. See for instance United Nations Development Program. Mitigación de la pobreza y desarrollo social, (Montevideo, Uruguay: UNDP project RLA/92/009/1/01/31, mimeographed); United Nations Development Program, Desarrollo

Humano y Gobernabilidad, (Montevideo, Uruguay: UNDP project RLA/92/030/I/01/31, mimeographed).

13. Gert Rosenthal, "Latin America and Caribbean Development in the 1980's and the Outlook for the Future" in *CEPAL Review*, No. 39, 1989, p. 1.

14. The Aspen Institute, *Convergence and Community: The Americas in 1993. A Report of the Inter-American Dialogue* (Washington: The Inter-American Dialogue of the Aspen Institute, 1992).

15. Adriana Puiggrós, *Sujetos, Disciplina y Curriculum en los Orígenes del Sistema Educativo Argentino* (Buenos Aires: Galerna, 1990). For an alternative explanation using a world system framework, see the work of representatives of the institutionalist school. For example, John Boli and Francisco O. Ramirez, "Compulsory Schooling in the Western Cultural Context," in Robert F. Arnove, Philip G. Altbach, and Gail P. Kelly, (editors) *Emergent Issues in Education. Comparative Perspectives* (New York: SUNY Press, 1992), pp. 25-38.

16. UNESCO. *Evolución Reciente de la Educación en América Latina* (Santiago de Chile: Unesco, 1974, mimeographed), pp. 167 and 227.

17. UNESCO, Conferencia de ministros de educación y ministros encargados de ciencia y tecnología en relación con el desarrollo de América Latina y el Caribe. Venezuela, December 6-15, Caracas, Venezuela (Caracas: UNESCO, 1971, mimeographed).

18. UNESCO/CEPAL/PNUD, *Desarrollo y Educación en América Latina: Síntesis General* (Buenos Aires: Proyecto DEALC, 4 vols, 1981).

19. Ernesto Schiefelbein, *Financing Education for Democracy in Latin America*, Chapter 1 of this book, p. 32.

20. Fernando Reimers concluded that the educational sector was proportionally more affected by cuts in expenditures than the overall public sector expenditures. See Fernando Reimers, *Educación para todos en América Latina en el Siglo XXI. Los desafíos de la estabilización, el ajuste y los mandatos de Jomtien* (Paper presented to the workshop on "pobreza, ajuste y supervivencia infantil" organized by UNESCO in Peru, December 3-6, 1990), p. 16.

21. Beatrice Avalos, "Moving Where? Educational Issues in Latin American Contexts," *International Journal of Educational Development*, 1986; Marlaine E. Lockheed and Adriaan Verspoor, *Improving Primary Education in Developing Countries: A Review of Policy Options* (Washington D.C.: World Bank and Oxford University Press, 1991).

22. Fernando Reimers, "The Impact of Economic Stabilization and Adjustment on Education in Latin America," *Comparative Education Review* , No. 35, May 1991, pp. 325-338.

23. Costa Rica see Martin Carnoy and Carlos Alberto Torres, *Educational Change and Structural Adjustment: A Case Study of Costa Rica* (Paris: Unesco Occasional Papers series-ILO Inter-agency Task Force on Austerity, Adjustment, and Human Resources, 1992).

24. Fernando Reimers and Luis Tiburcio, *Education, Adjustment and Reconstruction: Options for Change* (Paris: Unesco, 1993), p. 22.

25. Fernando Reimers and Luis Tiburcio, *Education, Adjustment and Reconstruction: Options for Change* (Paris: Unesco, 1993), p. 37.

26. See "Your New Global Workforce," *Fortune*, December 14, 1992, pp. 52-66.

27. Robert B. Reich, *The Work of Nations* (New York: Vintage Books, 1991).

28. See for example, Adam Przeworski, *Democracy and the Market: Political and Economic Reforms in Eastern Europe and Latin America* (New York: Cambridge University Press, 1991); Ken'ichi Omae, *The Borderless World: Power and Strategy in the Interlinked World Economy* (New York: Harper Business, 1990); Robert B. Reich, (n° 27 above); Lester Thurow, *Head to Head. The Coming Economic Battle Among Japan, Europe, and America* (New York: William Morrow, 1992).

29. Collier and Collier, Ibid.

30. Immanuel Wallerstein. *The Capitalist World Economy.* (London: Cambridge University Press, 1987).

31. For a good summary of these approaches see Jeffry A. Frieden, *Debt, Development and Democracy. Modern Political Economy and Latin America, 1965-1985* (Princeton, N. J.: Princeton University Press, 1991). The classic text is Cardoso, Fernando Henrique and Enzo Faletto. *Dependency and Development in Latin America.* Berkeley and Los Angeles: University of California Press, 1978. An extension of the analysis is Peter Evans *Dependent Development: The Alliance of Multinationals, State, and Local Capital in Brazil.* Princeton, NJ: Princeton University Press, 1979. An important work is Raúl Prebisch, "The Latin American Periphery in the Global Crisis of Capitalism" *Cepal Review*, N° 26, August 1985: 63-88.

32. Martin Carnoy and Joel Samoff, *Education and Social Transition in the Third World: China, Cuba, Tanzania, Mozambique and Nicaragua.* (Princeton, N.J.: Princeton University Press, 1990).

33. Ibid., page 10, footnote 4.

34. Ibid., page 20.

35. See Martin Carnoy, and Carlos Alberto Torres, "Education and Social Transformation in Nicaragua (1979-1989)." In M. Carnoy & J. Samoff, (Eds.), Ibid., pages 315-357; Torres, C. A. (1991) The State, Nonformal Education, and Socialism in Cuba, Nicaragua, and Grenada. *Comparative Education Review*, 35, (1), February, 110-130. For an overview of education in contemporary Latin America see also Daniel Morales-Gómez and Carlos Alberto Torres, (eds.), *Education, Policy and Change: Experiences from Latin America.* (Westport, Connecticut and London: Praeger, 1992).

36. Particularly in authoritarian governments usually resulting from military dictatorships, the sociology of fear, not the law, rules, and property rights always predominates over personal rights.

37. See his "Still the Century of Corporatism?" in F. B. Pike and T. Stritch (eds.) *The New Corporatism: Social-Political Structures in the Iberian World.* (Notre Dame & London: University of Notre Dame Press, 1974), pp. 93-94.

38. This is the central hypothesis of Daniel A. Morales-Gómez and Carlos Alberto Torres' book *The State, Corporatist Politics, and Educational Policy Making in Mexico* (New York: Praeger, 1990).

39. Ibidem.

40. Mark Ginsburg, Book Review of *The State, Corporatist Politics, and Educational Policy Making in Mexico* by D. A. Morales-Gómez and C. A. Torres (New York: Praeger Publishers, 1990). *Comparative Education Review*, Vol. 37, No. 3, August 1993, pp. 325-326.

41. Adriana Puiggrós, *Sujetos, Disciplina and Curriculum en los Orígenes del Sistema Educativo Argentino.* (Buenos Aires: Galerna, 1990).

42. UNESCO, *Anuario Estadístico*, (Paris: Unesco, 1988).

43. Phillip Coombs, *La Crisis Mundial de la Educación* (Barcelona: Península, 1971); Edgar Faure, *Aprender a Ser* (Mexico: Alianza Editorial, 1974).

44. CEPAL, *Transformación Educativa con Equidad* (Santiago de Chile, 1990).

45. Adriana Puiggrós, *Universidad, Projecto Generacional, e Imaginario Pedagógico* (Buenos Aires: Paidós, 1993).

46. Adriana Puiggrós, *Imaginación y Crisis en la Educación Latinoamericana* (Mexico, Alianza Editorial Mexicana, 1990).

47. Cited by David Held, *Political Theory Today*, (Stanford: Stanford University Press, 1991), page 9. Among other things, Held suggest that globalization is the product of the emergence of a global economy, expansion of trasnational linkages between economic units creating new forms of collective decision-making, development of intergovernmental and quasi-supranational institutions, intensifications of trasnational communications and the creation of new regional and military orders.

48. Ana María Ezcurra, *El Globalismo de la Post-guerra Fria.* (Buenos Aires: IDEA, 1991); José Luis Coraggio, *Economía y Educación en América Latina: Notas para una Agenda de los 90's*, Santiago de Chile, ECLA Papers No. 4, 1993.

49. ECLA. "Panorama social de América Latina," *Revista Iberoamericana*, No. 2, May-August 1993.

50. Moacir Gadotti and Antonio João Manfio, *Unidos ou Dominados: Pluriculturalismo, Diversidade Cultural e a Integração no Mercosul* (Foz do Iguaçu, Workshop on Education without Frontiers, Brazil, November 17-19, 1993, mimeographed).

51. Gramsci, Antonio, *La Alternativa Pedagógica*, (Barcelona: Fontanara, 1985).

52. Adriana Puiggrós et.al., *Interviews with Teachers.* (Buenos Aires: Instituto de Ciencias de la Educación, Universidad de Buenos Aires, 1992, mimeographed).

53. Ibid.

54. The study conducted at the Universidad Nacional de Entre Rios, in Paraná, Entre Rios, under the sponsorship of the project APPEAL (Alternativas Pedagógicas en América Latina) by pedagogues from the National Autonomous University of Mexico (UNAM), the Universidad de Buenos Aires (UBA) and the Universidad Nacional de Entre Rios (UNER) has used historical analysis to understand the rela-

tionships between education, modernism and postmodernism, and particularly the emerging university curricula for the XXI century. These researchers have reconstructed educational processes in recent history, discussing some of the crucial features of contemporary problems, and their future development. Amont other sources, this study draws from the theoretical proposals of Jacques Derrida and Jacques Lacan, and attempt to approach the problems from a postmodernist standpoint. They are particularly interested in the "deconstruction" of pedagogical discourses and in the analysis of the transformation of the subjects within those discourses. For a theoretical formulation and exegesis of Derrida's work which can be applied to education, see Rodolphe Gasche, *The Taint of the Mirror. Derrida and the Philosophy of Reflection.* (Cambridge, Harvard University Press, 1986).

55. The concept of social subject, and pedagogical subject refer also to the theoretical problematic of the social agency vis a vis structural determination.

56. Antonio Prieto, "Los hispanos en Estados Unidos. Las ficciones que nadie esperaba," *Primera Plana*, cultural supplement, Buenos Aires, July 26, 1992.

57. Jorge Luis Bernetti and Adriana Puiggrós, *Peronismo, Cultura Política y Educación.* (Buenos Aires: Galerna, 1993).

58. Domingo Faustino Sarmiento, *La Educación Popular.* (Buenos Aires: Banco de la Provincia de Buenos Aires, 1989).

59. Ivan Nuñez. "La Educación Chilena en el Período 1945-1990," in Claudio Lozano Seijas and Adriana Puiggrós (coordinadores) *Historia de la Educación en Iberoamérica.* volumen I (Mexico, García y Valadez, in press). Iván Nuñez, *Actores y Estrategias para el Cambio Educacional en Chile. Historias y Propuestas.* (Santiago de Chile, Proyecto Interdisciplinario de Investigaciones en Educación, PIIE, 1984).

60. Bernardo Kubler, *A World Bank Country Study. Argentina. Reallocating Resources for the Improvement of Education.* Washington, DC, The World Bank, 1991. First Sectorial Education Investment project MCE/Prov/BIRF, *Argentina. Proyecto de Educación Secundaria.* Buenos Aires, preliminary version, manuscript, 1993.

61. UNICRI, *Ser Niño en América Latina* (Buenos Aires: Galerna, 1991).

62. Ivan Nuñez, op.cit.

63. Néstor García Canclini, *Culturas Híbridas.* (Mexico: Grijalbo, 1990); *Las Culturas Populares en el Capitalismo* (Mexico: Nueva Imagen,1982).

64. Henry Giroux, *Border Crossings. Cultural Workers and the Politics of Education* (New York: Routledge, 1992).

65. Gregorio Weinberg, *Modelos Educativos en la Historia de América Latina* (Buenos Aires, Kapelusz, 1984).

66. Jacques Dérrida, *Cómo no Hablar? Y Otros Textos* (Barcelona: Anthropos, 1989).

67. This concept developed by Robert W. Connell refers to the historical association of masculinity with universalistic modes of thought. See R. W. Connell, *Gender and Power: Society, the Person and Sexual Politics.* (Stanford, CA: Stanford Univer-

sity Press, 1987); *Which Way is Up? Essays on Sex, Class and Culture.* (Sydney, London and Boston: George Allen & Unwin, 1983).

68. The notion of pedagogical subject is related to the notion of social subject developed by Ernesto Laclau in several of his works. See for instance Ernesto Laclau and Chantal Mouffe, *Hegemonía y Estrategia Socialista.* (Madrid, Siglo XXI, 1987); Ernesto Laclau, *New Reflections on the Revolution of our Times.* (London, Verso, 1991).

69. Paulo Freire, *Educación como Práctica de la Libertad* (Buenos Aires: Siglo XXI, 1978); *Pedagogía del Oprimido* (Buenos Aires: Siglo XXI, 1978); Carlos Alberto Torres, *Estudios Freireanos* (Buenos Aires: Ediciones del Quirquincho, 1995).

70. Lorenzo Vilches, *Teoría de la Imágen Periodística.* (Barcelona: Paidós, 1987); Jesús Martín Barbero, "Comunicación, pueblo y cultura en el tiempo de las trasnacionales" in Consejo Latinoamericano de Ciencias Sociales (CLACSO), *Comunicación y culturas populares en América Latina* (Mexico, Federación Latinomericana de Facultades de Comunicación Social, FELAFACS, 1987).

71. For a discussion of the implications of official knowledge for policy, see Michael Apple, *Official Knowledge* (New York: Routledge, 1993).

72. Carlos Pereyra, *El sujeto de la historia.* (Mexico, Alianza Universidad Mexicana, 1988); Mariflor Aguilar et al., *Crítica del sujeto* (Mexico, Facultad de Filosofía y Letras-UNAM, 1990).

73. Raymond A. Morrow and Carlos Alberto Torres, *Social Theory and Education: A Critique of Theories of Social and Cultural Reproduction* (New York: State University of New York Press, 1995).

PART ONE

The Political Economy
of Educational Reform
in Latin America

1

Financing Education for Democracy in Latin America

Ernesto Schiefelbein

In the past four decades Latin America has advanced several steps toward democracy by expanding access to education for most children. There are resources and public pressure for more equity in educational outcomes, but drastic changes in teaching methods and resource allocation are required for a democratic educational system to be viable. Educational improvements since the 1950s, the new desirable educational tasks, the new teaching methods required to meet the desired new tasks, and the feasibility of those new teaching methods are summarized in the next paragraphs and detailed in the corresponding sections.

Introduction

During the last four decades, Latin America has expanded both access to school and the years of schooling by replicating the "more of the same" model. In each neighborhood with more than 15 or 20 school-age children demanding education, classrooms were built and the required number of teachers were hired to operate the traditional primary schools. Eventually most of the teachers had some training and students gradually had access to a dull grind through a textbook. Growing family expectations on the power of schooling kept students bored for many years at school in spite of little learning and extremely high repetition levels.

Now that opportunity of access to and remaining in school are equitable, the next step is to make sure that all children have a fair chance to meet basic learning needs, but this step involves a drastic change from the traditional educational model. Meeting basic learning needs involves offering all students (specially those from deprived families) a fair chance to demand: that providing basic learning needs may require additional resources, as well as a drastic change in the allocation of available resources; careful strategies to cut off vicious circles developed by the traditional education model; and encourage a generation of virtuous circles with sequences of innovations and evaluations. The implementation strategy should eventually generate a new breed of innovative teachers willing to stimulate students to experiment and to observe, and to react to everyday life events, questions, and problems.

Advances Toward Universal Primary
Education in Latin America Since the 1950s

In the last four decades Latin America has taken large strides toward democratization by: (a) expanding access to education for most children reaching the school age; (b) extending the years of schooling; (c) improving timely admission to school; (d) providing early care to an increasing number of deprived children; and (e) increasing the provision of minimum inputs and eliminating tracks for social levels. The formidable advancements in these areas is detailed in the following paragraphs.

It was amazing to observe in Latin America that 93.3 percent of nine-year-olds were enrolled during the 1987 school year (Table 1). Another two or three percent of this cohort may enroll later or may have already dropped out after enrolling between the ages of six to eight. The balance, some four to five percent, is mainly formed by children in need of special care or living within an extremely isolated population. Therefore, the educational system supplies seats for all children requiring regular schools. There are enough teachers and classroom space, even though both may be improved (in number or quality).

The education systems have also increased their ability to keep students enrolled. Now students stay enrolled in school for six to seven years (Table 2). Students enroll in school at early ages (86.1 percent are already enrolled by the age of seven) and stay for an average of seven years. Dropping out starts at the age of 13. The average number of years at primary school is over 6.7 years (high school students are not included in the average schooling estimated in Table 2). However, the number of grades passed is much lower due to repetition and temporary dropping out, specifically for children who must be absent from school because they must work during the harvest season.

Timely entrance has also improved. In a typical age cohort half of the children join the school system at the age of six. Another third enrolls for

TABLE 1 Latin America and the Caribbean: Population and Enrollment Rates by Single Ages in Basic Education, 1987

Population Age (in years)	By Single Age[a]	Total Region[a]	South America		Central America and Panama	Gulf of Mexico	English-Speaking Caribbean
			Brazil[b]	Remaining Countries			
6	8,843,010	55.0	21.2	68.3	42.3	90.9	90.2
7	8,780,656	86.1	73.6	92.2	80.8	99.2	97.0
8	8,637,546	91.6	83.9	94.1	85.1	100.0	96.9
9	8,427,466	93.3	88.0	95.6	84.0	100.0	98.4
10	8,674,819	84.4	54.1	91.2	84.7	100.0	100.0
11	8,366,927	87.7	81.6	93.0	79.9	92.3	89.4
12	8,505,755	82.4	77.0	85.7	76.8	86.7	95.9
13	8,311,207	75.1	72.4	78.2	65.1	76.2	92.4
14	8,408,966	64.9	59.5	70.1	53.0	67.8	85.5
15	6,356,853	45.2	49.3	47.0	39.3	27.6	32.0
Access to school [c] (minimum estimate)	93.3		88.0	95.6	85.1	100.0	100.0
Age at which dropout begins[d]	13		10 and 13	10	14	14	15

[a]Twenty-five countries of the region have been taken into account. In the case of three countries (Montserrat, St. Kitts and Nevis and Trinidad and Tobago), only the six- to 11-year-old group was taken into account.
[b]1986.
[c]The highest percentage of students enrolled in an age group in a specific year corresponds to the minimum estimated access to school for that age group, given that some underage students who enter may have dropped out in the past.
[d]Point at which over 15% of maximum access drop out.
Source: SIRI-OREALC-Unesco Survey, 1987; CELADE. Population estimates by single age, 1987.

TABLE 2 Comparison of Average Primary Schooling and Average Number of Grades Approved

Country	Date	Cycle	Schooling	Average Grades	Average Gross Efficiency
Chile	1988	8	8.1	6.7	83.3%
Chile	1983	6	6.4	5.3	83.0%
Dominican Rep	1986	6	6.7	4.0	59.6%
Ecuador	1984	6	6.3	4.7	75.2%
Guatemala	1983	6	6.8	3.8	55.5%
Panama	1976	6	6.7	4.5	67.9%
Venezuela	1983	6	6.7	5.2	77.8%

Source: SIRI-OREALC-Unesco Survey, 1987, and E. Schiefelbein, Seven Strategies to Raise Quality and Efficiency of Education, Bulletin of the Major Project, No. 16, August 1988.

the first time one year later. At most only 10 percent join the school system with delay until the ages of eight and nine. The large age heterogeneity observed in Latin American classrooms is due to repetition rather than to late entrance.[1]

Latin American countries are also providing early care to an increasing number of deprived children. The percentage of children under the age of five attending preschool grew from 7.9 percent in 1980 to 15 percent in 1986. Many countries are now integrating preschool (kindergarten and pre-kindergarten) courses into primary schools where school space is now available. There are no enrollments by "age" at the preschool level, but in Latin America at least two-thirds of six-year-old children are in primary or preschool education.

Eventually most educational systems are able to provide access to regular education. Eventually most of the teachers receive some training and student gradually have access to more skills through textbooks. Differences between tracks specialized by social groups are gradually disappearing. Quality levels will be discussed in the context of goals for a more democratic education.

Tasks for Meeting Basic Education Needs of Democracies

Now that practically all children have access to school there is increasing public pressure for raising present achievement levels and becoming more equitable in terms of education outcomes. Demands for higher quality levels can be cast within a discussion of democracy. For example, President Perez said in Venezuela that "science must be built into the citizen's culture, thus science should be the axis supporting education, from preschool to higher education."[2] A solid quality of basic education is required to compete in the world marked economy. Latin American economic experts have recently agreed that better education is linked with sustained economic growth in democracies. Many more needs may surface, however, the challenge is to define reasonable and feasible goals that (as soon as achieved) are consistent with the design of more ambitious future educational goals.

Basic learning needs must be met before moving into more complex conditions of quality. Students (specially from deprived families) should have a fair chance to: (a) learn the educational tasks required for being promoted to the next grade and (b) make a meaningful use of school lessons in daily life. A fair chance for learning the minimum skills and contents is required for reducing segregation of those unable to meet basic standards for becoming a citizen, parent, worker, or church member. Four minimum skills are presented in the next section. Use of school learning in daily life is a simple and effective measure of the relevance of education. Given the low present quality level of education simple indicators should be used to measure quality.

Students Should Have a Fair Chance to Be Promoted to the Next Grade

Although there is now access for everyone, there are also huge differences in outcomes that should eventually be reduced to create a more democratic educational system. Only about five grades are approved (in school systems with six years of primary education), after remaining enrolled for six or seven years. Fragmentary evidence suggests that most middle- and upper-class students graduate from primary education, while primary students from the lower half of the socioeconomic distribution are promoted to less than four grades.[4] The large difference between socioeconomic groups observed in Latin American Countries is an indication of the inequity and poor quality of education delivered at public schools, and of the wastage of public funds due to repetition.

In spite of timely enrollment too many students are enrolled in first grade, and most of them are repeaters. In fact in the 1980-1987 period close to two age cohorts were enrolled in first grade (Table 3). Another way to look at the same problem: most children (all in many countries) are enrolled but repeat the lower grades (about half of the students spend two years in first grade).

Too many students repeating grades generate age-heterogeneity in classes and make it more difficult for the teacher to teach the age specific curriculum. The average age of the first grade student is higher than it should be (Table 3 suggests the increment is close to one year of age). The larger the age variance the more students that will find it difficult to follow teachers teaching the age-specific curriculum. Poor students cannot keep up with the pace of teaching and end up repeating grades. Studies in Mexico show that teachers choose who will learn (usually the middle-class children over the poor children), and teach those children.

Given that each repetition adds one year of age and the percentage of students enrolling at the standard age is known (86.1 percent is reported in Table 1 for the seven-year-old group), the difference between the "first grade students one year average or more" and the "maximum number students not enrolling in first grade at the standard age" correspond to the minimum number of repeaters. Table 4 suggests that there are at least 35 percent first grade students repeating the year, but the real number of repeaters must be much higher given that 55 percent of students enroll at the age of six (Table 1).

TABLE 3 Latin America and the Carribbean: Primary Education, Ratio Between Grade One Population of Normal Age and Enrollment in Grade One, 1980 and 1987

	South America		Central America and Panama	Gulf of Mexico	English-Speaking Caribbean	Total
	Brazil	Remaining Countries				
1980						
Grade one population of normal age	2,997,523	2,185,542	657,806	2,606,247	27,781	8,474,899
Enrollment in grade one	7,002,798	3,711,910	1,041,535	4,287,171	28,717	16,131,939
Ratio between enrollment and population	2.3	1.7	1.6	1.6	1.0	1.9
1987						
Grade one population of normal age	3,515,583	2,448,890	765,067	2,385,222	85,485	9,200,247
Enrollment in grade one	7,008,806	3,819,124	1,226,227	3,570,832	92,937	15,717,926
Ratio between enrollment and population	2.0	1.6	1.6	1.5	1.1	1.7

Note: This table does not include information on Argentina, Paraguay, Uruguay, Haiti; for the English-speaking Caribbean sub-region, figures refer only to Aruba, Dominica, Guyana, and St. Lucia; for 1987, they include Jamaica and Suriname as well.

Source: SIRI-OREALC-Unesco Survey, 1987; CELADE. Population estimates by single age, 1987.

TABLE 4 Latin America and the Carribbean: Primary Education, First Grade Enrollments, Overage and Repeaters, 1987

Variables	Brazil[a]	Remaining Countries[b]	Central America and Panama[c]	Gulf of Mexico[d]	English-Speaking Caribbean[e]	Total
First grade enrollment	7,888,886	2,942,888	863,676	3,570,832	93,718	14,479,912
Standard age	7	6-7	6-7	6-7	5-6	5-7
Students one-year average or more	4,081,428	1,227,882	448,481	1,397,995	28,932	7,168,638
Percentage	58.2	41.7	51.8	39.2	22.3	49.5
Maximum number of students not enrolling at age seven	926,368	159,588	99,452	18,199	3,365	1,286,964
Percentage of enrollment	13.2	5.4	11.5	8.5	3.6	8.3
Minimum number of repetition	3,155,868	1,868,294	340,949	1,379,796	17,567	3,961,674
Repetition rate	45.8	36.3	39.5	38.6	18.7	41.2

[a]1986
[b]Bolivia, Colombia, Chile, Ecuador, Uruguay, Venezuela
[c]Costa Rica, El Salvador, Honduras, Nicaragua, Panamá
[d]Dominican Republic, Cuba, Mexico
[e]Aruba, Martinica, Guyana, Jamaica, Sta. Lucia, Suriname
Source: Unesco/OREALC. Situación educativa de América Latina y el Caribe, 1980-1987. Santiago, Chile, 1990.

Using simulation models able to compute the minimum repetition rates consistent with the flowing through the education system of each age group of students, first grade repetition has been estimated at 47.5 percent for South American countries.[5] Results of the simulation models have been tested with two field studies[6] and with two follow up studies of age cohorts.[7] Estimated first grade repetition rates are presented in Table 5. A slow reduction of the repetition rates is observed in six countries, while increments are observed in two countries and the last two countries remain roughly at the same level throughout.

In summary, high repetition affecting deprived students is associated with students' expense time and lowered self-esteem; reduced teacher efficiency due to age-heterogeneity; and undemocratic inequity in educational outcomes related to membership in social class and wastage of public resources allocated to education. Although only first grade figures were commented above, average figures for the proceeding grades suggest that the repetition problems in higher grades may be of similar magnitude to the repetition problems in first grade (Table 6). Raising education quality for reducing repetition is probably the first task to be accomplished by Latin America countries vying for democratization in the 1990s.

Deprived Students Must Learn to Read
(Understanding What They Read)

Raising low reading levels should be the second task in advancing towards education for democracy. High first grade repetition rates show the percentage of students unable to read simple words and observations across schools in Latin American countries consistently show that even deprived students in grades five or six have difficulties in understanding what they read. Too many first grade students (over 50 percent of the students from urban-marginal or rural areas) are unable to read even simple words, are usually flunked, and must repeat first grade.

Learning to read (understanding what they read) is the cornerstone of education for democracy. It is the first step toward self-reliance (and to accessing campaign platforms and proposals from different political groups). However, literacy is usually taken for granted by curriculum designers, a highly selected group (usually university professors with five to 10 times the salary of the primary teacher), specialized in teaching future teachers how to teach to read, and their children are reading even before enrolling in preschool.

Normal Schools and Teachers' Colleges do not allocate enough resources to train future teachers how to teach reading skills but, ironically, remind future techers that an important task as educators is to identify and

TABLE 5 First Grade Repetition Rates Estimated with the Rates Model for Primary Education in the Indicated Periods (in percentages)

Year	Argentina	Bolivia	Brazil	Colombia	Chile	Ecuador	Paraguay	Peru	Uruguay	Venezuela
1970	36.3					36.7				
1971	33.6	37.0	55.8			36.7	40.1	41.8		15.6
1972	33.6	33.8	56.0	51.9	30.5	37.8	39.3	44.3	24.0	13.6
1973	35.7	34.4	54.4	50.5	32.6	34.4	37.2	41.2	20.3	20.8
1974	28.9	34.4	53.7	52.1	29.9	36.5	34.1	35.8	22.2	22.9
1975	28.8	35.0	54.6	54.0	27.0	35.7	39.3	33.5	23.7	26.9
1976	31.9	34.4	54.5	55.0	29.9	38.8	36.7	31.5	23.2	29.6
1977	30.5	33.2	57.5	57.3	30.0	35.7	37.8	37.7	19.8	27.0
1978	27.0	34.4	62.1	53.4	28.3	38.1	36.1	39.4	17.9	29.5
1979	27.7	33.7	57.4	45.8	25.1	40.0	35.2	43.3	17.9	29.8
1980	29.0	30.7	57.8	52.4	22.1	39.9	32.9	43.5	18.9	30.6
1981		32.8	57.9	42.4	13.8	39.1	32.6	45.8	17.6	30.1
1982		31.0	57.4	44.3	10.0	37.7	27.3	47.8	23.2	25.8
1983		34.2	57.6	42.0	10.0	36.2	29.1	45.2	21.7	26.5
1984		33.8	54.3	45.6	18.3		29.5	46.8	21.5	25.6
1985		33.5		35.7	14.0				19.1	
Change in interval										
(%)	7.2	3.5	1.5	16.2	16.6	-3.2	10.6	-5.0	4.9	-10.0

Note: Differences in last row are computed between values of the initial and last year of the period.
Source: Results of RATES Model with data of Unesco Data Bank.

TABLE 6 Latin America and the Caribbean: Primary Education, Distribution of School Enrollment in Initial Three Grades, According to Age of Students in Relation to Normal Age for Attending Each Grade,[a] 1987

Variables	South America[b]		Central America and Panama[c]	Gulf of Mexico[d]	English-Speaking Caribbean[e]	Total
	Brazil	Remaining Countries				
First grade enrollment	7,008,806	2,942,880	663,676	3,570,832	72,794	14,458,988
Percentage over age	39.0	29.0	26.9	17.7	4.5	30.8
Percentage under age	10.4	1.3	8.5	2.1	1.9	6.3
Second grade enrollment	4,639,855	2,323,391	581,011	2,980,439	69,949	10,594,645
Percentage over age	45.2	35.2	36.0	23.8	7.2	36.2
Percentage under age	8.5	4.8	11.2	4.9	4.1	6.8
Third grade enrollment	3,482,035	2,088,503	475,941	2,762,620	80,467	8,889,566
Percentage over age	47.4	38.2	36.9	21.3	21.3	36.3
Percentage under age	8.4	5.2	11.5	12.0	4.0	8.9
Total enrollment	15,130,696	7,354,774	1,920,630	9,313,991	223,210	33,943,199
Percentage over age	42.9	33.6	32.1	20.7	11.4	34.0
Percentage under age	9.4	3.5	10.0	5.9	3.4	7.1

[a]The official age for enrollment in a grade and the following ages were considered as normal age.
[b]Does not include Argentina, Paraguay, Peru, and Uruguay.
[c]Does not include Guatemala.
[d]Does not include Haiti.
[e]Corresponds to Aruba, Dominica, Grenada, Jamaica, and Suriname. In the case of Jamaica, the 12,700 children in the private sector are not taken into account.

Source: SIRI-OREALC-Unesco, Statistical Yearbook, 1988. Paris, 1988.

retain those first grade children not capable of decoding letters' sounds by the end of the school year. First grade repitition becomes a proxy for the long standing tradition of linking signs and sounds of the Spanish language to reading and writing skills.

In summary, the high level first grade repetition is an indicator that poor educational quality forces almost half of first grade students to spend two years of schooling associating sounds and letters. More resources in teacher training, designing child tutoring, and relating contents with daily life, extending the time available for learning and providing electronic equipment are strategies that should be explored to meet this second task, raising existing reading levels.

Children Must Learn to Communicate in Writing at Least Simple Messages

Citizen participation in a modern society that operates with written messages, requires the ability to process written messages. Unfortunately, urban-marginal or rural students that eventually pass the fifth or sixth grade are not able to understand or send even simple instructions. The only exercise in writing they have had once or twice per year is usually a one page description of what happened during vacations. Little practice of free writing is especially damaging given that writing is a process associated with a systematic thinking. The ability to follow instructions and send messages is the third task for meeting basic needs of democratic society and goes one step beyond reading and writing.

Every day activities such as the operation of modern telephones, microwaves or videotapes requires a 10-page manual; electronic mail and faxes that require written messages; toys and home equipment come in kits to be assembled following long (sometimes complex) instructions; and automatic vendor machines are operated with specific written instructions and messages. Children must learn the ability to communicate in writing if they want to become fully participating citizens.

The ability of children to communicate in writing varies widely according to their socioeconomic levels. Testing carried out in five Latin America countries in grades four to six detects large differences in achievement between children from different income groups. Achievement in rural areas is lower than the national averages, and because rural areas overlap economically deprived areas, the effects are magnified.[8] A study in Southern Chile detected 66 percent of urban students and 83 percent of rural students with problems in reading comprehension. These differences between urban and rural within Latin American countries may be as large as (or even larger than) the differences between Latin America and more developed countries. In summary Latin American countries must identify problems in communication when addressing the issues of poverty that have berring and students' promotion through school.

Children Must Be Exposed to Good Models of Democratic Behavior

The fourth task, to meet basic education needs of democracies is to expose children to good models of democratic behavior. Values are learned by role playing, rewarding experiences or opportunities to observe and interact with fine or skillful persons. For children to become agents of democracy they have to practice democratic values and be encouraged by school leader models. School government with periodical changes of responsibilities during the school year is a valuable mechanism where children may appreciate the advantages and constraints of a civic and democratic life.

Class observations have shown that about one quarter of class time in traditional schools is spent in controlling discipline and that these settings offer few opportunities for autonomous thinking.[9] Traditional schools do not design learning experiences that develop democratic practices like: tolerance for other's opinions; ability to work in groups; ability to make constrained decisions; ability to ask questions, or self-esteemed that is based in the value of the local culture. The traditional public school (urban-marginal or rural) is not actively using the opportunities for developing democratic values.

Children Must Be Able to Learn from Observing the Context

The fifth task for meeting basic education needs in a democratic society is to develop the skills of observation and learning from the context. Children must be able to observe for themselves, to describe accurately and to systematically think about what was observed. Education should enable the students to think for oneself, rather than to parrot received conventional beliefs. Once these fundamentals are well rooted they may be complemented with investigations in analogies, contradictions, inconsistencies, and exercises in information seeking, communication skills, and the willingness to learn from mistakes. Using the richness of the context in these learning experiences also helps ensure that school achievement be as independent as possible from the socioeconomic family level.

Most Latin America children know that "6 x 7" equals 42, but students in the last grade of primary education cannot estimate the number of square meters in a seven meters long and six meters wide classroom. Students may repeat the names of the elements of a flower, but have not looked at them in a real flower. Students may point to their country on a map, but have not prepared a map of their neighborhood. Students may show where is the north in the map, but have not identified the north in their classroom. Students may talk about health problems, but have not identified which are the illnesses in their families, and which are the usual treatments.

Learning from relevant experiences provides an ability to continue learning after graduating from school, but it also makes the process of learning itself much easy to learn. In addition, the society at large should realize that the school provides relevant tools that enable each person to live a creative and rewarding life. All citizens have the right to continue developing their potential and, at the same time, the potential of the community at large. Therefore, all children must be able to learn from observing their immediate surroundings and learn to value their culture in such a process.

Limitations of the Present Educational Model for Meeting the New Tasks

Available evidence suggests that the traditional "teaching the average student receives in the classroom" cannot deliver the quality of education required to meet the new tasks of an education for democracy in the Latin America of the 1990s. The traditional "teaching the average student receives in the classroom" will necessarily flunk the below-average (usually deprived) student and it will also not be able to successfully meet the new tasks described in the previous section. Therefore, suggestions for designated new teaching methods to meet the tasks and strategies for allocating the resources required to succeed in the implementation will be discussed in the next two sections.

Deprived students will not learn the five learning tasks so long as they attend a "typical" Latin American school. We define the "typical" Latin American school as a school that: (a) teaches to the more advanced children and ignores those children not capable of learning the curriculum; (b) follows simply a national curriculum, without using examples of daily local life as learning settings; (c) does not stimulate original questioning and reasoning; and (d) does not provide equal access and opportunity to learn computer skills now used in schools for the elite.

The analysis of the three main elements that limit the ability of the typical school model to meet the tasks of democratizing the educational system is presented in the rest of this section. The focus of the analysis is the impact of teachers' behavior and teaching methods on actual learning of socioeconomically deprived children.[10] The relevance of the analysis applies to identification of the typical school to be analyzed. Given that repetition problems mainly affect children in marginal and rural areas, these schools have been selected in this analysis.[11] The analysis of each of the three main elements concludes that few improvements can be introduced in the typical school when countries are supposed to raise their quality under severe economic constraints.

The Frontal Teaching Problem: Teaching the Average Student in the Classroom Has a Built-in Inequity

Teaching the "average" student when the talent of students is probably normally distributed, means that those with talent below the average student selected by the teacher will fail to pass at the end of the year (Table 7 shows the distribution of students from six to 13 years of age in first grade). The problem is even more serious given the peculiar Latin America age heterogeneity that flattens the distribution of talent and narrows the number of students near the "average" used as reference. Therefore, interest of students below the range of "average" to pay attention to the teaching effort is reduced (given that their only choice is to pay or not to pay attention to teacher instructions). Not paying attention equals increased misbehavior and, therefore, further reduction in the level of attention payed to teachers, higher repetition, and eventually higher age heterogeneity.

Probably half of the Latin America schools are reaching the maximum feasible education quality level for a traditional frontal teaching of the "average" student.[12] Many teachers try harder to improve as much as possible achievement of the average student, but sacrificing more challenging and interesting work for the brightest students and condemning deprived students to flunk the grade because they cannot keep the average pace.[13] Teachers try to compensate this basic flaw with remedial training and additional efforts to no avail. In spite of all teachers' efforts students' results are poor both in terms of high repetition rates and in terms of poor reading levels summarized in the beginning of this report.

Breaking the vicious circle of age heterogeneity means changing the frontal teaching model used in the typical school, but such a change goes against a long standing tradition. Most Latin American teachers (at least the 80 percent with a teaching diploma) have spent at least 12 years (and many up to 18 years) seated quietly in their benches or tables with a flat or sloping top for writing, while the teacher has been talking or writing at the chalkboard, mainly describing facts, definitions, and statements to be memorized. All the trained teachers that have been educated in Normal Schools or Teachers' Colleges know that they should use active methods of teaching and have memorized the steps for such an ideal practice or the characteristics of the available pedagogical models. But very few teachers

TABLE 7 Latin American Distributions of First Grade Enrollments

Age	Argentina	Bolivia	Brazil	Chile	Colombia	Costa Rica	Cuba	Ecuador	El Salvador
Year	1987	1988	1989	1989	1990	1986	1989	1988	1989
4	0.0%	0.0%	0.0%	0.0%	0.0%	0.0%	0.0%	0.0%	0.0%
5	0.9%	1.7%	0.2%	0.1%	2.7%	0.0%	7.6%	7.6%	0.7%
6	70.8%	39.1%	10.4%	39.2%	24.7%	34.0%	91.1%	50.5%	11.5%
7	16.0%	30.3%	30.5%	52.4%	29.9%	46.9%	1.2%	27.3%	33.8%
8	6.3%	16.2%	19.2%	6.0%	17.8%	12.1%	0.1%	8.4%	21.2%
9	3.0%	7.2%	13.0%	1.4%	10.2%	4.0%	0.0%	2.8%	12.5%
10	1.5%	3.0%	8.9%	0.5%	6.6%	1.7%	0.0%	1.4%	8.6%
11	0.8%	1.1%	6.2%	0.2%	3.5%	0.7%	0.0%	0.8%	5.1%
12	0.4%	1.2%	4.4%	0.1%	2.3%	0.4%	0.0%	0.6%	3.5%
13	0.2%	0.3%	2.9%	0.0%	1.2%	0.1%	0.0%	0.3%	1.8%
14	0.1%	0.0%	1.9%	0.0%	0.9%	0.1%	0.0%	0.2%	0.8%
15	0.0%	0.0%	1.5%	0.0%	0.0%	0.0%	0.0%	0.1%	0.3%
16	0.0%	0.0%	0.8%	0.0%	0.0%	0.0%	0.0%	0.1%	0.2%
	100.0%	100.0%	100.0%	100.0%	100.0%	100.0%	100.0%	100.0%	100.0%

(table continues)

TABLE 7 (continued)

Age	Honduras	Mexico	Nicaragua	Panama	Paraguay	Dominican Republic	Uruguay	Venezuela
Year	1986	1987	1988	1989	1990	1988	1989	1988
4	0.0%	0.0%	0.0%	0.0%	0.0%	0.0%	0.0%	0.0%
5	0.0%	0.9%	0.5%	2.0%	0.0%	0.0%	0.0%	6.1%
6	18.9%	60.0%	19.6%	57.6%	18.0%	14.8%	38.1%	48.9%
7	34.2%	22.3%	29.7%	24.6%	55.1%	32.1%	47.3%	25.4%
8	20.5%	8.4%	21.8%	9.2%	17.3%	21.5%	10.6%	10.8%
9	11.6%	3.1%	12.3%	3.7%	5.4%	13.3%	2.7%	4.7%
10	7.0%	5.1%	8.3%	1.7%	2.3%	8.7%	0.9%	2.2%
11	3.8%	0.2%	3.8%	0.7%	1.0%	4.7%	0.2%	1.0%
12	2.2%	0.0%	2.6%	0.4%	0.5%	2.9%	0.1%	0.5%
13	1.2%	0.0%	0.9%	0.1%	0.2%	1.3%	0.0%	0.2%
14	0.6%	0.0%	0.3%	0.1%	0.1%	0.5%	0.0%	0.0%
15	0.0%	0.0%	0.1%	0.0%	0.0%	0.2%	0.0%	0.0%
16	0.0%	0.0%	0.1%	0.0%	0.0%	0.1%	0.0%	0.0%
	100.0%	100.0%	100.0%	100.0%	100.0%	100.0%	100.0%	100.0%

Source: SIRI questionnaires, 1989.

A change in the frontal teaching model means a change in attitude rather than in knowledge. A fair number of teachers may talk about the active use of reality as the basis of learning; the emphasis on observation in relation to higher forms of reasoning; the linkage of new ideas with knowledge already possessed by the student; describe the importance of school government for civic values, the printing shop for writing, the humanistic value of technical training, the use of contracted projects, and the respect for children working at their own speed.[14] But very few have seen a real school operating something close to those creative approaches. Therefore, few Latin America teachers can teach with active methods, because those methods were not modelled during their teacher training nor were they used while they were primary or high school students.

In summary, the typical school has a built-in inequity mechanism and no further advances can be made toward an education for democracy by replicating the "more of the same" model. Such mechanisms are built in the frontal teaching model operation in the typical school and the only model most Latin American teachers have experimented with in their professional life. The combination of typical school teachers' characteristics and the invitation to parrot transcribed knowledge built into most textbooks creates an insurmountable barrier to quality improvement in the typical school. Such combination leads to a close ally, and the "personalized type of instruction" is required for increasing quality. Also, "additional time for learning" and more "students' choices that increase motivation" are also instrumental for reducing age heterogeneity and increasing time on task. Each of these three activities are difficult to implement in a typical school. Therefore, drastic changes in teaching methods and resources allocation are required for those dreams of providing more democratic education outcomes to come true.

The Present Available Learning Time Is Not Enough to Achieve the Desired Learning Tasks

There are no incentives for the typical school to reach minimum levels of time allowed for learning, let alone for time really spent on task. Little time is available for learning the desired learning tasks in the typical school due to a short school year with few hours per day, absences of the actors, and wastage of teachers' time. The real number of school days per year in the typical Latin American school is close to 160 and the daily schedule varies between three and five hours.[15] Teaching-learning time is reduced because the actors do not attend school all year long. Students, mainly rural students, leave the school during part of the year and teachers make use of sick leaves. Students' absences may be related with harvest time, loading-unloading from trucks or ships, or the weekly or monthly agricultural or commercial fair.

And the little amount of time available for learning is poorly managed. A Venezuelan study of classroom management found that only 40 percent of class-time was used in actual teaching. Half of the balance is idle time and the other half correspond to waiting between activities.[16] Between 50 and 64 percent of teachers' time has been used in teaching in Chile, and between 22 and 29 percent in controlling discipline.[17] and similar results have been found in other Latin American countries. Poor use of time is probably related to the lack of tutorial or individualized work traditions in the region. "Frontal" (preaching) teaching techniques do not allow students to keep working alone (or in groups) on a learning task to increase usage of available time; and lack of motivation increases students unrest and the amount of class time spent in enforcing discipline, and to age-heterogeneity commented above.

A curriculum reform to implement a "personalized type of instruction" should be based on a realistic assumption of the daily amount of time that a well motivated teacher will be willing to spend in implementing such reform. Such assumptions must be built upon responses to questions about their professional training level and questions about: how much time teachers will spend in preparing the next day's classes; in the classroom; actually teaching in the classroom (not including time for class management); at the school (but not the classroom); at home preparing for classes, grading tests, and commenting on papers. Realistic responses to these questions would give a profile of the real operation of the school (taking into account the amount of time required for a poorly trained teacher to create significant learning experiences). Such a profile would probably include very little extra time with respect to the regular schedule. That profile would probably be quite different from the activities carried out by the highly selected teachers reading this chapter. Therefore, the pressing question is how to introduce change without increasing the actual daily schedule of teachers. Fortunately, there are cases where this near miracle has been implemented.[18]

Given the constraint on teachers' time and the long-term task of remodeling teachers' attitudes the successful solution has been to produce an entirely new generation of self-instructional textbooks with step-by-step instructions. Several criteria must be met by those self-instructional textbooks. For example, if group work is programmed and tasks are of the "right-answer" variety, the group will rapidly discover that one person can do the job better and more quickly than the group. In that case there will be little interaction, and research has found that interaction is the source of learning in group work.[19] In summary, a new breed of textbooks must be produced including step-by-step instructions on how students would work with the best education specialists. This is a long run process that should be started as soon as possible and to be completed in many future editions.

Few Student Choices Reduce Motivation and Intellectual Skills

There are too few students' choices in the typical school to reach a high level of motivation, reduce age heterogeneity and increase time on task. Research reports on class observations suggest that students in typical Latin American schools have few opportunities for autonomous thinking.[20] Students think for sure when they ask questions, respond to meaningful questions, write essays, and make decisions about learning experiences, but these activities are not frequent in the typical school.[21] Most teachers only accept questions related with the (usually boring) topic being transcribed (or "covered" in the chalkboard or orally) and original questioning is stifled. Most of teachers' questioning asks for rote repetition and lack the meaning required to stimulate thinking.

Free student writing tends to be minimized, because the frontal teaching model uses classroom time for transmission of information and teachers must grade and comment those exercises later in their free time. Organization of typical schools does not allow teachers to do that work during the daily schedule. In fact the amount of free writing detected in visits to schools is reduced to only one or two pages per year (usually students are asked to write a one page description of mid-year vacation time). Finally, a frontal teaching method based on copying and rote learning does not allow students to make personal decisions regarding their learning

Students' choices (albeit constrained) involves several learning experiences going on at the same time in the same classroom, while frontal teaching only allows one. Choices are specially important in classes where there is high age-heterogeneity. Therefore, lack of choices is especially damaging to deprived students attending classes with high age-heterogeneity, improving education for democracy.

In summary, unless teachers' time spent on speaking or copying in the chalkboard is drastically reduced, there will be no opportunity for students to engage in actual thinking or in activities that attract their attention. This change in time allocation represents, in fact, the introduction of a whole set of different child centered teaching methods and the possibility of including real life knowledge in the design of learning experiences.

The Rationales for an
Effective Education for Democracy

The analysis of the previous section concludes that given the inequity built in the typical school, a new model should be implemented. The new model should deliver a personalized type of instruction, initially based (but eventually less dependent) on self-instructional-textbooks with step-by-step instructions of how students would work with the best education specialists. Therefore teachers would have time to spend with students in formative evaluation (specially on free writing), posing questions that trigger thinking processes, designing activities that increase their motivation and attention, or changing the instructions of the textbook when deemed necessary.

Assuming that there is agreement in this "new" model (that rephrase old principles) the real challenge consists in designing how to *operate* and *improve* such school model. Such a model is already in operation in some 20,000 Colombian schools. Its success has been tested several times and the model has been carefully described elsewhere.[22] Multigrade Escuela Nueva (EN) pass a higher proportion of students and in spite of that their students achieve better results than student in graded schools (Table 8). Therefore the aim of this section is to present the rationale of the EN Colombian model and to use this rationale both for thinking about the characteristics of an education for democracy, selecting among alternative school models, and for improving operating models. This first version of the rationale (or improved versions) may help in eventually moving towards better delivery systems of education for democracy that can operate with the resources that each Latin American country can allocate to education.

Although EN first mobilize teachers by developing a shared vision in the demonstration school, opportunities for ongoing teacher development are provided by exposing them to a set of principles built into the sequence of activities suggested in the instructional materials. EN operates as the combination of seven approaches that are present at the same time in all school activities (learning experiences) and that are gradually better implemented as the teachers become more and more comfortable in their new leadership role, in shared goals and in the promotion of solidarity in the profession. A description of those seven approaches follows.

Seeking the Involvement and Benefits of All Parties Concerned

The Escuela Nueva (EN) program seeks the involvement of each teacher, child, and member of the community not only in the educational process, but in improving the quality of life of all actors. The teacher is trained in a

TABLE 8 Colombian Repetition, Work, and Student Scores in Five Tests

		"Escuela Nueva"				Rural Graduada		
Indicator	Grade	N	Score	∂	N	Score	∂	%
Repeaters	All		47.2%			53.9%		6.7%
Working students	All		38.3%			40.2%		1.9%
Academic Self-Concept	All	1840	36.1	5.4	1166	35.8	5.5	100.8%
Social Self-Concept	All	1850	33.1	4.8	1176	32.4	5.0	102.2%
Social/Civic Attitudes	1st	1060	13.2	3.1	587	12.4	3.2	106.5%
Social/Civic Attitudes	3rd	735	15.4	2.7	466	14.8	2.5	104.1%
Mathematics	3rd	1143	15.3	7.3	681	13.7	6.7	111.7%
Spanish	3rd	1143	13.8	5.2	684	11.6	5.4	119.0%

Source: C. Rojas and Z. Castillo, Instituto SER de Investigación, 1988.

number of specific activities, professional rewards are raised, and opportunities for learning about the community and teaching methods are offered each class day and in monthly collegial workshops.

EN maximizes student involvement on several levels—whole-class discussion, cooperative groups, and individual projects—and brings students' cultural and personal experience to most learning situations in order to make the classroom safe and instruction relevant.[23] Feeling that their culture is valued increases their self-esteem and, therefore, achievement is also raised.[24] At the same time, students learn to learn by themselves and progress toward self-reliance by making decision and bringing their own knowledge into the learning environment.[25]

Confirming research results[26] the EN student's learning is greatly enhanced by actively involving parents in support of their children's learning. EN offers parents, relatives and the community at large the opportunity to: participate in debates on school activities; feel that they generate culture (as noted by Paulo Freire); feel that their culture is fully valued in daily school activities (through the many local examples included in learning experiences); and feel that they have possibilities for contributing.[27] For example, the local artisan able to prepare clay is asked to teach the small children to manipulate the clay for molding their first letters.[28] As a result of such activity the artisan participates in school activities and his work is valued, the teacher accesses other learning materials and the children learn to read in an interesting way. When the student can ask his/her mother about a recipe of a favorite dish (an activity that can be carried out in the classroom as a cooking demonstration); when the students asks his grandfather what was the town like 30 or 50 years ago; or when the student asks her father what his job consists of; and the student writes the responses down to further comment on them in class we create a natural encounter between school and daily life.

Linking Skills-Based Learning Tasks with Daily Life

Escuela Nueva (EN) links the teaching of discrete skills with appropriate daily life applications in order to give students a sense of purpose. Teaching skills linked with daily life examples encourages expression and analysis in writing, mathematical thinking, and comprehension of what is read. This approach is specially important for disadvantaged students that often see less purpose for or meaning in skills-based learning tasks than do more-advantaged students; consequently they need help to find meaning in what they do in school. The EN reading material reflects and respects the life experiences and backgrounds of the students.

The EN school asks the student to identify local objects and activities related with work, transportation, health, food, production, history, geography, stories, fables, riddles, lullabies, vegetable, animals, minerals, and all other topics included in the national curriculum. This close linkage with daily life of deprived students adds meaning and interest to the learning experiences, and serves as a mechanism for easily including local experience into day to day learning experiences.

Writing for Systematic Thinking and Exchanges of Opinions

The Escuela Nueva (EN) curriculum emphasizes meaningful written communication as the final step of a thinking process. EN has stressed the value of writing activities in helping students to explore, organize, and refine their ideas about themselves and to construct and present their own interpretations of environment and subject matter.[29] The self-instructional textbooks draw on the experiences and knowledge of students, as well as on the realms of experience that are less familiar to students (mainly in the materials used for self-evaluation). EN places less emphasis on learning the mechanics of written language (spelling, punctuation, or grammar,[30] in isolation from the act of communicating in writing. Moreover, EN recognizes the importance of linking reading, writing, and oral expression.[31] The self-instructing textbooks integrate all aspects of the teaching of literacy, by having students read and discuss what they've written, or write about what they read. The textbooks indicate each of the moments of learning processes when students must do some writing. Group rewriting of individual pieces is suggested in order to reduce teachers' time spent in grading or formative evaluation of written reports. Consequently, teachers have time for evaluating the progress of students since the basic instructions and information for the students to do their work are already available in the textbooks, there do not have to be delivered by the teacher to each group, and the teachers are more available to answer specific requests of the students.

Decisions for Enhanced Motivation and Thinking

Escuela Nueva (EN) encourages students' decisions (within constrained alternatives) for enhanced motivation and thinking. Each time students make a decision about their learning they become committed about its implications and through process of systematic thinking. EN students are deeply engaged, interested and hard workers because, among other things, they worked with examples they care about in ways that are interesting and meaningful to them. The instructional textbooks force students to make many choices within a global curricular framework that makes sure that everyone develops similar high level skills[32] in order to select from examples such as: What stories will we study? How can we express our ideas about the stories? Who can inform us about that problem? How much information can be balanced with artwork to make a great poster?

The rule is very simple: whenever the self-instructional textbook can give a student a choice of any kind, it does. The one thing better than having students choose from a variety of modes of learning is having them generate their own options. A test on students' options in traditional schools should include at least the following four questions: How often do students have choices in the classroom? How often do students feel in control, in charge of themselves? How many decisions that really count are students allowed to make? How often do students feel important in your classroom?[33] The 21st century requires new minds, and reading, writing and arithmetic are not natural acts of the mind.[34] Therefore, students' options may help in the creation of such a new mind, suited to the demands of the new world.

Making Sure That Teachers' Schedules Leave Time for Facilitation

The EN teacher may have a long interview with one student, because the rest of the students are engaged in their own work. If other students are busy sharing ideas and skills, the teacher can relax and be listening carefully to each student. Instructional material should reduce the amount of time teachers spend in giving instruction or providing standard information (that can be written in a textbook). EN teachers, as good surgeons or violinists, are able to adjust the surgical technique or the tempo of the concert, but are not expected to create a whole new technique in each class performance. In fact the more time they work with the EN model the more adjustments are expected. The more practice they have the more EN teachers will be ready to adjust to individual differences.

Implementing EN should not affect at all teachers' free time (beyond the regular work schedule) and even use of their regular work time is expected to be more relaxed than in the typical school.

Adopting a Mastery Learning Conception of Educational Achievement

EN presents the material divided into short units. Lessons are presented largely through written materials, but there are opportunities for teachers to present some lessons (in cases when no previous knowledge is required). Students move through these lessons at their own rates and self-evaluate their work against suitable materials or take formative tests on each unit.[35]

The teacher decides which students fail the final (active) evaluation and gives the student (or arranges for older students to give) individual or group tutorial help on the unit before moving on to new material. In summary, EN looks for an equilibrium between Bloom's Learning for Mastery (LFM) and Keller's Personalized System of Instruction (PSI).[36]

Learning from Evaluating Escuela Nueva's Past Experiments

The cornerstone of developing EN is systematic questioning of the current instructional practice and willingness to modify in order to improve learning. The six criteria commented in this section could be used for selecting future improvements.[37] The package has now three main continuous evaluation activities: reports prepared by supervisors and coordinators of local microcenters; empirical research on achievement and related input factors;[38] and observations of the frequent visitors of the project.[39] The microcenters and the training network have developed into a continuous source of rich evaluative information. This source represents a law cost mechanism to keep a check on quality throughout the process of going to scale in the rural Colombia. Research results and observations of international agencies will be commented in the next section as the final step of the development process of the EN experiment.

The implementation of the Colombian EN school model suggests that meeting the basic learning needs may require some modest amount of additional resources, a drastic change in the allocation of available resources, and a careful strategy to bridge vicious circles developed by the traditional education model. The Colombian experience also suggests that EN eventually creates a new breed of innovative teachers willing to stimulate students to experiment and to observe and react to everyday life events, questions and problems. Therefore, EN would be able to create a "virtuous circle" of sequences of innovations.

Feasibility of an Effective Education for Democracy

In spite of the budget constraints generated by the economic crisis and foreign debt there are resources in Latin America to implement a new teaching model that seems to be cost-efficient, but political consensus must be reached before designing the implementation strategies. The modest additional cost of the new teaching methods should be compared with the additional benefit in the reduction of repetition levels and the increment in students reaching upper grades with the same present total costs (assuming that no early drop outs are generated by graduating from primary education on time). Furthermore, teachers will find it easier to teach students in age-homogeneous classes.

Although the economic crisis of the early 1980s affected education in Latin America more than in other regions, changes in education inputs are not reflected in terms of less inputs, but in terms of lower teachers' salaries. The "public spending earmarked for education per inhabitant" dropped in Latin America from US$88 to US$60 between 1980 and 1986, while in developing countries as a whole it dropped from US$29 to US$27 (Table 9). Despite this major financial restriction, enrollment increased and, during the same period, there was an even larger increase in the number of teachers (Table 10). Therefore, teachers' salaries were drastically reduced during the 1980-1987 period. This salary reduction is affecting present school operation and Latin America is witnessing: lowering teachers' motivation; an exodus of teachers towards other sectors of the economy; and teachers spend less time on students' education as many will supplement their income by working second jobs. The salary reducation affects future school operation because it becomes more difficult to recruit good high school graduates interested in becoming teachers. However, there are teachers in the classrooms and new teaching methods can gradually be introduced if teachers can spend a few days in a demonstration school and see that the proposed changes will reduce their work load.

Start up and unit costs of the Colombian EN were much lower than expected. While the development of the EN package took 15 years and a high investment was carried out in those years present operation costs are quite close to costs in traditional schools. The cost of supplying one student with study-guides (self-instructing workbooks) for four subjects per grade level is US$15, though textbooks should be provided to students. The average 100 books per school/class library cost between US$150 an US$225. Average training cost per teacher is US$82 per year.[40] Textbooks and library books are used at the school during a four year period, therefore the annual cost per student (assuming 30 students per teacher is reduced to US$8.2, that is, some 10 percent of the present annual cost (US$4.5 per student if textbooks are not included as an increment, i.e., five percent of the annual unit cost).

Implementing new teaching methods (as the EN model) that reduce repetition seems cost-efficient. Eleven million repeaters in primary education in South America[41] and 17 million in Latin America (some 30 percent of enrollments) suggest that the annual budgeted cost of poor quality, only in terms of repetition, is close to $2 billion.[42] The estimation is immediate given that the average cost per student in Latin American primary education is over US$100. Even small increments in quality, resulting in reduction of repetition would probably make cost-efficient any massive effort to increase the quality of education. The Escuela Nueva (EN) "unassembled

TABLE 9 Estimation of Public Expenditures in Education in Latin America and the Caribbean

	Total (Millions of Dollars)	Percent of GNP	Public Expenditure per Inhabitant
Latin America and the Caribbean			
1975	13,477	3.5	43
1980	31,397	3.9	88
1985	25,392	3.8	63
1986	24,701	3.5	60
Developed Countries			
1975	289,684	6.0	270
1980	525,271	6.0	471
1985	585,349	6.0	471
1986	688,001	5.8	595
Developing Countries			
1975	40,433	3.6	14
1980	93,384	3.9	29
1985	95,846	4.1	27
1986	98,413	4.0	27

Source: UNESCO, Statistical Yearbook, París, 1988.

TABLE 10 Estimates of Teachers and Students per Teacher in Latin America and the Caribbean

Level	1980	1985	1986	*Annual Growth Ratio 1980-1986*
Preschool				
Total Teachers (thousands)	177	301	343	11.7
Number of Students per Teacher	27	26	25	
Elementary Education				
Total Teachers (thousands)	2,234	2,566	2,620	2.7
Number of Students per Teacher	29	27	27	
Secondary Education				
Total Teachers (thousands)	1,108	1,377	1,432	4.4
Number of Students per Teacher	16	15	15	

Note: There are few differences between the figures in Tables 6 and 10.
Source: *UNESCO, Statistical Yearbook 1988*, París, 1988.

kit" discussed above increases present unit costs in 5 to 10 percent and, therefore, makes it very appealing to study its characteristics and impacts specially in countries with high repetition rates. Society, as a whole, would obtain good profits for investing money in reducing repetition as part of the education for democracy strategy.

Additional resources and reallocation of present resources must be agreed with the Minister of Finance and the Congress to provide incentives for a more efficient handling of resources earmarked for education. The 5 to 10 percent additional resources required to implement new teaching methods must be bargained in terms of reduction of repetition, more relevant education, equity of educational outcomes and development of civic values. It is a package deal that requires a multipartisan mid-term political backing over five to ten years for the new teaching methods to really mature. Reallocation of resources from personnel (mainly from small increases of the teacher-student ratio) to textbooks, furniture and maintenance needs also some commitment of the Ministry of Finance that are not going to be wiped out in the next fiscal squeeze. Without the certainty for internal reallocation of savings in personnel there would be no incentives for the Ministries of Education to increase the teacher-student ratios to reduce the differences in unit costs per levels or to increase the percentage of resources allocated to primary education.

Private commitments would probably increase with teaching methods that encourage use of local content and active participation of parents. Eventually, a more relevant education should be assessed by the society and more resources (public and private) should be allocated to education.

Implementation of new teaching methods might be combined with other strategies for improving basic education.[43] Some of those strategies have also small costs (for example, bilingual education or "grade zero"), but better teaching methods may be assessed in terms of their own effects.

In summary, the economic crisis has affected education in the 1980s improving education quality in terms of reduced teacher-student ratios and worsening its quality in terms of lower salaries, but there are no restrictions for improving the efficiency of those teachers now working in each classroom. A small percentage of additional resources (5 to 10 percent), can be handled given the cost-efficient estimates in terms of reduced repetition rates via-a-vis the small increment in the annual unit cost as well as other benefits more difficult to express in money terms. However, implementation of changes requires long term, explicit political support.

Notes

1. *Bulletin of the Major Project in the field of Education*, No. 18, April 1989, p. 7-30, Unesco-OREALC, Santiago.

2. Carlos A. Perez, Discurso pronunciado por el Presidente de Venezuela en el acto de instalación de la III Conferencia General de la Academia de Ciencias del Tercer Mundo, Caracas, Octubre 15 de 1990.

3. ECLAC, Caracas, 1989.

4. In 1987 Chilean children in the lowest quintile of income groups had on average 8.5 years of school compared with 12.3 years of schooling of the highest income group (Tabulations from the household survey *CASEN II*).

5. E. Schiefelbein, *Repetition, the Constraint for Reaching Universal Primary Education in Latin America*, Bulletin of the Major Project No. 18, OREALC, April 1989, p. 19.

6. E. Cuadra and G. Ewert, *Comparison of School Records with Parent's Information on Enrollment, Repetition and Dropout: A Field Study in Honduras*, Project Bridges, Harvard University, July, 1987. Wynn Crowder, *Repetition in the Province of Ganzu, China* (draft), Unicef, 1988.

7. L.A. Alonso, *La Cohorte Etarea: Una via Alternativa para el Estudio de la Eficiencia Interna en Educacion*, Division de Estadisticas y Sistemes, Ministerio de Educacion Nacional, Bogota, August, 1988. E. Schiefelbein, Repetition, op cit. Table 1.

8. A. Repossa, 3. J. Araneda et al, "Nivel de Comprensión Lectora en Escolares Rurales de la Comuna de Valdivia y Algunos Factores Condicionantes," *Estudios Pedagógicos*, No. 15, 1989, pp. 43-56.

9. Nacarid Rodriguez, *La Educación Basica en Venezuela, Escuela de Educación* (Universidad Central, Caracas, 1990); J. Filp, C. Cardemil et al., "Control Social, Disciplina y Cambio: Estudio de las Prácticas Pedagógicas en una Escuela Básica Popular," *Documento de Trabajo del CIDE*, 1987 (RAE 4553); Johana Filp, "El Primer Año de Escuela en Chile," *Documento de Trabajo del CIDE*, 1988 (RAE 5145); Grabriela Lopez, *The Organization of Teachers' Practices Embedded in Chilean Cultural Forms*. Tesis (Universidad de Toronto, 1988); J Assael et al., "Alumnos, Padres y Maestros: La Representación de la Escuela," *PIIE*, Universidad de Humanismo Cristoiano, Septiembre 1989.

10. Finn Ch., "The Biggest Reform of All," *Kappan* 71, No. 8, April 1990, pp. 584-592.

11. CPEIP, "Resultados por Estructuras en la Asignatura de Matemática del 4° Año de Enseñanza Básica en 1982," *Serie Estudios*, No. 120, Julio de 1984.

12. Only 30 percent of primary teachers have no professional certificate or degree, but some 10 percent have obtained their certificates through on-the-job training. There are enough trained teachers, but salary incentives for attracting trained teachers to isolated or risky areas are still missing. E. Schiefelbein, J. C. Tedesco et al., Primary Schooling and Illiteracy in LAC: 1980-1987. *Bulletin of the Major Project*, No. 20, December 1989.

13. Remedial coaching with extra teachers, community monitors and mothers has been tried with a fair amount of success, but it does not prevent the generation of new failures. The cost tends to increase sharply when extra teachers are used.

14. The names of Aristotle , Pestalozzi, Herbart, Dewey, Freinet, Makarenko, Parkhurst (Dalton) and Montessori may also be associated to each of those educational approaches now accumulated as the curriculum legacy (learning as inquiry; interest and motivation; individual differences) in D. Tanner and L. Tanner, *History of the School Curriculum* (MacMillan, 1989), p. 400.

15. Once holy days are discounted, Colombia reaches 170 school days with four to five hours per day totaling 680 to 850 hours per year, in comparison with 1100 in USA, 1300 to 1600 in Europe, and even more in Japan. J. B. Toro, *Primero, mi Primaria*. Para triunfar Fundación Social, Bogota, 1988.

16. Nacarid Rodriguez, *La Educación Básica en Venezuela* (Escuela de Educación, Universidad Central, Caracas, 1990).

17. Two sessions with a total observation time of 180 minutes in a deprived school operating a personalized curriculum. J. Filp, C. Cardemil et al., Control social, disciplina y cambio; estudo de las prácticas pedagogicas en una escuela basica popular, *Documento de Trabajo del CIDE*, 1987 (RAE 4553). V. Espinola reports that teachers spend only 72.5 percent of the class time inside the classroom in Evaluación del sistema de marcado como estrategia para mejorar la calidad de la enseñanza basica subvencionada, *Documento de Discusion del CIDE*, No. 5, 1990, p. 42.

18. Redefining basic education for Latin America—Lessons to be drawn from the Colombian Escuela Nueva, *Fundamentals of Educational Planning Series*, IIEP, Paris, 1991.

19. Cohen, "Continuing to Cooperate: Prerequisites for Persistence," *Kappan* 72, No. 2, October, 1990, pp. 134-138.

20. Johana Filp, *El Primer Año de Escuela en Chile* (Documento de Trabajo del CIDE, RAE 5145). See also Gabriela Lopez, "The Organization of Teachers; Practices Embedded in Chilean Cultural Forms," *Tesis*, Universidad de Toronto, 1988. J. Assael et al., "Alumnos, Padres y Maestros: La Representación de la Escuela," *PILE*, Universidad de Humanismo Cristiano, September 1989.

21. Beyond paying or not paying attention mentioned above.

22. Redefining basic education for Latin, ... op cit.

23. Similar strategies have been used in personalization of school instruction. M.W. McLaughlin and J. Talbert, "Constructing a Personalized School Environment," *Kappan* 72, No. 3, November 1990, pp. 230-235.

24. Curriculum may also be made more relevant. For example, inclusion of child survival topics may disseminate valuable information and contribute to the survival of their siblings.

25. Awareness of the learning strategies seems to be a way of increasing active student participation and responsibility, helping to make education more satisfac-

tory and effective. See C. B. Chadwick, Estrategias cognoscitivas y afectivas de aprendizaje, *Revista Latinoamericana de Psicologia* 20, No. 2, 1988, pp. 163-205.

26. Rods H. Becher, *Parental Involvement, A Review of Research and Principles of Successful Practice* (National Institute of Education, Washington, DC, 1984).

27. The late 80s developments in the USA such as the Chicago plan for school reorganization and statewide programs for school choice clearly demonstrate the growing importance of parent and citizen involvement in school affairs. See Ann Lieberman and Lynne Miller, "Restructuring Schools: What Matters and What Works," *Kappan* 71, No. 10, June 1990, p. 761.

28. Here EN would be using the "Stage or Apprenticeship Model," Fleschsig and Schiefelbein, op cit.

29. Learning can in fact be learning in the sense of discovery, because children seldom know exactly what they are going to say before they come to say it (J. Britton, *Prospect and Retrospect: Selected Essays*, Boynton/Cook, 1982, p. 110).

30. Difficulties in direct writing assessment have led to test student writing ability indirectly with examinations on grammar and usage (See Brian Huot, The literature of direct writing assessment: major concerns and prevailing trends, *Review of Educational Research* 60, No. 2, pp. 237-263). Teacher time required to assess individual reports may also be a factor in emphasizing grammar, that is solved in EN by group writing after individual reports are prepared.

31. R. Durst and G. Newell, "The Uses of Function: James Brittons' Category System and Research on Writing, *Review Educational Research*, Vol. 59, No. 4, Winter 1989, pp. 375-394.

32. Observe, classify, describe, ordering, compare, draw inferences, deduct, evaluate, or make decisions.

33. Carolyn Mamchur, But ... the curriculum, *Kappan* 71, No. 8, April, 1990, p. 636.

34. Robert Ornstein and Paul Erhlich, *New World New Mind*, Doubleday, 1989.

35. Quiz feedback seems to increase achievement in primary education students. See E. Cabezon, The effects of marked changes in student achievement pattern on the students, their teachers, and their parents: the Chilean case, Thesis, University of Chicago, 1984.

36. C. Kulic, J. Kulic and R. Bangert-Drowns, Effectiveness of Mastery Learning programs: a meta analysis, *Review of Educational Research* 60, No. 2, Summer 1990, pp. 265-299.

37. An additional criteria could be the use of group work to reduce uncertainty generated by open-ended learning tasks. This criteria is well built into the EN package, but can be used for evaluating future developments.

38. C. Rojas and Z. Castillo, op cit.

39. The present chapter is an example of the latter.

40. US$30 for travel, five days per diem @ US$8; US$2 for materials, US$10 for the instructor/animator.

41. E. Schiefelbein, Repeating ... op cit, p. 19.

42. In addition to the money required to provide a seat for a second year, repetition also involves spending more time at school (and additional expenses related to attending school) in order to attain a given level of education. This personal cost is borne mainly by poor urban-marginal and rural students. Deprived students may have repetition rates twice as high as the national averages. For deprived students repetition involves more time at school, but also having less time to help to family work and postponing the entrance to the labor force.

43. Seven strategies for improving the quality and efficiency of the educational system, Unit for Co-operation with Unicef and FP, *Notes, Comments* ... No. 192, Unesco ED-90/WS-30, Paris, July 1990.

2

Education Policy and Human Development in the Latin American City

José Luis Coraggio

Foreseeable Trends and New Policies for Dealing with Them

If current trends continue toward the end of the century, 77 percent of the population of Latin America will reside in cities.[1] This seems inevitable. Another projection indicates that half the urban population will be poor or poverty stricken.[2] These developments might be avoided if proper action is taken. Their principal cause is that the globalization of power and markets will mean a reduction of formal employment, asymmetry in the freeing of markets in favor of the more powerful countries, growing deterioration of our terms of trade, and a continual drain on savings for the sake of the foreign debt.[3] Globalization also brings a shift in the political and economic interest in Latin America, first of all toward other markets of the industrialized world and subsequently toward countries of the former socialist world and regions suffering from extreme poverty, such as sub-Saharan Africa. At the same time, the reforms being imposed on Latin American states imply a drastic reduction of policies (primarily those affecting cities) aimed at off-setting the social effects of the free interplay of the market.

These prospects are already a matter of concern to the agencies whose task it is to watch over the new world or regional order. Thus, the development banking institutions have been elaborating a new line of reasoning aimed at addressing this situation: in the short term, it involves making the remaining resources for social policy efficient and concentrating them on extreme poverty (equity); and in the long term, creating conditions for new growth through attracting private transnational investment (competitiveness). The problem is to what extent such compensatory policies, at present minimized, will not become permanent, requiring increasing resources as the new economic structures intensify still further the exclusion of the majority of the population from the benefits of economic growth. In any event, the result of this entire process is highly unstable; indeed, as the banks themselves point out, in order to make structural adjustment sustainable (and, ultimately, socially profitable), there must be political stability, which is difficult to maintain by the democratic process in a society undergoing ever-increasing polarization.[4]

Furthermore, in view of the conflicts that have arisen from the social situation brought on by globalization, the concern with governability has led the agencies of the United Nations system to seek a new paradigm that goes beyond a stability which is ultimately vulnerable. This has led to new language about "human development," the motto of which is "invest in people." This is guided by moral reasons that do not admit the growing injustice in the world and is based on a projected technology revolution that will continue to substitute information and know-how for energy inputs.[5]

As the structural adjustment paradigm has already drastically changed our states and their relationship to society, this proposed new social paradigm is already having consequences that go beyond discourse: new priorities and new homogeneous guidelines for social policies have begun to affect the global and national allocation of resources. Caught between their lack of indigenous answers and the conditionality of international credits, governments are tending to adopt such policies. The problem is that, under the real conditions of world power and crisis, the human development paradigm seems to be producing proposals that in fact boil down to focusing public policies (primarily education and health) on the world's sectors and regions of extreme poverty.

From the standpoint of Latin American cities, it is a matter of urgency to critically analyze these new social policies which, together with economic policies, are crystallizing a "world-market-friendly" urban context rather than a "people-friendly market." In such a context, who may enjoy what privileges in our cities will be determined by anonymous global forces. And if the political system further develops its adaptive streak and loses its vocation for contradicting global processes, politics will lose its ultimate meaning for people. Politics will have to do with the administration (and corruption) of public affairs rather than the building of political wills to improve life in human society. How to balance the budget and avoid inflation will replace social projects as the platform of candidates aspiring to represent the people. If to this is added the overwhelming effect of the mass media, which are also subject to world-wide accumulation strategies, democracy and self-determination will be little more than utopian ideas. And without legitimate governments backed by the people, the probability of having an influence on a transformation of the world order that excludes us will continue to be minimal.

Already the privatization and deregulation imposed on our countries imply a gigantic transfer of power from the political sphere (in process of "decentralization") to the economic sphere (in process of a rare degree of centralization). This in turn implies an additional loss of power for the social majorities, for their control of political power was possible, albeit imperfectly, and that power was supposed to be legitimized by them. With all its limitations, it enabled them to apply pressure in the streets or vote for the maintenance of a benefit, but no such impact will be possible on the protectionist policies of the North or the exclusive strategies of the great conglomerates of world capital.

Within this adverse context, ways must be found to empower the popular sectors to defend the right to life, generate more autonomous bases of enhanced reproduction of that life and redefine national self-determination.[6] Given the fragmented state of the popular camp, one such way is to think and act strategically in the various concrete public spaces, in the interstices between the predominance of the exclusive market and the new public policies. Moving forward with both the immediate resolution of the needs felt by the popular sectors and the establishment of a horizon of development to nurture positive expectations. This may imply accepting the opening up of the economy and the reform of the state, while at the same time advocating transition interventions which favor the immediate development of human capital, the basis of the popular economy (urban, in particular). This involves fighting for a more equitable distribution of initial resources between the capitalist corporate economy, the public economy and the popular economy.[7]

Throughout the remainder of this chapter, we shall endeavor to illustrate this in relation to a concrete policy that has been made the focal point of Latin American development: education policy.[8] We shall try to analyze whether the proposal to focus that policy on providing universal access to an efficient primary education, is (1) consistent with the human development paradigm which purportedly justifies it[9] and (2) suitable for the sectors which it is supposed to benefit. We shall also attempt to define variants or alternatives for redirecting the resources channeled by that policy.

The Policy of Education for All

"Education for all" is a global guideline for education policies formulated at Jomtien, Thailand, in 1990 with the sponsorship of UNESCO, UNICEF, UNDP and the World Bank, and was officially adopted by the Latin American Ministers of Education in the Quito Declaration (1991).[10] Its principal goal is to efficiently invest the remaining public resources of the educational sector into the achievement of universal access to basic education, promoting the participation of the community and the private business sector in that task.

In its broader interpretation, its purpose is to guarantee that every individual has the opportunity for relevant basic education of good quality in an ongoing learning process throughout his life. However, under conditions of funding shortages and within the framework of certain pedagogic concerns of the learning process, these policies focused on the poorest, may be reduced to providing a compensatory package of knowledge and skills barely adequate to enable their recipients to survive and improve their learning ability. This would result in concentration of resources in primary schooling, entailing a reduction of public support to higher education and nonformal education.

As clearly shown by the Jomtien initiative, however, effective learning requires an appropriate learning context, in which all members of the community of education policy will require that other policies ensure the availability of jobs and services for all. In other words, to be effective in promoting development, education policy must be part of an integral social and economic policy. Conspiring against this are the legacy of decades of narrowly sectoral approaches.

Thus, if we adopt the paradigm of human development, education policy cannot be viewed as the compensation of selected individuals for the poverty produced by the economic structures; rather it must itself contribute to the development of new economic structures that will reverse the trends toward social disintegration and pauperization. Thus, the present focus on inorganic segments of the poorest strata, with the corresponding abandonment of the urban middle strata (which has been justified by the observation that they have benefited from the assistance that ought to have been directed to the neediest), does not overcome, but instead consolidates the structures that reproduce the exclusion of the majorities and will require continual compensatory interventions.

Beyond the declarations and the documents, the effective changes in educational policy will depend to a large extent on the allocation of flexible investment resources (generally of foreign origin), inasmuch as current expenditure (in the hands of the national or local public sector) by itself tends to reproduce earlier structures. This is why the World Bank or

IDB have great leverage in the interpretation of the uniform guidelines accepted by governments. What is more, although in this and other areas of social policy foreign aid and credos do not amount to even five percent of the total public expenditure, the two-fold IMF/World Bank conditionality multiplies the related impact, since, going hand in hand with credits, reforms of the education system and criteria for the allocation of resources are imposed.[11]

Furthermore, the organizations in question (and here one must include "socially sensitive" agencies such as UNICEF and UNDP) are guided by criteria of effectiveness based on indicators of the volume of credos (or donations granted) and of the attainment of quantitative goals. This, too, leads to priority being accorded to primary school, as possibly the best way to change the existing indicators of world education in a successful way. Although the new language concerning education emphasizes the question of quality, in fact, the concern with improving the indicators of access (which in Latin America is not the principal problem) persists, and this in many cases may result in emphasis on the poorest rural areas.

As for economic policy, the main thrust is on macroeconomic adjustment, in an effort to institutionalize a favorable framework for the free play of market forces. These forces, it is believed, will generate new economic growth, although all the forecasts indicate that, should an upswing take place in the world economy, it will be "growth without employment." As for the programs (of microeconomic inspiration) intended to modernize the urban informal sector, they are accelerating a process of Darwinian selection of new businessmen, with disregard for a macroeconomic view that would foresee the longer-range effects of such injections of funds and skills into that sector.

The Case of Latin America

Let us assume for a moment the decision has been made to invest in primary education. Its relevance is beyond question, when we recall, for example, the children of the streets in the cities of Brazil. But admission to school guarantees neither that the child will remain there nor that s/he will acquire knowledge useful for life as a producer and as a citizen. There is general agreement that the quality of primary education must be improved. This cannot be achieved, however, merely by concentrating resources on new texts or though internal evaluations of learning achievements or the administrative decentralization of the primary school subsystem. To improve the quality of primary education effectively, it is necessary: (1) to extend and improve initial education, which, according to UNESCO/OREALC research, is the principal educational achievement in the region and is of fundamental help in making up for the disadvantaged start of children from poor homes, in addition to improving the opportunity for mothers to carry on their own activities; (2) to continue to invest in the higher levels of education, inasmuch as the region has internalized the continuation of education as a value and a fundamental motivation for completing primary school; and (3) to invest in improving the capacities, status and salaries of teachers, without which other actions designed to improve quality cannot be carried out efficiently.[12]

On the other hand, it is proposed that educational curricula should be properly geared to the future demand for skills arising from the economy. However, in view of the fact that it is the world market which will determine our long-term production structures, the demands that national private business might formulate today in depressed economies may considerably miss the mark in terms of what will be required in the future.[13] Here, the need for another approach to the urban economy is evident if we are really to achieve external efficiency in education (measured in terms of the benefits society derives from investing in this sector).

The Latin American urban centers, in particular the major cities, have the potential to transform the present chaotic aggregate of domestic activities, whether informal or not, through the deliberate promotion of a third (popular) pole in the urban economy, acting coherently from the State and society, that is capable of interacting competitively with the private corporate economy and the public economy. But this requires a common strategy that will integrate and impart direction to public policies intended for the popular sectors and create a more equitable starting point in the distribution of resources, not only within the popular camp, (between the extreme poor and middle sectors) but also with respect to the privileged quarter of the population that is consolidating and emerging from structural adjustment.

Actually, from a global point of view, Latin America should have sufficient resources of its own to be able to invest autonomously in the training of its human capital. However, because of the extreme polarization of income and ownership (in metropolitan areas, more than 50 percent of the income goes to less than 25 percent of the population) and the fact that the surplus thus appropriated tends to be spent on luxury consumption or go into speculative investment. The region continues to be dependent on foreign resources to sustain social policies that are not in line with the interests of these minorities. To this is added the fact that the servicing of the Latin American foreign debt, the burden of which falls disproportionately on the popular sectors, siphons off every decade, the servicing of what is needed to achieve compulsory primary education throughout the world by the year 2000. Unless these internal and external restrictions (which are ultimately political in character) change, or a development process of a different order is embarked upon, the quality of urban life will continue to deteriorate.

Consequently sectoral policies such as education for all must be framed within a strategy directed toward urban development rather than being dispersed in an attempt to focus on the poorest inorganic segments, an approach apparently inspired by patronizing models for isolated rural communities. Even from the standpoint of the world's leadership this approach is erroneous. As even the World Bank concludes in its World Development Report 1990, "urban poverty will become the most significant and politically explosive problem in the next century,"[14] and this requires new approaches for an urban reality in which Latin America, as the most urbanized region of the developing world, is a critical example.

As a result of the crisis and adjustment policies, there has been an increase in social polarization, with a high percentage of what had previously been middle-range urban sectors now being situated below the poverty line and another considerable percentage living in conditions of great vulnerability These sectors have had educational opportunities but today it is recognized that it was of poor quality, and in any event, their know-how and skills are becoming obsolete in the face of the vertiginous economic and technology changes taking place. This, rather than making them privileged, adds them to the mass of those in need of high-quality education. Apart from this, if the point is to develop human capital, we must recycle and update the already existing capital and avoid falling into procedures characterized of the market, which creates new wealth by destroying existing wealth.

Conditions for an Education Policy Oriented Toward Human Development

Beyond the initial "big push," which implies drastic reforms—some of which are already being implemented (decentralization, adaptation of curricula to local conditions, improvement of school tests, etc.)—and fresh resources,[15] the policy of education for all, as the nucleus of a project for building a dynamic human capital, must be designed in such a way as to ensure the sustainability of human capital development in three ways: (1) by increasingly generating its own base of material resources; (2) by constantly feeding back into individual and collective motivation to learn and to produce new knowledge systematically; and (3) by keeping alive the political will to accord priority to education as an investment for multiplying development opportunities.

Accordingly, the following recommendations are made:

1. Education must be connected from the outset with economic development so that new knowledge skills and attitudes may have

the opportunity to be applied to the satisfaction of basic needs (work, health, nutrition, housing, habitat, participation, etc.) as part of the learning process. The experience (albeit in limited spheres) of NGOs and agencies such as UNICEF show this to be possible.[16] The complexity and magnitude of the large Latin American cities poses a challenge to this area.

2. Given the inability of the capitalist corporate economy and the public economy to provide opportunities for all, the development of an urban popular economy must be promoted. This will not only provide fresh resources for maintaining the material base of the educational system, but will also maintain and enhance the motivation for systematic acquisition of knowledge perceived as useful for life.

3. Curriculum design must be oriented toward the community as the elementary unit. This means working with and for local communities as integrated or integrable totalities (instead of focusing on isolated segments of the poorest, school-age girls, etc.). Attention must be paid to both rural and urban populations; however, in an initial stage it may be advisable to concentrate on urban settlements rather than on scattered settlements, where a favorable context for learning is greatly lacking. Consequently, the implementation of a policy of education for all in Latin America entails adequately delimiting existing or visual urban and rural-urban communities, a task that is beyond the possibilities of a sectoral view. These options are dictated by a number of reasons:

   a. In general, endeavors simply to alleviate extreme poverty by providing goods and services to the neediest individuals or families can be supported only through the continual injection of external resources and political will, which thus reinforces the economic and political dependency of the recipient groups. Self-sustained structural equity requires the establishment of new organic structures which, by their very nature, must be socially and ecologically heterogeneous;

   b. As already pointed out, poverty in Latin America is becoming more and more an urban problem. By the year 2000, it will no longer be a question of marginalized sectors or segregated zones within the city, but of urban masses of "chronically poor" and of the "nouveaux pauvres" coming from the middle segments;

   c. Poverty in Latin American cities does not take the form of Apartheid. Shanty-towns and slums—favelas—are inhabited by a broad spectrum of social strata; to try to single out only the cases of extreme poverty from among that spectrum would be highly costly and ineffectual and would contribute to the disintegration of society;

d. As recognized in a recent World Bank document on urban policy,[17] the competitiveness our economies are urged to develop will be connected more with urban systems than with the rural sectors or the productivity of isolated urban enterprises;

e. As soon as one looks at it within a development perspective, one readily grasps that education of school children suffice to bring about the changes in cultural patterns and basic knowledge that development requires. Only a synergistic approach to the implementation of education policy can render it effective and efficient. This requires puffing all the modules of education and learning to work at the same time, belonging in the various elements of the community as active components of teaching/learning: parents' associations, teachers' associations, NGOs, churches, corporate and social organizations, the mass media, etc., so as to create a community learning context.[18]

4. Whenever a choice is imposed by the shortage of resources education for all should focus on key urban or rural-urban communities having a multiplier potential. In other words, those capable of efficiently inducing similar developments in other communities through their horizontal and vertical techno-economic relationships and their cultural affinities and are also capable of and committed to making a contribution to the revolving fund of financial and human resources for universal education.

This necessary option, justified only if there exits the guarantee that an increasing portion of the resources generated by development will subsequently be directed toward promoting development in areas not accorded priority now, although in need of help, must be accompanied as an adjunct and not as a central policy, by the spreading of social safety nets to meet the needs of those areas momentarily relegated to the background. There are also political reasons to support this approach:

a. In general, it will not be possible to obtain lasting consensus on measures that eat up resources yet are mere stopgaps for alleviating the situation of less than a fifth of the population. This would imply leaving half the urban population (in large part the new poor and the remaining precarious middle-class segment in the hands of a hostile market. Thus, the political sustainability of such an education policy requires a broader distribution of benefits and, at the same time, a plausible promise of a more permanent solution to extreme poverty;

b. Focusing on the poorest rarely goes beyond compensatory approaches. This tends to reinforce the patronage system rather than promoting the autonomy of the popular sectors, as one would expect from a sustainable human development approach.

Some Consequences for the Definition and Operationalization of Basic Learning Needs

If, as advocated at Jomtien, the education process involves meeting basic learning needs, comprising "both essential learning tools (such as literacy, oral expression, numeracy, and problem solving), and the basic learning content (such as knowledge skills, values, and attitudes) required by human beings to be able to survive, to develop their full capacities, to live and work in dignity, to participate fully in development, to improve the quality of their lives, to make informed decisions, and to continue learning," then it is obvious that on the whole, such needs change with the actual context.[19] However, given the long-term nature of education, the investment to meet those needs must also take into account the development planned for that context. Thus, determining basic learning needs is an ongoing process in which fulfillment of the expectations and desires of the members of the community, objective analysis of empirical trends, and proposals for the transformation of the community and of society must all come together.

The role of education policy cannot, therefore, be viewed as responding to preconceived needs; rather, education actions are themselves generators of needs and demands, mobilizing (or paralyzing) the motivation to learn, nourished by the hope of personal or social development. For cultural reasons, in the case of Latin America, acquiring an education has not been so much an answer to a spiritual imperative as an instrument for social advancement. Thus, it is important that the traditional link between education and social mobility has been weakened by this crisis. It is necessary, therefore, to restore the tie between education and the material underpinnings of improved quality of life.

This being the case, determining basic learning needs does not amount simply to recording the demands or needs expressed or felt by the people. It requires determining, on a basis of participation, the development collectively desired by the community and the society. For the same reason, it is by nature a political process, in which the popular sectors must acquire the ability to represent their interests on the political scene and to assume a direct share in the management of the policies they seek to promote. Despite the complications that this may mean for education management, it is an inevitable course if education is truly to constitute a pivot for development. At present, Latin American experience shows that the market does not provide the right signals for orienting the educational system. It also shows that the opinions of experts cut off from the social base have not offered any guarantee of efficacy, either.

This renders more urgent the need for a strategic framework, democratically designed and approved, for grass-roots social development. Within such a framework, the question of programming the education sector becomes both more complex and more feasible. The political nature of the education programming process reminds us that other proficiencies are required, beyond the "work culture," to nourish a democratic social life: managing community services; designing projects and mobilizing resources to implement them; understanding and assessing the operation of local governments; helping to determine generalizable and feasible community objectives; recognizing and communicating with other members of the community and with members of other communities; making democratic decisions on questions involving conflicting interests; collectively finding meaning in a world undergoing change at a dizzying pace.

Conclusion

Urban specialists customarily reserve the term "urban policies" for public interventions involving physical infrastructure networks and the related local services (transport, water, sanitation, housing, waste disposal, etc.) and also some policies invoking processes considered local (urban real estate market, housing, property taxes, and local rates for services, zoning, regulations relating to environmental pollution, etc.).

However, if what we are discussing is the quality of life in the cities, we must admit that is affected by other policies of a national order (monetary policy, policies on employment and wages, technology, health, education, human rights, regulations relating to property rights in general, etc.), as well as other processes, of a global order (to such an extent that the local real estate market is being increasingly influenced by phenomena in other countries near and far).

The term "urban," therefore, has less to do with certain types of goods or services or with the spatial arrangements of cities than with a regionalization of societies less and less relevant in a world undergoing globalization in which the concepts of community and daily life are central.

Thus, if one attempts to have an impact on the living conditions of urban communities, an examination of global processes and national and global policies is essential for understanding and proposing development alternatives, as we have tried to illustrate here with the case of education policy.

Notes

1.   See Alfredo E. Lattes, "La Urbanización y el Crecimiento Urbano en América Latina Desde una Perspectiva Demográfica," in *La Investigación Urbana en América Latina, Tomo 3: Las Ideas y su Contexto*, José Luis Coraggio, ed. (Quito: CIUDAD, 1989).

2.   See ECLAC, "El Perfil de la Pobreza en América Latina a Comienzos de los Años 90," in *Notas Sobre la Economía y el Desarrollo*, No. 536 (Santiago, ECLAC, November 1992): ECLAC, "Panorama Social de América Latina, Edición 1991," in Notas Sobre la Economía y el Desarrollo, No. 517/518 (Santiago: ECLAC, November 1991); ECLAC/UNDP, *Magnitud de la Pobreza en América Latina de los Ochenta* (s.l., ECLAC/UNDP, 31 May 1990).

3.   See ECLAC, *Transformación Productiva con Equidad* (Santiago: ECLAC, 1990).

4.   See World Bank, *World Development Report 1990*. Poverty, (Washington, D.C., 1990); Inter-American Development Bank/UNDP, Reforma social y pobreza. *Hacia una agenda integrada de desarrollo* (Washington, D.C., 1993).

5.   See Boutros Boutros-Ghali, "So that the Poor, the Impoverished and the Suffering May Have a Better Life" (translated from the Spanish), Declaration of the Secretary-General of the United Nations, *Notas Sobre la Economía y el Desarrollo*, No. 530 (Santiago: ECLAC, June-July 1992); UNDP, Human Development Report,

6.   Here we are referring to the shaping of a popularly based political will capable of formulating and backing an alternative project on the national or world development.

7.   On this, see José Luis Coraggio, *Ciudades sin Rumbo* (Quito: CIUDAD-SIAP, 1991); *Economía Popular y Políticas Sociales* (Quito: Instituto Fronesis, forthcoming).

8.   See *Educación y Conocimiento: Eje de la Transformación Productiva con Equidad* (Santiago: ECLAC/UNESCO, 1992).

9.   See José Luis Coraggio, *Desarrollo Humano, Economía Popular y Educación (El papel de las ONG Latinoamericanas en la Iniciativa de Educación para Todos)*, CEAAL Papers (Santiago, 1993).

10.   See UNDP/UNESCO/UNICEF/WORLD BANK, *Meeting Basic Learning Needs*, background document of the World Conference on Education for All, Jomtien, 5-9 March 1990; *World Conference on Education for All: Meeting Basic Learning Needs*.

Final Report (New York, 1990); José Luis Coraggio, "Economia y educación en América Latina. Notas para una agenda de los 90," CEAAL Paper No. 4 (Santiago, 1993).

11. Although the World Bank has conducted and made use of an important volume of research in the field of education, the theoretical and methodological bases of that research must be put to the test, not only from the standpoint of practice (which may take a decade before conceptual errors are detected), but also from the point of view of other pedagogic concepts and notions regarding the relationship between education and economy (see the study referred to in note 9).

12. Furthermore, the teacher is by nature a part and a crucial multiplier of the human capital whose development is sought. Here it is obvious that adjustment policies aimed at reducing public expenditure, and in particular the payroll, have an adverse impact on the effectiveness of the main policy of human development.

13. For that reason, a significant voluntary contribution of that sector to the education system cannot be expected.

14. See World Bank, *Urban Policy and Economic Development: An Agenda for the 1990s* (Washington, D.C.: World Bank, 1991), p. 4.

15. Here it must be pointed out that a large portion of the new funds allocated to primary education by international agencies come from the reduction of other lines of investment in education or other social policy sectors that have lost their priority.

16. In view of the enormous effort that the effective implementation of a policy of education for all would entail, the resources and skills of NGOs can play a fundamental role here. However, this poses a number of challenges for them: working with heterogeneous communities in a pluralistic manner; going beyond small local projects, which while qualitatively important, are unable to bring about structural changes in the life of the target groups; learning to coordinate with one another and/or become more multifaceted in their skills and interests; changing their ideological stances with respect to the state, the school, international agencies and social organizations, being more pragmatic in the endeavor to contribute effectively to sustainable human development; agreeing to be more transparent and adapting their institutional behavior to new relationships and the types of resources they imply; and contributing to the national and local capacity to design their own alternatives in a dialogue with foreign agencies.

17. World Bank, *Urban Policy and Economic Development: An Agenda for the 1990s* (Washington, D.C.: World Bank, 1991).

18. Community participation is often understood in the narrow sense of providing schools with material resources.

19. See *World Conference on Education for All Meeting Basic Learning Needs. Final Report* (New York, 1990), p. 43.

3

Neoliberal Education Policies in Latin America: Arguments in Favor and Against

Robert F. Arnove

A tidal wave of conservative thought swept over Latin America in the 1980s. Originating in the metropolitan centers of North America and Europe, the wave extended all over the world. Its impact changed the familiar landscape of the state's relations to civil society. According to McLean, "The era of state concentration, centralization, and equalization was replaced by one of state withdrawal. Privatization, localization, and consumer choice became the slogans of the new age."[1] Education policies also were dramatically altered to reflect changed economic policies.

While conservative in nature, these policies are frequently denominated "neoliberal." The term derives from the neoclassical economic theories expounded by major international donor agencies like the World Bank and the International Monetary Fund (IMF) and their consultants. The theories are based on work of classical economists Adam Smith and David Ricardo, who believed that the role of the state consisted in establishing the conditions by which the free play of the marketplace, the laws of supply and demand, and free trade based on competitive advantage would inevitably rebound to the benefit of all. Government policies, based on these notions, have led to a drastic reduction in the state's role in social spending, deregulation of the economy, and liberalization of import policies. The educational counterparts of these policies have included moves to decentralize and privatize public school systems.

Fiscal stabilization and structural adjustment policies associated with neoliberalism are designed to reduce a country's budgetary deficits and external debt while bringing inflation under control. These were serious problems throughout Latin America in the 1980s, where, in certain countries, the annual inflation rate exceeded one thousand percent. The indebtedness of two Latin American countries alone, Brazil and Mexico, exceeded $200 billion. The servicing and repayment of external debts was crippling the capacity of countries to grow economically. In need of foreign capital, the countries of Latin America (similar to those of Africa and Eastern Europe) turned to the IMF and the World Bank to obtain a good credit rating and access to foreign capital on reasonable terms. The "conditionalities" imposed by these external donors, while necessarily involving, in the short-run, cuts in social spending, a tightening of the belt and economic hardships for frequently the poorest members of a society, in the medium-run are supposed to lead to economic stability, and in the long-run to economic growth. The argument also is made that in the absence of such economic stability and growth, democracy is unlikely to flourish.

Education policies recommended by the staff of the World Bank also are supposed to favor democratization of school systems and more efficient use of scarce public resources to reach the neediest members of a society, while requiring elites to pay for the most costly levels of education that have the lowest rate of economic return.[2]

This chapter examines the arguments in favor of and against such education policies (i.e., decentralization and privatization) with regard to how they affect three central challenges facing all Latin American countries as well as most societies around the world. These challenges involve the need to increase the equity, quality, and efficiency of an education system.[3] Moreover, the chapter examines the extent to which these policies have contributed to improving literacy and basic education opportunities for the adult populations of Latin America.

Challenges to Education

Concerns associated with *equity* include the need to improve access and retention rates of school-age children and youths, particularly from the most disadvantaged sectors of society. As we see in Table 1, repetition and dropout rates are particularly high. In many countries, approximately one-third of students typically repeat first grade, and in some countries a majority do not complete the fifth or sixth grade of primary education. In 1989, the percentage of students graduating from sixth grade without ever having to repeat a grade ranged from a low of one percent in Brazil to a high of 54 percent in Uruguay, which, according to Table 1, clearly is an exception. It should be noted that the figures presented in the table do not indicate the percentage of students who never enter the formal education system. In the case of Brazil, this figure was 15 percent for the entire country, and as high as 35 percent for the impoverished Northeast Region.[4] Similar rates prevail in many countries in Latin America, and especially for rural and indigenous populations. Failure to extend a basic education that provides the fundamental skills of literacy and numeracy significantly weakens the prospects for achieving economic growth and a democratic political system.

TABLE 1 Latin American Repetition and Completion Rates in Primary Education in 1989 by Percentage

Country	First Grade Repeaters	Sixth Grade Graduates	Sixth Grade Non-Repeating Graduates
Argentina	31	83	17
Bolivia	33	47	9
Brazil	53	34	1
Chile	10	85	41
Colombia	31	87	26
Costa Rica	22	79	31
Dom. Rep.	58	38	3
Ecuador	33	81	34
El Salvador	54	50	4
Guatemala	55	59	9
Honduras	53	66	12
Mexico	33	77	23
Peru	28	76	21
Panama	-	86	33
Paraguay	33	71	20
Uruguay	15	91	54
Venezuela	28	62	14

Source: Wolff, Laurence, Ernesto Schiefelbein, and Jorge Valenzuela, 1994, *Improving the Quality of Primary Education in Latin America and the Caribbean.* Washington, DC: The World Bank.

The challenge of *quality* is related to what is learned in school: what skills and knowledge are acquired in school and how does the cognitive achievement of students in one school system compare with those in others. Notions of excellence and effectiveness enter the discussion at this point. A common argument suggests that a too rapid expansion of educational systems will result in lower standards and diminished quality. Since the 1950s, arguments over equity versus quality have raged throughout the world with different societies placing emphasis on one goal over the other at a particular historical juncture. In Latin America, the pendulum has swung from the pole of quality in the 1950s and early 1960s, when higher education was emphasized, to the pole of equity, from the late 1960s to the mid-1980s, to attempts to balance both over the past decade.[5] However, the momentum now appears to be swinging in the direction of an emphasis on quality.

International comparisons of educational achievement over the past three decades indicate that even more prosperous Latin American countries with very well developed education systems, such as Chile, lag far behind the industrialized countries of North America, Europe, and the Pacific on reading and science tests.[6] In 1994, the Educational Testing Service found that among a sample of thirteen-year olds who had completed fifth grade, only the Mozambican student population scored lower than Brazil on measures of mathematics and science achievement. The top five percent of mathematics students in São Paulo, the most industrialized city in the country, achieved scores that were barely comparable to the average score of students in Formosa, Korea, and Hungary.[7] Such results alarm educational policy makers who believe that their countries need workers more highly skilled in mathematics and the sciences if they are to compete more effectively in the global economy.

The challenge of efficiency is imperative in the face of the economic stagnation that characterized much of the region during the period 1980-1995, and the corresponding reductions in education budgets. In fact, the 1980s have been termed the "lost decade" for development in Latin America. Economic expansion, experienced at high rates from the 1950s through the 1970s, slowed considerably in the 1980s and 1990s. In the 1960s, the average annual GNP growth rate for Latin American economies was 5.7 percent. In the 1970s, the growth rate was 5.6 percent, despite difficulties caused by the oil crisis. By the 1980s, the average annual GNP growth rate for Latin American countries dropped to 1.3 percent.[8]

As a result of this economic downturn, significant improvements in education spending made during the 1960s and 1970s were effectively negated by drastic spending cuts in education. According to Fernando Reimers:

> On average, (unweighted) per capita expenditures in education in Latin America increased by 4.29 percent per year between 1975 and 1980, while they decreased by 6.14 percent between 1980 and 1985. The progress in educational finance made in the seventies was undone in the eighties.[9]

For example, in Bolivia, between 1975 and 1980, per capita expenditure on education increased at an annual rate of 3.62 percent. But, between 1980 and 1985, per capita expenditure on education decreased at an annual rate of 42.03 percent.[10]

With regard to the issue of adult illiteracy: although Latin America and the Caribbean has the lowest illiteracy rate of any developing region—27 percent overall, as compared with 57 percent for Africa, and 44 percent for Asia—there are notable disparities in literacy attainment. Women are at a disadvantage relative to men: in 1990, they had an illiteracy rate of 30.4 percent, compared with 24.2 percent for men.[11] Indigenous populations and rural populations frequently have illiteracy rates double or triple that of urban, *mestizo* populations; and it is not uncommon for less than one-third of rural women in a number of countries (for example, Guatemala and Bolivia) to be literate.

Even countries with a history of national literacy campaigns continue to have high levels of illiteracy. In Brazil, there have been a series of literacy initiatives over the past four decades, beginning with the pioneering work of world-renowned adult educator Paulo Freire in the early 1960s. Despite such efforts, the overall illiteracy rate in the country in 1995 was approximately 18 percent, and in the northeast, where Freire initiated his program of adult education for cultural freedom, the rate reaches 35 percent.

The 1980 Nicaraguan National Literacy Crusade (CNA) is internationally recognized as one of the most dramatic and successful campaigns of the twentieth century. The Crusade is credited with reducing the illiteracy rate in the country by more than one half—from approximately 50 percent of the population over the age of 10 to under 23 percent.[12] But by 1995, due to a series of factors—the war situation in the country during the Sandinista period, many individuals losing the minimal literacy skills they acquired during the CNA, the continuing high dropout rate among primary school children, and population growth—the number of illiterates was not only approaching, once again, 50 percent of the population over the age of 10, but the number of illiterates had grown from approximately 723,000, in 1980, to over one million in 1995.

The magnitude of the illiteracy problem is growing not only in Nicaragua, but in many countries of Latin America, such as Argentina, once considered to have achieved near universal levels of literacy. The question is whether or not countries will consider literacy and adult basic education as a priority, when compared with the levels and types of education favored by the major international and national donor agencies. Indeed, in light of the following arguments, it appears to be highly unlikely that adult education will be accorded much in the way of public resources.

Arguments in Favor of Neoliberal Education Policies

Essentially, neoliberal education policies favor investing in the first four years of schooling as against investing in secondary and higher education, which, according to cost-benefit analyses, register a lower social rate of return.[13] The policies advocate charging user fees at the secondary and especially tertiary levels of education. Subsidizing private provision of schooling as cost effective for governments is a further tenet. In addition to such moves, which facilitate privatization of schooling, neoliberal policies favor decentralization of education systems, characterized by hierarchical, bureaucratic structures with most administrative functions located in a capital city.

The arguments in support of these policies follow.

1. A decentralized and privatized education system is more likely to be democratic, efficient, and accountable than a centralized, state-directed system. The state in Latin America has been historically authoritarian, inefficient, and corrupt.

Many countries in the region are emerging from repressive military regimes (Argentina, Brazil, Chile, Uruguay, Honduras, and Guatemala) or socialist regimes (Nicaragua), where the state was all powerful and intrusive. In authoritarian regimes, school systems are more likely to be used as instruments of indoctrination with curricula and textbooks being heavily censored to permit the expression of only a narrow range of ideas. The strengthening of civil society vis-a-vis the state is critical to the creation of a pluralistic, democratic society.

Even where nominally democratic regimes exist, state bureaucracies, at all levels of government (from the federal to the municipal), are characterized by graft. All too often public office is considered an entitlement to personal enrichment. Cronyism under various names and guises leads to incompetent and unnecessary personnel being hired—often to ghost appointments—to kick-backs and payoffs that ultimately mean that needed funds and equipment may never reach schools and school children, unless they reside in areas with the greatest political clout.[14]

A decentralized system, although not immune to corruption, is likely to be more accountable, if only because the actions of public officials are more visible to proximal constituencies. Indeed, the argument may be made that the abuses of bureaucratic, state monopolies of education can only be tempered or eliminated by privatizing education as much as possible.

Market forces represent the most efficient means of allocating scarce resources among competing claims for educational provision. If families were allotted the equivalent of public per capita expenditures on education, they would tend to send their children to the best schools they could. Good schools would attract more students and flourish, and bad schools would close or attempt to reform themselves.

Closely aligned with notions that decentralization and privatization are conducive to more democratic and accountable education system is the following argument.

2. Decentralized education systems make more educational sense because they are more responsive to local community needs and realities.

In countries with heterogenous populations and vast differences in geography, it makes little sense to have a uniform curriculum and a central bureaucracy making decisions that govern daily routines. While a core of common knowledge, concepts, and values should be taught in all schools, there is need for substantial variations in curricula and texts to reflect differing regional/local contexts. The role of the state can be normative in establishing basic standards for all and in guaranteeing, for example, the rights and responsibilities of teachers. However, the state cannot possibly be responsible for administering the internal, day-to-day affairs of schools. Decisions concerning which teachers to hire, how to expend monies, and what improvements to make in programs and facilities should be determined at the level of each school. Parental and student choice combined with distinctive learning environments shaped by each school community represents an ideal approach to diversifying curricula and fostering a pluralistic, democracy.

3. These moves to dismantle the role of the state in education contribute to the (a) empowerment of teachers as well as parents and communities, and (b) to the likelihood of effective school reform.

Empowerment involves giving people a voice to articulate their interests and the means to solve the pressing existential problems facing them and their collectivities. Decentralized structures that involve teachers, parents, and major stakeholders in important educational decision-making is empowering.

Furthermore, the empowerment of teachers is closely related to the professionalization of teaching. If autonomy is an important characteristic of an occupation considered to be a profession, then, more decentralized or site-based management will certainly strengthen the ability of teachers to determine how best to serve their clients (students).

Teachers, however, also need the input and support of parents and other important education stakeholders. Their participation in school councils as well as community-level decision-making bodies enhances the like-lihood that locally based educational reform efforts will be successful because they are more representative of community interests. Furthemore, such locally-based decision-making contributes to the possibility of consensus-building in societies frequently characterized by deep divisions.

4. In a poor country, various moves to decentralize and privatize education represent a principal means to obtain additional funds to raise teacher salaries and improve school physical plant.

Given the economic setbacks suffered by most Latin American economies during the period 1980-1995, most of the cuts in education budgets have been at the expense of teachers. Teacher salaries fell 34.8 percent between 1980 and 1989 for the region as a whole. Particularly striking cases are El Salvador, where teachers' annual salaries fell 68.4 percent (from $7,980 to $2,514), and the Dominican Republic, where teacher salaries experienced a 60 percent reduction (from $2,432 to $974).[15] Major cuts generally have been made in funds for school supplies and equipment, and the construction and maintenance of school buildings.

Instituting minimal user fees, especially beyond the first four years of basic education, represents a means of supplementing limited budgets for teacher salaries and school improvement. In destitute countries like Nicaragua, the Ministry of Education (MED) has signed agreements with individual high schools that grant them substantial administrative and budgetary autonomy. The schools are required to charge a monthly fee of 10 *córdobas* (less than $2.00) per student. The MED supplements these fees with an allocation of 15 cs. per student, which it estimates to be the cost per pupil at the most efficiently operated schools in the country.

The MED reasons that these arrangements benefit both the individual schools and the education system in general. The receipt of per pupil allocations contingent upon average daily attendance rates induces teachers to give greater attention to the quality of instruction in order to reduce dropout rates. If the school is efficient in its operations, maintaining a high ratio of students to teachers and staff and conserving energy costs, extra funds will be available to increase teacher salaries.[16]

Moreover, the MED calculates that it will save approximately 7cs. per student by means of these arrangements with individual schools. This savings is based on the discrepancy between the national average monthly per student expenditure of 22cs. and the 15cs. per student allocation to autonomous schools. With the greater efficiencies introduced by such site-based management, the MED estimated that it would save approximatley

15 million cs. (approximatley $2.65 million in 1993), which could be used to support primary teachers, the poorest paid educators.[17]

5. Policies that emphasize primary education and involve charging fees that approximate the true cost of a university education are both more equitable and economical.

Primary education provides the basic literacy and numeracy for a productive workforce and an enlightened citizenry. It is the least costly level of education and the best investment for a country. According to Psacharopoulos, a leading economist of education at the World Bank, "the so-called rate of return to investment in primary education in developing countries is around 25 percent compared to 12 percent for higher education." He goes on to note, "Such a rate does not mean that a country should invest only in primary education, but there should be a bias toward primary education. What would be the point of allocating 40 percent of the state's budget for university education if the country has an illiteracy rate of 90 percent among women in rural areas?"[18]

Indeed, in a number of Latin American countries, higher education expenditures represent over 40 percent of the national education budget, while tertiary-level students comprise usually less than five percent of all enrollments. In some countries, as much money may be spent on one or two hundred thousand university students as on more than a million rural school children or the millions of illiterate adults. It is not uncommon to spend twenty to 30 times as much money per capita on a university student as on a primary school student.

Furthermore, higher education students generally come from elite urban and middle-to-upper class backgrounds. In many cases, they may attend private schools that better prepare them to pass rigorous entrance examinations, which then entitle them to attend public universities where they pay little, if anything, in the way of tuition and fees (often under $25 per year). In effect, the children of the elites are being susidized by the poor of a country to obtain an education degree that solidifies their class position and guarantees opportunities in employment, status, and income not available to the majority.

Frequently, higher education students accorded these privileges waste the public monies spent on them. Dropout and repetition rates are very high. Students often need an additional three or four years to graduate because of disruptions in their studies caused by strikes and other political activities. In many cases, students do not complete their studies; and when they do, they often are in fields of study unrelated to development priorities.[19]

Higher education institutions have very low student to faculty ratios, and, like central ministries of education, are typically top heavy with administrators. Moreover, political patronage is rampant in many higher education institutions, where faculty are often appointed on the basis of their party affiliation, and students, as well, receive scholarships or positions on the basis of nonmeritocratic considerations.[20]

For these reasons, in a number of Latin American countries, there have been moves to charge income-contingent tuition fees and to facilitate the creation of private universities which can meet the growing demand for higher education. In Brazil, more than 60 percent of higher education students are enrolled in private institutions; and, in Chile during the Pinochet regime (1973-1989), there was a decisive move to strengthen private universities vis-a-vis public universities.

Arguments Against Neoliberal Education Policies

Each of these arguments is countered by those opposed to the decentralization and privatization of education. The opposition argues that education should be viewed as a continuum from preschool through higher education and adult education. The state's role in public education is fundamental to the creation and maintenance of a nation-state and to the exercise of citizenship rights in a democratic polity. Given the prevalent levels of poverty throughout the southern hemisphere of the Americas, government policies designed to charge user fees for previously free services are likely to bar poor children access to schooling or drive them out of the school system. Decreasing participation rates in schooling, combined with the lack of priority given to adult education in the current policies of the World Bank and many national governments, is contributing to rising rates of illiteracy throughout the hemisphere. Any responsiveness to local needs and concerns these policies are supposed to promote is countered by attempts to impose national curricular standards and assessment procedures in a number of countries. Further, according to critics, instead of empowering teachers, parents, and community members, and improving the status of educators, these policies are divisive and attempt to erode the power of teacher unions. Finally, the failure of the state to allocate sufficient funds to higher education, based on misleading cost-benefit analysis, poses a danger to the scientific and technological advancement of Latin American countries.

The specific arguments are as follows.

1. The role of the state in educational provision is critical to national consensus-formation and the creation of a democratic polity. There is little evidence to suggest that decentralizing and privatizing

education will lead to greater efficiency and less corruption. Since the nineteenth century Wars of Independence (1810-1825) that liberated Central and South America from colonial rule, education has been called upon to help create a sense of nationhood. In countries like Argentina, Chile, and Uruguay that received a large influx of immigrants from Europe in the latter half of the nineteenth century, education, very much as in the United States, was used by state authorities to forge national unity.

Although education was viewed by nineteenth century statesmen and educators like Domingo Faustino Sarmiento of Argentina and Andres Bello of Venezuela and Chile as a "civilizing" influence in the creation of citizens, mass-based public education systems available to all from preprimary through higher education remained an elusive goal well up to the second half of the twentieth century.

In the post-World War II period, the state has assumed the principal role in providing and extending education to the great majority of school-age children and providing opportunities for advanced education. Latin America, despite high repeater and dropout rates, has the highest school participation rates of any developing region, as indicated in Table 2.

TABLE 2 Percentage of Appropriate Age Group Enrolled in Different Levels of Education, for All Developing Areas and Latin America, 1975, 1985, and 1992

	Level 1	*Level 2*	*Level 3*
All Developing Areas			
1975	92.8	31.4	4.1
1985	98.6	37.6	6.1
1992	97.9	44.5	7.7
Latin America			
1975	96.6	36.9	11.8
1985	105.9	51.1	15.6
1992	106.3	53.2	17.7

Source: UNESCO, *1993 and 1994 Statistical Yearbooks*, Table 2.8.

Note: This table is explained largely by high repetition rates and a substantial number of overage youths absorbed into the school system when opportunity was extended to previously excluded populations.

Although there are significant discrepancies across and within countries, decentralizing and privatizing education will lead to even greater inequities.[21] The poorest regions will fall even farther behind the wealthier ones, unless the state plays a role in equalizing educational expenditures. In countries like Chile, a model of privatization of both the economy and education system, achievement scores of school children reflected such growing disparities. According to Prawda, "The introduction of market mechanisms in the educational sector to allow consumer choice and introduce cost containment incentives, such as in Chile, has resulted in unfair policy practices, mainly for lower income rural groups, that are deprived of information and school alternatives to make appropriate selections, It has also significantly widened the gap in cognitive achievement results between students attending privately paid schools and those in high-risk municipal, mostly rural schools, and also between those attending old, traditional, privately subsidized schools and those going to recently established subsidized institutions fostered by the Chilean decentralization reform."[22]

Although many private schools cater to the children of elites and provide a quality education, it also is the case that many private schools are essentially a business enterprise with little concern for quality. In Brazil, for example, although a majority of higher education students attend private institutions, it is widely recognized that the best universities tend to be the public ones. The private institutions often are diploma mills turning out students principally in fields that do not require much investment in laboratories and equipment—such as law, the social sciences, and business administration. Unless private schools, at all levels of education, are carefully supervised by the state and subject to national laws governing the teaching profession, they will generally pay teachers less and have substandard facilities.

Indeed, if the state is considered corrupt, what evidence is there that the private sector is any less prone to greed and self-enrichment at the public expense? Certainly, the evidence of civic mindedness on the part of industry is not that strong. Moreover, in the absence of oversight by some regulatory body, opportunities for graft and corruption are just as likely in decentralized as in centralized systems of education.

2. In a context of growing poverty, policies that charge user fees have a deleterious impact on attainment of universal primary education and literacy. As indicated above, economic growth throughout the Latin American region decelerated in the 1980s. A falling Gross National Product (GNP) translated into decreasing per capita income for the majority of Latin Americans. On average, Latin

American per capita incomes fell nine percent. In more dramatic cases such as Argentina, per capita income fell 22 percent.

Not only has income dropped, but class differences have intensified. In the 1980s in metropolitan Buenos Aires, 25 percent of the poorest households lost 15 percent of their income, while five percent of the richest households increased their income by almost 20 percent. In the metropolitan areas of Rio de Janeiro and São Paulo, 25 percent of the poorest households lost almost 13 percent of their income, while five percent of the richest gained approximately 25 percent.

Income losses were not only experienced by the poorest of the poor; 50 percent of the households located in the middle of the scale lost between three percent and 10 percent of their income.[23] As a result, in Latin America, class structures have become more polarized with the rich and poor sectors separated by an increasingly wider gap. This is also true in Mexico and Chile which have served as models of structural adjustment for other countries in the region. Despite the apparent economic success of Chile in particular, and Mexico until recently, the poor are becoming poorer and more numerous, and the gap between the rich and poor is growing.[24]

In countries like Brazil and Nicaragua, over 70 percent of the population is living in poverty, over a quarter of the population in situations of extreme destitution. In such conditions, charging even a nominal user fee of approximately one dollar a month for a family with three or four children (often the norm) presents a dilemma: to pay the fee or buy needed medicines, clothing, even food. The situation is so desperate for so many families that these fees are barring access to or driving poor children out of "public" school systems. At the same time, a free nutrition program that provides a daily glass of milk and a snack may induce a family to send a child to school.

Although ministry of education officials in countries like Nicaragua claim that such fees are not charged to children in the first four years of primary school, and there are exemptions for rural and poor children as well as children with exceptionally good grades, school practices belie such declarations. School authorities introduce fees in a variety of guises—charges for laboratories and equipment or special programs or even the administration of examinations—and place great pressure on parents to donate resources or labor to assist their schools.

One result of the dire economic situation and such educational policies and practices is that as many as 20 percent of school-age children in a number of countries do not even enter the school system. This generation of youth will swell the number of totally or functionally illiterate adults whose needs have traditionally been neglected in Latin America.

As previously discussed, the number of illiterates in Nicaragua increased between 1980 and 1995, despite a widely acclaimed literacy campaign that taught over 400,000 youths and adults to read. In 1995, the illiteracy rate represented approximately one-half the population over the age of 10. Brazil, another country with a history of innovative literacy programs and large-scale national efforts in adult basic education, still has over 18 million illiterate adults.

The response of the World Bank and national governments in the region has been to emphasize the responsibility of the private sector (nongovernmental organizations, NGOs) in addressing the illiteracy problem. NGOs are likely to be more responsive to local community needs. Many literacy and adult based education (ABE) programs sponsored by NGOs are based on the notions of Brazilian educator Paulo Freire concerning education as a process of consciousness-raising that empowers people to name the word and change the world.

The problem is that these programs tend to be small-scale reaching at best a fraction (less than 10 percent) of those in need of systematic instruction. It is unlikely that any major inroads will be made in reducing high levels of illiteracy without major efforts on the part of national governments and international donor agencies to mobilize people and provide adequate resources and technical assistance. But the World Bank and a number of Latin American countries have decided not to invest such resources in adult education, which they consider a poor investment. In Nicaragua, in 1992-1993, the government allocated less than $25,000 for literacy and ABE to address the needs of over one million youths and adults. A 1995 agreement between Brazil and the World Bank to provide over $700 million in aid for primary education in the Northeast Region did not include a single dollar for literacy and ABE. Although UNESCO and UNICEF do provide funding for adult education, especially for community-based education directed at women and their children, the amounts of money they command are infinitesimal compared with those of the World Bank and major national overseas agencies like the United States Agency for International Development (USAID).

The implications of illiteracy for citizenship are evident when a country makes literacy a requirement for voting. Such was the case in Brazil which, until the promulgation of a more democratic constitution in 1988, denied the franchise to illiterate adults.

3.   Neoliberal policies that decentralize and privatize education administratively and economically are complemented by neoconservative policies that dictate curricula and textbooks. As such, current curricular policies are not responsive to local varia-

tion. While neoliberal policies favor the application of marketforces to the governance, financing, and administration of education systems, neoconservative policies emphasize the return to traditional values, to a cultural "canon" as a way of combatting the breakup of the family and other social crises. Neoconservatives are especially concerned with reintroducing rigor and notions of excellence into the curricula.[25] This concern is manifest in the movement to articulate national curricula standards.

The neoconservative movement in education, not surprisingly, is taking place in parallel fashion in the United States and a number of Latin American countries. In Nicaragua, the new policy directions of the Chamorro government (1990-1995) contain many of the key ideas and buzz words related not only to parental choice but to excellence, standards, and model schools that formed part of the conservative education agenda of Reagan and Bush administrations.[26] Similarly, in 1995, the Brazilian Ministry of Education and Culture initiated efforts to develop a core national curriculum, national standards, and national assessment procedures and instruments.

Emphasis on greater accountability of schools and external assessment also has been applied to the higher education level. In Argentina, introduction of a new Higher Education Law triggered an extraordinary student mobilization that brought tens of thousands of students, professors, staff of universities, and parents to the National Congress in Buenos Aires, in July 1995, to protest its passage. The legislation paved the way for a system of fees and tuition in the public universities and created a number of accountability measures that threatened the autonomy of public universities. These measures include, for example, mechanisms for evaluation by an outside national level commission of teaching loads and scientific productivity of faculty and quality of degrees. It is alleged that approval of this legislation was a precondition for a $165 million loan from the World Bank for the Program of Reform of Higher Education. The government disputes such charges, but recognizes that it is highly unusual for the World Bank to lend any resources for higher education in Latin America.

4.   Neoliberal reform policies do not empower teachers, nor do they improve their status and salaries. They tend to be divisive and erode the power of teacher unions. The brunt of cuts in social spending has fallen disproportionately on health and education services, and within education on teacher salaries. Teacher salaries have fallen throughout Latin America not only relative to private sector employees but relative to other public sector employees.

It is not uncommon in many Latin American nations to pay teachers little more than what is paid to domestic employees. In some countries (e.g., Nicaragua) teachers receive even less than domestic employees. Unable to support their families, many teachers have left the profession for higher paying jobs. Many ministries of education prefer to replace veteran faculty with younger, uncertified teachers, and then certify or upgrade them through inservice courses.[27]

Generally unfavorable working conditions also are likely to worsen. Because World Bank officials believe the internal efficiency of education systems can be increased by having instructors teach more students and longer hours, demands on teacher productivity are increasing while their wages are either frozen or decreasing.

The power of teacher unions to negotiate salaries and working conditions also has been eroding. Policies that decentralize decision-making to the municipal or school level greatly curtail the influence of teacher unions. National level negotiations concentrate the power of a union; decentralized policies fragment efforts and lead to divisiveness. The divisiveness occurs not only between various organizations representing teachers but within the same unions.[28]

There is no question that in a number of countries, conservative governments have instituted such policies with this goal in mind. Placing parents and community members on school councils, while ostensibly a move to democratize education decision-making, also has the effect of limiting rather than augmenting the power of teachers, individually and collectively.

These councils often are given the authority to hire and fire teachers and shape curricular decisions. While teachers believe that parental and community input are important components of successful schools, they view the authority accorded some of the councils as excessive and an infringement on their autonomy to determine what education best serves their students. Moreover, teacher wages, benefits, and working conditions, guaranteed in the past by nationally negotiated agreements, are undermined by decentralization. In effect, these policies have not provided a framework for different stakeholders to come together and reach a consensus on educational priorities, but have pitted them against one another.

5. Neoliberal policies threaten the quality of higher education and curtail its ability to serve the national interest. The presidents of Latin American universities have been meeting at the regional level in the 1990s to address threats posed by the neoliberal agenda and policies advocated by international donor agencies. Latin American university officials warn of the dangers of falling into the trap

of *primarización*, emphasizing primary education to the neglect of higher education. Rather than pitting primary and secondary education against higher education, ministries of education should view education as a continuum with each level contributing to the commonweal.[29]

Advocates for the university community argue that cost-benefit analyses are highly misleading in that they do not accurately reflect the many benefits of a higher education to individuals and the society—benefits not calculated by these analyses that nonetheless are very real. They include the contributions of a higher education to improvements in the health, longevity, satisfaction, and creativity of individuals—all of which may be reflected in higher levels of productivity in the workforce. Externalities (often not calculated by economists) include the contributions of universities to the intellectual and cultural life of a country, to its sense of national identity.[30] Also missing from such analyses are the role that higher education institutions have played in opposing dictatorships, in being the critical conscience of a nation, and in providing the political and civic leaders of a country.

Central to any discussion of the economics of education should be the role that universities play in the creation of scientific and technological knowledge. If Latin American countries are not to be scientific backwaters—dependent on the metropolitan countries of the North for the knowledge needed to generate jobs, improve the quality of life, and conserve the environment—then, what the region needs is world-class institutions of higher learning.

Throughout the region, many higher education institutions are now grappling with the issue of charging income-contingent fees. They recognize the legitimacy of students from affluent backgrounds paying a fair share of the costs of a higher education. But they also point out that in many cases a majority of the students are not from elite backgrounds, that they and their families are barely surviving economically.

According to Xabier Gorostiaga, rector of the Central American University of Managua, a central question is this: how in a situation of economic depression to make a university education available to all students of ability while also constructing a university of quality that would be a fundamental agency for overcoming the national crisis?[31] Thus, the higher education leadership in Latin America today advocates policies that democratize access to higher education on the part of all students of talent, while gearing university activities more towards the resolution of pressing national problems.[32] Accountability, for them, is a matter of making higher education institutions responsive to meeting the needs of their societies.

This view is contrasted with that of governmental authorities who view accountability in terms of devising a set of regulations and procedures for external control of matters previously within the purview of the university community.

Conclusions

Although the arguments presented in this chapter represent diametrically opposed points of view, it is possible to think of a more consensual and eclectic approach that draws upon the strengths of each side of the debate. For example, it is not uncommon to find educators arguing for a combination of more centralized, and adequate, financing of education with less centralized curricular decision-making.[33] Unfortunately, governments, such as that of Brazil, are proceeding to decentralize financing of education while nationalizing curriculum development and assessment procedures.

There are approaches that do involve a complementariety of local and national efforts in the area of financing. Prawda, for example, notes that "... incentives and disincentives can be built into the decentralization process to stimulate the good performance of smaller units of government and discourage inefficiency and mismanagement (corruption)." One incentive involves "... allowing local governments to raise revenue and proportionally complementing their effort with [national] fiscal resources to finance additional educational spending ... to improve quality." One disincentive involves "Making local authorities legally accountable if they career into unreasonable budgetary deficits."[34]

Similarly, with regard to curricular development, the national government could provide a basic framework of core content to be covered by all schools, while allowing substantial local variation. A package of incentives and disincentives could be adopted that promoted decentralized curricular development. Incentives would favor the development of curricula that reflected the diversity of a society but also recognized the forces and factors that united people in pursuit of a common good. Disincentives might be applied for not implementing policies that guarantee greater equality of educational opportunity for the poorest children.

In every country in the region there is a need for a national dialogue to determine what education policies to pursue and, of necessity, what economic model to adopt to achieve sustainable development that benefits the vast majority of people. Such a dialogue must involve all the principal stakeholders and be guided by the opportunity for all to be heard and respected. It is hoped that such a bottom-up and democratic approach to decision-making will lead to multiple models of development, each appropriate to its particular context.[35]

By contrast, current approaches to economic and education policy formulation represent an imposition of "conditionalities" by international donor agencies like the World Bank and the IMF. They are the antithesis of democratic decision-making and the design of development models appropriate to differing national contexts.

In presenting the arguments in favor and against neoliberal education policies, I have attempted to be as neutral as possible. However, on the basis of my experience, I have reached the conclusion that these policies, overall, have not improved the education or the life chances of the majority of Latin American children and adults. Within a context of increasing impoverishment and a growing gap between the rich and the poor, they lead to increasing inequities in educational access and outcomes. They are unlikely to meet the challenges of providing universal primary education and eliminating large-scale illiteracy. Moreover, certain cost-cutting measures designed to increase the "efficiency" of school systems lead instead to tremendous waste of human potential—to continued high dropout and repeater rates—and to a failure to provide a set of conditions that favor teachers' professional work and the learning of children.[36] If maximizing the value of educational resources and their outputs is an important goal, then, such policies are inefficient in the extreme.

Despite the deceptive promise of neoliberal policies to effect substantial reforms in education, their limitations are serious and many of their consequences deleterious. I argue, instead, for a process of democratic deliberation and consensus building that is likely to lead to education systems more responsive to their national contexts and the challenges of equity, quality, and efficiency.

Notes

1.   Martin McLean with Natalia Voskresenskaya, "Educational Revolution from Above: Thatcher's Britain and Gorbachev's Soviet Union," *Comparative Education Review* 36 (February 1992), p. 71.

2.   See, for example, George Psacharopoulos, "Comparative Education: From Theory to Practice, Are you A:\neo* or B:*ist?" *Comparative Education Review* 34 (August 1990): 369-380.

3.   See, for example, Beatrice Avalos "Moving Where? Educational Issues in Latin American Contexts," *International Journal of Educational Development* 7, No. 3 (1987): 151-172.

4.   Ralph Harbison and Eric Hanushek, *The Educational Performance of the Poor: Lessons from Northeast Brazil* (New York: Oxford University Press, 1992), p. 32; cited

in Anthony Dewees and Steve Klees, "Social Movements and the Transformation of National Policy: Street and Working Children in Brazil," *Comparative Education Review* 39 (February 1995), p. 82.

5. Robert F. Arnove, Stephen Franz, Kimberly Morse, and Carlos Torres, "Education and Development in Latin America," in Richard S. Hillman (ed.), *Understanding Contemporary Latin America* (New York: Lynne Reinner Publications, 1996).

6. Alex Inkeles, "National Differences in Scholastic Performance," *Comparative Education Review* 23 (October 1979): 386-407.

7. "*Encino só supera Mocambique,*" *La Tarde* (Salvador, Brazil), July 31, 1995: 3.

8. CEPAL. *Panorama social de América Latina* (Santiago de Chile: Comisión Económica para American Latina, 1991); and CEPAL *Transformación productiva con equidad* (1992); and World Bank, *Brazil: Public Spending on Social. Programs, Issues and Options.* (Washington, D.C.: World Bank, 1988, Report 7086-BR).

9. Fernando Reimers, "The Impact of Economic Stabilization and Adjustment on Education in Latin America," *Comparative Education Review* 35 (May 1991), p. 332.

10. Ibid., p. 323.

11. Gabriel Cárceles, "World Literacy Prospects at the Turn of the Century: Is the Objective of Literacy for All by the Year 2000 Statistically Plausible?" *Comparative Education Review* 34 (February 1990), pp. 7-16.

12. Robert F. Arnove, *Education and Revolution in Nicaragua* (New York: Praeger, 1987), chap. 2.

13. See George Psacharopolous, "The Cost-Benefit Model," in G. Psacharopolous (ed.), *Economics of Education: Research and Studies* (New York: Pergamon Press, 1987), pp. 342-347.

14. For example, see David Plank, "The Politics of Basic Education Reform in Brazil," *Comparative Education Review* 34 (November 1990): 538559.

15. Laurence Wolff, Ernesto Schiefelbein, and Jorge Valenzuela, Improving the Quality of Primary Education in Latin America and the Caribbean (Washington, D.C.: The World Bank, 1994), p. 154.

16. Robert F. Arnove, *Education as Contested Terrain: Nicaragua, 1979-1993* (Boulder, CO: Westview Press, 1994), pp. 105-105.

17. Ibid; and Celso Canelo Candia, "MED fija metas para 1993," *La Prensa*, March 24, 1993, p. 2.

18. Psacharopoulos, "From Theory to Practice," p. 372.

19. Such statements, for example, were made by the Nicaraguan Minister of Education, Humberto Belli, and the Presidential Minister, Antonio Lacayo, during the university strike of 1992; see Arnove, *Education as Contested Terrain,* pp. 140-149.

20. Ibid.

21. See, for example, Robert F. Arnove, Stephen Franz, and Kimberly Morse, "Latin American Education," in Jack Hopkins (ed.), *Latin America: Perspectives on a Region* (New York: Holmes & Meier, 1996).

22. Juan Prawda, "Educational Decentralization in Latin America: Lessons Learned," *International Journal of Educational Development* 13, No. 3 (1993), pp. 262-263.

23. CEPAL, *Programa Social.*

24. Jorge Castañeda, *La utopia desarmada* (México: J. Mortiz/Planeta, 1993).

25. For further discussion, see Jim Carl, "Parental Choice as National Policy in England and the United States," *Comparative Education Review* 38 (August 1994): 294-322.

26. See, for example, Ministry of Education (MED), *Lineamientos del Ministerio de Educación en el Nuevo Gobierno de Salvación Nacional* (Managua: MED, 1990). Furthermore, papers by two of the principal ideologues of this period Dianne Ravitch and Chester Finn have been distributed by the Center for Education and Democracy, associated with the MED. For further discussion, see Arnove, *Nicaragua*, pp. 70, and 98-100.

27. See, for example, Martin Carnoy et al., *The Impact of Structural Adjustment Policies on the Employment and Training of Teachers* (Stanford, CA: Stanford University, School of Education, 1995).

28. See, for example, Arnove, *Education as a Contested Terrain*, pp. 116-122.

29. Xabier Gorostiaga, "Falso y peligroso dilema," *Barricada* (Managua), March 12, 1993, p. 3; and "New Times, New Role for Universities of the South," *Envío* 12, No. 144 (July 1993): pp. 24-40. Also see CEPAL, *Educación y conocimiento, eje de la transformación productiva con equidad* (Santiago, Chile: Economic Commission for Latin America, November 1991). It should be noted that in Latin America, ministries of education typically represent preuniversity and adult education, while separate ministries or councils represent postsecondary education.

30. On externalities, see W. W. McMahon, "Externalities in Education," in George Psacharopoulos (ed.), *Economics of Education: Research and Studies* (New York: Pergamon Press, 1987), pp. 133-141. McMahon defines externalities in this way: "The external benefits of education are those benefits to society that are above and beyond the private benefits realized by the individual decision maker, that is, the student and family" (p. 133).

31. Xabier Gorostiaga, "Referendum para qué?" (Managua: Central American University, UCA, April 1993, p. 11; cited in Arnove, *Education as a Contested Terrain*, p. 152.

32. See, for example, Gorostiaga, "New Times, New Role," as to how Latin American universities might contribute to the attainment of sustainable development that benefits the majority.

33. Such was the case when I organized a two-day graduate seminar for inservice teachers at the University of Espirito Santo, in Northeast Brazil.

34. Prawda, "Educational Decentralization" (p. 263). To Prawda's mention of efforts to improve quality of education should be added a concern with the equity of schooling financing formulas.

35. Xabier Gorostiaga, "Copenhagen: The Potential Success of a Failure," *Envío* 14, No. 166 (May 1995): 40-45.

36. For a critical discussion of how efficiency may be variously defined see, Joel Samoff, "The Reconstruction of Schooling in Africa," *Comparative Education Review* 37, No. 2 (May 1993): 207-208; 215-216.

Basic Education in Latin America

4

Dewey Under South American Skies: Some Readings from Argentina

Inés Dussel and Marcelo Caruso

Summary

Dewey's repercussions in Argentina will be considered in this chapter from a point of view suggested by the theory of articulation and modern literary theory. Pedagogical fields operate as "translation matrices" which include foreign pedagogies within peculiar constellations of meaning. In Argentina, despite the liberal impulse of the nineteenth century, pragmatism was always confined to the margins of the school system. Dewey's work was generally considered as equivalent to practical curriculum and vocationalism, and thus it was contested by the prevalent humanist trend. Two closely-related problems are dealt with in this work: the scope and limits of educational liberalism and the evolution of the New School movement in our region.

Introduction

Some years ago, Borges wrote about the impossible endeavor of Pierre Ménard, trying to re-write the book of Cervantes, "Don Quixote," exactly in the same way it had been written in the eighteenth century. Even in the act of literally transcribing it, Borges remarked, Pierre Ménard was already producing a different book.

This warning, however, has not been sufficiently accounted for by those who make comparative history. Seeking the traces of the original in the copy, the links between educators of diverse countries and historical moments have been talked about in terms of maladjustments, infidelities or degradations of the first version.

Recent work on Dewey's repercussion in the Third World suggest other approaches. Ronald Goodenow finds significant transferences between progressive Latin American educators and Dewey's pedagogy.[1]

In this article, however, we intend to look at Dewey's readings in Latin America from a different point of view, as suggested by the theory of articulation[2] and modern literary theory, particularly the aesthetics of reception.[3] Dewey's pedagogy and Latin American pedagogies will be considered as open discursive systems whose elements are permanently re-articulated, creating new series of meanings. Latin American pedagogical fields[4] operate, in our view, as "translation matrices" for ideas and proposals which are integrated in a particular constellation of meanings and/or discursive positions.

Our proposal can be illustrated by putting upside down Robert Escarpit's assertion: "to know what a book is, it must be first known how it was read," and say: "to know what a reader is, it is necessary to know how and which books he reads."[5] As much as the possibilities and limits of Dewey's discourse are included by conservatives, liberals or radicals, the analysis of Dewey's readings in Latin America can enlighten particular features of Latin American pedagogical fields. With this particular interest, we will try to define the "horizons of reading"[6] from which Dewey was read, the "quotation system" on which he was included, by whom and how he was quoted, which aspects of his work were emphasized and which ones were disregarded or unknown. It is our hypothesis that the Argentine horizon from which Dewey was read confined his pedagogy to the margins of the school system. When he was finally accepted as a pedagogical authority, during the fifties, it was at the cost of blocking his curricular orientations. Two closely-related problems seem to be central to guide us in our approach: the scope and limits of educational liberalism and the evolution of the New School movement in our region.

Dewey and Educational Liberalism

It has been said that the concept of liberty, be it in its negative or Rousseauian version, equality, propriety, and security constitute the pillars of the classic liberal political imagery.[7] The particular articulations they have established within concrete situations of structural modernization and capitalist extension may help to characterize different views of liberalism as social imagery,[8] according to the predominance and interplays among these fundamental concepts of liberalism.

Dewey's particular version of liberalism is deeply rooted in a model of capitalist expansion with peculiar notes. Modernization tied to cultural modernity, the openness of the social frontier, the regulations of imagery built under the sign of Protestantism, were specific conditions that characterized the society he lived in. Perhaps it was all this that helped the emergence, from the University of Chicago and later from Columbia, of the most inclusive proposal to link school, democracy and social subjects that liberalism has ever produced.

Some recent works do not share this optimism on Dewey. Bowles and Gintis have argued that Dewey's work cooperated in the settlement of advanced industrial capitalism.[9] On the other hand, studies from curriculum history consider his links with strictly disciplinary tasks or blend his impact on school practices.[10] Henry Giroux has revitalized Dewey's image in the construction of public spheres and ethics to oppose neoconservatives' attacks in the '80s.[11] W. Feinberg, in a suggestive critical review of Westbrook's *John Dewey and American Democracy*, points out Dewey's silences on ethical and normative issues engaged in liberal democracy.[12]

The multiplicity of readings on Dewey is related both to his prolific work and life, during which he was part of and witness to great social and political changes, and to his role as a "folk hero" or compulsive referent for most of American educational literature.[13] We would like to emphasize the fact that, probably due to this multiplicity, John Dewey's work has articulated an active and reformist pedagogical imagery which included other initiatives, such as the Winnetka Plan, the Dalton Plan, and other methodological innovations of the period.[14] Most of all, this pedagogical imagery articulated different subjects, knowledges, and activities with the aim of relating democracy to school life.

This complex of meanings began to be read early in Latin American societies, which were characterized by variable subordinate but constitutive connections to the world system, weak modernization processes and an increasing cultural hybridization.[15] Given these conditions, Latin American liberalism was, as a Brazilian scholar said, an "idea out of place":[16] it combined the adoption of the formalities of liberal social philosophy with the defense of an oligarchic system.[17] It had become the élite's rationalization for political domination, justifying the exclusion of the political and cultural backgrounds of the great majority of people.[18]

It is hardly surprising then that Dewey's proposal, based on the inclusion of differences, appeared deeply contradictory to them. To know what, how and under which conditions Dewey was read could give some clues to understanding the limits inclusive proposals had in our region.

Pedagogical Horizons of Reading in Argentina

When William Brickman wrote about Dewey's foreign reputation as an educator, he needed just one paragraph to define that "it is in Brazil and

Argentina that Dewey appears to have attracted his greatest following in Latin America."[19] Brickman holds that since Sarmiento and José Pedro Varela's works (liberal leaders of the nineteenth century), Latin American pedagogues have generally regarded their colleagues of the north with respect.

For our part, we would not be so positive about the leadership of the south of the continent in the diffusion of Dewey's ideas in Latin America, particularly in consideration of the Mexican process—about which Dewey himself was particularly concerned.[20] But we can affirm that due to the relative educational progress and the vigorous publishing industry in Argentina during the first half of the twentieth century, this country turned out to be a powerful and relevant cultural center for the whole of the Latin American world.

The essential guidelines of the modern educational system was settled in the second half of the nineteenth century. Sarmiento, the fourth president of the Argentine Republic,[21] pushed the polarity "civilization vs. barbarism" as the basis for the building of the Nation-State. It can be said that this polarity had obvious pedagogical connotations: on one side, the "modern" and "civilized" country of the agricultural exporting oligarchy; on the other side, the "backwardness" and "ignorance" of the provinces' caudillos, in many cases representatives of local oligarchies with conflicting interests. This definition of the national problem reserved a crucial place for education: Sarmiento's call to "educate the sovereign," because "an uneducated people will always vote" caudillos.[22]

Soon after, "education" was also given the task of achieving national unity, which was, in the minds of political leaders, threatened by immigration.[23] A "patriotic crusade" was held in 1908-1910 by the national educational board, trespassing on local autonomies and initiatives. To pursue these ends of political homogenization and national unity, the educational system received a lot of support. According to the national census, by 1914 almost 48 percent of the children went to school; in 1930, school attendance reached 69 percent.[24]

In the meantime, various struggles among different projects took place. Adriana Puiggrós has shown clearly how different groups emerged and fought to shape the Argentine curriculum.[25] She identifies two main pedagogical trends: the "normalizers," who thought education was the best way of "keeping people on the right track" and wanted a centralized and homogeneous system; and the "radical democrats," who claimed to be for self-government and political and pedagogical pluralism. The first group won the battle, settling the hegemony of the traditional humanist curriculum whose rituals and content showed a surprising resilience during this period.[26] Despite their differences, both groups agreed on a pedagogical optimism which sustained the expansion of the educational system and which constituted the "sens du jeu" (Bourdieu) in the pedagogical field.

This consensus began to decline in the second decade of this century due to an increasing social and political mobilization. Universal suffrage was established in 1912 and four years later the first democratically elected government, a nationalist popular movement, came to power. When students took over the government of the very conservative University of Cordoba in 1918, a process which was known as the "University Reform" only a few among the pedagogues supported the movement and the great majority became suspicious of the political consequences of freedom in the classroom. For some of them, the students' demands to share the government were unbearable; for others, it was a sign that more prudent reforms should be developed to prevent such commotions. "Modernization" and "democratization," together or separately, were the new keywords in the pedagogical field.

The 1930 world crisis caused deep changes in Argentine economic and social structure. It had strong repercussions in the pedagogical field too. The Catholic Church mounted a renewed offensive to include religious content in the school curriculum. The inclusion of religion was part of a proposal for "spiritualizing the Argentine school" directed against scientificism and intellectualism. This offensive found interested interlocutors in the government, as evidenced by the educational policies of José Evaristo Uriburu (1930-1931) and those of the military governments (1943-1946). In the meantime, conservative educational reforms between 1931 and 1943 tended to link school to the incipient Argentine industry.[27] The pluralistic versions of liberalism and the pedagogical left concentrated their struggle on the defense of the secular state and the humanist curriculum. They did not paying attention to the new scénario which was emerging after the crisis.[28]

Argentina Readers: Pragmatism in the Margins

Some years before the first Spanish translations of Dewey's books in 1915 and 1917,[29] his work was well-known among Argentine educators. Dewey's European readers seem to have taken part in this early diffusion—especially German readers—but first-hand contact with North American education appears to have been the primary way they came to know him.

At the beginning of the century most of the intellectual field concentrated its attention on Europe, especially on France. On the educational front, in spite of Sarmiento's devotion to Horace Mann, the "official line" of the educational system which claimed to be his legacy was in fact opposed to his convictions: increasing centralization and homogenization, and the prevalence of the traditional humanist curriculum. Those who wanted alternative models looked towards Germany and, only in a few cases, to the United States.

There are a number of reasons to explain this weakness in Latin American intellectuals and pedagogues at that time who favored a North American orientation. One important feature is the close economic dependency Argentina had on Great Britain. Another relevant issue was the ruling classes' conviction, favored by a striking social and economic expansion until 1930, that Argentina would play an important role in the concert of nations. This led to a sharp competition between Argentina and the U.S. to influence the rest of the American countries.[30] Argentina refused for a long time to constitute a Pan-American union, confronting Monroe's "America for the Americans" with the slogan "America for humanity."

Along with economic and political relationships, the intellectual climate in Latin America was influenced by an anti-North American movement called "arielism." Influenced by the Spanish defeat at Cuba in 1898, the Uruguayan José E. Rodó addressed to Latin American youth denouncing the perils of the imperialist expansion of the U.S. over Latin America, which was already being experienced in the materialist temptation pervading our culture; the spirit of Caliban represented by North American values and fashions. Largely discussed in the literature[31] was the question of whether his sermon was modernist or not. In regard to our subject, his view favored anti-liberal responses and weakened the support to alternative educational models based on the U.S. experience.

Not surprisingly, during the first decades of the century the diffusion of Dewey's ideas was led by liberal and radical pedagogues who, in many respects, confronted the educational status-quo. Most of them considered the U.S. educational system and pedagogies as a model example for reforming a country where oligarchic landowners ruled a fraudulent democracy. Industrialism and popular participation were like city lights for them. However, their global admiration probably led them to disregard the differences and struggles that shaped the North American curriculum.[32]

Two of these "radical democratic" pedagogues who admired Dewey deserve special consideration. Raúl B. Díaz (1862-1918), one of the chief inspectors of federal education, quoted Dewey frequently in the articles he wrote for the official journal of education. He was invited by the national board of education to the U.S. in 1907-1908.[33] He returned deeply impressed by what he saw and brought with him a lot of experiences on school government by children. He emphasized Dewey's commitment to democracy and consideration of both social and psychological aspects of education.

Ernesto Nelson (1873-1959) was probably the most resolute propagandist of Dewey in Argentina in the first decades of this century. His Pro-North-Americanism was centered on his trust in Fordism and liberal democracy. For him, the market was the most fair judge of abilities and capacities, so he persistently attacked the colonial tradition of a centralized state that controlled the educational system.

Nelson himself had studied at Teachers College, Columbia University in 1902-1905, but he never got a degree. In 1906, being inspector of secondary schools, he spent some time at Columbia University, where he probably met Dewey himself, although he has left no testimony to this. Some years later he became a member of the National Education Association in Washington, DC.[34] In Argentina, Nelson was one of the founders of the North American-Argentine Cultural Institute, and wrote a lot of books and papers on North American culture and institutions.[35] He was kindly accused by one of the establishment pedagogues of "inflamed yankeeism."[36]

Nelson was especially fond of Dewey's ideas. First of all, he shared the view that democracy in education implied respect for the child's nature and freedom as well as school access for all social classes. Education would be for Nelson, as for Dewey, a privileged way for social improvement. In his presentation to the Pan-American Congress, he denounced Argentine education as "a system of organized restriction," which perpetuated social injustice. The term "educated class," he said, "is still suggestive of autocratic privilege."[37] This problem was much more acute at the secondary and university than at the primary level. In his view, Argentina had to unify secondary schools as the U.S. system had done.[38]

As Inspector of Secondary Education, he proposed a plan for reforming secondary schools which found little support. He criticized the traditional humanist curriculum and defended the ideal of an active school. Every genuine idea is a result of action, said Nelson, but in current education kids get into the habit of following the authority of teachers or texts. He was desolated by the fact that during his work he saw "thousands of children among whom there is no one who carries his own truth, not even his own mistake."[39] He believed that secondary school should be conceived as a system of activities through which the pupil can obtain information by himself. He proposed not so much a change in the content of the curriculum but in the direction of activities. As in Dewey's Pedagogical Creed, the task of the professor should be to select the appropriate contexts for learning.[40]

Nelson's efforts to include the adolescent daily life and culture were remarkable. As the principal of the Secondary School of the University of La Plata, before being appointed inspector, he promoted the inclusion of newspapers and excursions as a means for learning. He also organized a football team for developing both physical and cooperative education.[41]

Although Dewey's egalitarian liberalism was adopted by Nelson as his own creed, two points of his proposal differ from Dewey's ideas: the notion of "occupations" and the preparation for life. Dewey himself was particularly emphatic about the latter issue: school did not prepare for life, but was part of life itself. Nelson, on the contrary, spoke of secondary school's function as preparing for life and not exclusively for a university career.[42] He was arguing against a firmly-rooted anti-pragmatism which was entrenched in the humanist curriculum, and he was probably looking for allies among the partisans of industrial and vocational education. However, Nelson's shift towards vocationalism deepened when he dealt with the notion of "occupation": he believed it equivalent to manual training for the masses.[43] Nelson complained,

> ... to put it bluntly, the schools betray the working classes by denying them the practical, manual training that would fit them to increase their efficiency...."[44]

The best education for the masses should be the one that made them more efficient within a taken-for-granted world (liberal capitalism) and not a provider of alternative views, as Dewey intended with "occupations."[45]

The work of both Díaz and Nelson purveys insightful clues to understanding following readings on Dewey in Argentina. Liberal democracy, school government, school related to life, utilitarian pragmatism, practical curriculum, efficiency, manual training, Fordism, became the "key words" with which Dewey was most frequently associated, even if some of them were not his own words. No distinction was made between Dewey and other North American pedagogues.

Nelson and the school inspectors' influence seems to have been important in the constitution of the discursive plot of the New School in Argentina. They were widely known among primary and secondary teachers, and were quoted and respected even by those who rejected North American imperialism.[46] Nelson's textbooks on "Inventive Mathematics" and "Active Geography," guides for active teaching, were used all around the country until 1950. More importantly, recent works[47] suggest that Nelson encouraged the reading of Dewey to Rosario Vera Peñaloza, Olga Cossettini, Amanda Arias, and Bernardina and Dolores Dabat. All were teachers who led alternative experimental schools in Buenos Aires, Santa Fe, and Córdoba during the '20s and the '30s. They combined Dewey's pragmatism and democratic plea with the aesthetic bias of the Italian *Scuola Serena*, Décroly's centers of interest, and the Montessori system. This mixture of readings produced a peculiar synthesis which has been deeply studied.[48] As Dabat said, "it is in our language, in the language of our pedagogues ... that we shall explain Ferrière and Dewey, Miss Parkhurst, or Lounacharsky to ourselves ..."[49] They were seeking to blend foreign pedagogies with native culture and experience in the field, surpassing a traditional failure of liberalism in our region.

These alternative experiences were part of a wider movement of reform in Argentine education, which became significant after the abovementioned students' University Reform held in 1918.[50] The educational battle between conservatism and activism tainted the cultural climate, and traditionalist newspapers and intellectuals accused the latter of promoting moral and political subversion.[51]

Even if contested, activism tended to be assimilated "in a definitive and silent way to school practices"[52] in a long period which goes from the '20s to the '40s. Most of the educational reforms in those years invoked its name, like the "Sistema de Labor y Programas" led by José Rezzano in the first district of the Argentine capital, or the utilitarian "Escuelas de Nuevo Tipo" briefly developed by the popular national government of the Unión Cívica Radical in 1928-1930.[53] But both had more ties with vocationalist trends than with pragmatism, its main concern being to develop manual skills.

During this period, official educational journals and teachers' union magazines published a lot of articles from and on European and North American pedagogues who ascribed to the New School movement. Dewey's "How We Think" and "The Child and the Curriculum" were among them.[54]

It has been said that along with this silent incorporation of hegemonic discourse, it was the voices of teachers criticizing the traditional school which was also silenced.[55] What turned out to be the official New School discourse was an abstract child-centered pedagogy without any trace of social critique, something quite different from the legacy of Dewey, Díaz, or Nelson. Furthermore, it had strong ties to Catholicism, through an open attack on the laic core of Argentine educational laws.

Juan Bautista Terán (1880-1938) constitutes a singular example of this shifting, which could be defined more properly as a reaction within the New School movement. As president of the National Board of Education from 1930 to 1932, under the military government of José E. Uriburu, Terán led a movement "to spiritualize the school."[56] He criticized both positivism and pragmatism, which he accused of reducing the child to a "beam of instincts and tendencies." "School should not only be a gym to awake and give full shape to child spontaneousness," as Dewey and Montessori sought.[57] The aim of education, in Terán's view, should be to form a moral being with freedom and responsibility, and project it to a transcendent level.

Terán considered Dewey a naturalist philosopher, heir to Rousseau. "Dewey's practicism sets aside the purely intellectual and ethical aims (of education), or includes them in the teaching adapted to the conditions and conveniences of the environment in which the child is going to develop. (His philosophy) is a strict application of pragmatism, of the doctrine characteristic of his own race and country, according to which utility is the supreme aim of philosophy."[58] For Terán, not only was this philosophical system ethically wrong but it was also condemned to historical failure, as the recent crisis of the U.S. shows. In his view, its incapacity to achieve material commonwealth and its disdain for pure culture had led that country to bankruptcy. Obviously, he did not recommend following the model but fighting against it.

Terán defended spiritualism as educational philosophy. It implied a return to intelligence in opposition to the pragmatist's "cult of life."[59] He advocated the traditional humanist curriculum and denied the value of vocational schools because they "condemn people to live in empiricism and close their access to the highest possibilities of intelligence."[60] In his argument, activism was subordinate to discipline, order, and respect to the rules. The latter being the government's pedagogical principles. The New School that Terán and his partners had in mind was similar to the one developed in fascist Italy. Terán's appeal in 1930 opened a decade in which alternative experiences within the New School were to be persecuted, and radical teachers exonerated.

It may then be surprising to find some resemblances, at first sight, between Terán's and Aníbal Ponce's views of Dewey, the last of the professors to be expelled in that period. Ponce (1898-1938), as a member of the pedagogical left, condemned Dewey's pedagogy as utilitarian and a purely methodological expression of American bourgeois civilization. He developed his criticism based on a roughly deterministic Marxism. He considered Dewey part of the "methodological trend" of the New School, which sought to increase the performance of students adjusting pedagogy to child's personality, both biological and psychical.[61] Dewey's claim for collective work at school was a response to changes in capitalism. Fordism required a new school centered on children's socialization, instead of the traditional school's individualism. According to Ponce, Dewey, and Montessori implied the capitalist rationalization of teaching.

Ponce's condemnation of Dewey and the whole New School movement was probably related to the class reductionism that structured his discourse, which led him to disregard national issues as well.[62] This bias may have prevented him from deconstructing the equivalences between Dewey's pedagogy, efficiency, and manual training settled years ago. Another important issue involved in his rejection of Dewey is the traditional admiration that Argentine leftist political parties had devoted to Sarmiento's "civilizing" endeavor, sharing the official pedagogical grammar.[63] Thus the left had criticized all the reforms which intended to dispute the classical bachillerato's legitimacy. Briefly put, the left constituted an unexpected ally in the subsistence of traditional humanist curriculum. Unable to distinguish between official discourse and teachers' praxis[64]—a distinction that, if made, could have contributed to the emergence of a curricular alternative—Ponce could not include Dewey's "inclusiveness."

Attacked by right-wing pedagogues as well as by leftists, Dewey had few followers in those years. Among them there was another man from the left who was distinctively and firmly engaged in the New School Movement. The teacher Jesualdo Sosa (1905-1982), born in Uruguay and with vast experience in Argentina, had a different view on Dewey and New Education from Ponce's. He considered Dewey as "one of the most progressive bourgeois partisans of the school of work,"[65] the school of socialist tomorrow. Dewey's proposal linked school work to knowledge and democracy, both issues eschewed by Kerchensteiner. Jesualdo considered the influence of Fordism and Taylorism in Dewey's work but he qualified his concepts as "evidently progressive"[66] with respect to his predecessors' educative means and objectives. One of the negative remarks Jesualdo had for Dewey was the presence of religion, a fact that in South America was associated with conservatism. Once again, Jesualdo stood out among leftist pedagogues when he recognized that the term "religion" could include some kind of constructive mysticism "necessary for human perfection,"[67] Jesualdo was one of the few pedagogues framed in the political left who laid bridges to religious spiritualism.

Returning to the pedagogical field, it was Terán's reaction which was the one that articulated and defined the prevailing reading of Dewey in the '30s and the '40s, and not Jesualdo's. In the pedagogical field, humanist curriculum was strengthened by the aim of "cultivation of intelligence" and authoritarian discipline, and by the condemnation of vocationalist and professional schools. Dewey's legacy tended to be contested by the official New School discourse; evidence of the latter's narrow borders. However, evidence has been found that teachers studied Dewey's work in courses they organized by themselves.[68]

With the Second World War, Americanism in general and Dewey's readers particularly received new impulse. The war acted as a nodal point[69] that reorganized all the meanings of political and cultural struggles and created new ones. Liberal democracy and laic spiritualism gained support against the menace of fascist nationalism. The polarity benefited pro-NorthAmericans, who received unforeseen favors, as those of the left, engaged in Earl Browder's bend. At the end of the war, the North American influence in Argentine economics and politics had increased so much that the 1946 polls showed the U.S. ambassador openly favoring one of the candidates.[70] The eruption of Peronism, a national populist government, completely changed the political and pedagogical scene, putting the question of social justice and political democracy at the center of the debate.[71]

Another important issue for the renewing of Dewey's reading was the Argentine exile of Lorenzo Luzuriaga after the Spanish Republic defeat. Luzuriaga was a prominent liberal republican pedagogue who had translated the bulk of Dewey's books and articles, many of which he published in the *Revista de Pedagogía*, which he edited in Madrid. In his long exile, he wrote a lot of textbooks on contemporary pedagogy and especially on the New School movement, in which he always enhanced the relevance of John Dewey.[72] Luzuriaga filled a vacant place in the pedagogical field since the decline of positivism, that of a liberal and democratic alternative to the official spiritualist discourse. He re-edited most of the Spanish publications on Dewey in Argentina.

But it was Juan Mantovani's reading that would mark Dewey's entrance to the Argentine pantheon of pedagogical heroes. Mantovani (1896-1961) was a representative of laic spiritualism, a trend in official discourse which sought to reconcile spiritualist anti-positivism with laicism. Having passed through all the steps in the school system (professor, headmaster, inspector, member of educational boards, and reformer), Mantovani built a pedagogy with loans from activism, German and Italian spiritualism and Luzuriaga's liberalism.[73] During Perón's government, he resigned and finally joined the opposite front. His influence among teachers and pedagogues was considerable.

Not being a pragmatic, Mantovani underlined Dewey's ideal of democracy: it was not a given achievement but a way of life that had to be continually rebuilt through education and social mobilization.[74] He also underscored Dewey's critiques towards U.S. imperialism and social injustice. However, he said, "it is possible that Dewey's thoughts are less adaptable to the spiritual environment of Latin America, in which prevailing categories and mentalities are different from those characteristic in Dewey's country."[75] This was due to the Latin Americans' inclination to the sensitive and the spiritual instead of the intelligible and material. Dewey's work would never be well adapted to Latin American conditions. Anyway, Latin Americans could learn his democratic faith and his views on children's interests and freedom from him. Remarkably, Mantovani consecrated Dewey in the hall of great pedagogues while at the same time he excluded the possibility of his playing a role in specific curricular orientations. In the midst of the century, once again, Dewey's legacy and pragmatism was relegated to the margins of the Argentine school system, in professional schools, adult education or education for disabled people.

Some Final Remarks

We would like to conclude by pointing out the most relevant of the conditions of reception from which Dewey was read in Argentina in the first half of our century.

The spread of liberalism was undoubtedly one of the conditions for reception of Dewey's work. But Latin American liberalism, at the end of the nineteenth century, was in fact quite different from European or North

American versions. As Roberto Schwarz has said in the Brazilian case, the adoption of liberalism supposed that "liberal ideas could not be practiced but were all the same un-rejectable."[76] Progress was a disgrace due to wild modernization processes, but backwardness was not bearable either: this was one of the most constitutive paradoxes of our societies. Oligarchic land-owners, political fraud and disorganization, were among the characteristics of South American societies that claimed to be organized and governed on liberal grounds. This was recognized as problematic as early as 1880 in Argentina, and new integrative ideals were proposed quickly: the nation, the people, the class. Liberalism evolved into positivistic conservatism, creating a new series of equivalences; doctrinarians were left alone with an industrialist utopia.

The development of the Nation-State was another relevant issue. The quantitative dimension of the Nation-State was already looked after by the centralized board of education. The disputes took place in an organized system and addressed effective democracy and modernization. Dewey's readings were fragmented and emphasized limited aspects, generally the technical and practical ones. Dewey's authority opened the possibility of critique of the educational status-quo, a critique that reached its peak in the '20s. The diffusion of his ideas was dispersed and more capilar than hierarchic. It was included in the discursive plot of the New School among others.

The third remark refers to the role Americanism played in international references, whose place in Argentine culture has already been outlined. In our view, the scattered character of Argentine readings is also related to the fact that Dewey has never been the legitimating pedagogical authority for official or alternative discourses. His readings were inscribed in a beam of influences which made it very difficult to follow the North American pedagogue. Except for Nelson, none of the pedagogues considered followed Dewey organically. Pragmatism was confined to the margins of the school system. Still, it affected the core of the humanist curriculum on which a powerful alliance was built.

The pedagogical field's configurations were also important for defining the horizons of reading from which Dewey was analyzed. In our opinion, the journey through Dewey's Argentine readings shows a multiplicity of images which act as mirrors of the pedagogical field. Dewey as renewer, Dewey as anti-democratic manual trainer, Dewey as pragmatic, Dewey as democratic philosopher, are images constructed both by his partisans and his opponents. They speak of the possibilities Dewey's concepts opened to discursive articulation, but most of all they refer to the struggles for structuring the Argentine curriculum, in which Dewey was invoked both to promote reforms and to prevent them. The Argentine pedagogical field acted as a matrix for translation, and each translator built different sets of meanings and equivalences. Despite their differences, a distinctive feature of the field appears in the difficulty to firmly include Dewey's inclusiveness. In the '30s, he was reduced to a methodologist and practioner, and thus rejected. In the '50s, he was frozen out as a general philosopher. The operation made by Mantovani is a symptom of this freezing: while he produced the final reconciliation of Argentine spiritualism with Dewey, he blocked an effective intervention of his ideas in the renewing of pedagogy. Despite Sarmiento's original appeal, egalitarian liberalism and pragmatism were not to have a privileged role in the Argentine curriculum in the twentieth century.

The authors would like to thank Elisabete Cruvelho, Terri Catlow, Amalia Martínez and Isabel Copello for their help with content and translation; also to Pablo Cafiero and Torsten Lösel for their support.

Notes

1.   Goodenow, Ronald, "The Progressive Educator and the Third World: A First Look at John Dewey" *History of Education* 19, no. 1 (1990):23-40.

2.   For Ernesto Laclau, articulation is constitutive of all social practices and social identities. Subjects are constituted by systems of differences (institutions) and the fissures or gaps they reveal. "Our whole analysis goes against an objectivistic conception and presupposes the reduction of 'fact' to 'sense,' and of 'the given' to its conditions of possibility. This 'sense' is not a fixed transcendental horizon, but appears as essentially historic and contingent," as a result of articulation (Laclau, *New Reflections on the Revolution of Our Time*, London, Verso, 1990, pp. 212-213). This articulation is not infinite: it is limited both by history and politics. On the historicity of meanings, see Bakhtin, Mikhaíl, *Estética de la Creación Verbal* (México: Siglo XXI, 1984); on the impossibility of a complete sense, see Laclau, op.cit..

3.   See especially, Jauss, H. R., *Pour une Esthétique de la Réception* (Paris, Tel-Gallimard, 1978); Altamirano, C. and Sarlo, B., *Literatura/Sociedad* (Buenos Aires, Hachette, 1983) and Selden, R. and Widdowson, P., *Contemporary Literary Theory* (London: Harvester/Wheatshef, 1993).

4.   "En termes analytiques, un champ peut être défini comme un réseau, ou une configuration de relations objectives entre des positions. Ces positions sont définies objectivement dans leur existence et dans les déterminations qu'elles imposent à leurs occupants, agents ou institutions, par leur situation (situs) actuelle et potentielle dans la structure de la distribution des différentes espèces de pouvoir (ou de capital) dont la possession commande l'accès aux profits spécifiques qui sont en jeu dans le champ, et, du même coup, par leur relations objectives aux autres positions (domination, subordination, homologie, etc.)" (P. Bourdieu, *Réponses*, París, Du Seuil, 1992, pp. 72-73).

5. Altamirano and Sarlo, p. 101.

6. Altamirano and Sarlo talk about "horizons of reading" that both shape and limit the reception of any given text. They borrowed this concept from Jauss, who uses the term "horizons of expectations" to describe the criteria readers use to judge literary text in any given period. These criteria refer to the reader's previous experiences on reading, the literary norm and the distinction (submitted to historical change) between the imaginary world and everyday life. See note 5.

7. Vachet, Los Fundamentos del Liberalismo (Madrid, Catálogos, 1980).

8. The social imaginary is a set of representations and images that categorize the social world (self/other, thinkable/unthinkable, real/illusory, meaningful/ senseless) and work out social identities and formative models for that world. They include multiple temporalities and discourses (scientific, fictional). As Baczko has said, it is the arena of social conflicts as well as one of the issues for which there is constant struggle. See Baczko, B., *Les Imaginaires Sociaux. Mémoirs et Espoirs Collectifs* (Paris, Payot, 1984).

9. Bowles and Gintis, *La Instrucción Escolar en la América Capitalista* (México: Siglo XXI, 1986).

10. Popkewitz, Th.S. (ed.), *The Formation of the School Subjects. The Struggle for Creating an American Institution* (Philadelphia: The Falmer Press, 1987).

11. Giroux, H., *Schooling and the Struggle for the Public Life. Critical Pedagogy in the Modern Age* (Minneapolis: University of Minnesota Press, 1988).

12. Feinberg, W., "Dewey and Democracy at the Dawn of the Twenty First Century: A review of Robert B. Westbrook, John Dewey and American Democracy" (Ithaca: Cornell University Press, 1991), *Educational Theory* (Summer 1993).

13. Popkewitz, Th. S., "Política, Conocimiento y Curriculum en la Educación," *Propuesta Educativa* 8 (1993), 36-43.

14. See for example, Lorenzo Luzuriaga's introduction to his translation of *The Child and the Curriculum* (Buenos Aires, Losada, 1967); or Lourenço Filho's review in *Introdução ao Estudo da Escola Nova* (Sao Paulo: Cia. Melhoramentos, 1930).

15. García Canclini, N., *Culturas Híbridas* (México: CONACULTA, 1989).

16. Schwarz, R., *Ao Vencedor as Batatas* (Sao Paulo, Duas cidades, 1977). Schwarz gives an example: the inclusion of the French "Déclaration des Droits de l'Homme" in the Brazilian Constitution of 1824, while the slavery system was still in vogue.

17. For the definition of the Oligarchic State, see: Allub, L., "Estado y Sociedad Civil: Patrón de Emergencia y Desarrollo del Estado Argentino (1810-1930)," in Ansaldi et al., *Estado y Sociedad en el Pensamiento Nacional* (Buenos Aires: Cantaro, 1989), 109-157; Cavarozzi, M., "Elementos para una caracterización del capitalismo oligárquico," *Revista Mexicana de Sociología* 78, no. 4 (1978).

18. See Hale, Ch., "Political and Social Ideas in Latin America, 1870-1930," *The Cambridge History of Latin America* ed. by L. Bethell (Cambridge: Cambridge University Press, 1985), 367-441; Terán, O., *En busca de la Ideología Argentina* (Buenos Aires: Folios, 1986).

19. Brickman, W., "John Dewey's foreign reputation as an educator" in *School and Society* 70 (no. 1818, October 22, 1949, New York), 261.

20. See *John Dewey's Impressions of Soviet Russia and the Revolutionary World. Mexico-China-Turkey*, 1929, Introduction and notes by W. W. Brickman (New York: Teachers College, Columbia University, 1964).

21. Domingo Faustino Sarmiento (1811-1888) was an intellectual and political leader of his time. He was a great admirer of the United States, especially of Horace Mann's work in Massachussetts.

22. Quoted by Tedesco, J. C., *Educación y Sociedad en la Argentina, 1880-1945* (Buenos Aires: Ed. Solar-Hachette, 1986), 31.

23. The 1914 Census showed that almost 80 percent of the population was immigrant or son of immigrants.

24. Tedesco, p. 248.

25. See Puiggrós, A., Sujetos, *Disciplina y Curriculum en los Orígenes del Sistema Educativo Argentino, 1885-1916* (Buenos Aires: Galerna, 1990).

26. Part of its hegemony was based in the support received by subordinate social groups, who considered humanist curriculum as a sign of social distinction (in Bourdieu's terms) and fought mostly for its widening instead of its replacement.

27. See Tedesco, J. C., "La Crisis de la Hegemonía Oligárquica y el Sistema Educativo Argentino, 1930-1945" in Tedesco, J. C., *Educación y Sociedad en Argentina, 1880-1945* (Buenos Aires, Solar, 1986).

28. For a detailed discussion on the period, see Puiggrós, A., "La Educación Argentina Desde la Reforma Saavedra Lamas Hasta el Fin de la Década Infame. Hipótesis para la Discusión," *Escuela, Democracia y Orden, 1916-1943* ed. by A. Puiggrós (Buenos Aires, Galerna, 1992), 15-97.

29. The first one was *The School and the Society* (Madrid, Beltrán, 1915), translated by Domingo Barnés; and *How We Think* (edited in Boston in 1917 under the title of "Psicología del Pensamiento"), translated by Alejandro Jascalevih. Cf. Brickman, p. 263; Sánchez Reulet, A., ed. by John Dewey en sus *Noventa Años* (Washington, D.C.: Unión Panamericana, 1949), 27.

30. See Escudé, C., 1942-1949. *Gran Bretaña, Estados Unidos y la Declinación Argentina* (Buenos Aires: Ed. de Belgrano, 1988).

31. See Hale, Ch., "Political and Social Ideas in Latin America ...," pp. 414 and ss.

32. See Kliebard, H., *The Struggle for the American Curriculum, 1893-1958* (New York: Routledge and Kegan Paul, 1986).

33. Díaz, Raúl B., *Ideales y Esperanzas en Educación Común* (Buenos Aires Talleres Gráficos de L. J. Roso y Cía., 1913). In his view, the U.S. were the only country in the world which could show a school being "the center of the life and happiness of the child, close to his home ... guided by the nation's ideals of democracy and greatness" (p. 1).

34. In 1915, he shared the tribune with Charles W. Eliot at the Pan-American Congress and some years later the Pan-American Union and the Carnegie Foundation for International Peace published some of his works.

35. See Nelson, E., *The Spanish Reader* (Boston: D. C. Heath and Co., 1916); *Las Bibliotecas en los EE.UU* (Dotación Carnegie para la Paz Internacional, 1929); *La Salud del Niño, Su Protección Social en la Legislación y en las Obras* (New York: La Nueva Democracia, 1929).

36. Mercante, V., *Charlas Pedagógicas* (Buenos Aires: R. Gleizer, 1927), 12.

37. Nelson, E., "The Secondary School and the University," in Department of the Interior, Bureau of Education Bulletin, *Needed Changes in Secondary Education* 10 (Government Printing Office, Washington DC, 1916):21-32, p. 24.

38. Nelson, E., *Filiación Histórica de la Educación Argentina* (Buenos Aires: Confederación de Maestros, 1939). Here he repeated almost the same arguments held by Dewey in *The Educational Situation* in 1902.

39. Nelson, E., *Plan de Reformas a la Enseñanza Secundaria en Sus Fines, Su Organización y Su Función Social* (Buenos Aires: A. Mentruyt, 1915), 13. See also Gagliano, R., "Aportes para la Construcción de una Historia Crítica de la Adolescencia en la Argentina," *Escuela, Democracia y Orden, 1916-1943*, pp. 299-341.

40. Nelson, E., "The Secondary School ...," p. 27.

41. Nelson, E., "Un Experimento Trascendental en la Educación Argentina. El Internado del Colegio Nacional de la UNLP," *Boletín del Museo Social Argentino* (Buenos Aires, Coni Hnos., 1912), 3-27. On the other side of the educational battle, Victor Mercante, writer of the official Plan of reforms for secondary education in 1915, reproved football and popular culture as educational activities.

42. Nelson, p. 31.

43. Nelson, p. 32.

44. Nelson, "A Problem for the Americas," *Points of View* 5 (August 1942), Panamerican Union, Washington, D.C., pp. 3-8.

45. See Kliebard, chapter 3.

46. See Barcos, J. R., 1928. *Cómo Educa el Estado a tu Hijo*, Ed. Acción, Buenos Aires, 2da. edición, especially Preface.

47. See Ziperovich, R., 1992, "Memorias de una Educadora," in Puiggrós (ed.), op.cit., pp. 161-256; and Carli, S., 1992. "El Campo de la Niñez. Entre el Discurso de la Minoridad y el Discurso de la Educación Nueva," in idem, pp. 99-160.

48. See Etcheverry, D., 1958. Los Artesanos de la Escuela Moderna. La Lucha por la Libertad Creadora en la Escuela Argentina, Galatea-Nueva Visión, Buenos Aires; also note 47.

49. Quoted by Carli, "El Campo de la Niñez ...," p. 131.

50. "Political pedagogical reformism had gained strong support among primary and secondary teachers, even though it may have reached more institutionalization and public expression at the universitary level." Puiggrós, A., "La Educación Argentina Desde la Reforma Saavedra Lamas ...," p. 37.

51. Ibidem. See also Gálvez, M., *En Defensa de Nuestra Cultura* (Buenos Aires, 1924).

52. Clotilde Guillén de Rezzano, quoted by Carli, S., op.cit., p. 148.

53. See Puiggrós, A., 1992, op.cit., pp. 49-65.

54. The majority of the articles referred to european writers, as Ferrière, Montessori, Décroly and Claparède. As one article devoted to Dewey said: "It is familiar to us the work developed in Europe under the direct inspiration of Rousseau ...; but we do have only loose information from the northamerican crusade to establish the New School ..." Salas Marchan, M., 1920. "John Dewey y la escuela norteamericana," in *El Monitor de la Educación Común* (Año XXXIX:No. 576, Diciembre 1920), 219-225; 219.

55. Ibidem.

56. Terán, Juan B., *Espiritualizar Nuestra Escuela. La Instrucción Primaria Argentina en 1931* (Buenos Aires: Librería del Colegio, 1932).

57. Terán, p. 4.

58. Terán, p. 12.

59. Terán, p. 13.

60. Terán, p. 42.

61. Ponce, A. *Educación y Lucha de Clases* (Buenos Aires: Cartago, 1984): 163. He considered the existence of a second trend, "doctrinarian," which he also criticized. In Ponce's view, the doctrinarians held that the methodological tendency wanted to prepare children for present times and not for the future, as it was its own aim. According to Ponce, Terán's pedagogy could be inscribed in this second type.

62. See Terán, O., "Aníbal Ponce o el Marxismo Sin Nación," in *En Busca de la Ideología Argentina* (Buenos Aires: Catálogos, 1986):131-178.

63. We have borrowed this term from Bernstein's work on the structuring of pedagogic discourse. The official pedagogical grammar refers to the hegemonic set of "rules which regulate the production, distribution, reproduction, interrelation and change of legitimate pedagogic texts (discourses), their social relations of transmission and acquisition (practice) and the organization of their contexts (organization)." Bernstein, B., *The Structuring of Pedagogic Discourse. Class, Codes and Control*, Vol. IV (London & New York, Routledge, 1990), 193.

64. Carli, p. 152.

65. Jesualdo, *Los Fundamentos de la Nueva Pedagogía* (Buenos Aires: Ed. Americalee, 1943):132.

66. Jesualdo, *Diecisiete Educadores de América. Los Constructores, los Reformadores* (Montevideo, Ed. Pueblos Unidos, 1945):198.

67. Jesualdo, p. 199.

68. See Puiggrós, "La educación argentina ...," p. 95.

69. See Laclau, New reflections ...

70. Braden supported Tamborini, who confronted Juan Domingo Perón's nomination. Skupch, P., 1971, gives insightful evidence on the increment of U.S. influence on argentine economy along the first half of twentieth century.

71. See Bernetti and Puiggrós. *Peronismo, Cultura Política y Educación, 1946-1955* (Buenos Aires: Galerna, 1993).

72. See *La Educación Nueva Facultad de Filosofía y Letras,* Universidad Nacional de Tucumán, 1943; *La Pedagogía Contemporánea* (Buenos Aires: Losada, 1960).

73. He met Aníbal Ponce and Ernesto Nelson at the "Colegio Libre de Estudios Superiores," where they all taught in 1930-32. This coincidence shows him distant from Terán's intolerance and more proximate to democratic pedagogues. See Puiggrós, 1992, op.cit., page 95.

74. This was obviously related to the post-war context as well as to the argentine political situation after the emergence of peronism, which put "democracy" as a privileged signifier. Mantovani, J., "John Dewey. Su fe en la democracia y en la educación," *Filósofos y Educadores* (Buenos Aires: Librería El Ateneo, 1957):45-53.

75. Mantovani, p. 53.

76. Schwarz, R., *Ao Vencedor as Batatas* (Sao Paulo: Duas cidades, 1977), 22.

5

Contemporary Brazilian Education: Challenges of Basic Education

Moacir Gadotti

Historians usually divide the history of Brazilian education into three distinct periods:

1. From discovery through 1930: a period marked by the dominance of traditional education, centered around the authority of adults and teachers, and predominantly influenced by religion and private schooling;
2. From 1930 to 1964: following a period of confrontation between private and public education there is a dominance of liberal ideas with the rise of the "new school," which focused on the child and on renewed methods, in opposition to traditional education.
3. The post-1964 period: established during a long period of authoritarian education during the military regime, this phase of Brazilian education is dominated by a technical approach to schooling. There has been from 1985 to present a transitional period which reveals an enormous gap in the access of education to all people.

During the populist period (1930-1964), the Brazilian State became permeable to certain popular demands as part of electoral obligations stemming from a system of political representation. The post-1964 period, however, was characterized by increasing separation between state and society (e.g., the suspension of elections, the closing of Congress) which hindered further educational development. Beginning in 1985, with Brazil's democratization process underway, the country became hopeful for solutions to its educational backwardness. However, these solutions by and large have not emerged.

The call for a new Constitution in the following year and its subsequent approval in 1987, brought together a large number of Brazil's socially organized groups, both in the public and private spheres, to hammer out the basic principles of a new plan for education which could put an end to illiteracy and universalize primary education. These principles are now part of the Constitution promulgated in October of 1988, but have not been translated into practice thus far. The new LDB [Lei de Diretrizes e Bases], which has been under examination in Congress since 1989, should eventually supplement the constitutional principles established in 1988.

Landmarks in the History of Brazilian Education

In 1549 the Jesuits—from the Catholic religious order known as Company of Jesus founded by Inacio de Loyola in 1534—landed in Brazil and stayed until 1759. During this period they led the country's education using the methods and content of the Ratio Studiorum, inspired in the scholastic.

From the city of Salvador, Bahia, where they arrived, the Jesuits rapidly fanned out across the various regions of Brazil, first toward the South and then toward the North.

Marquis of Pombal, then Prime-minister for Portugal (1750-1777), defending the ideas of *enlightened despotism*, undertook educational reforms with an incipient struggle for public schooling. In 1759, the Jesuits were expelled from the Portuguese Kingdom under the allegation of cultural obscurantism and excessive political involvement. By the time the Jesuits were expelled from Brazil, they controlled 36 missions, 25 residences, and 18 secondary schools scattered throughout the country.

Beginning in 1808, with the coming of the Portuguese Royal Family to Brazil (which was fleeing the Napoleonic invasion), the educational concerns from the Portuguese monarchy were limited to training the governing elite and the military cadre. The main initiatives undertaken by the government during this period were: the creation of the School of Surgery and Anatomy (1808), the rounding of the Royal Naval Academy (1808), the creation of the Public Library (1810), the creation of technical schools as well as the establishment of the teaching of arts through the hiring of French artists.

In the year of 1820, the Portuguese bourgeoisie seized power in Portugal and forced D. Joao VI to return to his homeland (April 26, 1821). In 1827, five years after independence from Portugal, Brazil rounded two schools of Law: one in Sao Paulo and another in Recife, where the Brazilian elite was trained to occupy the main posts in public administration, politics, journalism and law.

According to the Imperial Constitution, decreed in 1824, it was the responsibility of the Local Assemblies [Assembleias Legislativas] of each province (today, states) to legislate over public instruction. In spite of the fact that the Imperial Constitution defended the principle of free elementary instruction to all citizens, elementary education was ignored. At the end of the Empire, 85 percent of Brazil's population of about 14 million was illiterate.

Brazil became aware of its educational backwardness through the legal proceedings by lawmaker Rui Barbosa in 1882 in which he compared our performance with that of the European and North American countries.

The First Republic (1889-1930) was a period which put in check the educational model inherited from the Empire. In 1890 the republican transitional government established the Ministry of Public Instruction, Postal Services and Telegraph, inspired in the positivist ideas of August Comte and put forth by Benjamin Constant. However, two years later, this same Ministry was abolished, thus transferring educational matters to the jurisdiction of the Ministry of Justice and Interior Businesses.

The 1891 Constitution instituted the secularization of public education. During the first 20 years of this century, inspired by liberal ideals, by faith in the power of education and by the maxim that the "ignorance of the people" was at the root of all crises in the country, successive governments established numerous Normal Schools to train elementary school teachers. This period also gave rise to the civic-patriotic movement, associated with the name of Olavo Bilac, which advocated combating illiteracy.

Within this context ABE (The Brazilian Education Association) was founded in 1924, which included well-known Brazilian educators such as Fernando de Azevedo and Paschoal Lemme. This association propelled an educational reform movement in Brazil the apex of which was the "Manifesto of the Forerunners of the New Education" (1932) which supported public, secular, free and mandatory schooling. The 1934 Constitution consecrated these ideas in a specific chapter on education.

This period is also marked by numerous educational reforms which sought to establish the structure and the functioning of basic and higher education: the Benjamin Constant reform (1890); the Epitacio Pessoa's reform; the Rivadavia Correia's (1911); the Carlos Maximiliano's; and the Joao Luis Alves' reform (1925). The states also promoted various reforms, including the Sampaio Doria reform, in San Paulo (1920); the Lourenco Filho reform, in the state of Ceara (1923); the Anisio Teixeira reform in Bahia (1925), the Francisco Campos reform, in Minas Gerais (1927); and the Fernando de Azevedo reform, in the Federal District (1928). These reforms were sparked by the creation of ABE and the national investigation on education triggered by "the State of São Paulo's Newspaper," in 1926, and led by Fernando Azevedo. They contributed both to the theoretical debate on education and the concrete development of this sector.

The 1930 revolution produced important transformations in the field of education. In particular it led to the creation the same year of the Ministry of Education and the writing of a special chapter on education in the 1934 Constitution. Francisco Campos, the first Brazilian minister of education, ordered the creation of the Statute of the Brazilian Universities (Campos reform, 1930). In 1934 was founded the University of Sao Paulo (USP).

The 1937 Constitution introduced the formation of professional schools in Brazil which are followed by the Secondary Schooling Organic Laws (1942). The period from 1930 through 1945 was marked by the rapid evolution of public education and the stagnation of the private sector, especially in primary education.

The 1946 Constitution established State and Federal financial contributions to education, including the principle that the Union should never invest less than 10 percent of its budget in the maintenance and development of education and that the states, the Federal District and the municipalities should never invest less than twenty percent. It also determined the need to forge new legal guidelines for education. In 1948 Clemente Mariani, minister of education, sent in the first project on the national guidelines for education (LDB) which was only sanctioned and turned into law in 1961. During this long period of discussions on educational reform in Brazil, two polarized positions prevailed: a) the defense of public schooling; and b) support for private education. The LDB from 1961 finally reconciled these two positions in an ambiguous document.

During the democratizing period from 1946 to 1964, various popular movements emerged in support of education, which in turn spearheaded successive mobilization campaigns: the campaign for the improvement and dissemination of secondary education; the eradication of illiteracy; the adult education campaign; rural education; education for the hearing impaired; education for the rehabilitation of the visually impaired; campaign for school lunches; and the campaign for instructional material.

This debate was intensified at the end of the 1950s and early 1960s. The success of the "Paulo Freire Method" caught the attention of President João Goulart (1963) who tried to expand its application throughout the country. The military coup of 1964 halted this ambitious project and sent Freire into exile.

The military regime became famous in the educational field for two reforms: the higher education reform act from 1968, and the overhauling of basic education in 1971. Basic public education became lower and upper elementary education, and technical knowledge was stressed in contrast to general education. The military rule decided to reinstate Civic and Moral Education as mandatory disciplines in all levels of schooling, including in graduate studies. The National Student Union (UNE), after being accused of promoting "subversive" activities, was substituted by the National Student Directorship (DNE). In 1969, the military regime approved Decree Law 477 which restricted the rights of professors, students and staff to organize by classifying these activities as subversion.

These were the years of the so called "economic miracle" and of "educational inertia." In 1967, the government founded MOBRAL (Brazilian Literacy Movement) which, in fact, did not get off the ground until 1970. The plan was to eliminate illiteracy in Brazil in ten years. At the time of the founding of MOBRAL, official illiteracy rates were at 32,05 percent. In 1980, census data from IBGE (the Brazilian Bureau of the Census) continued to show the persistence of illiteracy: 25.5 percent of people 14 years of age or older.

To many Brazilian educators today, the 1980s are considered a lost decade. In spite of the relative expansion in educational opportunities during this period and despite the reorganization of educational workers, teaching quality deteriorated enormously. Drop-out rates and grade repetition grew to alarming proportions. Because of drop-out rates and grade repetition, only 44 percent of students graduate from elementary school, which in turn takes an average of 11.4 years to complete. Furthermore, only 3 percent finish eighth grade without having to repeat a grade and just 65 percent of all students complete fifth grade.

The 1990s began signaling hopes for education; however, up to the present (1996), all plans to confront the Brazilian educational challenge—and there have been many—have not left the drawing board.

The Brazilian Educational System

The 1988 Brazilian Constitution establishes that education is a right to all, and an obligation of the State and the family. It aims at the whole development of the individual and his/her preparation for citizenship and work. According to the constitution, schooling should take into consideration equal access and continuity in the schools, freedom to learn, the pluralism of ideas, a free public school system, the valorization of all professionals of education, democratic practices and standards of quality. Further, investment in education in Brazil is open to private initiative as long as entrepreneurs abide by the general educational principles established by the constitution.

The Union, the states, the federal district, and the municipalities are responsible for the organization of their respective educational systems in a regime of "collaboration" (Art. 211). The Union organizes and finances the federal system of education through technical and monetary assistance to the states and municipalities, which must offer mandatory education.

The national education system encompasses the public systems and other public or private institutions which deliver educational services. Its objective is to guarantee the unity of the various systems and the same standard of quality throughout the national territory. The state system of education includes the public and private schools as well as administrative, legislative, and technical support state institutions. The municipal system of education includes the public and private schools, as in the case of the state system, and institutions and educational services within its jurisdiction.

All policies converge around the improvement of quality in the schools, putting at the disposal of the different systems the means to perform their functions with academic, administrative and financial autonomy.

In recent years, public schools have been constituting school councils (CE) with the power to deliberate more freely over educational matters. The school councils are the most important normative and executive organizations in the administration of any particular school. They have either substituted the former APMs (Teacher and Parent Associations) or incorporated them as financial departments of the CEs. Participation is open to students as well although in many private and public schools students voice their concerns through their own organizations.

From the legal perspective, there is a sharing of responsibilities within the various spheres of public power which should act in a coordinated manner. In practice, however, this coordination is still very problematic.

The administration of education in Brazil encompasses federal, state and municipal institutions:

- Federal: Ministry of Education (MEC) and the National Council of Education (CNE), which in 1995 was sub-divided in two Councils: a) the Council of Basic Education; and b) the Higher Education Council;
- State: State Secretary of Education (SE) and State Council of Education (CEE);
- Municipal: Secretary or Department of Education and Municipal Council of Education (CME).

The State Secretaries of Education define their political and educational agendas through the CONSED (Council of State Secretaries of Education) and the Municipal Secretaries through the Association of Leadership to Municipal Education (UNDIME).

The Brazilian Universities are represented by the Council of Rectors for the Brazilian Universities (CRUB).

The Ministry of Education, as part of the Executive Branch, is responsible for enforcing the educational laws and rules of the Federal Council of Education. The Federal Council on education, in turn, has the normative function of handling education at the national level through the establishment of general educational guidelines and standards.

The State Secretaries of Education are responsible for coordinating educational policy at the state level pursuant to the norms established by the State Councils of Education. These, in turn, perform normative functions in education at each state.

The Municipal Secretary of Education coordinates the activities of education within the jurisdiction of the municipality. Beginning with the 1988 constitution, several municipalities have gradually been reorganizing their educational structures, particularly with the creation of Municipal Commissions of Education. Any municipality which does not invest 25 percent of its taxable income toward the development of basic education is subject to intervention by the Federal government.

Private elementary and secondary education are also subject to supervision by state agencies, and early childhood education is inspected by municipal administrations.

Financing Education

The union must invest at least 18 percent of its tax revenues and money transfer on the maintenance and development of education annually, and states and municipalities are required to spend at least 25 percent. Public resources are destined to public schools, but money can also be allocated to community, parochial and philanthropic schools. Nutritional programs as well as health, transportation, and instructional materials are expected to be financed by other budgetary sources.

In addition to mandatory investment in education from revenue mandated by the constitution, primary education is also supported by funds from compulsory taxation of businesses which is earmarked for education (the current proposal for new national educational guidelines contains a provision for collecting business contribution for expenditures related to child care services). Currently, industrial and commercial enterprises contribute 2.5 percent of the sum of all employees' salaries to education. Rural producers and agricultural businesses contribute with a share of 0.8 percent over their production.

Even though Brazil's investment in education is far less than the actual needs of its educational system, it has increased its expenditures in the last ten years compared with the authoritarian period. In 1972, for example, according to World Bank's statistics (Reduccion de los Costos Unitarios en los Sistemas Educativos de Latino-America, Centro de Investigacion Educativa, Costa Rica, 1974, quadro 6, p. 168), Brazil was the country which, proportionally, invested least in education in Latin America. In 1972, Brazil invested only 6.5 percent compared to countries like Costa Rica, Mexico, Panama, Uruguay which spent more than 25 percent of their budgets on education. This profile placed Brazil even behind Haiti, the next to the last country in level of investment in education with 11.3 percent of its budget. Today Brazil spends 3.7 percent of its GNP on education, a relatively low average if compared with countries such as Canada (6.2 percent), Egypt (5.2 percent) or the United States (5.0 percent).

Private schools in Brazil depend almost exclusively on student monthly tuition and fees, which due to constant increases have caused protests, strikes and the closing of some schools.

Levels of Schooling

Brazilian formal schooling is divided into two levels.

Basic Education. This includes early childhood education (ages 0-6), elementary education (ages 7-14), and secondary education (ages 15-17). Before the educational reform of 1971 (LDB), the last two were considered part of primary and secondary education.

Higher Education. At the beginning of 1991 the Brazilian government established through a federal law that the school year should have a minimum of 200 days, and at least four hours of daily schooling. Given the huge negative reaction to this measure decree was rejected a few months later. This mandate is also included in the new LDB (National Guidelines for Education) which was approved in 1990 by the Education Commission of the House of Representatives. This is a rather controversial issue because in practice the ruling of 180 school days still prevails regardless of the 1991 educational law.

The LDB has also established an adequate ratio of students per classroom teacher:

- childcare, 20 students;
- preschool and literacy education, 25;

- other grades and levels, 35 students.

Elementary and secondary curriculum necessarily encompass the Portuguese language, mathematics, knowledge of the physical and natural world, as well as political and social realities, particularly in Brazil. Physical and artistic education is also mandatory. Environmental education does not constitute a specific discipline on its own and must be integrated across all subject matter. Technological initiation should also begin at the elementary level.

Religious studies are supported by law in Brazil and are offered as electives among disciplines available in public elementary schools.

Early childhood education must promote children's physical, psychological and intellectual development, supplementing the education received from the family.

Early childhood education may be offered at child care facilities to children up to three years of age, and through preschools for children of four to six years of age. In the new LDB the integration between childcare and pre-schools has been called "Centers for Early Childhood Education." In 1990 there were 50,957 pre-school facilities—of which 11,792 were privately run and 39,165 run by the government—with a total initial enrollment of 3,740,512.

Elementary education aims at the progressive mastery of reading, writing and arithmetic as basic tools for assessing human environments, and developing an understanding and appreciation for solving human problems. Teaching at this level must be carried out in the Portuguese language. In fifth grade all students are expected to begin studying a modern foreign language. In 1990, there were 208,934 elementary school sites in Brazil (11,512 private and 197,422 public), and a total enrollment of 28,943,619 pupils.

Secondary education aims at deepening and consolidating the knowledge acquired in elementary schooling, preparing the student to continue learning, to think independently and to grasp the basics of technological and scientific productive processes.

Secondary education may be extended to include technical education. For example, a teacher education program for elementary school teachers (former Normal Schools) might last four years altogether. Technical [professional] education can be attained from institutions specifically tailored to deliver technical-professional training at the high school level and which issue certificates of proficiency for industry, commerce, agriculture, and services. These are the so-called "Technical schools." These schools are open to students who have successfully completed their elementary education.

For young men and women of the working class who did not have access to elementary education at the appropriate school age, there have been created the supplemental education courses [cursos supletivos], some of which have been offered through distance education programs. The new LDB project provides for a special working schedule to the working-student population (e.g., reducing the daily shift to two hours), [tele-education] programs in the work place, regular course offerings in the evening, a flexible school organization, subject matter centered around the worker's social practice and work, and teaching-learning methodology adequate to these students' experience and intellectual development. In 1990 there were 10,160 secondary schools (3,926 private and 6,234 public) in Brazil with a total enrollment of 3,498,777.

Higher education, managed by public institutions (federal, state and municipal) or private (parochial or secular), accomplishes its goals through teaching, research, cultural events, and extension. Its goal is to promote critical reflection, participation in material production through the specific professions, systematization, and the advance of practical and theoretical knowledge.

Higher education shall supply every individual with the indispensable basic preparation to participate in society as informed citizens, and also the means to progress in the work place as well as in further education.

The universities and other related higher education institutions, pursuant to their social function, aim at contributing, through research and extension, to the solution of regional and national socio-economic and political problems, and disseminating their findings and accomplishments.

The Brazilian higher education system encompasses three types of schools and programs:

- undergraduate courses;
- graduate study programs;
- post-doctoral programs.

The proposed new LDB contains a provision to supersede the current 180-day school year for 200 days.

In order to guarantee the constitutional principle of democratic governing, the higher education institutions which had not yet formed their partnership governing bodies (orgaos colegiados de gestao) are now beginning this process which will allow for the participation of teachers, staff, students and community members in university governance. This constitutional norm, however, is not mandatory for private institutions.

The universities in Brazil enjoy pedagogical-scientific freedom as well as organizational and financial autonomy.

In 1988 there were 871 higher education institutions, of which 26.75 percent were public. The remaining 638 were owned by private organizations. Among the public higher education institutions, 54 were federal, 87 state universities, and 92 were owned by municipalities. Only two out the 92 municipal higher education institutions were universities. The remaining 90 were defined as independent colleges [instituicoes isoladas]. From the total of 871 higher education institutions mentioned above, only 84 have university status. The remaining 787 (approximately 91 percent) are classified as independent colleges. Over 61 percent of a total enrollment of 1,505,360 in higher education pertain to the private schools.

Special Education

Increasingly scholars and educators have recommended that children with disabilities be offered special education, preferably within the regular classroom setting. This same recommendation points to the need of using specialized resources beginning at the cohort of zero to six years of age. Special education can also be handled by offering classes with specialized teachers who visit various participating schools involved or who work in special settings.

The State Secretary of Education usually disseminates information regarding its special education programs. In addition, the Association of Parents of Children with Disabilities (APAEs) has contributed enormously to enhance special education. In 1988 there were 4,091 special education schools in Brazil and 1,206 specialized support institutions. In the same year, enrollment totaled 87,968 disabled children and 20,555 teachers. The great majority of these schools were public, with only 94 belonging to the private sector. Conversely, most specialized entities were owned by individuals and private organizations: 973 out of 1206.

Indigenous Communities Education

Since initial contact between Western and pre-Columbian cultures, indigenous peoples have been systematically decimated. In Brazil I estimate that at discovery in 1500 there were approximately 2 million indigenous people. In contrast, there are fewer than 200,000 survivors today.

The awareness of this reality compelled Brazilian lawmakers to include in the 1988 Constitution a provision to guarantee that indigenous communities maintain the use of their languages and their specific learning processes (Art. 210). This constitutional right was intended to preserve and strengthen the indigenous peoples' social organization, cultures, customs, beliefs and traditions.

The new proposed LDB anticipate the creation of specific programs tailored to educating indigenous communities, developing instructional materials and a school calendar appropriate to the needs of diverse indigenous groups. Brazil has about 600 indigenous schools.

Distance Education

A form of teaching amongst Brazilians which is not well-developed but of great potential today is the so-called distance education. Distance education provides students with the opportunity for independent study, choice of schedules and combining self-teaching instructional materials with access to modern means of communication without leaving the home.

Because of its specific characteristics, distance education when applied to early childhood and elementary schooling exerts only a supplemental function. It is predominantly offered to young men and women and to working class adults. Distance education has the characteristics of continuing education, professional training and cultural enrichment.

Statistics on Brazil's Educational Backwardness

Despite the progressive nature of the Brazil's legislation on education and despite the often progressive thinking of Brazilian educators, this country still has one of the lowest performance indices in the world. Brazil is among the nine countries with more than ten million illiterates. The greatest contingent of illiterates is concentrated in the urban areas: nine out of 10 illiterates live in Brazilian cities. Sao Paulo is the Brazilian capital of illiteracy with more than one million of illiterates.

Alarming Statistics

Illiteracy is linked to the school dropout rates and to high grade repetition. As a side effect of this phenomenon I also point to the distortion grade/age which feeds illiteracy: 69 percent of the total first grade students are too old for their grade level. At fifth grade this percentage increases to 80.4 percent.

By the year 2000 Brazil will have a population of approximately 180 million inhabitants. If nothing changes until then 14 percent of Brazil's population (23 million people) will be illiterate, and half of these people will be adults. In September of 1990—the International Literacy Year—the federal government announced an ambitious literacy program called National Literacy and Citizenship Program (PNAC). This program, however, was abandoned in 1991 without any concrete results and without any explanation to the general population, nor to the educational community in particular. This episode exemplifies how the Brazilian authorities deal with educational matters. In 1994, another ambitious program began implementation through a partnership between the Federal, State and Municipal governments: The National Plan of Education for All. The government that rose to power in 1995 has overlooked this National Plan while undertaking new educational policies, the results of which are obviously hard to predict.

The deficiencies in Brazil's educational system have clearly accumulated over the years. In the 1950s Brazilian educator Anisio Teixeira developed a now popular "pyramid" to demonstrate that education in Brazil constituted a "privilege" if compared with countries such as the United States. In the United States 33 percent of the student population which started elementary school entered the American universities as opposed to 2.3 percent in Brazil. The narrowing of educational opportunities in Brazil occurred especially when the students reached "ginasio" (today's first through eighth grades). Only 18.1 percent of all students who entered first grade would finish this level.

In drawing comparisons between income level and educational access I can easily conclude that schooling in Brazil does not constitute an instrument of democratization, but continues to maintain privileges and barriers which stem from unequal income distribution. Although the population with monthly family income below two minimum salaries represent 44.3 percent of the total Brazilian families, they account for only 3.5 percent of the student population in universities.

Data from UNICEF/IBGE (1990) revealed that dropout and grade repetition rates rose 24 percent and 14 percent between 1979 and 1985, respectively. The dropout rate rose from 10 percent in 1979 to 12.4 percent in 1984.

In 1989, the Supreme Electoral Court [Tribunal Superior Eleitoral] published research on the degree of schooling amongst the 75 million Brazilian voters: 68 percent were illiterate or semi-illiterate, or had never completed elementary education.

In comparison to the economic potentials of the country, the level of Brazil's elementary education lags far behind the rest of the world. According to a UNICEF report (1994) 88 percent of all Brazilian children should finish fifth grade, but only 39 percent reach this level.

Contemporary Brazilian Education: Challenges of Basic Education

In the 1950s Brazilian educator Anisio Teixeira developed a now popular "pyramid" to demonstrate that education in Brazil constituted a "privilege" if compared with countries such as the United States. In the United States 33 percent of the student population which started elementary school entered the American universities as opposed to 2.3 percent in Brazil. The narrowing of educational opportunities in Brazil occurred especially when the students reached "ginasio" (today's first through eighth grades). Only 18.1 percent of all students who entered first grade would finish this level.

CIEPs and CIACs

These figures speak for themselves, and show that Brazil's educational backwardness is putting its own development at risk. It was hoped—and mandated by the Constitution—that by the last decade of this century, Brazil's Municipal, State and Federal governments would undertake drastic reforms and devise social policies to tackle this reality which puts Brazil closer to the fourth than to the first world. Nevertheless, the most recent developments in education in Brazil are not very encouraging.

In contrast to the official discourse of Brazilian President Coilor de Mello, which promised a "revolution in education" in 1991, that year was marked by a total abandonment of education. Despite all the promises, nothing of significance happened. On the contrary, the "great" project (National Literacy and Citizenship Plan) announced in 1990 to eradicate illiteracy was totally forgotten.

As far as private education, the fluctuation in tuition and fees became totally chaotic. With expectations for uncontrolled inflation, some schools increased students fees up to 500 percent. Due to this trend in the private schools in 1992 many parents began transferring their children to public schools.

Since former-President Collor's first government Plan of March 1990, fees and tuition adjustment policies have been changed eight times, and tuition was frozen or negotiated between parents and owners of these schools countless times. As the rules for these actions were never made clear—whether, for example, negotiation was under the jurisdiction of the Ministry of Education and Culture or the Finance Ministry—the union of private school operators disregarded the rulings from the State Councils of Education. The controversy over monthly tuition and fees displeased parents and students, teachers and educational entrepreneurs, but united the educational business sector with the parochial schools, thus consolidating the private sector in education.

During the first half of this decade two controversial educational projects, with the same basic conception, were particularly important because they represented a political-educational strategy involving the various state authorities and the federal government: these were the CIEPs

(Integrated Centers of Public Education) and the CIACs (Integrated Centers for Children Support).

The CIEPs (integrated Centers of Public Education) were created during the first government (1983-1987) of Governor Leonel Brizola, in the State of Rio de Janeiro, with the objective of offering 'comprehensive' education to underprivileged children. These school complexes included medical and dental services, libraries, sports, cafeteria, etc. The site project was authored by architect Oscar Niemeyer. Amongst the educational goals of the CIEPs, which were conceived by educator Darcy Ribeiro, included student promotion without grade repetition. The systematic student repetition by grade in Brazil's public schools is considered elitist. Yearly examinations are being substituted with other forms of evaluation. Instead of exams, the students are evaluated by objectives. Objectives which are not attained by students during the school year will be worked out in the following year, without making the students repeat the grade. [This is a system also used in France.]

The CIACs (Integrated Centers for Children Support), with a built area of approximately 4,000 m 2 were inspired by the CIEPs. Their cost is approximately the same (US$1 million) per unit and each unit attends approximately the same number of children (750 to 1,000). The first CIAC was inaugurated in November 1991 at Vila Paranoa, in the periphery of Brasilia. According to the government, the CIACs were formed to implement children's constitutional rights as expressed in the Federal constitution and in the Statute for Children and Adolescents. They are not only schools, but centers of integral attention to children, including in the same space form al schooling, nutrition, culture, sports activities, childcare, education to labor, safety and community development.

The cost per pupil at CIEP is three times as much as at conventional schools. in both projects—CIEPs and CIACs—the student is motivated, through sports activities or entertainment, to stay in school full-time in order to guarantee better performance. But were it not for the new evaluation system at CIEPs, student failure would be at the same level as the conventional schools.

The Coilor government had promised to build 5,000 CIACs in partnership with the States and Municipalities by the end of its term (1994); however, the President Coilor was impeached under charges of corruption in December of 1992.

The CIACs project was criticized by many educators who considered it just a "promotional" rather than educational project. They argued that the distribution of these five thousand new schools throughout the states and municipalities was motivated by political interests. As a consequence, at the start of 1995 the construction of new CIACs was interrupted and today there are fewer than two hundred of these schools in operation. But for the promoters of both CIEPs and CIACs, these projects represented a true revolution in education, introducing a new concept of schooling which is already being "exported" to other countries. The CIEPs project, in spite of the criticisms outlined above, continue to be defended by the Labor Democratic Party (PDT), led by Leonel Brizola and, in education, by senator Darcy Ribeiro.

Despite the controversy they have generated, these projects are rare examples of the few educational alternatives happening concretely in the past few years.

The Statute of Children and Adolescents

At the institutional level, the approval of The Statute of Children and Adolescents in 1990 represented a great victory that resulted from a long history of struggles by various private and public groups for concrete actions in support of Brazilian children. This is an example of how positive outcomes result when the public and private sectors unite in a common effort. Without a doubt, the dualism of the Brazilian educational system into public versus private interests, the antagonism which has been developed within each of these broad sectors, and the historical neglect of the Brazilian governmental authorities towards education, are principal reasons of our educational backwardness.

There has been no lack of debate, in the last years, over issues related to children and "disenfranchised" adolescents—the well-known street boys and girls. These debates have engaged and even sometimes united governmental and non-governmental organizations.

Among the concrete results stemming from the engagement of the Brazilian civil society around the issue of children, are the Funds and Forums of Children and Adolescent Rights, and the Tutelage Councils responsible for enforcing the law. According to art of the Constitution, the society and the state must give "absolute priority" to guaranteeing children and adolescents the right to life, nutrition, education, leisure, professionalization, culture, dignity, respect, freedom, and familial and community life.

According to data from UNICEF (United Nations International Children's Emergency Fund) and IBGE (The Brazilian Bureau of the Census), Brazil has approximately 58 million children and adolescents ages 0 to 17, which represent 41 percent of the total population. Over half of these children are in families whose income is less than half the current minimum wage (US$100). UNICEF estimates that of these young children in Brazil 25 million are considered at risk; 15 million suffer from malnutrition; 12 million are abandoned or unassisted orphans; 10 million are forced into working precociously; 9 million are at school age but without access to school; 7 million are physically or mentally ill and without specialized care; hundreds of thousands are confined in boarding house-prisons, living in subhuman conditions (The Children and Adolescent Statute has provisions to deinstitutionalize these boarding houses); tens of thousands are unlawfully imprisoned, victims of abuses of all kinds; several thousand are mutilated by accidents in the working place; and several hundred are killed annually due to violence in big cities.

As the current economic crisis deepens in Brazil, these children and adolescents will be its first victims. It has been demonstrated by DIEESE (Inter-Union Department of Statistics and Socio-Economic Studies), for example, that a clear correlation exists between low wages and high infant mortality: when the purchasing power of people decreases, the rate of infant mortality predictably increases.

Although mortality for children under one year of age in Brazil has decreased and the level of schooling has increased, the precarious conditions of life in Brazil, especially in the household, continues to be alarming. Confronted with this appalling social situation there have been some positive initiatives such as the Children and Adolescent Statute which represents considerable progress. This statute is a ray of hope to all Brazilians.

The New LDB

Until September of 1995, the date at which I am writing this chapter, the Lei de Diretrizes e Bases da Educacao (LDB) was pending a vote in Congress. Currently it is being discussed by the Senate, which has approved a new document, authored by Senator Darcy Ribeiro. Contrary to the original text submitted to the House of Representatives, this amended proposal was not open to discussion by society at large. Therefore, there are two proposals being considered. The proposal developed by the House of Representatives had been discussed during half a decade by virtually everyone dealing with education in Brazil. Nevertheless, this negotiation effort ended up incorporating the participation of a small fraction of society, in a similar fashion to what happened with the 1988 Constitution. I refer, for example, to the members to the National Council of Education by teachers' and students' unions. The more concise Darcy Ribeiro project was designed by the Senator himself with the assistance of specialists from the Ministry of Education. While it tries to eliminate corporatist interests in education, the project overlooks past victories such as teachers' career plan, and opposes the financial and administrative autonomy of the public schools. The discussion of the new LDB can be traced back to 1988 when the Constitution chapter on education was written. With the approval of the 1988 Constitution the debates about the New National Guidelines for Education were intensified which involved three years of work and negotiations by political parties, the scientific community, labor unions, union federations, professional organizations and numerous educators. The decisions emerging from this process of social participation have not been respected even under the protests of prominent educators, and former Constitution writers (constituintes) such as the late sociologist Florestan Fernandes, who participated in the design of the first version of the LDB, originated in the House.

The LDB encompasses all levels of schooling, from pre-school to graduate studies, from public and private to special education, and education of Brazilian ethnic-cultural minorities. For this reason, it is called the "Constitution of Education."

In 1988 Federal Deputy Octavio Elisio submitted the first proposal for a new LDB, and eleven other projects by various other Deputies followed suit. At the same time, the special House Education Commission for Education, Sports and Tourism began an exhaustive public hearing process and many organized groups brought in alternative proposals for a new LDB.

In August of 1989 the first amended project was presented by Deputy Jorge Hage, the House Education Commission' reporter, which incorporated numerous ideas from previous proposals. Thus began a long process of hearing and discussion procedures. By 1991 this project had received none less than 1,200 amendments. These numerous amendments were combined into a single document which was approved by the House in 1993 and forwarded to the Senate. As it stands, it contains two LDB proposals, one of which will be sent to the House for approval or rejection without the possibility of further amendments. If the House approves the version sent by the Senate, the President will have the power to sanction or veto it. Nevertheless, the impass created by the Darcy Ribeiro proposal still haunts Brazil's educational politics.

Contemporary Brazilian Educational Challenges

As in all of the world, the political and economic transformations which took place towards the end of the last decade, in particular the changes in eastern Europe, have had profound repercussions in Latin America. At this time Brazil began to suffer from hyper-inflation which reached an average of 30 percent a month. Several anti-inflationary plans were experimented with, and it was not until the last one which was launched in 1994 by then Finance Minister Fernando Henrique Cardoso on the tail of restructuring policies from the World Bank that anti-inflationary measures succeeded (at least up to this moment). This success earned Cardoso the Presidency the following year.

Brazil's Socio-Political Reality Today

The success of the economic stabilization plan of 1994—Brazil's monthly inflation rate is now estimated at 2 percent—caused some Brazilian intellectuals and many politicians to think of neo-liberal policies as the panacea for solving all the social and economic ills of the country.

However, it is conceivable that Brazil might follow the same pattern of crisis which has taken place in other Latin American countries where similar forms of economic restructuring have been adopted:

1. Bolivia—which has implemented International Monetary Fund restructuring policies since 1985 and has adopted a rigid orthodox stabilization plan—has ended up stagnating and ruining its economy with high rates of unemployment. A clear illustration of the crisis of economic restructuring in Bolivia was the firing by COMBOL (Bolivian Mining Corporation) of twenty three thousand of its 28 thousand workers.
2. In Venezuela, in 1989, the populist President Carlos Andres Perez adopted neoliberal orthodox policies and had to confront a popular uprising where 300 died, just one week after he was sworn into office.
3. The same year Peru elected Alberto Fujimori under a neo-liberal political platform and the numbers of poor people jumped from 8 to 12 million out of a total population of 23 million.
4. In Argentina and in Mexico economic stabilization plans have also been threatened by unemployment and low wages.

All these countries today experience high levels of social tension triggered by the rise of poverty.

The conclusion to this seems evident: the neo-liberal structural adjustments solve the problem of inflation and, in some cases such as the Peruvian one, promote economic growth. Nevertheless, they cannot improve the situation of the working poor in Brazil. Indeed, such readjustments will inevitably worsen their plight because neo-liberalism does not provide answers to social questions. President Fernando Henrique Cardoso therefore still owes the nation a sound social policy.

Today Brazil's relatively good economic performance is contrasted with great regional disparities and very low social indicators. It is unfortunate that the notorious phrase "Brazil is doing well, but its people are not" (coined by former President Gal. Ernesto Geisel) continues to strike a meaningful chord among Brazilians. The economic modernization we are witnessing today does not conceive of human beings as subjects and active citizens, but rather as commodities and as mere consumers.

Elementary Education Challenges

The first public announcements by Cardoso's government about autonomy and the strengthening of school unity—including the decentralization of financial resources—the creation of basic national curricular standards and the emphasis on distance education, were received with enthusiasm. Nevertheless, these plans have not gotten off the ground. Instead, the first 100 days of the government were spent heavily on publicity, which saw the President delivering lectures in several public schools in the country. But the government is still lacking a policy which is consistent with the demands of education and other social needs. Contrary to what many expected in Brazil, the Cardoso government has cut important ties which had been developed in previous governments between the State and Civil Society in education. The CNTE (National Confederation of Education Employees), for example, had forged an agreement with the government for a Ten-Year Plan [1993-2003] (piano decenal) of Education for All. This agreement involved the following three points, which I consider the greatest educational challenges in Brazil:

- the need to implement a basic national curriculum;
- a countrywide mandatory starting salary for teachers of at least US$300 (today's national average equals US$100);
- a clear definition of responsibilities within and between the various government organizations. Today, the three governmental administrative spheres—the Union, the States and the Municipalities—supposedly take care of elementary education but in a very inarticulate way.

Instead, the government has chosen the perils of administrative discontinuity. Consequently, if the government does not correct this mistake in the educational sector it is doomed to face serious resistance—especially by educators—as has recently occurred in Bolivia.

Thanks to widespread popular mobilizations for the rights to education today, access to elementary education has been guaranteed to the majority of the population, but the quality of education has not. The culture of grade repetition continues to prevail in our schools: of every 100 young children who enter first grade, only four finish eighth grade without any repetition.

Faced with these challenges, the Federal government counter attacked in 1995 by arguing that it would focus on a limited number of real and consequential improvements in education. It added that it would not intervene directly in education because it believed action should be taken by the states and municipalities. The Ministry of Education and Culture (MEC) should be considered basically as a policy-making institution in order to clear the way for the actions of states and municipalities. In keeping with this promise, the government proposed the following actions:

1. "Mobilization campaign: education, a national priority," with the goal to reform education and raise the morale of teachers as a fundamental theme for the national agenda on education;
2. "Implementation of basic curriculum standards." The definition of these standards shall supply subsidies to policies on textbooks, evaluation procedures and on projects of distance education;
3. "Resource decentralization program," which will begin with the allotment of financial resources directly to the schools;
4. "Textbook program," which emphasizes a gradual decentralization of choice and acquisition of textbooks, and the organization of a "handbook for evaluating textbooks."

In a meeting with all state governors at the beginning of September 1995, President Fernando Henrique Cardoso launched a project entitled "Fund for the Development of Elementary Education and Teacher Valorization" with the joint contributions of the Union, the states and municipalities, the goal of which is to invest R$12 billion in elementary education during the first year. For 1995 alone, there is a mandatory cost of RS$17.83 billion, half of which would be used for teachers' salaries.

The goal of this project is to spend at least R$300 per capita on elementary school children, and also that this same amount be the minimum teachers' wage for weekly working hours. This investment is 39.5 percent higher than the minimum recommended by the United Nations' CEPAL (Economic Commission for Latin America, ECLA), which is US$215.

Because Brazilian society, particularly those segments mobilized by parent and teacher associations, has already seen similar plans in the past that never went off the ground, the expectations and hopes for concrete actions are now even greater. At the same time society is skeptical about these governmental intentions, citing their limited scope in relation to the enormous challenges facing elementary education in Brazil.

Educational Innovation at the Grassroots Level

The hope for education of better quality depends essentially of society's participation and input. In recent years, Brazil has witnessed the emergence of civil society, in particular at the municipal level, where the best educational innovations have been developed. These innovations are not always strictly attached to any political perspective. They are part of a movement which bypasses political parties, unions, social movements, and which involves the public administration, the private enterprise, individuals and groups interested in improving education in several of the country's regions. Though these initiatives are not yet linked by a common and concerted effort to improve education in Brazil, they point to a new tendency dominated by increased participation from civil society.

These new experiences in educational reform point to the elimination of two problems I believe are critical to understand the current crisis in education in Brazil: a) the dichotomy between public and private schooling; and b) the centralization and bureaucratization of the educational system.

The antagonism created between public and private schools, since the dawn of education in Brazil, has systematically produced low quality in both spheres.

The second problem addressed by the new municipal reforms refers to the preponderance of administrative centralization and bureaucracy, with its heavy intermediate government powers. This centralized system emulates educational models from the past. Therefore, the path to efficiency and quality includes the radical decentralization of governance.

The above innovations, on the one hand, have helped de-mystify pedagogical dreams from the 1960s which considered education as the lever of social change. On the other hand they have overcome the acute pessimism of the 1970s, when schools were described as mere reproducers of society. In this respect, these initiatives also point to a new paradigm in education.

Educating for Active Citizenship

Today, after more than one hundred years of their establishment, educational systems in many parts of the world are living an explosive trend in decentralization.

In the current context where political pluralism has become a universal value, I witness an increasing globalization of the economy, on the one hand. But on the other, I see the emergence of unprecedented local powers in the history of Brazilian education.

In the last few years the theme of school autonomy has emerged with more frequency in educational debates and in school reforms. This theme, in turn, is linked to a discussion over participation and self-rule which have dominated the educational debate during the last two decades.

The principle according to which education is the state's obligation does not imply inactivism on the part of the population and individuals: education is an obligation of parents, students, and the community. With this mobilization in defense of public education, it has been possible to press the state even further to fulfill its obligation in assuring free public and high level schooling to everyone. A population accustomed to good quality services will continue to mobilize to maintain what it now perceives as a right.

It is within this context that new proposals have emerged such as the Project of the Citizen School, from the Paulo Freire's Institute, the principles of which have been adopted by some municipalities. These principles include: a) preparation for active citizenship—the schools can incorporate millions of Brazilians into citizenship and shall improve participation of organized Civil Society in institutional power; and b) prepare individuals for the country's economic development—education is the sine qua non for Brazil's self-sustained development. Elementary education is a precious commodity and of greater value to development than the country's natural wealth, of even greater value than the control of technology.

We cannot transform history without knowledge, but we do need to discipline knowledge and educate people so that they can become subjects of their history and act in society as participants in constructing their destiny, as opposed to being manipulated by the internal logic of economic reasoning. The market ought to be submitted to the citizenry.

Schools do not distribute income, but distribute knowledge, and knowledge is power. A citizenship school is one which places knowledge—intellectual capital which is just as important as financial capital—at the disposal of all citizens, especially the disenfranchised, and educates the whole citizen for competence and solidarity. It surpasses educating a competitive individual as conceived of by bourgeois education.

Brazil's social apartheid will not be overcome simply by imposing a better income distribution on the country, nor by securing solidarity from the middle classes. W e need to prepare our youth for the work force. It is my belief that only through basic quality education for all can we rid Brazil of poverty. This has already been demonstrated through examples of countries such as South Korea, Hong Kong and Taiwan. Thirty years ago these nations were in a similar situation as Brazil and today they are far better off economically thanks to intensive investments in education.

Public schooling has been threatened internally and externally in many Latin America countries. To dismantle it means to cut one of the last links of a democratic pact from which the modern state has been born. To threaten public schooling—whether through the incompetence of those who believe in it or through the arrogance of those who oppose it—is to place one of the pilars of our civilization at risk. However, it needs a comprehensive, system-wide reform. Brazil needs to rescue the state schools as institutions supported by public resources. But we must also turn the state schools into real public schools, administered by all citizens and without discrimination. Furthermore, it is essential to transform state schools so that they can become community schools, conceived of and administered by a society which is effectively responsible for their operation and results.

As previous efforts at educational reform in Brazil have shown, this ideal citizen school cannot and will not be constructed over night. No magic—nor any new theory—can deliver this to us instantly. We cannot push through this new educational reality in a short period of time if this means that only few privileged segments of society will partake of positive changes in education. We must arrive there together, before it is too late.

References

Alves, Maria Helena Moreira. 1984. *Estado e oposicao no Brasil* (1964-1984). Petropolis, V ozes.

Beisiegel, Celso de Rui. 1974. *Estado e educacao popular.* Sao Paulo, Pioneira.

Brasil, Republica Federativ a do. Ministerio da Educacao e Desporto. 1989. *Politica nacional de educacao.* Brasilia, MEC.

—. 1991. *Diretrizes gerais e recomendacoes para form ulacao de proj etos pedagogicos dos CIACs.* Brasilia, MEC.

Cardoso, Fernando Henrique. 1994. *Mao a obra, Brasil: proposta de governo.* Brasilia, s. ed.

CENPEC/UNICEF. 1993. *A democracia do ensino em 15 municipios brasileiros.* Sao Paulo, CENPEC.

—. 1995. *Raizes e asas.* Sao Paulo, CENPEC.

Cunha, Luiz Antonio. 1991. *Educacao, estado e democraci no Brazil.* Sao Paulo, Cortez.

Faria, Lia. 1991. *Ciep: a utopia possivel.* Sao Paulo, Livro do Tatu.

Fernandes, Florestan. 1966. *Educacao e sociedade no Brasil.* Sao Paulo, Dominus.

—. 1989. *O desafio educacional.* Sao Paulo, Cortez.

Ferreira, Nilda Teves. 1993. *Cidadania: uma questao para a educacao.* Rio de Janeiro, Nov a Fronteira.

Franco, Maria Laura e Dagmar Zibas (orgs.). 1990. *Final de seculo: desafios da educacao na America Latina.* Sao Paulo, Cortez.

Freire, Paulo. 1991. *A educacao na cidade.* Sao Paulo, Cortez.

Freitag, Barbara. 1979. *Escola, estado e sociedade.* Sao Paulo, Moraes.

Gadotti, Moacir. 1987. *Pensamento pedagogico brasileiro.* Sao Paulo, Atica.

—. 1990. *Uma so escola para todos: caminhos da autonomia escolar.* Petropolis, Vozes.

—. 1992. *Escola cidada: uma aula sobre a autonomia da escola.* Sao Paulo, Cortez.

—. 1993. *Organizacao do trabalho na escola: alguns pressupostos.* Sao Paulo, Atica.

—. 1993. *Historia das ideias pedagogicas.* Sao Paulo, Atica.

—. 1995. Pedagogia da praxis. Sao Paulo, Cortez.

Garcia, Walter Esteves (org.). 1980. *Educacao brasileira contemporanea: organizacao e funcionamento.* Sao Paulo, McGraw-Hill, 3a. ed.

—. (org.). 1995. *Inovacao educacional no Brasil: problem as e perspectivas.* Campinas, Autores Associados. Jaguaribe, Helio e outros. 1986. Brasil, 2000: para um novo pacto social. Sao Paulo, Paz e Terra.

Lei de Diretrizes e Bases da Educacao Nacional: texto aprovado na Comissao de Cunha, Luiz Antonio. 1991. *Educacao, estado e democraci no Brazil.* Sao Paulo, Cortez.

Mello, Guiomar Namo de. 1986. *Educacao escolar: paixao, pensamento e pratica.* Sao Paulo, Cortez.

—. 1993. *Cidadania e com petitiv idade: desafios educacionais do terceiro milenio.* Sao Paulo, Cortez.

Paiva, V anilda Pereira. 1973. *Educacao popular e educacao de adultos: contribuicao a historia da educacao brasileira.* Sao Paulo, Loyola.

Ribeiro, Darcy. 1986. *O livro dos CIEPs.* Rio de Janeiro, Bloch.

Ribeiro, Maria Luisa Santos. 1987. *Historia da educacao brasileira: a organizacao escolar.* Sao Paulo, Cortez, 7a. ed. rev. e ampi.

Rodrigues, Nejdson. 1982. *Estado, educacao e desenvolvimento economico.* Sao Paulo, Autores Associados e Cortez.

Romanelli, Otaiza de Oliveira. 1978. *Historia da educacao no Brasil: (1930-1973).* Petropolis, Vozes. Romao, Jose Eustaquio. 1992. Poder local e educacao. Sao Paulo, Cortez. Prefacio de Moacir Gadotti.

—. e Moacir Gadotti. 1994. *Projeto da escola cidada.* Sao Paulo, Cortez, IPF.

Saviani, Dermeval. 1987. *Politica e educacao no Brasil.* Sao Paulo, Cortez.

Silva, Luiz Heron da e Jose Clovis de Azevedo (orgs.) 1995. *Paixao de aprender II.* Petropolis, Vozes.

UNICEF. 1993. *Todos pela educacao no municipio: um desafio para dirigents.* Brasilia, UNICEF.

Werebe, Maria Jose Garcia. 1994. *Grandezas e miserias do ensino no Brasil: 30 anos depois.* Sao Paulo, Atica.

6

The Problems of the Decentralization of Education: A View from Mexico[1]

Sylvia Schmelkes

Educational decentralization in Mexico will first be approached by reviewing attempts at decentralizing education through educational policy and the present educational situation in Mexico, the context in which decentralization actually takes place. Next, the chapter reviews some conditions which recent literature on decentralization establishes for enterprises of this nature to be successful. These will serve as a basis for analyzing, in the third part, what has happened as a consequence of the decision of the federal government to decentralize education in 1992: both the problems it has faced and the possibilities that it has opened. Lastly, I will reflect on some of the risks for the future and the implications for educational policy.

A Brief Review of the Recent History of Mexican Education

Mexico is a very centralized country. Some authors have explained this phenomenon by comparing the case of Mexico with the United States. Mexico was first a State, then a Nation.[2] Even though after its independence from Spain in 1821, and after heated and lasting discussions between centralists and federalists, Mexico decided to constitute a Federation of States, this was more a fiction derived from the desire to imitate what had recently happened in the North than a true federation since the states as such were, in many cases, arbitrary territorial divisions of the country. In this case, first the country as a whole achieved its own independent status and then it created the states which it called upon to federate.

Educationally, the first Constitution (1824) established the privilege of "promoting illustration" exclusively to the General Congress. However, each State was free to organize its own public education. The second Constitution, in 1957 (after the Reform), very influenced by liberalism and preoccupied with the individual liberties, does not attribute any right to the Federal Congress in educational matters, and this implies that these affairs are the responsibility of each of the states. This explains why the first Ministry of Education, the Secretaría the Instrucción Pública y Bellas Artes, which was founded at the beginning of the century, was suitable only in the federal district and in the territories.[3] It is also the root of profound educational inequalities among the different states, which is at present one of the principal educational problems in the country.

After the Revolution, the 1917 Constitution gives the municipalities the responsibility of public education. This, of course, did not work. The municipalities had no resources with which to operate their educational systems, and only the large cities were able to develop educationally. Fortunately, this situation did not last. José Vasconcelos, the rector of the National University, was convinced that education had to be a national endeavor. The federal government had to have the ability to establish schools all over the country, without this meaning that the individual states could not operate their own schools in their own territories. His project was successful, and he became the first Secretary of Public Education in 1921.

Ever since this date, and up to very recently, the power of the federal government over education has grown steadily, both legally and in practice. By 1982, 65 percent of total enrollment was federal. In this year, the federal government participated with 80.6 percent of the total educational budget, while the states participated with 13.2, the municipalities with 1.1 percent and the private sector with 5.1 percent.[4] Also, during all this time, the educational system in the country grew very rapidly. Between 1950 and 1990, the number of children enrolled in primary education grew fivefold, from 2.9 million to 14.4 million. The number of teachers was multiplied by six, and the number of schools went from 23,000 to 84 ,000.[5]

The consequence of both of these phenomena (the concentration of power in the federal government and the rapid growth of the system) was the constitution of a very complex bureaucracy in the central Ministry, which Reyes Heroles, the Secretary who started the decentralization process, called "a rheumatic elephant." This structure is characterized by being pyramidal, rigid, without a valid communication network and very slow in processing both information and decisions.

Another feature of the Mexican educational system, which must be added to the previous discussion, is the existence of a very strong, corporative and also centrally dominated teachers union. The Union is said to be the most powerful one in Latin America (in general, not only among teachers unions), with around 1,000,000 subscribers, and with a monthly income that represents 1.5 percent of their salaries.[6] The federal bureaucracy and the union have historically constituted a symbiosis. The government lets the union act—vertically, corporatively and corruptly—as well as designate educational officials, supervisors, and even school principals. The union participates in "mixed" committees that decide on positions and movements of teachers all over the nation. The power this gives the union can be easily imagined. In exchange, the federal government expects political tranquillity on the side of the teachers, as well as several other duties such as "overseeing" national and local election processes.

This combination of a strong and inefficient central bureaucracy and a strong central and exclusive union made the educational system very difficult to administer. Educational policies that implied important but needed changes in the educational system were met with almost certain opposition from the union, who was happy with the status quo. In addition, information took a very long time in reaching decision-makers, and decisions took even longer in being executed as expected. The federal government began to realize the need for a decentralization of the Mexican educational system in the middle of the seventies.

In 1978, Delegations of the Ministry were instituted in each of the 31 states, which were later transformed into "Educational To-Be-Decentralized Units." These Units began to administer the federal resources destined to education in each of the states, for the pre-school, primary, secondary and normal school levels. However, this was defined by the Mexican authorities only as a "de-concentration" process, which only decentralizes administration but reserves decision-making for the central level.

During the De La Madrid regime, which began in 1982, more serious attempts at decentralizing education were carried out. Agreements were signed with each of the 31 states and the Educational To-Be-Decentralized Units are transformed into Units of Coordinated Services. These Units fully administered federal resources, but the idea was for them to begin assuming certain attributions, to begin making certain decisions, to initiate a process of integrating basic and normal education (federal and state) services and, in the long run, to take charge of the labor relations with teachers and education workers in general.

Of course, the union was not happy with these reforms, mainly because they represented a serious menace to its traditional and power-delivering centrality, as well as to the "national unity" of the union. The union was, in fact, the main reason why these initial attempts at decentralization could proceed no further. The tension created with the union when the first 12 agreements were signed with an equal number of states was evident in the Union's Secretary General's (Miranda) speech in this ceremony, in which he sustained that practice was the ultimate test of any reform, and that, in practice, decentralization ould reveal a great number of problems to be faced, and demand a greater participation of organized teachers in the decisions that would have to bemade to face them.

By 1988, the basic and normal educational levels of the system were deconcentrated at a national level. A new regime took office in December of 1989, but no further steps were taken towards decentralization until May, 1992. This surprised many of us, because the union was showing signs of weakness. The democratic movement, a dissident movement within the union, had already indicated strength in certain regions of the country, including the Federal District. The Union leader, who had been declared by his backers as a "life-long" leader, was ousted. The Secretary of Education considered that it was time "the Union gave us back our Ministry."

But it was precisely these factors that made it possible in 1992, with now President Zedillo as Secretary of Education, to actually make the decision to decentralize education. After a few months of intense negotiations, and with the assurance that the union would remain national, even though the labor relations in each state would be conducted by the state government, the union signed the famous "Agreement for the Modernization of Basic Education." This Agreement was also signed by the President of the Republic, Carlos Salinas de Gontari, and by the governors of each of the 31 states of the Union.

One of the main points of the agreement was the "federalization" of basic and normal education. Federalization is understood as the transfer to the state governments of the administration and operation of these levels of education. The Federal Government maintained in exclusivity the normative, evaluative and compensatory functions.

It is important to say that the decision to decentralize education was initiated in a reality in which the educational development of the states of the Republic is very unequal, and closely correlated with the levels of economic development and urbanization of each of the states. Differences between the states have been enormous. The illiteracy rate, for example, was 12.4 percent for the country as a whole in 1990. However, it was only 4 percent in the capital, 4.6 percent in Nuevo León (one of our richest industrial states), 26.8 percent in Guerrero (the second poorest state), and 30 percent in Chiapas. In this same year, the population over 12 years of age without lower secondary education represented 56.8 percent of this age group in the country as a whole. However, in the Federal District (the capital) it represented one third of this population (36.1 percent), while in Chiapas it constituted three fourths of this age group (74.8 percent).

Terminal efficiency rates (percentage of children that finish primary education in six years with respect to those enrolled in first grade six years earlier) are now 61 percent for the country as a whole, but only 20 percent in Indian and disperse rural schools. These differences can be found in almost all indicators of educational development, and are very consistent.

At the same time, we must say that federal contributions to education in the different states seems to have responded to negotiations political in nature rather than to fixed criteria of a compensatory nature. It is not necessarily the poorest states that receive a greater proportion of the Federal budget. Neither is it, necessarily, the states that contribute more (or less) to their own education.[7] The efficiency (or the problems in the efficiency) of the educational system in each of the states is not consistent either with the proportion of federal funding they receive. It is mostly political reasons that seem to explain the evolution of the amounts the federal government apportions each state for maintaining education. The proportion each of the 31 states receives from the federal budget varies from a little bit over 1 percent in some states, to more than 9 percent. The differences between the states regarding the proportion of the state budget dedicated to education are also enormous: 10 states have no state system of education, and therefore allocate very small proportions of their budget (less than 20 percent); 16 allocate between 21 and 39 percent; five dedicate more than 40 percent.[8] The Federal District (the capital) dedicates nothing to education; everything comes from the Federal Government. This is the basis from which federal funding in the context of "federalization" stems. With the exception of specific compensatory projects, now being carried out with loans from both the World Bank and the Interamerican Development Bank, no great changes in this allocation scheme are to be expected.

Inequalities, of course, are not only present when comparing the states among themselves, but they are also present within each of the states of the Republic. This is in fact the case in most Latin American countries, where education has suffered a process of segmentation, and different educational systems, in terms of the quality of their results, coexist.[9] And inequalities, between and within states, are of course not only quantitative, but qualitative as well: what children actually learn in the different states, and in different regions within the states, has been shown to be vastly different. This is partly due to the socio-economic and cultural differences of the families from which the children come. But it also depends, to a greater degree than we had recognized before, on the quality of educational supply. The most important aspect of educational supply is, of course, the training and the attitudes of teachers. Problems regarding teacher training must also be considered as part of the picture within which decentralization takes place.[10]

Some Conditions for Successful Decentralization Processes

Let me make this commentary regarding the Mexican process a look into the conditions, derived from recent experiences in decentralization world-wide, that seem to allow for a successful decentralization process. A review of a very small part of the extensive literature on decentralization that has been produced in recent years allows us to point out to the following seemingly favorable conditions for decentralization.

Decentralization of education is more successful when it takes place within a context of decentralization of the life of the country than when it is an isolated adventure in decentralization. The case of France is an example of educational decentralization that occurs within a context of decentralization of basic and social services administered by the State.[11] One of the most important reforms that must accompany a decentralization movement is a fiscal (tax) reform that allows for states, andparticularly municipalities, to have the resources needed to be able to adequately attend to and maintain local educational systems.[12]

Additionally, decentralization of education is more successful when it is conceived as a systemic transformation, rather than as single change in the system. Decentralization fails when it is isolated from other transformations within the system. To recognize educational change as systemic change does not necessarily mean that everything must be transformed at the same time. However, it does imply that it is necessary to take responsibility for the consequences of the changes in one of the factors on the rest of the factors involved. Institutional transformation will have a very limited impact on educational outcomes if it does not consider the appropriate time to introduce decentralization.[13] Nothing will happen at the schoolroom level if decentralization limits itself to the subdivision of a macrosystem into meso or minisystems, without carrying out changes in the operation of the systems.[14]

Successful experiences in decentralization, paradoxically, also require strong central governments, in part for the reason stated above. The role of the State changes when profound institutional transformations take place. Government policies have to be transformed into State policies, and that implies a strong participation on the part of civil society, particularly on the part of parents and community. Also, true decentralization means transferring power not only to the state governments, but granting autonomy to the local authorities and to the individual schools. But precisely because of the depth of these implications, a strong, if transformed, central government, is required.[15]

Finally, decentralization must allow for parents to exercise some level of social control. Further, decentralization must include precise technical standards and procedures for assessing student achievement.[16] In the absence of precise technical standards, and of mechanisms for their frequent assessment, a process of decentralization will most certainly produce greater inequality. Hannaway and Carnoy contend that, even if these conditions are met, decentralization will not solve, at least in the short term, the problems of the very poor.[17] Other measures are needed to provide adequate educational attention and more equal learning opportunities to the children in this situation, which unfortunately represent a very large percentage of school-age population in Mexico.

Decentralization in Mexico: Problems and Opportunities

The Agreement signed in 1992 led to reforming Article III of the Constitution and to the approval of a new General Law of Education, which clearly stipulates the attributions of the federal and state governments. Further, the law introduces two very important innovations. The first is a whole chapter dedicated to equity in education. The second is another chapter dedicated to social participation in education. The chapter dealing with equity establishes the responsibility of the federal government compensating for the differences in educational development among the different states of the Republic. The chapter dealing with social participation legislates the existence of Participation Councils at the school, municipality and state levels.

If we analyze the way the conditions are being met in Mexico, we would have to note the following. Practically the only sector that is being decentralized in Mexico is the educational sector and, as we mentioned, only at the basic and normal school levels. In the late 1980s there was an attempt to decentralize the health sector, which was unsuccessful and therefore interrupted. Even though the issue of "federalism" and the federalization of national life has been much discussed recently,[18] and even though persons holding elective posts and belonging to the opposition have lately been vociferous regarding the financial rights of municipalities, there have been no changes up to now in the tax laws of the nation that would allow for greater local responsibility in educational services.

Nevertheless, decentralization in Mexico has been understood as part of a more complex process of educational reform. In an attempt at summarizing the scope of the "modernization" process, suffice it to say that the agreement included three areas of reform: reorganization of the system, curricular reform, and upgrading of teachers' training and the teaching profession.

The reorganization of education includes decentralization and as such, social participation. The latter is based on a recognition that education cannot continue to be considered as pertaining exclusively to the government. The need for a more active role on the part of society in the operation and evaluation of basic education is emphasized. In a way then, at least theoretically, the process includes the question of accountability ans social controls.

Curricular reform was carried out over a period of three years and is now almost complete for primary and secondary education. The reform was aimed at strengthening: the exercise of reading, writing and oral expression; of mathematics, emphasizing the ability of posing and solving problems; the substitution of the curricular area of "social sciences" with the subjects of geography, history and civics (previous programs had been criticized because allegedly children did not learn well either history or geography or civics in the social science area); and of contents aimed at health care and environment. It is a "back to basics" approach to curricular reform.

Regarding the upgrading of teachers and the teaching profession, the Agreement promises a complete reform of the initial training of teachers, an emergency program for their updating, special efforts for recuperating the social value of the profession, and the establishment of a "teaching career." However, the only reform that was carried out during the previous regime was the latter, the teaching career, which is a horizontal promotion mechanism for teachers based on performance evaluation. The problems of teacher training and teacher formation which, as we have mentioned, are considered crucial for the improvement of the quality of education, have not been addressed. Curriculum may have been reformed, but without pertinent and effective teacher training processes there is nothing to insure that things will change at the classroom level. We are certain that the reform of teacher formation and teacher training is long overdue, and a program for its transformation is expected to be the most important project to be announced by this six-month-old regime when it eventually publishes its educational program.

Even though in theory the federal government is responsible for the evaluation of the system, no progress has been made towards a national evaluation system, and no "precise" standards have been defined that could be orienting performance towards educational achievement. Meanwhile, decentralization has been going on for almost three years. A look at what has happened allows us to draw a picture of the problems and the opportunities that have arisen during the process.

Problems

These are some of the most important problems that have arisen during the process of implementing decentralization are the following.

First, it has been very difficult for the states with both a federal and a state educational system to integrate funds, particularly because the teachers of both systems had different salaries and, especially, fringe benefits. The state teachers are, in general, in a much better financial situation than the federal teachers, but the federal teachers are more numerous than the state teachers. Integrating signifies, for the organized teachers, the homologation of their labor conditions. The states have not had the resources to take on this responsibility and, rather than risk political problems with the union, have maintained the two systems operating simultaneously, much the way they were before. Nevertheless, this is seen as a time bomb in all the states, since maintaining both systems, now administered by the state government, clearly duplicates structures and expenses.

Second, the aggravation of educational inequality, though expected and feared as a consequence of decentralization, is beginning to manifest itself in several circumstances. Perhaps one of the most important is the difference in the institutional capacity of the states to face what decentralization implies. The states that have adequate human resources capable of carrying out diagnostic research, of planning, of evaluating, of developing curriculum, and of designing innovative programs for the solution of specific local or regional problems, are able to take advantage of decentralization for furthering their educational systems. Unfortunately, these states are also the ones that had a relatively developed educational system before decentralization.

On the contrary, these human resources—as well as the political will of obtaining or developing them—are absent in the poorer states, which are overwhelmed with the administrative implications of decentralization and have not been able to go any further than administratively maintaining and reproducing a very deficient educational system. In general, we can say that these states did not want the Mexican educational system to be decentralized because of the administrative and political problems it implied. In a sense, decentralization in Mexico was, paradoxically, a central decision, especially for these poorer states.

From the central point of view, decentralization has implied a certain loss of control. This has been observedwithin two substantive issues. The first has to do, again, with human resources. The federal government had invested in the development of human resources especially for planning (microplanning) and information (statistics) functions at the state level. When the state governments took over, many of these trained persons had to leave the system. Repercussions on the quality of information and on the possibility of microplanning are beginning to be noted in some states.

The second one has to do with contents. Decentralization opened up the possibility of introducing all kinds of innovations—most of them sold to the government by private institutions, others emerging from personal convictions of state governors—at the state level. Thus, for example, in one of the states a method that insures literacy in 30 hours is being rapidly expanded and is now being transferred from adult education to schools.

Another example is the case of a governor who has been much influenced by oriental philosophies and who decided to introduce meditation as compulsory in all schools. A program for "value formation" that consists in working on 52 different "values," one a week, is being implemented in primary and secondary schools in more than one state. Many of these innovations are, of course, pedagogically unsound, or at least highly questionable. The federal government has found it hard to stop these initiatives, and has let many of them continue.

Up to now, the decentralization process has only reproduced, at the state level, what was before happening at the central level. The mechanisms that are supposed to bring decentralization down to the very local municipal and school levels have not been put in practice, and they are exceptionally only an object of planning in very few states. The School Participation Councils and the Municipal Participation Councils have not been set up, or if they have, remain only as formal entities without activity. The transfer of power to the districts and schools is still only a desire placed on paper in only a few exceptional states. As we have seen, it is difficult to expect effects of decentralization on what goes on in schools and classrooms and mechanisms such as these are not developed as part of the decentralization process.

Opportunities

Nevertheless, decentralization has also opened up the possibility of very important innovations in the states that have the adequate human resources and the interest in developing their own educational systems. Perhaps the best way of discovering these possibilities is to look at what is happening in two states that meet these conditions.

Aguascalientes

This is a very small, relatively rich and very well communicated state in the center of the country. It had no state system of education, so decentralization implied only assuming the administration of the previous federal system. Aguascalientes has an excellent university that has been training students at the undergraduate and graduate level for many years. Teachers and graduates of the university are now employed by the state government in the educational sector. Decentralization coincided with the beginning of a local government term (that lasts six years) and, fortunately, with the political will to take on the educational responsibility. In fact, education was defined as the first priority of the new government, and its main objective is that of enhancing quality of education. The state has a very detailed middle-term educational program.

According to the central actors of educational decentralization into Aguascalientes, pedagogical practice and what goes on in the classroom has not changed much. However, education has become a social concern and has acquired a political importance that it did not have before. Education is in the news every day. Society is now informed and has become interested in what is going on.[19]

The educational sector has introduced important structural innovations in the system. Probably the most important is the transformation of the system of school supervision and of the conception and operation of school principals. Supervisors are now able to make a good diagnosis of their zone, which is translated in a zone project that, among other things, looks at school coverage and efficiency, the need for internal compensation, and local-level teacher training processes. The objective is to create the needed leadership for attaining the objectives of universalizing basic education, integrating the basic education system (preschool, primary, and secondary), and enhancing the quality of educational results.

Another innovation is the creation of the Aguascalientes Foundation for Educational Excellence. This foundation offers individual and school-level awards to teachers and schools that can demonstrate an increase in the levels of efficiency and quality of their students. There is an award for every level of education and for every region, so teachers and schools do participate. This is an example of how, with relatively few resources, quality improvement can be stimulated.

Aguascalientes has also been able to take advantage of the spaces left in the curriculum for regional contents. Educational materials dealing with regional history, geography, artistic production, ecological problems, have been produced for both teachers and students are being used in the classroom.

Guanajuato

This is also a state in the center of the country. Even though it borders Aguascalientes, it is a very diverse state, where there is an important industrial region and, at the same time, some of the poorest municipalities in the country. The educational indicators of Guanajuato are among the lowest nation-wide. The government of Guanajuato is the second oppositional government in the history of the country. From 1989 to 1992, a special graduate program for officials in the Secretariat of Education and in the university was carried out. Graduates from this program are now in charge of the state educational system (this included the Secretary until the recent change in the local government), which, in the case of Guanajuato, has already been integrated into the former federal system.

Due to the peculiar political conditions of Guanajuato, the government decided to drastically transform the educational system. Internally, the system is being deconcentrated—administration is being handed over to the 42 municipalities. The supervisors will no longer be in charge of administrative matters, in order to be able to dedicate their time completely to educational advisory. The basis for planning in the system is to be the School Project, which is to be designed and carried out by each school, with the participation of the community. The Secretariat of Education concentrates mainly technical groups: planning, curricular development, evaluation, and a unified teacher formation and training system.

It is still early to know how this program will prosper. Guanajuato changed government in June of 1995, and even though the opposition won and is again in office, there is no guarantee of continuity. The reform has met with strong opposition on the part of the supervisors and of the union. Supervisors were key persons in the administration of human resources, and thus very important for the union. They are not happy with the division between educational and administrative functions, because it is the latter that imply power. Nevertheless, these reforms give us an idea of what kind of initiatives are possible through the decentralization process.

Needless to say, these innovations are being carefully studied by other states interested in retrofitting their educational systems, and a strong cross-fertilization is occurring among the states that have been able to go beyond merely administering the system.

Decentralization is, of course, only just beginning. It is too soon to be able to assess its consequences and results. And there is a need for a long transition period in which short-term problems are solved, initiatives are filtered, and more structural problems are attended to. In what follows, I will refer to some of the risks that will have to be consciously faced by educational policy in the near future.

The Risks Involved—Policy Implications

There is one general risk that I would like to refer to first. Given the innovative character, at least for Mexico, of many of the changes that have recently taken place in education in the country, it would seem that these constitute working hypotheses that have only just begun to be put to the test. If it is so, then the greatest risk is probably that of not considering them as such, as working hypotheses, and therefore not treating them as such. This implies the need for monitoring, assessing and following up on their consequences—both foreseen and unforeseen—and result, so that the problems that arise can be timely discovered and corrections made when possible, and so we can be sure that what is being carried out is actually producing the desired effects. Unfortunately, the innovative regime ended without mechanisms for monitoring and assessing the effects and consequences of these transformations being set in place. The fact that this can be an indication of a weakening central government, when we are aware of the need for a strong and renovated, central government, is one of the main worries.

Other risks involved include the following: the risk of deepening educational inequality as a primary focus. As we have seen, decentralization takes place within a profoundly differentiated, heterogeneous and unequal context. It is true that the central government has reserved for itself the function of compensating for educational differences. However, up to now this has only meant the possibility of directly operating in the poorer states through special programs limited to a few years and geared towards some of the poorest schools in the region. There is no doubt that these programs are necessary. But they cannot solve the problem of inequality because they do not create internal capacity for planning, assessing, administering and doing research on their educational systems.

Further, these programs cannot solve the problem of inequality because educational inequality is not something that only occurs between the different states, but within each state, within a school district, even within a single school. The central government should be able to monitor the educational system in order to discover inequalities within the states, and to make sure that the states have the capacities to act against them. Again, these systems have not been set up, even though our present information system would make it relatively easy to do so.

The risk of greater inequality with decentralization is real. As decisions affect the place where educational activity is taking place, they also approach the interests of groups that are able to put pressure on decision makers in order to insure that local educational development meets their own particular needs.

The risk of "privatizing" public schooling is another challenge. It is well known that some experiences in decentralization have actually resulted in a privatization of what before was considered and operated as government responsibility. Such was the case in Chile when Pinochet municipalized education.[20] The risk is seen in the model that has been designed for social participation. The capacities of actually participating in educational affairs are as unequally distributed as the opportunities for enrolling, remaining and learning in school. The system has to take on the task of "educating the demand." Greater still is the risk of limiting participation to financial support of the school.

Two injustices emerge from this limitation. The obvious injustice is that the richer communities have richer schools. On the contrary, the poor communities are the ones that limit their accessibility to financial support, and these communities, therefore, end up paying more for the education of their children than the communities whose greater cultural capital allows for diversifying social participation.

A third risk of a weakened central government is perpetuating the imposition of uniformity. The curricular reform delivers equal contents for all. We know, however, that uniform models for diverse populations only produce unequal results. The new curriculum has not foreseen ways in which contents and methodologies may begin to diversify. It is difficult to imagine how we are to strengthen a country that believes its unity is a product of its plurality if we do not design mechanisms for fostering and assessing innovations in this direction. The way to open up curriculum to regional, cultural and social diversity is yet to be designed.

In many countries there has been a historical pendular movement in which centralizing and decentralizing trends alternately gain control. We cannot say that in Mexico this has been the case, since previous attempts at decentralization date back to the beginning of the century but were never really put in practice. Mexico is a large, rich and diverse country which deserves a strong, decentralized educational system. However, since we have been a truly centralized country throughout our history, a strong central government is needed in order to insure a process toward strong decentralized structures of education. The central government has unfortunately not shown signs of moving in this direction. Perhaps, then, the most important policy implication of the risks that we have mentioned is one that refers to the need of carefully planning, assessing and graduating the transition and what this implies for the central government in the middle and short term. It would be unfortunate if, due to the lack of vision and/or of capacity of strengthening local decision-making and administration, we would find ourselves in a position in which centralist trends would again gain control.

Notes

1. This article is based on a presentation in the 43rd Canadian Education Association Short Course for Educational Leaders, on Educational Leadership in a Knowledge-Intensive Society, held in Banff, Alberta, May 13-20, 1995.

2. Prawda, Juan. *Logros, Inequidades y Retos del Futuro del Sistema Educativo Mexicano.* México: Grijalbo, 1989, p. 26.

3. Latapí, Pablo. "El Federalismo en la Educación." Conferencia presentada en el Foro Nacional: Hacia un Auténtico Federalismo. Guadalajara: mimeo, 1995.

4. Noriega, Margarita. "La Descentralización Educativa: Los Casos de Francia y México," in *Revista Latinoamericana de Estudios Educativos,* Vol. XXIII, No. 1 (first quarter), 1993, p. 60.

5. Guevara Niebla, Gilberto. "El Malestar Educativo," en *Nexos,* Vol. XV, No. 170 (February), 1992, p. 21.

6. *Prawda,* op. cit., p. 241.

7. See Camacho, Juan Carlos. "Financiamiento, Descentralización y Equidad." Guanajuato: mimeo. 1995, and Latapí, 1995, op. cit.

8. Latapí, 1995, op. cit.

9. See Rama, Germán. "Educación y Cambios en la Estructura Social the América Latina," in *Boletín del Proyecto Principal de Educación para América Latina y el Caribe,* No. 35 (December), 1994, p. 14.

10. See Schmelkes, S. *The Quality of Primary Education in Mexico: A Study of Five Zones.* Paris: IIEP. 1995.

11. Noriega, op. cit., pp. 47-48.

12. Ibid, and Latapí, op. cit.

13. See Tedesco, Juan Carlos. "Tendencias Actuales de las Reformas Educativas," in *Boletín del Proyecto Principal de Educación para América Latina y el Caribe,* No. 35 (December), 1994, p. 6.

14. Martínez Rizo, Felipe. "La Función Docente en México Antes y Después de la Descentralización," in *Hacia Dónde va la Educación Pública?* México: *Fundación para la Cultura del Maestro Mexicano,* Vol. II, 1994, p. 283.8m 0.

15. See *Tedesco,* op. cit., p. 7.

16. Hammaway and Carnoy, quoted by Martínez Rizo, F., 1994, op. cit.

17. Hannaway and Carnoy, quoted by Martínez Rizo, 1994, op. cit.

18. A National Forum on Federalism, presided by the President and attended by most of the governors of the 31 states, was held in Guadalajara in March, 1995.

19. Zorrilla Fierro, Margarita. "Aguascalientes," in ¿*Hacia Dónde Va la Educación Pública?,* Vol. II. México: *Fundación para la Cultura del Maestro Mexicano,* 1994, p. 258.

20. Núñez, Ivan. "Rumbos de la Descentralización en Chile," in ¿*Hacia Dónde Va la Educación Pública?* op, cit., pp. 273-274.

References

Camacho, Juan Carlos. 1995. "Financiamiento, Decentralización y Equidad." Guanajuato: mimeo.

Guevara Niebla, Gilberto. 1992. "El Malestar Educativo," *Nexos*, Vol. XV, No. 170 (February).

Latapí, Pablo. 1995. "El Federalismo en la Educación." Lecture presented in the Foro Nacional: Hacia un Auténtico Federalismo. Guadalajara: mimeo.

Martínez Rizo, Felipe. 1994. "La Función Docente en Méxcio Antes y Después de la Descentralización," in *¿Hacia Dónde Va la Educación Pública?* México: Fundación para la Cultura del Maestro Mexicano. Vol. II.

Noriega, Margarita. 1993. "La Descentralización Educativa: Los Casos de Francia y México," in *Revista Latinoamericana de Estudios Educativos*, Vol. XXIII, No. 1 (first quarter).

Núñez, Ivan. 1994. "Rumbos de la Descentralización en Chile," in *Hacia Dónde va la Educación Pública?* México: Fundación para la Cultura del Maestro Mexicano.

Prawda, Juan. 1989. *Logros, Inequidades y Retos del Futuro del Sistema Educativo Mexicano*. México: Grijalbo.

Rama, Germán. 1994. "Educación y Cambios en la Estructura Social de América Latina," in *Boletín del Proyecto Principal de Educación para América Latina y el Caribe*, No. 35 (December).

Schmelkes, Sylvia. 1995. *The Quality of Primary Education in Mexico: A Study of Five Zones*. Paris: International Institute for Educational Planning.

Tedesco, Juan Carlos. 1994. "Tendencias Actuales de las Reformas Educativas," *Boletín del Proyecto Principal de Educación para América Latina y el Caribe*, No. 35 (December).

Zorilla Fierro, Margarita. 1994. "Aguascalientes, ¿Hacia Dónde Va tu Educación?" in *Hacia Dónde Va la Educación Pública?* México: *Fundación para la Cultura del Maestro Mexicano*, Vol. II.

7

Teacher Education Reform Initiatives: The Case of Mexico

Maria Teresa Tatto and Eduardo Velez

Introduction

The lack of systematic knowledge about the effectiveness of old and new teacher education approaches in Mexico complicates policy making and threatens to weaken the quality of education teachers receive. Yet evaluative studies that comparatively assess the merits of past and current approaches to educate teachers are non-existing. Currently, Mexican education authorities while recognizing the need to develop comprehensive information systems to make informed decisions regarding teacher education, are not willing—in part because of limited resources and in part because of the complex political ethos surrounding teachers—to undertake an empirical study to assess teacher education approaches in Mexico. In this paper we develop an alternative way to comparatively assess the merits of teacher education based on document analysis and interviews that may provide valuable preliminary information and may help set the basis for future empirical studies. Two research questions guide our analysis: (1) What are the structure and programmatic character of teacher education in México? and (2) How does this structure seem to contribute to developing the professional knowledge and abilities teachers need in order to effectively teach? After developing a framework for analysis we suggest plausible policy alternatives to increase teacher education's contributions to teachers' professional knowledge and skills. The results of our analysis make evident the need to develop evaluative studies that comparatively assess the merits of past and current teacher preparation approaches in order to develop sound teacher education policy in Mexico.

The latest wave in Mexico's educational reform began in 1978 having as its main objective the decentralization of the educational system, and is characterized by a strong concern for advancing the quality of basic education.[1] Raising the quality of teaching has emerged as a government priority and as key factor in the improvement of education across the country.[2] As a consequence, there is a growing interest in developing new or supporting existing approaches to effectively educate teachers in the knowledge, skills, and attitudes necessary to increase the quality of their teaching.[3] In addition to the long-standing Normal de Maestros, new approaches have evolved over the years in an ad hoc manner to fill perceived gaps or to respond to the state agenda or to union and teachers' demands.[4] Systematic knowledge about what strategies have proven successful in Mexico's teacher education, and how they have affected the quality of teaching relative to context and costs is lacking (D.I.E., 1990). The lack of well founded knowledge in this regard, has contributed in part to the development of teacher education policy in an ad hoc manner. Although recently, prompted by government mandates, a number of teacher education approaches have carried out internal implementation studies, there are no evaluative studies in Mexico to date that assess in a systematic and comparative fashion, the effectiveness of different approaches to educate teachers. To the extent that teacher education in Mexico is likely to involve more participants and more expenditures in the future, analysis of the substance and character of these programs as well as their potential and actual effects will be important for public and also private decisions and for differential investment in modifying or developing approaches to educate teachers. Nevertheless, Mexican education authorities, while recognizing the need for more knowledge in developing teacher education policy, are not currently willing to undertake a study to assess how effective teacher education has been to date. The reluctance to assess teacher education effects is due in part to the expensive nature of such a study and in part to its implicitly politically loaded character for both the Secretariat of Public Education (S.E.P.) and the teacher's union (Sindicato Nacional de Trabajadores de la Educación or S.N.T.E).[5] The situation in Mexico is not different from that of other early industrialized nations, in fact, few of these countries to date have had the resources, or the political stability to implement studies of this kind and those that have done so have received professional and financial support from international aid agencies such as USAID or the World Bank in the U.S., or SIDA in Europe.[6] In this paper we present an alternative method at developing preliminary understandings of the comparative merits of teacher education in Mexico by using analysis of documents describing the structure, curriculum, objectives, and philosophy as well as evidence of implementation results gathered by the programs themselves.

We have also used limited interviewing in an attempt at gaining a better understanding of the documents reviewed and of actual implementation practices among the programs examined. Because the data source is limited, this paper's conclusions should be seen as hypothetical and as providing the basis for future empirical research on teacher education impact. We believe that empirical studies of comparative effects of teacher education are especially important in México because of the limited nature of our knowledge regarding ways to improve teaching, due in part to the private ethos around teaching and teacher education perpetuated by the teachers themselves and by the teacher union.

Based on an original document analysis methodology for assessing teacher education approaches' potential influence, this study shows what are the structure and programmatic character of different teacher education approaches in México, and how this structure may contribute to developing the professional knowledge and skills of teachers. The objectives of this paper are: (1) to contribute to a better understanding of the potential influence of different approaches to educate teachers in a developing country, and (2) to provide an illustration of a plausible method to analyze the possibilities and limitations of teacher education in a context dominated by economic and political constraints. The rest of the paper is divided into four sections. After presenting a brief background information on Mexico's educational system and teachers we present an account of the reform movements in teacher education to date. Next, we develop a conceptual framework to analyze in a comparative manner the structure and programmatic character of teacher education approaches in México, and discuss how these features may contribute to developing the professional knowledge of teachers. We briefly discuss plausible policy strategies to increase teacher education's contributions to teachers' professional knowledge and skills. We conclude that in the absence of an actual empirical study this type of analysis may help unmask the extent to which different approaches to educate teachers may be successful and widen the range of informed choices in teacher education policy making.[7]

Educational Quality, Teachers, and Educational Reform in Mexico

Historically, México has been successful in providing educational services for its population. At the preschool level the coverage is 70 percent, and for primary and secondary education is 98 and 80 percent respectively (D.I.E., 1990). México was the first among developing countries to successfully implement progressive educational policies such as the provision of free textbooks to the population attending basic education in the 1950s.

Over the past two decades a series of educational reforms have been designed to strengthen basic education at all levels. One such reform was implemented in 1972 at the primary education level, achieving important advances in the redesign of the textbooks, in the development of a new pedagogic orientation emphasizing student centered instruction, and in the integration of scientific thought in the day to day curriculum (D.I.E., 1990).

In spite of these achievements, the terminal efficiency and quality of basic education provided in México is low in the view of government officials and educational scholars alike (D.I.E., 1990). Only 54 percent of the students who start primary education graduate. Only 34 percent of those who enter primary education graduate from secondary education. The annual drop-out rate in primary education is five percent and there is a 15 percent repetition rate in the first and second grades of primary education. The situation in rural areas is more severe where only 25 percent graduate from primary education. Sixty-one percent of the schools located in rural areas serving mostly indigenous populations do not have the required six grades of primary education. In one out of three primary schools in the country one teacher is expected to teach two to six grades. The low quality of basic education in México is mostly seen as caused in part by the inefficient use of time by the schools, the growing bureaucratization of education, and the lack of educational materials other than the free textbooks, and in part by the mechanistic and reproductive character of the instructional process, the poor conditions under which teachers work, the poor preparation of teachers, and the lack of in service training programs for teachers (Centro de Estudios Educativos, 1990). These problems of educational quality are often associated with the context (geographical and socioeconomic) in which schools are located.

Low teacher salaries, poor school conditions, and lack of real democratic participation in school governance are seen as major contributing factors reducing the quality of teaching as well as teacher's dedication to their profession. Due to the worsening economic situation in the country teacher salaries have decreased by more than 33 percent since 1983 and lack of effective incentives for rural teachers have pressed teachers to work double time, to look for a second job or in some cases to work as temporary labor in the United States (Torres, 1990). Teachers in México have little control over their work conditions. Their work is isolated and fragmented and evolves in a politicized environment, under administrators that are removed and ignorant of teachers needs and dilemmas, and implementing a curriculum over which they have no input and in many occasions seems inadequate to the context and pupils teachers teach. Because of the historically centralized and hierarchical structure of authority prevalent in the educational system and schools in México, teachers seem to have few possibilities for democratic participation in school governance, for active participation in their own professional development, for deciding curricular content, and for implementing strategies to improve the quality of education in their schools.

Mexican teachers not only confront a politically turbulent environment, work under poor conditions, and have no decision making power in school governance, they also lack a good preparation that would enable them to successfully teach. According to a Report by the World Bank, only about 50 percent of the close to half a million (565, 328) basic education teachers in México have the qualifications that are currently required to teach (World Bank, 1991). Many seem to lack the basic knowledge of the subject they teach as well as the pedagogical skills to appropriately address the learning needs of their pupils. Deficient teacher preparation is even more pronounced among those teachers who teach in rural or poor areas. These teachers are usually beginning teachers with little classroom experience and who understand little of the community where their school is located. These teachers also confront a number of issues that have gone largely unexplored in teacher education programs such as the complexities involved in teaching children in multi-grade or unitarian classrooms. Because teacher education programs have been traditionally located in urban or semi-urban areas many of these teachers can not easily access them. In addition systems that have been created to help teachers develop professionally are underutilized. For example a study by the Centro de Estudios Educativos (CEE), found that among 243 teachers surveyed only 2.1 percent were currently taking advantage of the open programs for teacher upgrading to the Licenciatura (or bachelors) level at the Universidad Pedagógica Nacional (UPN) even though only 12.4 had completed the required Licenciatura in basic education (66.5 percent had at least studied the Normal Básica) (Farres and Noriega, 1993). Because this sample was drawn from urban areas, the researchers suspect that the situation in rural areas regarding teachers' schooling is significantly lower. Teachers expressed that the training received in the Normal School "included very few hours of practice and that this practice was reduced to visits to schools where their role was to support administrative tasks or development of teaching materials" (Farres and Noriega, 1993, p. 28). The study points to the need to provide teachers with education in subject matter contents "since it has been observed that teachers capacity to communicate, read, and write is very basic specially among those teachers who work in areas far away from the cities" (Farres and Noriega, 1993, p. 20). In this same study teachers who are currently teaching as well as those who dropped out of the profession saw in-service training as essential in improving the quality of education in schools.

Paradoxically, the increase in years now required to become a teacher has had a negative effect on the number of teachers who enroll in the Normales. According to the World Bank, "in less than 10 years (between 1981 to 1990) the enrollment declined by close to 36 percent and continues to decline at a rate of 10 percent every year to a point in which now the low student teacher ratios in the Normales (9:1) make this particular system of teacher training highly inefficient" (World Bank, 1991, p. 17).

The current system to train teachers in service is recognized as being somewhat inaccessible (too bureaucratic, with complicated scheduling and requirements) and of low quality.[8] Mexican educators suspect that the effectiveness of these programs is also low, it is however difficult to ascertain this since there is an endemic lack of systematic evaluations of both pre-service and in-service teacher education programs in México. In summary, a general criticism of teacher education in México has been that it has failed to bridge the gap between the curricular content of the programs and the real practice of the teacher.

The poor preparation of teachers before, during, and after they become teachers is in part reflected on the level of achievement of their pupils. In a study conducted by SICEM (Sistema de Información de la Calidad de la Educación) and reported by the World Bank in 1991, shows that "between 1987-89, 69 percent of Mexico's primary students scored 6 or lower on an academic performance scale from 1 to 10 [... A]nd in the four principal subjects: Spanish, mathematics, social and natural sciences [...] out of a possible score of 100 only first grade students averaged over 50 points. In grades four through six students' average scores were just above 20. At the secondary level students did even worse, averaging between 11 and 16 out of a 100" (World Bank, 1991, p. 37). These results are evidence of the deterioration of basic understandings of subject matter and are even more compelling when examining teacher education curricula which reflects this lack under the possible assumption that teachers come into training with an acceptable level of subject matter knowledge.

Among the major initiatives in the modernization agenda of the Salinas De Gortari (1988) government (spanning from 1988-1994) has been a major revamping of the educational system.[9] The reform proposed to address a wide range of problems affecting the quality of education, such as redesigning the school curriculum towards a more conceptual orientation, encouraging the family and community to take part in improving the quality of basic education, supporting teachers who work in difficult contexts, reforming and strengthening the education of teachers, creating mechanisms to provide in service training to teachers, and, although not explicitly stated in the reform agenda, to diffuse the influence of the SNTE by decentralizing power to the states thereby decentralizing the teacher union as well (S.E.P., 1992c).

Whether or not these initiatives have the force or substance to achieve such changes, they have provided the space for educators to reconsider the current approaches to educate teachers and to design alternatives that are expected to respond more fully to the educational needs of teachers and pupils in the country. Similarly they have open opportunities for teacher participation in their own professional development, and have encouraged a subtle questioning of the existing school structures and their role on teacher and pupil growth.

Although this paper's focus is on teacher education we recognize that as important as teacher education may be in improving the quality of teaching, it cannot by itself address the myriad of problems we have discussed above such as the difficulties and constraints teachers confront in their workplace. Workplace conditions have been recognized by educators as including mechanisms of control that may further subordinate teachers and may defeat the aims espoused by "professionalism" strategies (Densmore, 1987).

A review of teacher education reform in the following section provides the context for understanding the contributions that teacher education brings to what teachers need to know and be able to do in their teaching practice.

Teacher Education in México: Layers of Reform

Teacher education in México has been subject to a number of reforms since its origins in the last century (S.E.P., 1990). In the early 1920s along with the creation of the Secretariat for Public Education (S.E.P.) after the Mexican Revolution, emerges in 1925 the National School for Teachers (Escuela Nacional de Maestros) in both rural and urban areas.[10] These schools have served as a model for the training of pre-service primary school teachers in México.

According to Alvarez García, the first significant reform in teacher education in México occurred in 1945 to unify the curriculum of the urban and rural normal schools in an attempt for national unity and equality for rural and urban teachers (Alvarez García, 1991, cited in Farres and Noriega, 1993). A consequence of this reform was the development of an urban curriculum at the expense of a rural oriented teacher education even though the population at that time was more than 55 percent rural. The curriculum was designed to be equivalent to high school studies. In 1961 and as a result of a 1954 resolution, normal schools began to require the secondary school diploma as a precondition to enroll in them. The primary school reforms of 1969, 1972, and 1975 were specially important for teacher education because of the impact they had in the curricular changes of the Normal Schools (S.E.P., 1990). Initially the Normal Schools' curriculum was oriented towards a traditional pedagogy based on the relation of the teacher with contents and later on with methods using as focus the principles of educational technology which assumed that the improvement of education resided in learning *how to teach* rather than in *what to teach*. The effects of this philosophy currently affects the impact of teacher education in general and specially at the Normal level. The Normal School was drastically reformed in 1984. In an attempt to improve the quality of basic education, and as result of union pressures over the characteristics of a higher education program for teachers, a presidential decree was issued in which the Normales would provide a bachelors degree (licenciatura) over eight semesters, raised the criteria for admitting candidates to high school level, and revamped the curriculum to emphasize the learning of curricular contents of preschool, elementary and secondary education, as well as pedagogy. In addition to these curricular changes, the aims of the reform were to give research and diffusion of knowledge in education a major role in these institutions. The goal of the Normales was stated by the reform as the education of professionals with scientific, critical and participatory attitudes.

The Mexican educational community has criticized the effort to reform pre-service teacher education as one that has caused a great deal of confusion, and has drastically decreased the number of individuals who would like to become teachers. Raising the requirements from secondary to high school for example, has stopped many, and granting of the Licenciatura has created discontent among teachers who graduated before 1984 since now they have to upgrade their degree to that of Licenciatura to be considered fully qualified.

An informal evaluation of the 355 Normal Schools (with a reported 77 percent rate of response) carried out by the CONACEN highlights the most relevant challenges regarding the improvement of pre-service teacher education in México as their large degree of heterogeneity—in origin, development, norms, administration, and resources—which has brought about a series of problems such as lack of coherence, duplication of tasks, failure to follow a normative criteria, lack of comprehensive planning, and lack of communication and academic exchange among themselves and with other institutions of higher education (S.E.P., 1991). The Normales have a strong bias towards attending urban populations since more than 80 percent are located in urban areas, and are evidencing a declining level of enrollment as a result of the high school requirement and the weak support given to the students through the program. Normales are also seen as having a weak academic level which seems to be a result of the predominance of teaching as the main faculty activity with very little emphasis on research, curricular and professional development, diffusion, assessment, tutoring, scholarly activities, academic exchange, planning, and evaluation. Teacher educators in these institutions seem overwhelmed by the large number of subjects that constitute the curriculum. The highly diverse curriculum makes coherence difficult, the Licenciatura for preschool education for example has 65 courses, for primary education 63 courses, the one for secondary education 48, and in special education 63. The poor level of preparation of teacher educators and the lack of availability of appropriate resources and materials further complicates the adequate development of these institutions' tasks.

The development of new alternatives to educate teachers has been subject of political demands by the union and teachers. The creation of the National Pedagogic University (UPN) in 1978 represented a response to the perceived need by the SNTE leaders and members for a post-secondary education approach for teachers.[11] But while this was an initial proposal of SNTE the López Portillo administration made this project its own, overriding the original proposal of the SNTE.[12] SNTE's response to this attempt at weakening its influence was to close job opportunities for the graduates of the UNP (Pescador and Torres, 1985).

The lack of union support to UPN's graduates regarding job placement effectively sabotaged the mission of the UPN envisioned by the government, and insured that the level of preparation of those teaching in schools remained the same.[13] The UPN has been affected by a number of problems that have impaired its functioning. These problems seen as of structural nature by the SEP have affected UPN's capacity to provide full coverage to teachers in need of courses to complete the licenciatura now required for basic school teachers. In addition, the UPN has a high dropout rate in part due to UPN's inability to carve a place for its graduates within the professional and salary structure of the SEP, and in part to its failure to reach a satisfactory agreement with the teacher union regarding job placement for its graduates.[14] The current yet unfulfilled plan for the UPN includes the development of a professional curriculum, educational research and diffusion of knowledge capacities, and extension services for teachers and administrators. The UPN approach has relied on semi-institutionalized and in-service programs based in the distance education approach to provide bachelors, Masters and specialization courses. The UPN has a principal unit in México City and 74 units and sub-units distributed throughout the country. According to educational authorities, there is a need to "re-define" the role and social responsibility of the UPN. Whether the UPN will be able to truly re-define its role and to improve its efficiency is an open question. There seems to be, however, promising directions that are being proposed as part of this transformation. A central aspect of such proposed changes is the re-conceptualization of in-service training in the teachers and administrator's work place as well as the linkage of research and practice through the school and the school community. This transformation—it is argued—requires the understanding of teaching practice from the teachers perspective, and resorting as much as possible to the productive use of the school structures already in place such as the Technical Councils.[15]

Another approach to in-service education are the CAMs.[16] The origin of the in service Teacher Actualization Centers (CAMs) dates back to the creation of the Federal Institute for Teacher Training in 1944 and later with the Local Study and Consultation Centers created as a response by the central authorities to the rapid expansion of the educational system in México which largely increased the number of hired teachers with no proper training and pressed the already overcrowded system to educate teachers. These programs are coordinated by the SEP and have expanded to the point that there are about 200 courses that attempt to provide knowledge on pedagogy and upgrading in curricular contents specially regarding changes produced by the different educational reforms implemented in México. These programs provide non-certified teachers with credentials that directly affect their salary and job placement. In general these programs are recognized as of low quality and because of both their coverage and relevance to current requirements for teachers are likely to be restructured into a more coherent teacher education approach.

A more recent initiative to in-service teacher education is the PEAM (now Program for Teacher Upgrading or PAM). The Emergent Program for Teacher Upgrading (El Programa Emergente de Actualización del Maestro or PEAM) evolved within the context of the Educational Modernization Program as a response by the government to the perceived need to introduce the new curricular contents and programs and for upgrading the knowledge of all multi-grade, preschool, elementary and secondary teachers in the country (S.E.P., 1990; S.E.P., 1992a; S.E.P., 1992b; S.E.P., 1992c; S.E.P., 1993c; S.E.P., 1993d). Developed and implemented by the central S.E.P. in collaboration with state level coordination, this program's objectives were to strengthen in the short term, the knowledge level of teachers in order to support their work, and to motivate them to participate in long-life skills' upgrading; to support the decentralization process by encouraging states to create their own structures, strategies, and upgrading mechanisms within national norms frameworks; to consolidate a national framework for a permanent teacher upgrading system based on follow-up and evaluation strategies that will contribute to the diversification of alternative teacher education strategies in the country (S.E.P., 1992a, p. 2).

According to reformers, the philosophy and structure of the PEAM reflected an attempt to bring about a fundamental change in the way the teacher's role and work is understood (S.E.P., 1992a, p. 2). Teacher upgrading was seen by program developers as a continuous flexible and systematic process oriented to strengthen teacher knowledge and improve the day to day work at the school. Important characteristics of this program included an emphasis on collegiality, reflection or self-analysis based on teaching experiences, development of didactic materials and resources, development of different options to contribute to the improvement of proactive teaching and learning processes in pupils (S.E.P., 1992a, p. 3).

The program's implementation conceptualized in three stages (the preparatory, the intensive and the extensive) attempted to develop at the state level the infrastructure (physical, material, and human) to carry out the training in a period of about three months. From May to August 1992 a massive effort began to print and distribute training guides, manuals and materials, and to develop TV programs to be distributed in all the states in the Mexican Republic. A "cascade" technique was used to train conductors (at the central level), and instructors, supervisors, and school principals in that order (at the state level). The training implemented during July to August 1992 attempted to inform teachers about the plan and process of The National Modernization Agreement, and to inform and supply teachers with the new curricular programs and materials and guidelines for their application.[17] The extensive phase had as an objective to deepen the knowledge of the contents, methods, strategies and educational resources emerging from the curricular reform; to strengthen the functions of principals and supervisors as "academic organizers and promoters" of school development projects; to understand the common problems in the teaching learning process and child development as well as the relationships with parents, family, and community (S.E.P., 1993c).[18] The end of this extensive phase was to be marked by the beginning of the "Permanent Program for Teacher Upgrading," currently on hold due to the change in government.

The PEAM's attempt at "professionalizing" the Mexican teaching force can be seen from a critical perspective as a symbolic attempt by the State to incorporate teachers into its modernization initiatives, a perception that is reinforced by the fact that no important changes have been introduced in the traditionally hierarchical structures of authority in schools. Nevertheless, the SEP's effort at reaching every teacher in the country to provide them with short education courses and new educational materials—albeit within the modernization framework of the state—cannot be easily dismissed. An evaluation of the preparatory and intensive phases by SEP, shows an acceptable level of satisfaction among the participants while also makes evident the limitations of a short-term upgrading program (S.E.P., 1992c; S.E.P., 1993d). The evaluation points out that the larger aims for training teachers and school administrators such as reflection on their own practice, the development of new roles and self-image, need a longer and continuous process.

Another approach by-product of the Modernization Program but functioning relatively independent from SEP is the Compensatory Program to Address Educational Lag (Programa para Abatir el Rezago Educativo or PARE) (Hicks, 1993; S.E.P., 1993a; S.E.P., 1992d; S.E.P., 1992e; S.E.P., 1992f; S.E.P., 1992g; S.E.P., 1993b). The PARE Teacher Education Program, is part of a comprehensive program to improve the quality of education in México, it is currently implemented by the National Council for Educational Advancement (Consejo Nacional de Fomento Educativo or CONAFE) through their State Coordination Groups (GCE) and with a loan from the World Bank. The PARE focuses on elementary education and its activities have been programmed in four year periods beginning in 1992 with the purpose of better serving populations who have been traditionally difficult to reach through educational services. The objectives of this program are to address educational issues in marginalized populations by supplying physical infrastructure, educational materials for the classroom and libraries, educational courses for teachers and administrators (principals and supervisors), as well as incentives for those who serve in marginal areas. The PARE's Teacher Education Component attempts to offer opportunities to receive pre-service and in-service training to teachers and administrators who work at the elementary level in marginal areas (in practice the program also attempts to include teachers in urban areas), teacher educators from both the Normal Schools and the CAM's as well as those in the UPN. Based on a constructivist philosophy, the program follows two mandates: one, to consider teaching practice as object for study and transformation, and two, to encourage self-learning assuming teachers desire to transform their own practice. The program relies on a "cascade" technique to provide education to teachers and their principals and has involved supervisors and teacher educators in the process. The PARE has developed high quality materials to introduce teachers to constructivist teaching in mathematics, language (Spanish and Indian languages), alternative models to evaluate learning, the use of teaching resources found in the community, and strategies to teach multigrade groups. The program is organized into two semi-schooled courses throughout the year and three intensive courses during the Summer months.

As of mid June 1993, the PARE's Teacher Education Program had been implemented in four of the poorest states in the country: Chiapas, Guerrero, Hidalgo, and Oaxaca. According to evaluators, in all these states except Oaxaca the goals of the program "had been reached in more than an 80 percent" (Hicks, 1993). A formal evaluation revealed that the perception of the teacher education component of the PARE was positive among participant teachers. Further feedback indicated that educators believed that this program should be implemented on a "permanent" basis (i.e. every month or every two months) specially for teachers who work in indigenous or difficult to access locations, since these teachers need permanent support and advice.

The PARE teacher education program represents one of the most successful attempts to date at reaching teachers in poor regions. In the two years since its implementation, it has created an unprecedented demand for its courses among teachers in the four different states, has overcome organizational, political, and union hurdles, and has positioned itself as a legitimate and credible alternative for teacher education in México. The success of the program seems to be closely related to the support it has received from the World Bank and to its organization by state teams which while operating relatively independent from SEP, use for program implementation the historically ingrained hierarchies currently operating in the educational system. This hierarchical organization according to program implementors is a very efficient system of communication and knowledge diffusion.[19]

In contrast with official initiatives, different approaches to educate teachers are emerging from alternative sources. The Educational Research and Teaching Program of the CEE and SECyR, was developed by educational researchers in the Center for Educational Research in México (CEE) and adopted as an in-service training program for teachers (Fierro, Farres, and Irene, n.d.). This program was implemented as an integral part of the Direction of Higher Education of the Secretariat of Education Culture and Recreation (SECyR) of the State of Guanajuato and was part of the Specialties offered by the Normal School in that State in 1989 and was linked with credits in the study program with participants receiving points for the teachers' tenure system. The goal of the program was to develop a strategy to help teachers address the educational needs of rural communities in the state. With a duration of two years the program was based on the methodology of action-research as the mechanism through which the teachers would be able to make sense of their experiences in schools, improve their practice and develop curricular innovations that incorporate the needs of pupils in rural areas. In addition the program looked to provide teachers with historical, economic and sociological perspectives in education in relation to their work in the school and as a way to help them develop better understandings of the contexts where they work. Teachers were expected to work in groups to develop the tasks assigned during the course as well as in shared school projects.

A formal evaluation of this program developed by the Centro de Estudios Educativos (CEE) revealed that the program did stimulate critical reflection on teaching practice and on the factors that contribute to educational lag in the rural areas (Fierro, Farres, and Irene, n.d.). Probably the most significant impact of the program, according to teachers' self-evaluation, was an enrichment of the theoretical framework they had to think about their practice and on the causes of educational lag in their pupils. Additional benefits were the ability of teachers to implement innovative approaches to their work such as team work, reading and analyzing texts, developing dialogs with teachers, principal, supervisors, and instructors, and implementing action-research with their pupils allowing them to link theory with practice.

The CEE program—probably because of its length, its relative independence from the central SEP/SNTE and its emphasis on action-research—seems to be well attuned to the teachers' needs and their problematic in a multiplicity of contexts. In spite of these important characteristics, this program's shortcoming is the lack of developed networks and infrastructure (such as the ones developed by PARE) for successful generalized implementation, and its highly theoretical content.

The progression in the development and implementation of teacher education in Mexico reveals that although these strategies are in some cases motivated by political aims they may also have the effect of helping teachers improve their knowledge and skills in teaching. Moreover ethnographic studies of teaching in Mexican schools reveal that teachers do in fact lack basic knowledge required for teaching and curriculum development, their situation regarding salaries and working conditions is poor, and there are few incentives to work hard in schools (Fierro, 1991; Rockwell and Mercado, 1986). Thus the current efforts by the government may also be seen as legitimate attempts at improving the conditions of teachers and as having the potential to stimulate teachers to acquire new knowledge, to work together in their schools, and to effectively participate in school governance. Moreover, the PARE for example, is seen by teachers, principals, and supervisors, as a legitimate alternative to improve their knowledge and create collegial working groups in and outside schools. This fact serves as a reminder of the importance of looking at the programs and their contributions in their own terms acknowledging the teachers themselves as actors within political, social, economic and organizational contexts. The following section examines the impact of teacher education approaches in México underlining the value of analyzing programs' possible contributions to teachers' knowledge and of discussing programs' potential to address teachers' needs. The driving forces of this analysis are: an attempt to understand why teachers' knowledge of the subject matter in México is so low; where are teachers expected to learn; what they need to know to do a decent job; and, acknowledging the politics and dynamics surrounding teacher education and teaching, how to make informed decisions as to the approach or approaches that better serve the needs of teachers and those of their pupils.

Teacher Education in México: A Preliminary Exploration

Developing an Analytic Framework

In order to understand teacher education in Mexico it is important to determine how different approaches vary in relation with one another in a particular context, given the needs and resources of that context. The design of teacher education in addition to including goals, determining program duration and approach, providing incentives or support, targeting a specific population, working out the program's content, and plans for keeping costs at a reasonable level, usually includes a conception of the degree to which teachers should be able to manage a variable mixture of the knowledge they need to be able to teach. This mixture may include knowledge of subject matter, knowledge of pedagogy or the principles and strategies of classroom management and organization, knowledge of the curriculum such as educational materials and programs, pedagogical content knowledge (teacher's professional understanding that brings together subject matter knowledge and pedagogy), abilities to teach diverse learners, knowledge and understanding of the context where teaching occurs (including group and classroom dynamics, governance and financing of schools and the school system, and the character of communities and cultures), as well as knowledge of educational ends, purposes and values (Shulman, 1987). If these categories of knowledge are accepted as valid across cultural contexts, it is therefore possible to think about teacher education in terms of the extent to which different approaches will provide teachers with the knowledge required to teach. Although this categorization of teaching knowledge represents more an ideal than a reality in current teaching and teacher education across international contexts it provides a useful framework and point of departure to examine the reach of the different approaches to educate teachers in México. The impact of teacher education approaches in México can also be examined under other equally valuable frameworks. A historical perspective, for example, would serve to uncover the role of teacher education throughout the years in the formation of a massive and cohesive teaching force in a large and diverse country.[20] Similarly a political framework would be useful in explaining the formation of political—or apolitical—positions in teachers and the degree to which teacher education can be seen as serving—or not—the aims of the state.[21] Our emphasis throughout the paper is in the contribution of teacher education to teacher knowledge. In our analysis we look at the different approaches on their own right and point at the characteristics that seem to address the unique needs of teachers in the Mexican context.

The evolution of teacher education in México, signals that teaching is increasingly being re conceptualized as involving a degree of complexity warranting a higher quality and level of preparation for teachers especially when they are being asked to teach within a constructivist framework. Paradoxically and in spite of this recognition teacher education is currently limited in structure and design to help teachers respond to the complexity of their work.

The results presented in the next section are based on document analysis of the curriculum of the different teacher education approaches in México following the framework outlined above. Further work in this area would need to test empirically the arguments put forward in this section, and would also need to explore program implementation and effectiveness relative to its costs (refer to Table 1 for an abridged description of the different programs' characteristics, and to Table 2 for a description of these programs' curricular emphasis areas).

Teacher Education and Teachers' Knowledge of the Subject Matter

The lack of preparation on the subject matter teachers will teach seems to be an endemic weakness of teacher education programs not only in México but worldwide.[22] The problem may lie on the assumption that teachers are supposed to have acquired their knowledge of subject matter elsewhere and that teacher education's task is to help them learn how to teach such knowledge.

In our analysis of the curricula of the different approaches to teacher education in México, the lack of emphasis placed in the learning of subject matter by teachers is evident (see Table 2). This lack is appreciated in the pre-service preparation of elementary school teachers (the curriculum for secondary school teachers does include more subject matter knowledge though the extent to which teachers and pupils' knowledge is impacted by this curriculum is unknown and suspected to be low) and in the other in-service approaches with the exception of the PARE material reviewed.

Congruent with a constructivist approach to teaching, the PARE curriculum presents an interesting combination of subject matter and pedagogy or what we have referred to as pedagogical content knowledge in the materials developed to teach mathematics and language instead of the overemphasis on curricular content that seems to be typical of in-service programs in México (see Table 3). Although the PARE materials are noticeable because of their high quality and their inclusion of subject matter material they only cover a limited number of topics for both mathematics and language. Following the same strategy developed by PARE, an effective long-term in-service program (for more than two years) could conceivably be designed to provide teachers with the subject matter knowledge they need.

The poor knowledge that teachers have of subject matter needs to be recognized as a weakness of the educational system in México. To address and recognize such weakness brings about expensive but necessary solutions if the quality of education is to be improved.

In short, it seems necessary but not sufficient to provide teachers with curricular guides on the different subjects in the study plan. The capacity to teach the subject appropriately requires conceptual understandings that go beyond guidelines and require long term learning experiences. Learning of the necessary subject matter does not necessarily imply a drastic raise in costs of teacher education, an important consideration specially when dealing with the large number of teachers as they exist in México. Other countries have already successfully experimented with low cost in-service alternatives such as the distance education approach.[23] México has, through the PARE, the PEAM, and the Telesecundaria system, developed the necessary infrastructure to carry out in-service distance programs to provide subject matter knowledge for teachers, schools administrators, and teacher educators. The challenge for distance education is the predominantly oral culture prevalent in México in general and in Indian communities in particular.

Teacher Education and Teachers' Knowledge and Critical Involvement in the Development of the Curriculum They Teach

Teacher education both pre-service and in-service (specifically the Normal de Maestros and the PEAM) in México seems to have been quite successful in designing and implementing programs to help teachers gain a good level of information about the curriculum (see Tables 2 and 3). Furthermore the teacher guides recently developed as part of the PEAM effort are good resources teachers have available to help them improve their teaching. Less attention has been paid to creating mechanisms to facilitate teachers involvement in the development and/or critical review of curricular

TABLE 1 Different Approaches to Teacher Education in Mexico

Program/Goal/ Philosophy	Duration/ Location	Entry Conditions	Content
Normal De Maestros (basicas y superiores): To educate professionals with scientific, critical, and participative attitutes. Provides initial training to teacher candidates for primary and secondary education. At the end of their training they have a secured position in a school guaranteed by the state and the teachers union, SNTE. Normales are the only PRE-SERVICE training institutes in the country.	Full-time Institutional Duration for preschool and primary school teachers: Four years Duration for secondary school teachers: Four years	No recruit-ment or selection, but can-didates present an entrance exam.	Traditional with emphasis on educational foundations and peda-gogy. After 1984 includes the teaching of subjects taught at the university level but disconnected with the daily lives of schools. The new cur-riculum attempts to depart from the trad-itional lecture method to a more participative one, encouraging critical thinking.
Universidad Pedagogica Nacional: Actualization and upgrading. Began in 1978. INSERVICE	Duration: ? Institutional-based. It has a distance modality.	Recruitment and entrance exam. Low standards of admission in contrast with universities.	Includes teaching of subjects at the uni-versity level but dis-connected with pedagogy.
Centros De Actualización Del Magisterio (CAM): With origins in 1944, these centers constituted a new system to provide initial training to teachers in-service. Currently they also provide updating services to teachers. Provides credentials to non-certified teachers. INSERVICE	Not clear.	Teachers who did not graduate or receive formal ini-tial teacher training.	Traditional with em-phasis on educational foundations and peda-gogy. Similar to those provided by Normales. Plus updating on curr-icular and instructional plans originated by the reforms.

(table continues)

TABLE 1 (continued)

Supervised Practice and Follow-up	Approaches to Training	Target Group	Incentives to Enter Teaching	Quality Level	Costs
Normal De Maestros (basicas y superiores):					
Limited, poorly coordinated and traditional. Teachers are left to "sink or swim" during this experience. Lack of contact between faculty from Normales and practicing school teachers.	Teacher-centered; lecture format. After 1984 there is an attempt at creating a participatory learning environment for prospective teachers.	After 1984 high school graduates; before 1984 secondary school graduates.	A secured position in a state school backed by the teachers union.	Nationally recognized as providing low-quality instruction.	Moderately high, considering the recognized low-quality of instruction and the low teacher/ student ratio of 9:1. Receive state support.
Universidad Pedagogica Nacional:					
Nonexistent: There are few or no formal connections with schools.	Teacher-centered; lecture format; attempts at developing a "university-like culture."	Graduates Normales with or without teaching experience.	Grants a B.A. degree. Few go into or back to teaching.	Low-quality criteria with curriculum distanced from teaching.	High; very low student: teacher ratio. State support.
Centros De Actualización Del Magisterio (CAM):					
Not clear.	Teacher-centered; lecture format and self-learning, self-paced materials.	Inservice teachers who need to obtain a teaching credential or update their knowledge.	Since these teachers are currently inservice, the incentive is to obtain a teaching credential.	Recognized as of low quality.	Not clear.

(table continues)

TABLE 1 (continued)

Program/Goal/ Philosophy	Duration/ Location	Entry Conditions	Content
Programa Emergente De Actualizacion De Maestros (PEAM): Actualization and up-grading to preschool, elementary, and secondary teachers, their principals, and their super visors.	Intensive phase: Short periods varying from two weeks to one month throughout two years (?) In-site, school-based.	None. Attempts to reach all teachers in the country. Teachers are asked to participate on a volun-tary basis during the intensive phase.	Curriculum that departs from the traditionally-oriented to encourage problem solving in pupils. The intensive stage pre-sents information on the National Agreement on the Modernization Process, updates on the curricular and program changes, and in the contents of the new textbooks for elementary and secondary grades. In-cludes materials for multi-grade teachers. Resorts to Technical School Councils and Principal and Super-visor's support for suc-cessful implementation. The extensive stage pre-sents strategies for pro-moting school change, and collaborative work among school personnel. No clear provision for self-sustained learning.
Attempts to strengthen in the short term the knowledge of teachers, principals, and super-visors, to support the process of decentralization and modernization at the state level, and to consoli-date a national framework for long-term teacher upgrading. INSERVICE			

Supervised Practice and Follow-up	Approaches to Training	Target Group	Incentives to Enter Teaching	Quality Level	Costs
Programa Emergente De Actualizacion De Maestros (PEAM):					
Not clear whether pro-gram instruc-	Carefully de-signed self-instructional	Attempts to give full coverage to	Supported by the current Carrera	Varies depending on context.	High. National scale. State

(table continues)

TABLE 1 (continued)

Supervised Practice and Follow-up	Approaches to Training	Target Group	Incentives to Enter Teaching	Quality Level	Costs
tors actually observe and provide feedback to teachers in their classrooms.	materials; on-the-job training; group activities; within a modernization philosophy.	all the teachers in the country. Also includes the training of school principals and eventually supervisors to train teachers.	Magisterial in which teachers obtain "points" per course passed which translates in salary increases and/ or promotions.	Lack of coordination and follow-up between the state level and the center after the first year of activities.	support under the Modernization Program and the decentralization reform.

Program/Goal/ Philosophy	Duration/ Location	Entry Conditions	Content
Programa Para Abatir El Rezago Educativo (PARE): Actualization and upgrading. Begun in 1992, this is a compensatory program that attempts to give a new impulse to those schools or populations who are at risk of being left behind in the modernization process by providing additional resources and servuces, The program repre sents an integrated conception to teacher and school improvement which aims to, in addition to providing training and	Short periods depending on the number of modules included in the training program. Insite, school-based.	Selected by the state SEP in conjunction with the sponsoring/supervisory agency CONAFE. emphasis. Includes materials for multi-grade teachers. Looks to be relevant to teachers and teaching in rural areas.	Innovative curriculum based on current research on education and teaching; co-curricular activities; teaching methods and some subject-matter. The guide provided to the instructors recommends that instructors "schedule with teachers follow-up visits and technical advisory meetings [... to] verify that change in the teaching priactice has occurred."

(table continues)

TABLE 1 (continued)

Program/Goal/ Philosophy	Duration/ Location	Entry Conditions	Content

incentives to teachers,
support principals and
supervisors' develop-
ment, provide texts,
educational spaces,
and teaching materials
among others.

IN-SERVICE

Supervised Practice and Follow-up	Approaches to Training	Target Group	Incentives to Enter Teaching	Quality Level	Costs
Programa Para Abatir El Rezago Educativo (PARE):					
Not clear whether program instructors actually observe and provide feedback to teachers in their classrooms.	Carefully designed instuctional materials in modules; on-the-job-training; group activities with a pupil-centered philosophy; problem solving, constructivist approach to pupil learning.	Teachers and administrative personnel (principals and supervisors) who work in schools located in poor or rural areas. Also offers a course for for teacher educators.	Supported by the current Carrera Magisterial. Possibilities for improved work conditions. Other incentives such as increased salaries.	Varies depending on context. Overall good coordination follow-up and cohesion across sites.	Moderate. Moderate scale. State support with a loan from the World Bank.

(table continues)

TABLE 1 (continued)

Program/Goal/ Philosophy	Duration/ Location	Entry Conditions	Content
Centro de Estudios Educativos y SECyR Teacher Training Program (CEE&SECyR) (pri vate and local state support): Actualization and up-grading. Provides teachers with the possibility of obtaining their teaching credential. Attempts to provide teachers with the research to improve their practice, and to participate critically in this process. The goals of this program also include the development of strategies by teachers to work with parents and the school community.	Two-years or four semesters. In-site and self-guided.	Selected the teachers participating in the Rural and Community Education Project. Selection by CEE along with the state SEP. Teachers participated on a voluntary basis. Preschool and primary school teachers.	Innovative curriculum-based on the idea of teachers as reflective practitioners and on teacher learning as a self-initiated, self-sustained activity. The curriculum em-. phasizes theoretical teaching foundations, curricular innovations in rural basic education, and practice and methods of participative research. Emphasis on teachers working in cohorts within schools.

IN-SERVICE

Supervised Practice and Follow-up	Approaches to Training	Target Group	Incentives to Enter Teaching	Quality Level	Costs
Centro de Estudios Educativos y SECyR Teacher Training Program (CEE&SECyR) (pri vate and local state support):					
Not clear whether program instructors actually	Careful de-signed ma-terials. Emphasis on	Small scale limited to a small group of teachers	Development of collegiality within schools and a sense	Good. With 80% success rate. Carefully	Low/small scale. State SEP and pri-vate support.

(table continues)

TABLE 1 (continued)

Supervised Practice and Follow-up	Approaches to Training	Target Group	Incentives to Enter Teaching	Quality Level	Costs
observe and provide feed- back to teach- ers in their classrooms. but the pro- gram seems organized so that teachers provide feed- back to each other.	theory and on teachers as researchers. Teachers spend half of the program in contact with the in- structors, and half in indivi- dualized or independent study.	who work in schools se- lected by the Rural and Community Education Project.	of ownership/ empower- ment to teachers. Cre- dits added to their record allowing for possibilities of promotion, upper mobility and for improv- their quality of life and work conditions.	controlled and mon- itored.	

IN-SERVICE

TABLE 2 Areas of Emphasis in Five Approaches to Teacher Education in Mexico

Teacher Education Approaches	Normal De Maestros* + Clock hrs. total= 238 (does not include individual-ized study hours).	Universidad Pedagogica Nacional Clock hrs. total = NA	PEAM Intensive phase = 40 hrs. Extensive phase = 60 hrs.*** Clock hrs. total = 100 for elementary teachers; and 120 for secondary teachers	PARE Clock hrs. total =293****	CEE/SECyR Clock hrs. total = 880 of contact time. Plus assumes 1088 individualized study hours.
Areas of Emphasis			Percentage of total time/modules allocated to the areas of emphasis in each of the approaches		
Professional Foundations: Psychology, Sociology, Economics, History	24	NA	Intensive phase: 0 Extensive phase: 0	0	44
Curricular Contents of Preschool, Primary or Secondary Education	35	NA	Intensive phase: 50** Extensive phase: 33	0	0
General Education: Subject Matter Knowledge	10	NA	Intensive phase: 0 Extensive phase: 0	56 (combines pedagogy and subject matter content)	0

(table continues)

TABLE 2 (continued)

Teacher Education Approaches	Normal De Maestros* + Clock hrs. total= 238 (does not include individualized study hours).	Universidad Pedagogica Nacional Clock hrs. total = NA	PEAM Intensive phase = 40 hrs. Extensive phase = 60 hrs.*** Clock hrs. total = 100 for elementary teachers; and 120 for secondary teachers	PARE Clock hrs. total =293****	CEE/SECyR Clock hrs. total = 880 of contact time. Plus assumes 1088 individualized study hours.
General Pedagogy/ Teaching Methods	31 (includes courses on child development)	NA	Intensive phase: 50** Extensive phase: 67 (includes statements regarding the importance of children, parents, and community involvement in education)	44	11 (curricular innovation to incorporate contextual understandings in pupil's learning and teachers' work)
Methods and Practice of Educational Research	0	NA	0	0	45 (80% is dedicated to practice and 20%to the study of research methods)

(table continues)

TABLE 2 (continued)

Teacher Education Approaches	Normal De Maestros* + Clock hrs. total= 238 (does not include individual- ized study total = NA	Universidad Pedagógica Nacional Clock hrs.	PEAM Intensive phase = 40 hrs. Extensive phase = 60 hrs.*** Clock hrs. total = 100 for elementary teachers; and 120 for secondary teachers	PARE Clock hrs. total =293****	CEE/SECyR Clock hrs. total = 880 of contact time. Plus assumes 1088 individualized study hours.
Teaching Practice	Not explicitly mentioned. Possibly achieved through "teach- ing laboratories" course series.	NA	For both phases: Not explicitly mentioned. May assume that teachers make connections on their own since all are in-service.	Not explicitly mentioned. May assume that teachers make connections on their own since all are in-service.	Teachers are ex- pected to carry out their research projects in school cohorts" as part of their pro- gram. Not clear whether they are supervised by their in- structors.
Co-Curricular Activities	Not explicitly mentioned.	NA	For both phases: Not explicit, though mention is made of the "virtues" of teachers' work with parents, families, and community.	Not explicitly mentioned. Makes reference to extra- class activities, but these seem to allude	Not mentioned as such, though through teachers' work in their re- search projects,

(table continues)

TABLE 2 (continued)

Teacher Education Approaches	Normal De Maestros* + Clock hrs. total= 238 (does not include individualized study hours).	Universidad Pedagogica Nacional Clock hrs. total = NA	PEAM Intensive phase = 40 hrs. Extensive phase = 60 hrs.*** Clock hrs. total = 100 for elementary teachers; and 120 for secondary teachers	PARE Clock hrs. total =293****	CEE/SECyR Clock hrs. total = 880 of contact time. Plus assumes 1088 individualized study hours.
				to periods of self-instruction and individual problem solving.	they develop work with families and communities.
Internship	Not mentioned.	NA	For both phases: Not explicitly mentioned.	Not explicityly mentioned.	Not explicitly mentioned.
Examinations	"Qualitative" in characters	NA	For both phases: No references to examinations, but teachers and principals are expected to develop teaching materials, and plans for organizational change to improve educational quality.	Carefully designed diagnostic, progress, and final evaluations of the course itself and the participants as well. Clearly delineated guidelines to accomplish the course objectives,	No reference to examinations though teachers have to complete work as part of their practice-research assignments to pass the course.

(table continues)

TABLE 2 (continued)

Teacher Education Approaches	Normal De Maestros*	Universidad Pedagogica Nacional	PEAM	PARE	CEE/SECyR
	+ Clock hrs. total= 238 (does not include individualized study hours).	Clock hrs. total = NA	Intensive phase = 40 hrs. Extensive phase = 60 hrs.*** Clock hrs. total = 100 for elementary teachers; and 120 for secondary teachers	Clock hrs. total =293****	Clock hrs. total = 880 of contact time. Plus assumes 1088 individualized study hours.
				emphasizing: team and group participation, willingness to work, contributions, carrying out the proposed activities in and extra-class (20%); the results of the seven-course evaluations (20%); the final individual and written evaluations measuring understanding and application of contents (60%); attendance to all sessions.	
Methods of Instruction	Participative learning in a "democratic	NA	Intensive Phase: "Cascade" techniques to train teachers, beginning with	An instructor or "Assessor" who has been carefully	Programmed materials or "self-study guides."

(table continues)

TABLE 2 (continued)

Teacher Education Approaches	Normal De Maestros* + Clock hrs. total= 238 (does not include individualized study hours).	Universidad Pedagogica Nacional Clock hrs. total = NA	PEAM Intensive phase = 40 hrs. Extensive phase = 60 hrs.*** Clock hrs. total = 100 for elementary teachers; and 120 for secondary teachers	PARE Clock hrs. total =293****	CEE/SECyR Clock hrs. total = 880 of contact time. Plus assumes 1088 individualized study hours.
Methods of Instruction	Participative learning in a "democratic classroom environment," lectures, observations, "teaching" laboratories.	NA	Intensive Phase: "Cascade" techniques to train teachers, beginning with training of conductors, instructors, school principals, supervisors, and finally, teachers within a period of more than two months. Lectures based on guides centrally provided to all participants, programmed materials, 40 TV programs, lectures, and workshops in "teacher centers." Extensive phase: The teacher as the center for solutions of teaching-learning problems, emphasis on involving principals and teachers working together to improve school quality.	An instructor or "Assessor" who has been carefully trained and has a written guide to carry out the course in addition to the materials that are given to the course participants. The course is carried out through contact sessions, team and group work, and self-instructional time including readings, and written exercises. The experience of the teacher is seen as the beginning	Programmed materials or "self-study guides." Lectures, group work, and individual work. "Action-research" activities.

(table continues)

TABLE 2 (continued)

	Normal De Maestros* + Clock hrs. total= 238 (does not include individualized study hours).	Universidad Pedagogica Nacional Clock hrs. total = NA	PEAM Intensive phase = 40 hrs. Extensive phase = 60 hrs.*** Clock hrs. total = 100 for elementary teachers; and 120 for secondary teachers	PARE Clock hrs. total =293****	CEE/SECyR Clock hrs. total = 880 of contact time. Plus assumes 1088 individualized study hours.
Teacher Education Approaches					point for instruction. In each session of the course participants are expected to "recover" their teaching experience, analyze it, and evaluate it with help from the instructor.

* Although the percents provided here are based on the Primary Education Bachelor curricula, it is very similar to the Pre-school Education Bachelor curricula with the major difference in the area of "curricular contents" which have been developed for pre-school age children. The emphasis regarding the subjects included in the curriculum for the Normal Superior for training secondary school teachers is approximately 63% dedicated to general subject matter knowledge, 12% to specialized subject matter knowledge, 20% to foundations, and 5% to pedagogy.

+ Based on the 1984 Study Plan.

** These percents are based on my own calculations since its is not explicit in the documents I have studied.

*** Preschool and primary school teachers attend 60 hrs.of training. Secondary education teachers, principals, and supervisors attend 20 more hrs. allocated to the knowledge of "Curricular Contents," which will transform the emphasis in 50 percent dedicated to contents, and 50 percent to pedagogy.

**** Includes 35 optional hours proposed in the Module: "Written language in primary school." Does not include the hours from the module "Methodology for teaching multi-grade groups."

NA Comparative information not available for this approach.

TABLE 3 Possible Impact on the Base Knowledge of Teachers of the Five Approaches to Teacher Education in Mexico

Teacher Education Approaches	Normal de Maestros	Universidad Pedagogica Nacional	PEAM IP=Intensive phase EP=Extensive phase	PARE	CEE/SECyR
			Possible Impact of Different Teacher Education Approaches in Mexico on the Knowledge Base of Teachers:		
Knowledge Base of Teachers:					
Subject Matter Knowledge	-	-	IP - EP + ?	+	-
Curriculum Knowledge	+	?	IP + EP ?	+	-
Gnrl. Pedagogical Knowledge	+	+	+	+ ?	-
Pedagogical Content Knowledge	?	?	EP ?	+	+
Knowledge of Learners and Context	-	-	-	+	-
Knowledge of Educational Ends, Purposes and Values	?	?	EP ?	+	+

+ Positive Impact

- No Evident Impact

TABLE 4 Different Characteristics that May Increase the Impact of the Five Approaches to Teacher Education in Mexico

Teacher Education Approaches	Normal de Maestros	Universidad Pedagógica Nacional	PEAM IP=Intensive phase/ EP=Extensive phase	PARE	CEE/SECyR
Characteristics			Possible Impact of the Different Characteristics of Teacher Education Approaches in Mexico		
1) Coherence Between Stated Goals and Program Actions	-	-	IP +/ EP -	+	+
2) Comprehensive Strategy	-	-	+?	+	- ?
3) Relevance to Context	-	-	?	+	+
4) Balance of Institutional and Field Components	-	-	IP -/ EP +	+?	+?
5) Meaningful Connections with Schools and Teachers	-	-	IP ?/ EP +	+?	+?
6) Tutoring, Supervision or Follow-Up	-	-	IP -	+?	+
7) On-the-Job Training and Field-Based Programs	-	?	IP -/ EP +	+	+
8) Good Quality Self-Paced Materials	-	?	+	+	-
9) Innovative Curriculum: Problem Solving/Constructivist Approach	-	-?	IP -/ EP +	+	+
10) Preparation of Teachers and School Administrators	-	-	EP +	+	-
11) Preparation of Teacher Educators	-	-	-	+	?
12) Organized within School Improvement Efforts	-	-	IP ?/ EP +	+	+
13) Capacity for Self-Sustained Learning and Future Growth	-	-	IP ?/ EP +	+	+

+   Positive Impact
-   No Evident Impact
NA Not Applicable

materials. The tendency by teachers and educators alike to disregard *what is taught* and its implications for social equality and justice is a major short-coming of teacher education approaches not only in México but in other contexts as well (Beyer and Zeichner, 1987). Such omission may be the cause of some teachers' reluctance to use the PEAM materials in their day to day teaching.

The provision of materials to teachers and the intensive training carried out by the PEAM, for example, has proven not to be sufficient to persuade some teachers to actually use the material in the manner it was intended. In addition to the resistance expressed by some teachers to the modernization program, and teachers' lack of input in the curriculum, other factors may have influenced this outcome. Because the materials were actually delivered several weeks before the intensive phase of training was carried out there was a "discontinuity" between one and the other (a brief introduction by the supervisor or school principal regarding the nature and purpose of the materials at the moment of delivering them, may have alleviated this situation). This—according to an evaluation study carried out by PEAM—has resulted in some teachers leaving these guides and other materials in the shelves or using them only sporadically. An additional reason for this lack of use may be that the training did occur separately from the actual practice of teachers. Little effort if not at all was devoted to "critically put in context and in practice" the new curriculum. In fact during the PEAM training periods the task was more one of information about the curriculum and the modernization strategy than of giving teachers the opportunity to critically act upon curricular materials and other elements conducive to help them improve their practice.

Among the materials reviewed for this paper, the "package" prepared by the PARE seem to have been particularly successful in integrating different areas of teacher knowledge with curricular knowledge by selecting an important section of the elementary school curriculum (i.e., in mathematics teaching fractions) and treating it in depth (this we have called pedagogical content knowledge). Though the PARE's intent was not to inform teachers about the new curricular materials alone (as can be observed in Table 2), the PARE strategy does not only cover part of the curriculum but increases the likelihood that teachers *understand* the curricular topic in question (see Table 3). Even though the treatment of curricular knowledge in this manner requires a considerable time investment when designing the materials as well as when learning them, understanding the curriculum and having the possibility to critically analyze it, may increase the use that teachers make of the new developed materials. Though this approach may seem more time consuming at first, it may be possible to resort to a combination of in-service and distance education strategies such as the ones mentioned above to familiarize teachers with the curriculum helping them understand and critically analyze its contents. Similarly, teachers grass-roots efforts to improve education in their school if supported may present a good opportunity to discuss and learn more about the curriculum. Mentoring, and follow-up as well as on-the-job training seem good ve-hicles for this task. A more democratic version of the technical councils such as teacher learning groups could conceivably facilitate curriculum knowledge and discussion.

Regarding the pre-service modality (the Normal) a disproportionate amount of time seems to be allocated to learning the elementary school curriculum (35 percent of the time spent in the program) (see Table 2).[24] It is questionable whether this is a good use of time specially given the fact that the connections between the curriculum and actual teaching practice are sporadic or absent in this institutionalized setting. It is conceivable that pre-service training may be better used as a setting to gain a better mastery of the subject matter, pedagogical knowledge, and knowledge of ends, purposes and values in education. If meaningful connections between these institutions and schools are achieved, pre-service programs may be a good vehicle for acquiring pedagogical content knowledge, gaining a better grasp of the context of schooling and critically looking at what is being taught.

The Mexican in-service programs have developed a strong infrastruc-ture to keep teachers abreast of the latest curricular changes and educa-tional innovations (see Table 3). Short in service training programs and the use of the distance modality, as well as school based teacher learning groups with tutoring from teacher educators in the field, may be good vehicles to achieve this purpose in a cost-effective manner.

Teacher Education and Teachers' Pedagogical Skills

Pedagogical knowledge or skills has been defined as those principles and strategies of classroom management and organization that make pos-sible the learning and teaching of subject matter. Many teacher education programs in México and other countries allocate a large amount of their time and resources to developing teachers' pedagogical skills. This is one of the areas that figures prominently in all the approaches to educate teach-ers in México (see Table 2). The Normal de Maestros for instance allocates 31 percent of its time to teaching general pedagogy and teaching methods. The PEAM intensive phase allocates 50 percent and the extensive phase projected an allocation of 67 percent of the program's time. The PARE allo-cated 44 percent, and the CEE/SECyR program 11 percent to this area.

Although it may be important for teachers to be able to manage and organize instructional environments as well as to understand how to address the needs of complex classroom settings (i.e., such as multi-grade classrooms), the fact that this typically seems to occur independent from other areas such as subject matter knowledge should be cause for concern. The artificial separation between what teachers should know and what teachers should be able to do transforms teachers into technicians able to control behavior and organize a classroom, but who lack the essential knowledge and understanding of concepts that bring substance to their teaching. Teaching then is transformed into an uncritical task where the main goal is to cover a curriculum that sometimes teachers do not fully understand or have had any input on. Furthermore by having a heavy concentration in pedagogy at the expense of subject matter knowledge, teacher education programs sacrifice the understandings and critical thinking teachers need to help students achieve self sustained learning and problem solving capabilities.

The recognized failure of teacher education programs designed to improve the quality of teaching and learning—specifically the Normal de Maestros and the Universidad Pedagógica Nacional—in addition to school, SEP and SNTE politics, may be caused by the disproportionate time dedicated to pedagogy and curricular contents at the expense of subject matter knowledge and meaningful connections with schools and classrooms (see Table 3). The PEAM a new attempt at compensating the knowledge deficiencies detected on teachers in-service, seems to follow the same problematic pattern since this program's main emphasis is on pedagogy and on learning of curricular contents. PEAM's expectations that connections will occur with schools and classrooms through the participating teachers, supervisors, and school principals using as vehicles the Technical School Councils further decreases the likelihood of lasting change due to the difficult task of monitoring and enforce this role for the Councils. Alternative structures more organic to teacher lives in schools may facilitate the formation of forums where teachers discuss, and reflect on their practice with the goal of improving education in their schools.

The PARE also has an important emphasis on pedagogy but it does so by combining it with subject matter learning and understanding. The PARE, however, also shares some of the problematic features with the PEAM such as an over reliance on Technical School Councils.

The CEE/SECyR program attempts to link pedagogy with contextual understandings of pupil learning and teachers work. By encouraging and preparing teachers for a reflective attitude towards their practice, this program enriches the technical aspect observed in other programs by giving teachers the tools for improving their own practice.

In summary, teacher education programs in México all have developed strategies and the technology to help teachers acquire pedagogical knowledge. They have done so through pre service as well as in service approaches. These approaches however need to find connections between this knowledge and other knowledge areas, and most importantly with knowledge of subject matter.

Teacher Education and Teachers' Pedagogical Content Knowledge

A number of educators and educational researchers have argued that the manner in which teachers understand the subject and develop effective ways to teach this subject to pupils distinguishes good from bad teaching (Kennedy, 1991; Shulman, 1987). Because teachers cannot develop understandings about how to better teach the subject without previous knowledge of both subject matter and pedagogy these two are prerequisites for the former. Among the programs reviewed only one—the PARE—seems to have been able to develop teaching materials and strategies that may help teachers develop this important aspect of their role (see Tables 2 and 3). The importance given to this aspect of teacher preparation is evident by the significant amount allocated in the program (56 percent of the program's time). The PARE's philosophy based on a constructivist approach to teaching and learning may play an important part on why this is so. In order to achieve program coherence, a constructivist approach to teaching and learning requires the development of conceptual understandings of the subject matter as well as pedagogical techniques and knowledge of the students and the context where teachers teach. It also requires a vision of teachers and pupils as actors and developers of their knowledge and understandings. Therefore, for at least the two topics addressed in the PARE in Mathematics and Language, teachers have an opportunity to acquire the necessary pedagogical content knowledge. Although the PARE materials in this area are limited to only two subjects and within those two subjects to two topics, the technology and approach already developed may serve to set the basis to further pursue this approach to teacher education. The fact that these materials were developed as part of an in-service program makes them more likely to be implemented effectively if the appropriate support is given to participant teachers. The fact that the materials are self-paced may allow for use as part of a longer term distance education program aimed at providing teachers with the pedagogical content knowledge they need to teach.

Teacher Education and the Preparation of Teachers to Teach Diverse Learners

Good teaching is intrinsically interactive (Cohen, 1988; Dewey, 1938; Freire, 1989; Lampert, 1985). In order to provide successful learning experiences for students, teachers need to constantly seek feedback from them and to plan their teaching in a flexible manner to accommodate different needs and learning styles. In a traditionally centralized educational system such as Mexico's with standard curriculum and textbooks, it is the teacher who carries the responsibility for pupils to see relevance in what they learn. The teacher becomes in this sense the only flexible vehicle through which students will make sense of their learning experience. Moreover Mexico's diverse student population and multi-grade classroom arrangements makes it a priority for teachers to learn how to develop strategies that will allow them to address students needs through the curriculum, and to manage productively the diversity in their classrooms.

To fulfill the reform aims of encouraging an active involvement of the community in the school, teachers also need to know the dynamics of their classroom and school contexts, as well as those of the community where the school is located.

The importance of helping teachers understand their student's as well as their immediate and mediate contexts should not be underestimated. According to recent statistics, Mexican teachers who work in rural or remote areas show a high rate of absenteeism which may be due in part to the lack of familiarity with contexts different from those where they grew up or where they learned to teach.[25]

Among the programs reviewed, all of the in service approaches have goals that include statements referring to the "virtues of teacher's work with parents, families, and communities," in attempts at familiarizing teachers with the community and to get to know their students in a deeper more significant manner (see Table 3). The CEE/SECyR program, however, specifically dedicates a large part of their program to this enterprise (see Table 2). The program incorporates efforts to develop curricular innovations using as a starting point teacher's understanding of learners and their cultural and social context (allocating an 11 percent of the program's time to this area. Furthermore this program trains teachers to act as reflective practitioners increasing the possibility for a closer "match" between what students learn at school and their experiences in their community (allocating 45 percent of the programs time to this activity). The program is specifically directed at teachers in rural or poor communities and aims to use their experience in these schools to help them develop better understandings of the pupils and places where they work.

Other programs such as the PARE includes in its curriculum a module dealing explicitly with management of multi-grade groups. In addition and as part of its comprehensive strategy to improving education in the most disadvantaged regions in the country, the PARE involves the community in the implementation and monitoring of the teacher's incentive system through which teachers receive an additional salary.

The PEAM extensive phase planned to encourage teachers, principals and supervisors, through class assignments and conversations, to think about a new design for the school organization to involve parents, families, and community in improving the quality of education.

The pre-service Normal de Maestros, includes in its curriculum courses on child development and other psychological approaches to understand children. It is unclear, however, how—if at all—these understandings are incorporated into curricular innovations or how teachers are expected to use them in classroom management.

Although it may be assumed that teachers get to know their students and families by the mere act of teaching and being in the school, actual understandings of pupils' learning needs and the incorporation of these understandings to curricular and classroom practice needs to be guided and constantly re-evaluated. Strategies for facilitating learning of this knowledge on teachers may be on-the-job-training, supervised practice and follow-up in combination with seminars and the use of videos for analyzing teacher-student interactions.

Similarly getting to know the immediate and mediate contexts of schools requires a combination of field experiences as well as periods of reflection that could be provided through seminars, workshops, or through conversations with teacher educators, or supervisors.

Teacher Education and Teachers' Understandings of the Educational Ends, Purposes, and Values Involved in Teachers' Practice

Knowledge of the philosophical and historical basis underlying the ends, purposes and values of education in a particular context is essential for teachers' conceptualization of their role, and in a country as large and diverse as México, for nation building and cohesiveness (Feinberg and Soltis, 1985). Furthermore, understanding the ends and purposes of education provides teachers with a framework to guide their teaching. Developing understandings in this area may help teachers negotiate their status vis a vis authorities and union leaders. A recent study on the teaching force in México, reports that among the population of teachers surveyed, teachers' perception of their role is more that of a blue collar worker than of a professional in education (Farres and Noriega, 1993). The tension that exists regarding the proletarian versus the professional character of teaching is a historical one and has been extensively manipulated. The government offers teachers the promise of professionalism in exchange for loyalty and compliance however teachers' proletarian status rarely changes. In the rhetoric of the PME (Programa de Modernización Educativa), teachers are referred to as professionals and as initiators and promoters of educational and social change, and the new approaches to educate teachers are said to reinforce such role. Structures within schools, however, continue to control the work of teachers without truly providing them with the space and opportunity to participate as actors in school improvement, school governance, and professional development. This situation runs against the rhetoric of the current educational reform stated as raising the status of teachers as that of professionals by helping them become more reflective and "the central actors in their own transformation process" (Farres and Noriega, 1993, p. 17). Although it is clear that the proletarian versus professional character of the teaching profession in México runs deeper than the rhetoric of current educational reforms may reach, it is possible that by understanding in more depth the history and philosophy behind education teachers may have a more solid base to make professional decisions that are congruent with their role as children advocates. These understandings, however, are rarely acquired through readings or lectures alone. A reflective process in which practice and theory merge are more appropriate settings for the development of these concepts.

The philosophical and historical basis of education is an area that figures prominently in the pre-service training curriculum (the Normal de Maestros) (see Table 2). However, because teaching in this program has been characterized as traditional and divorced from practice it is not known whether and how teacher candidates apply this information to their teaching practice and their professional lives.

Whereas the Normal de Maestros deals with these foundations at a more theoretical level, the CEE/SECyR program, connects theory and practice. The CEE/SECyR program, allocates 44 percent of its time to the discussion and understanding of history, philosophy, and sociology, among others and how these relate to education, to teachers, and to their work (see Table 2). After going through this program teachers themselves express a new sense of self and of their role in community, school, and classroom contexts (Fierro, Farres and Irene, n.d.). The CEE/SECyR program has therefore developed and implemented a program that seems to have been successful at helping teachers improve their knowledge and insights in this area. Future innovations in teacher education in México may want to explore the possibilities for adopting this model.

The PEAM and PARE in-service programs, do not treat these contents directly in their curriculum. Three obvious reasons for this are the limited time frame in which these programs attempt to reach teachers, the assumption that teachers already posses such knowledge, and the belief that knowledge and understandings of philosophy and history are not as relevant for teacher's performance given the current knowledge needs of Mexican teachers (see Table 3). In addition given the current politicized character that surrounds teachers and teaching, SEP and union elites may have decided to leave that terrain untouched.

Expanding the time frame for in-service teacher training may allow the incorporation of this important area into the curriculum and if complemented with tutoring and in school discussion may provide excellent opportunities for teachers to acquire this knowledge. Self-paced materials can serve this purpose in combination with seminars or workshops as well as with conversations among teacher educators, teachers and other school personnel.

Throughout this paper we have discussed how teacher education needs to be re conceptualized in order to better support teachers' work. Our main foci has been the analysis of teacher education's contribution to teacher knowledge and skills as essential factors teachers need in order to appropriately enact their role within a politically turbulent and hierarchically organized context. In what is left of this paper we further explore the conditions that may account for the differential responsiveness of the approaches reviewed to teachers' needs in the Mexican context.

Plausible Policy Alternatives to Increase Teacher Education's Contributions to Teachers' Professional Knowledge and Skills

The approaches to teacher education in México that seem to more fully respond to the professional needs of teachers (PARE, PEAM, and CEE/SECyR) share a number of characteristics that are distinctive of approaches that have proven effective according to the research literature (Tatto, 1993) (see Table 4). Findings from research on teacher education indicate that a strong sense of purpose in programs that educate teachers may have an important impact on future performance and dispositions (Tatto, Kennedy and Schmidt, 1992). One of the problems that have been widely acknowledged regarding teacher education in México is what seems to be the duplication of purposes and curricula across a number of programs. The UPN program seems to duplicate what others do, such as the approach offered by the Normales, yet knowledge of subject matter and reflection over what is taught for instance, seem to go largely unattended. Similarly, the programs created by the CAM's seem to be quite large, and disjointed. In contrast—and likely because of its historically distinctive origin—the newer PARE, PEAM, and CEE/SECyR programs present a higher degree of coherence between goals and actions (see Table 4, line 1).

It is clear through a number of studies reported in the literature that issues of teacher quality cannot be resolved through teacher education programs alone (Tatto, 1993). A comprehensive strategy to improve the qual-

ity of teaching is necessary. In addition to training teachers, other support-
ive mechanisms such as incentive packages, on-the-job support strategies
implemented through principals, teachers, school based teacher groups,
and change in the organizational structures of schools among others may
help improve the quality of teaching. The PEAM and the PARE both resort
to a number of strategies such as the Carrera Magisterial,[26] in and out of
school support, and the provision of materials and other resources to help
improve teaching and learning.[27] The CEE/SECyR has linked training with
promotion mechanisms as well as the development of informal structures
of collegiality within schools to support teachers innovations while they
attempt to improve their practice (see Table 4, line 2). By mutually reinforcing each other, these strategies—albeit with some problems and limitations—may bring some improvement to the quality of teaching in México.

The lack of understanding of the context and lack of developed abilities by teachers to deal with unexpected or unfamiliar circumstances has
proven to contribute to teacher's sense of ineffectiveness and failure in challenging situations, poor teacher performance, high rates of teacher absenteeism and lack of commitment to the profession (Mitchell, Ortiz, and
Mitchell, 1987; Moore-Johnson, 1990). The PARE and the CEE/SECyR programs have developed specific strategies to attend to the needs of those
teachers who work in rural and difficult areas. PARE materials have been
designed to help teachers develop skills for multi-grade teaching, and both
programs include a strong emphasis in the development of positive and
productive relationships with parents and the larger school community
and the PEAM extensive phase includes similar provisions (see Table 4,
line 3). Understanding and working in collaboration with the school community may support teachers' work and increase their—and their pupils'—
possibilities for success in the classroom.

Prospective and experienced teachers need both class time to understand and assimilate new knowledge, and opportunities to apply what they
are learning, while critically reflecting on both the theory and practice of
teaching. Given the large number of teachers to be trained and Mexico's
large territory, a realistic way to achieve the desired balance between classroom and field experiences seems to be provided by the new models of in
service teacher education such as the PARE, the planned PEAM extensive
phase, and the CEE/SECyR (see Table 4, line 4). In all these programs a
combination of face to face contact with instructors and current school teaching seem to present the conditions conducive to learning and applying
new teaching knowledge. The fact that the conditions are present, however, does not guarantee that the "connections" between learning and practice will occur. Teachers need guidance for these connections to be meaningful in their learning process and for critically reflecting upon them. In

the materials reviewed for this paper for each one of the programs, it was difficult to find evidence that teachers are receiving guidance of this type (see Table 4, line 5).

According to research in teacher education, in both pre-service and in-service programs, tutoring or follow-up during and after training seem to be effective in helping teachers make the transition between what they have learned in their preparation program and its application in the classroom (Tatto, 1993). Usually teacher educators are in a good position to do this task, however principals or supervisors can take on this role provided they have had at least the same or a higher level of preparation than that of the teachers. In addition, principals and supervisors need to be sensitized as to the most productive and collaborative ways to provide feedback to teachers, including a more participatory and democratic style of governance in schools and a more critical perspective over the curriculum they teach.

Both the PARE, and the PEAM in the intensive and specially in the planned extensive phase, have envisioned the training of supervisors and principals in an attempt to make them partners with teachers in the learning process, as well as to facilitate a shift in their conception from their role as administrators to that as "instructional leaders." The perpetuation so far of the traditionally hierarchical structures of schools may make this objective less attainable (see Table 4, lines 6 and 7).

The effectiveness, format, cost, and coverage of a teacher education approach are all important elements to consider for the continuity of a program (Tatto et al., 1993). Although distance education approaches in a number of countries have proven a viable alternative, the traditionally oral culture prevalent among Mexico's most disadvantaged populations represents a challenge for an approach with a heavy reliance on documents. Nevertheless, the development of good quality self-paced materials such as the ones prepared by the PARE, and the CEE/SECyR programs, and for the PEAM projected extensive phase, as well as continuous face-to-face contact with the teachers may enhance the possibilities of developing a variant of a distance approach to teacher education with relatively low costs (in part because of the economies of scale, and in part because of the strong infrastructure that has been developed as seen in the three in-service programs recently implemented in México).

Although the UPN has been operating a distance education program for teacher upgrading for some time, this program does not seem to be specially successful or appropriate to fulfill the most urgent educational needs of teachers such as subject matter learning. Important lessons however may be learned by examining the UPN experience (see Table 4, line 8).

In summary, planning a comprehensive strategy to develop the capacities of teacher education institutions, schools and their personnel for self sustained learning, needs to be seen as a first and essential step towards improving the quality of education. This is specially important when there is a concerted national movement towards the development and implementation of an innovative curriculum focused towards problem solving and following a constructivist approach to teaching and learning. The development of these capacities does not only require the initial training of teachers but also of school personnel and their supervisors recognizing the potential for team work and democratic school governance. In addition the development of collegial structures within and outside the school may provide spaces for self-reflection and discussion that seem essential in helping teachers and schools improve their practice. In the PARE and in the PEAM, a conscientious attempt has been made to involve principals and supervisors in the teacher education dynamics by both providing them with specific skills to improve their performance, and by asking them to serve as the actual educators of teachers. Collaborative work among teachers along with the shift in the role of principals and supervisors is expected to stimulate teacher growth, school reorganization, and improvement. Similarly, the CEE/SECyR program attempts to develop connections between teacher education and the day to day workings of the school with the expectation that these will continue after the teacher education period is over. In contrast with what can be seen as the more "organic" approach to teacher education and school improvement followed by these three programs discussed above, both the Normales and the UPN seem to lack the infrastructure that would allow them to help teachers and school administrators to develop the much needed capacity for self-sustained school improvement (Table 4, lines 9, 10, 11, 12 and 13).

Conclusions

While teacher education has remained dormant for more than half a century reflecting in part the stagnant status of teachers, the State has recently begun a vigorous effort to educate teachers without precedent in México. Although a number of policy options have been used to improve teachers' knowledge and skills, these options may not lead to an effective improvement of teaching in México if previous and current experiences with teacher education are not systematically and comparatively recovered. Our preliminary analysis of teacher education's past and current innovations revealed six problematic trends that potentially contradict and may defeat the purposes of the current teacher education reform: (1) the lack of emphasis on teacher education programs on subject matter learning and subject matter pedagogy; (2) the lack of tutoring mechanisms in teacher education and in schools to help teachers implement in classrooms what they have learned in their preparation programs; (3) the lack of teacher input in the design of teacher education programs; (4) the lack of preparation provided by teacher education programs regarding how teachers can effectively bring input in the curriculum and in the development of strategies to re-organize and govern their schools; (5) the little attention given to the education of teacher educators in the new curricular innovations and new pedagogy promoted by the reform; and (6) potential contradictions involved in implementing reform mandates encouraging professionalism in teachers on the one hand while in the other tacitly supporting the historically dominant top-down structures of authority within schools and the SEP. Given the highly political environment surrounding teachers and teacher education in Mexico, unless decision making is guided by systematic knowledge about teacher education effectiveness, policy on the education of teachers may continue to evolve in an ad hoc manner and the quality of teacher preparation and teaching may remain weak.

The views expressed here are those of the authors, and should not be attributed to the World Bank. The interpretation of the information contained in the documents analyzed are the sole responsibility of the authors. We gratefully acknowledge the help of Eva Hicks, consultant, and Silvia Schmelkes and Lesvia O. Rosas from the Centro de Estudios Educativos. We thankfully acknowledge the helpful comments of Susan Street, and three anonymous reviewers.

Notes

1. For a detailed account of the educational reform and its dynamics see Prawda (1989) and Prawda (1985). The tendency to improve educational quality in México is not unlike those in other early industrialized countries where expansion of their educational systems after World War II, was made at the expense of quality. See Fuller (1985) and Fuller (1986).

2. Salinas De Gortari (1988) gave a high priority to teaching as part of his agenda developed during his term as president in the last six years. The new Mexican President Ernesto Zedillo also from the Institutional Revolutionary Party (PRI) is expected to continue a similar policy regarding education after assuming power in December 1, 1994; moreover Zedillo himself helped design the educational agenda as one of the four Secretaries of Education appointed during the Salinas government.

3. The latest wave of educational reform in México reflects world-wide trends towards improving the quality of education after a period of expansion to increase

educational access, and consequently focuses in improving the knowledge and skills of teachers (see Meyer, Nagel and Snyder (1993), for an illustration of world-wide explanations of educational expansion). The recognition that high quality teaching is an important element in the improvement of the quality of basic education has world-wide acceptance. See for example Biniakunu (1982); Dove (1982); Chapman and Snyder (1989); Fuller, and Snyder (1991); Henderson (1978); Tatto, Nielsen, Cummings, Kularatna, and Dharmadasa (1993); Verspoor and Leno (1986).

4.   The national teachers' union or SNTE organizes a large number of the federal teachers in México and is an important and powerful political force in México's educational arena. The union under the leadership of one single individual for many decades, collaborated with the government in developing and implementing policy in education. The SNTE has been recognized by educational scholars as managed by few leaders in the top and as giving little or no representation to teachers' concerns. For a more extensive treatment of these issues see Street (1992a) and for a detailed discussion of SNTE and its dissident group the CNTE dynamics see Loyo (1992). Also see Ginsburg (1995).

5.   Empirical research on teacher education is currently being done by the Departamento de Investigaciones Educativas del Centro de Investigación y de Estudios Avanzados del Instituto Politécnico Nacional (D.I.E.) but only on the PARE Program. One of the four Secretaries of Education during the Salinas regime was Ernesto Zedillo who is Mexico's currently president. Empirical research on educational institutions would be equivalent to an evaluation of Zedillo's former actions/ agenda.

6.   See the series of BRIDGES studies on teacher education in Sri Lanka (Tatto et al., 1993); in Indonesia (Nielsen and Tatto, 1992); and in Pakistan (Warwick, 1992).

7.   While for the purposes of this paper we look at the different approaches to educate teachers from an "ideal" teacher education perspective, the historical significance of the different approaches should not be overlooked. Particularly the Normal Schools have played an important role in the formation of a national teaching force as it currently exists in México.

8.   The large number of organizations, programs, and courses developed to provide the necessary education for new and experienced teachers has created confusion, inefficiencies, and duplication of tasks. The creation in 1979 of the National Advisory Council of Normal Education (CONACEN) was an unsuccessful effort to facilitate the coordination of initial and in-service training mechanisms (World Bank, 1991).

9.   Reformers argue that a valuable outcome of the Programa de Modernización Educativa or PME's vision is the National Agreement regarding the Modernization of Basic Education which represents a commitment between the Federal, State governments and the National Teacher's Union to work together to improve educational access and quality.

10. There are currently 341 Normal Schools. Ninety-four are federal operated, 134 are state operated, and 113 are private with either federal or state affiliation. Among these about 39 percent train preschool teachers, 58 percent train primary education teachers, 27 percent train secondary education teachers, and 8 percent and 7 percent train physical and special education teachers respectively. These are classified into urban, rural, experimental, or regional centers.

11. There are 74 units distributed around the country which provide the Licenciatura or bachelor's degree in basic education, pre-school and primary education through distance education and partially institutionalized education.

12. For example the SNTE's plan included a large university that would be part of the Normal Schools' network with a traditional bachelors degree and a conventional pedagogy whereas the SEP's vision included a smaller university with a carefully planned growth that operated in a distinctive way from the Normal Schools with an innovative and modernist orientation to the bachelors degree and a focus departing from the traditional pedagogy that dominated education in these schools (Pescador and Torres, 1985).

13. For a more detailed discussion of the very complex dynamics regarding the UPN see Pescador and Torres (1985), Street (1992a), and Street (1992b).

14. The SNTE provides a guaranteed position in schools to teachers from the Normales after graduation but not so to the graduates of the UPN.

15. The Technical Council is usually conformed by the teachers in a particular school, the principal and the supervisor, and is expected to function as the school governance mechanism. There are also technical councils for a school sector, zone, and for particular schools. Justa Ezpeleta (1991) a Mexican scholar points out these councils are not organic to the day-to-day workings of the school, they require from teachers to do extra work with little or no extra pay, and lack many teachers conviction of its relevance and usefulness.

16. Under the responsibility of SEP's General Directorate of Normal Education and Teacher Upgrading or DGENAM.

17. In this way the government advances its modernization agenda under the symbolic policy of professionalization of the teaching force. Accordingly it is questionable whether teachers actually acquired or whether provisions will be made in the future for them to acquire new professional knowledge under this program. This is especially true given that the program has already fulfilled its "political mission."

18. This phase was to be implemented from July to September 1993 but was still in the planning stages as of June of 1993. As of September 1994 the extensive phase was never implemented and it is likely that it will never be implemented.

19. Interview with PRGO2.

20. See Street (1992b) for a historically oriented perspective.

21. See Ginsburg and Tidwell (1990), for an analysis of teacher education's influence on the political views of teachers in México.

22. Although we do not have empirical confirmation of this aspect since the S.E.P. has just recently tested the teachers and the information is not available yet, the dramatically low achievement level reported of pupils in the study carried out by the SICEM (Sistema de Información de la Calidad de la Educación en México) mentioned above cannot be blamed entirely on the student. The teacher and most importantly the system, share responsibility for such failure. Furthermore the teachers are themselves graduates of such schools which seems to perpetuate and multiply the problem.

23. See Tatto and Kularatna (1993), where the authors describe a distance education approach which relies on well designed self-paced study materials and tutors (usually field instructors from teacher education institutions) to provide needed feedback and guidance during the training period.

24. Farres and Noriega argue that only 10 percent of the program's time is allocated to the actual mastering of the "contents of elementary education" (Farres and Noriega, 1993, p. 16). This is what I have called knowledge of subject matter and my calculations are consistent with those of the CEE researchers. In addition the Normal program does include time (35 percent) to acquaint the student with the primary education *curriculum* which does not guarantee teachers' conceptual understandings of the subjects they will teach.

25. Another factor may be the lack of appropriate incentives to work in rural or remote/difficult to access areas.

26. The carrera magisterial represents a system of horizontal promotion to raise the status of the teaching force and the quality of teaching by moving away from the seniority criteria as the only mechanism for promotion and salary increases to one of professional development and improved classroom performance. It is directed to: classroom teachers, principals, supervisors, and teachers with commissions, and teachers involved in education/technical activities. The carrera magisterial has five steps in the promotion ladder: (1) Evaluation of teachers' professional performance; (2) Accumulation of credits in the "professional development" courses (includes upgrading courses regarding knowledge of the curricular changes and the new study programs, as well as professional development courses); (3) Seniority in the system; (4) Academic preparation; (5) Seniority as teacher. In addition the S.E.P. has determined that in order for teachers to receive credit in this system they need to present an assessment of their knowledge and skills through an exam administer by the S.E.P. Teachers are to be monitored as to their regular attendance to and performance in the courses in order to be promoted to the following level.

27. The problematic nature of a meritocratic system of promotion and salary raises has already been discussed in this paper and by others in different contexts see Moore-Johnson (1984). The adoption and impact of the carrera magisterial, however, should be judged against Mexican teachers' low levels of education, poor living and working conditions within the highly politicized and centralized Mexican context vis a vis the conditions of teachers in more industrialized countries such as the U.S.

References

Beyer, L. and Zeichner, K. 1987. "Teacher Education in Cultural Context: Beyond Reproduction," in T. Popkewitz, ed., *Critical Studies in Teacher Education*. Pp. 298-334. Philadelphia, PA: The Falmer Press.

Biniakunu, D. D. 1982. "Inservice Teacher Training Improves Eighth Graders' Reading Ability in Zaire." *Journal of Reading* 25(7): 662-665.

Centro de Estudios Educativos. 1990. *Proyecto Inter-Regional para la mejora de los servicios de educación primaria. Diseño del Estudio para México* (México, D.F.: Centro de Estudios Educativos).

Chapman, D. and Snyder, C. 1989. *Is Teacher Training Associated with Teachers' Classroom Behavior in the Third World?* (Unpublished manuscript). Albany: State University of New York, School of Education.

Cohen, D. 1988. "Knowledge of Teaching: Plus que ça Change ...," in P. Jackson, ed., *Contributing to Educational Change*. Pp. 27-84. Berkeley, CA: McCutchan.

Densmore, K. 1987. "Professionalism, Proletarianization and Teacher Work," in T. Popkewitz, ed., *Critical Studies in Teacher Education*. Pp. 130-160. Philadelphia, PA: The Falmer Press.

Departamento de Investigaciones Educativas del Centro de Investigación y de Estudios Avanzados (D.I.E.). 1990. *Educación Básica: La Reforma como un Proceso Integral* (Documents DIE, 18). México, DF: Instituto Politécnico Nacional .

Dewey, J. 1938. *Experience and Education*. New York: Macmillan.

Dove, L. 1982. "The Deployment and Training of Teachers for Remote Rural Schools in Less-Developed Countries." *International Review of Education*. Hamburg: UNESCO Institute for Education.

Ezpeleta, J. 1991. *Sobre las funciones del consejo técnico: Eficacia pedagógica y estructura de poder en la escuela primaria*, México, D.F.: Departamento de Investigaciones Educativas, Centro de Investigación y estudios avanzados del Instituto Politécnico Nacional.

Farres, P. and Noriega, C. April 1993. *Estudio Exploratorio sobre el Magisterio*. (mimeo) México, D.F.: Centro de Estudios Educativos.

Feinberg, W. and Soltis, J. 1985. *School and Society*. New York: Teachers College Press.

Fierro, C. 1991. *Ser maestro rural. ¿Una labor imposible?* México: Secretaría de Educación Pública, Libros del Rincón.

Fierro, C., Farres, P., and Irene, J. (n.d.). *Informe final del programa de especialidad en investigación educativa y docencia*. México, D.F.: Centro de Estudios Educativos.

Freire, P. 1989. *Pedagogy of the Oppressed*. New York: Continuum.

Fuller, B. and Snyder, C. W. 1991. Vocal Teachers, Silent Pupils? Life in Botswana Classrooms. *Comparative Education Review* 35: 274-294.

Fuller, B. 1985. *Raising School Quality in Developing Countries. What Investments Boost Learning?* (Staff working paper). Washington, DC: The World Bank .

Fuller, B. 1986. Is Primary School Quality Eroding in the Third World?" *Comparative Education Review* 30: 491-507.

Ginsburg, M. and Tidwell, M. 1990. "Political Socialization of Prospective Educators in México: The Case of the University of Veracruz," *New Education* 12(2): 70-82.

Ginsburg, M. 1995. "Contradictions, Resistance, and Incorporation in the Political Socialization of Educators in México," in M. Ginsburg and Lindsay, B., eds., *The Political Dimension in Teacher Education*, Garland.

Henderson, E. S. 1978. *The Evaluation of Inservice Teacher Training.* London: Croom Helm.

Hicks, G. E. 1993. *Estudio evaluativo sobre actualización de maestros e incentivos al docente del programa para abatir el rezago educativo (PARE)* (Reporte final, mimeo). México, D.F.: Consejo Nacional de Fomento Educativo y Banco Mundial.

Kennedy, M. 1991. "Policy Issues in Teacher Education." *Phi Delta Kappan* 72: 658-665.

Lampert, M. 1985. How do Teachers Manage to Teach? Perspectives on Problems in Practice. *Harvard Educational Review* 55: 178-194.

Loyo, A. 1992. "Modernización educativa o modernización del aparato educativo?" *Revista Mexicana de Sociología*, Mexico, D.F.: Instituto de Investigaciones Sociales-UNAM 2: 339-349.

Meyer, J., Nagel, J., and Snyder, C. 1993. The Expansion of Mass Education in Botswana: Local and World Society Perspectives. *Comparative Education Review* 37(4): 454-475.

Mitchell, D., Ortiz, F., and Mitchell, T. 1987. *Work Orientation and Job Performance. The Cultural Basis of Teaching Rewards and Incentives.* New York: State University of New York Press

Moore-Johnson, S. 1984. "Merit Pay for Teachers: A Poor Prescription for Reform," *Harvard Educational Review* 54(2): 175-85.

Moore-Johnson, S. 1990. *Teachers at Work. Achieving Success in Our Schools.* New York: Basic Books.

Pescador, J. A. and Torres, C. A. 1985. *Poder político y educación en México.* México, D.F.: UTHEA, p. 20-21.

Prawda, J. 1985. *Teoría y praxis de la planeación educativa en México.* México, D.F.: Grijalbo.

Prawda, J. 1989. *Logros, inequidades y retos del futuro del sistema educativo Mexicano.* México, D.F.: Grijalbo.

Rockwell, E. and Mercado R. 1986. *La escuela, lugar del trabajo docente*, México: Departamento de Investigaciones Educativas, Centro de Investigación y estudios avanzados del Instituto Politécnico Nacional.

Salinas De Gortari, C. 1988. *Plan Nacional de Desarrollo 1988-1994* (National Development Plan 1988-1994). México, D.F.: Presidencia de la República. Policy document.

Secretaría de Educación Pública (S.E.P.). 1990. *Programa de Formación y Actualización de Docentes* (Program for instructing and upgrading teachers) PEAM. México, D.F: Secretaría de Educación Pública .

Secretaría de Educación Pública (S.E.P.). 1991. *La Evaluación en las Instituciones que Forman y Actualizan Docentes: La experiencia de las escuelas normales* (Evaluation of institutions that train and upgrade teachers: The experience of the Normal Schools). México, D.F.: Consejo Nacional Consultivo de Educación Normal.

Secretaría de Educación Pública (S.E.P.). 1992a. *El Programa Emergente de Actualización del Maestro* (PEAM) (Program for teacher upgrading). México, D.F.: Coordinación Nacional del Programa Emergente de Actualización del Maestro.

Secretaría de Educación Pública (S.E.P.). 1992b. Guía de apoyo para el conductor (Support guide for teacher trainers). PEAM. México, D.F.: Secretaría de Educación Pública.

Secretaría de Educación Pública (S.E.P.). 1992c. *Informe del Seguimiento de las fases preparatoria e intensiva del programa emergente de actualización del maestro* (follow-up report for the preparatory and intensive phases of the teacher upgrading program PEAM). PEAM. México, D.F.: Coordinacion Nacional del Programa Emergente de Actualización del Maestro.

Secretaría de Educación Pública (S.E.P.). 1992d. *La lengua escrita en la educación primaria* (Written language in Primary Education). Manual del asesor y Documento del Docente. PARE. México, D.F.: Secretaría de Educación Pública.

Secretaría de Educación Pública (S.E.P.). 1992e. *La matemática en la educación primaria* (Mathematics in Primary Education). Manual del asesor y Documento del Docente. PARE. México, D.F.: Secretaría de Educación Pública.

Secretaría de Educación Pública (S.E.P.). 1992f. *Manejo de grupos multigrado* (Multigrade groups management). Manual del asesor y Documento del Docente. PARE.México, D.F.: Secretaría de Educación Pública.

Secretaría de Educación Pública (S.E.P.). 1992g. *Recursos para el aprendizaje* (Resources for learning). Manual del asesor y Documento del Docente. PARE. México, D.F.: Secretaría de Educación Pública.

Secretaría de Educación Pública (S.E.P.). 1993a. *La evaluación en la educación primaria* (Assessment in Primary Education). Manual del asesor y Documento del Docente. Programa para Abatir el Rezago Educativo (PARE). México, D.F.: Secretaría de Educación Pública.

Secretaría de Educación Pública (S.E.P.). 1993b. *Pedagogía. Teoría y práctica educativa* (Pedagogy, theory and educational practice). Guía del asesor y Guía del Estudiante. PARE-UPN. México, D.F.: Secretaría de Educación Pública.

Secretaría de Educación Pública (S.E.P.). 1993c. *Programa de Actualización del Maestro. Documento de Información General* (Program for teacher upgrading. General Information document). PAM. México, D.F.: Secretaría de Educación Pública.

Secretaría de Educación Pública (S.E.P.). 1993d. *Síntesis de Actividades 1992-1993* (PEAM Summary of activities 1992-1993). PEAM. México, D.F.: Coordinacion Nacional del Programa Emergente de Actualización del Maestro.

Shulman, L. 1987. "Knowledge and Teaching: Foundations of the New Reform," *Harvard Educational Review* 57: 1-22.

Street, S. 1992a. "El SNTE y la política educativa: 1970-1990," *Revista Mexicana de Sociología*. Mexico, D.F.: Instituto de Investigaciones Sociales-UNAM 2: 45-72.

Street, S. 1992b. "Maestros en Movimiento. Transformaciones en la Burocracia Estatal (1978-1982)," Mexico, D.F.: Centro de Investigaciones y Estudios Superiores de Antropologia Social.

Tatto, M. T. 1993. "Policies for Teachers Working in the Periphery: An International Review of the Literature," in W. Cummings, ed., *Reaching Peripheral Groups: Community, Language and Teachers in the Context of Development*. Pp. 57-124 (Special Studies in Comparative Education, No. 31). Buffalo, NY: State University of New York.

Tatto M. T., Nielsen, H. D., Cummings, W. C., Kularatna, N. G. and Dharmadasa, D. H. 1993. "Comparing the Effectiveness and Costs of Different Approaches for Educating Primary School Teachers in Sri Lanka," *Teaching and Teacher Education. An International Journal of Research and Studies* 9(1): 41-64.

Tatto, M. T. and Kularatna, N. G. 1993. "The Interpersonal Dimension of Teacher Education: Comparing Distance Education with Two Other Programs in Sri Lanka," *International Journal of Educational Research* 19(8): 755-778.

Tatto, M. T., Kennedy, M. and Schmidt, W. 1992, April. *Understanding the Core and Challenges of Teacher Education: An Analysis of Faculty, Experienced and Prospective Teacher's Views of Teaching, Learning, and Learning to Teach*. Paper presented at the Annual meeting of the American Educational Research Association, San Francisco, CA.

Torres, C.A. 1990. *The Politics of Non-formal Education in Latin America*. New York: Praeger.

UNESCO. 1986. *School Based Inservice Training: A Handbook*. Bangkok, Thailand: Regional Office for Education in Asia and the Pacific.

Verspoor, A. M. and Leno, J. L. 1986, November. *Improving Teaching: A Key to Successful Educational Change. Lessons from the World Bank Experience*. Paper presented at the Annual International Movement Towards Educational Change Seminar, Bali, Indonesia .

World Bank. 1991. *Basic Education in Mexico: Trends, Issues, and Policy Recommendations* (Report No. 8930-ME). Washington, DC: Human Resources Operations Division, Country Department II, Latin America and the Caribbean Regional Office.

PART THREE

Higher Education in Latin America: Argentina in Comparative Perspective

8

The Paradox of the Autonomy of Argentine Universities: From Liberalism to Regulation

Marcela Mollis

University autonomy refers to the capacity of university institutions to self-govern. However, this definition does describe the complexity of the political, normative and organizational, and its practical consequences for the Argentine institutions. Part of that complexity remains because "autonomy" is not a self-explanatory concept. It arises from multiple interpretations of actors with divergent interests, which enrich the concept with multiple historical meanings.

This chapter will intend to show the incidence of diverse historical meanings in the Argentine university autonomy through the process of building its organizational identity. To achieve this purpose, the dynamic interaction between actors and interests (individuals and public) shaping the present state of the university autonomy in Argentina, will be introduced. The inner changes produced from the liberal conceptualization of university autonomy to the regulated concept of autonomy recently prescribed in the promulgated Law of Higher Education in Argentina will also be discussed.

The University Autonomy: A History of Dependence of the Medieval Powers

Universities, traditionally, like churches, have usually had a degree of autonomy from political and economic control that is quite remarkable, partly because they have been protected by the upper classess, however, constituted, at nearly all times in almost every society. They have on ocassion, through what has gone on within them, helped to change the world but have themselves been much less changed than most of the rest of the world (Kerr, C. 1994:45).

University autonomy was not only provided as a constitutive characteristic of medieval institutions of higher learning but it helped in shaping its ecumenical and universalistic tradition as well. Based on an analysis of the relationship between autonomy and public powers (empires, principalities, communes, etc.), it is necessary to go back to the birth of universities in the Twelfth Century. The creation of the University of Bologna (the university of students) it is particularly relevant to understand the organizational model of the Argentine University Reform movement in 1918, basically because it gave students so much influence and power that dominated faculty organization.

In medieval times intellectuals organized themselves, as members of any other medieval guild, and identified with a forum that provided them with corporative privileges to act with certain independence. The University whether of masters or of students, was only a particular kind of guild (Rashdall, 1936:97 in Clark, B.1977:8).

In the case of the University of Bologna, given its imperial origin, it gained independence from the power of the Church and other local powers. That is how some universities began to develop a "constitutive autonomy," that is to say, an autonomy that was intrinsic to, a precondition for the development of their medieval nature as corporations of higher learning. They gained autonomy with respect to certain powers enjoying a set of corporative privileges, and also depending exclusively from the public power that allowed them those same privileges. There were historical tensions, however.

As Burton Clark describes in the case of old Italian universities:

> The towns, no longer to be intimidated by threats of secession, took over basic control from without, while the masters, now permanently employed by the state, where no longer dependent of students and student approval for their income. What had been an essentially commercial relationship bettween buyers and sellers of service was replaced by a more hierarchical one, based on state support of the professor, in which the consuming student was now subordinate (Cobban, 1971:35, in Clark, B, 1977:10).

Historically considered, university autonomy does not mean total independence from all power. On the contrary, it does imply a relationship of searching for legitimacy between actors with a determined "vocation including scholars, students, and representatives of the public power" (Le Goff, 1983).

Universities institutionally considered, emerged by the hand of the public powers as corporations, sought to achieve a monopoly of schooling, and particularly a monopoly in granting degrees, that put them against the authorities of the Church but not in conflict with the public power. As a consequence of the control they had on the school trade, the public power found advantages in generating a dependent relationship with universities, both in terms of their professional skills and in terms of the regulation of public social order in general. Though, these academic guilds, sought juridical autonomy whose recognition was obtained from the public power according to the tradition set by Federico Barbarroja for Bologna, the Authentica Habitat, was considered to be the legitimate source for all academic freedom.

Usually, members of the majority of corporations were independent from the public power due to the fact that they lived off the income of their trades. In the case of scholars guilds, even though they enjoyed sufficient legitimacy for students to pay for their salaries, such collectae was not enough.

It is today relevant to acknowledge that historical payment to the academics, emerged together from the ecclesiastical benefits, from the salaries and rents given by the cities, princes and sovereigns. In exchange, the public powers demanded the right of presentation together with patronage. This particularity, since the moment it was founded, prevented the university corporation from enjoying one of the essential privileges of the corporations: self-recruitment of their membership. However it is evident that they accepted the limitation of their independence in exchange for the material benefits of the financial underwriting of the "chair" by the public power.

The relationship between universities and public power was not defined only by antagonisms, struggles and crises. On the contrary, they have also been defined by reciprocal services, mutual respect and a system of privileges in exchange for the prestige gained by the university intellectuals financed by public powers.

One can conclude that universities were centers for professional training, as well as institutions which concentrated a particular socio-demographic group such as "intellectuals." They provided a degree of prestige to the public powers in exchange for receiving all sorts of privileges, which in turn, guaranteed their independence from other powerful individuals (Le Goff, 1983:193-205; Mollis, 1994:179-210).

Considering this tradition, what mutual services do Latin American higher education and the State provide each other today? What type of State do they need to produce "intelligence," and what type of university does the State need to be more capable, fair and equitable? (Hilderbrand, M. and Grindle, M., 1994).

Dependence of the State and
Independence of the Central Government

> While governments may centralize control and rule from the center, they ought not to atttempt to administer from the center. (Alexis de Tocqueville: 1954, in: Clark, B., 1977:36)

Alexis de Tocqueville, admirer of American federalism, established early in 1830, the beforementioned strategic principle in what administration concerns. Administrating from the center means to concentrate authority in the central bureaus of national agencies, instead of expanding it among several local centers and offices. Following Robert Fried's interpretation of the Italian historical tradition in this matter (an appropriate approach to understand the Argentine situation) "to rule from the center is to centralize political control, moving authority from local and provincial government to the national level. To administer from the center is to concentrate authority in the central offices of the national agencies. ... The tendency to do both has run deep in Italy" (Fried, R., 1963, in Clark, 1977:37).

The text of the first Argentine University Law (1597 Law) recognised as Avellaneda's Law, has been influenced by a model inspired by the French Napoleonic university, as in the Italian case. This organizational type results from the organization of a confederation of schools or colleges, headed by a Rector who has in practice merely honorific functions. The so called Avellaneda's Law shows that Tocquevillian spirit, which justifies the liberal tradition of our institutional autonomy. It reads as follows:

First Article: The Executive Power will decree that the superior councils of the Universities of Cordoba and Buenos Aires will dictate statutes in each of these universities, subject to the following rules:

1. The University will be composed by a Rector, elected by the University Assembly, which will have a duration of at least four years in his post, and could be re-elected;
2. By a Superior Council and by the departments that function now or are to be created by laws to be enacted later on. The University Assembly is formed by all the members of all the departments.
3. The Rector is the representative of the university. He presides over the sessions of the Assembly and the Council and executes

its resolutions. It will correspond to the Rector to enjoy the position of honor in all those solemn acts that the schools celebrate" (UBA, 1959, 75). The key item to understand the liberal spirit of the decentralized administration, is one that refers to the designation of professors, the initiative remained in the hands of the schools.

4. Each school will exert the police function and disciplinary jurisdiction within their respective institutions, project the study plans, grant the certificates to authorize academic examinations, and according to the results in the examinations, to exclusively award the diplomas of each scientific profession, approve or reform the study program presented by the professors, dispose of the university funds assigned for their expenses giving account of these to the Superior Council every year, and set the conditions of admission for students that enter their classrooms.

5. In the composition of each school government there will be at least a third of the professors that head their classes, corresponding to each department nominated by all the active members. All schools will have the same number of members which must not exceed 15.

6. The vacant chairs will be filled in the following way: the faculty will vote a slate of candidates which will be presented to the Superior Council, and if this Council approves it will be taken up to Executive Power who will design which professor will be in charge of the chair.

7. The university rights (that is, the resources appropriated for the functioning of each chair position) will constitute the "university fund," with exception of the part that the Superior Council assigns, with approval of the Ministry of education, for its expenses and for those of the schools and colleges. Every year, the Congress will be informed of the existence and investment of these funds" (UBA, 1959:76).

Since then, Argentine public universities, and particularly those of large size, embody the idea of a university as a "confederation of schools or faculties." President Julio Argentino Roca, during his second presidency (1898-1904) and the Minister of Public Instruction Osvaldo Magnasco, were representatives of a liberal thought which conceived the Argentine state as the "political representative of society," and as such, the only one responsible for public instruction at the three educational levels: elementary, intermediate and higher education. The liberal conception of that Executive Power in 1899, described the University as the institution that was responsible for two essential functions: professional training on one hand, and scientific training, on the other. According to each one of these, the State had different responsibilities and attributes. As to the first, it had to supervise and control, and as to the second, it had to respect the unconditional liberty and the necessary autonomy to carry out scientific investigation. As it is expressed in the Message and law project on the general and university instruction plan:

> To the Honorable National Congress: (...) The State cannot consent in that respect: public education must respond not to private ambitions, but to the highest requirements of national interest, and in such a way, break away from the old empiricism and conform to the healthy rules of the natural science of education, particularly in the first school years. Now well, isn't it true that the university should lose the promiscuous character that it routinely holds among us? The natural rule prescribes another order, ... higher education must also be successively characterized by a double and clear tendency. The first is the professional or immediately economic; the other, the merely scientific or speculative. The former ends up in the individual trade ..., the latter is of pure investigation and its economic role would be of auxiliary contribution towards the encouragement and progress of the applied sciences or just the delight of the spirit. That's why the double role of the university work; the one that conducts towards professional exercise and the one that transports intelligence to the higher studies, to the greatest perfection of mental discipline, to the most subtle investigation of the methods, to the discovery of the great principles, thus, to the refinements of the application. (...) The State cannot, either theoretically, legally or economically, renounce to its immediate intervention in whatever concerns studies or careers of this type; if not the political precept that enables the Congress to prepare the university plans and confers the Executive certain absolute attributions in this respect and which they can't decline. If the State is the political representation of the society it cannot be indifferent to professional production. (...) It is logical to think that only the State must elaborate those plans, give them character and tendency, and organize the teaching of this class in accordance to the social goals. (...) The tasks of scientific investigation, in as much as they constitute not a factory of professionals but a high intellectual culture, are tasks which are alien to the functions of the government and, on such grounds, it could not, without injustice and danger sometimes, deny the erudite which sustain autonomy, the truth of their demands and the need for emancipation. The university must have, in this aspect, ample faculties and such complete independence as the nature and the objectives of this last higher discipline requires: organize and distribute the studies, select the methods, establish their regimen, desig-

nate the teaching staff, set conditions, grant certificates and patents, without more restrictions than the natural and constitutional restriction of any liberty, the discreet observance of the State just to defend and ensure social order and public interests that the workers and scientific doctrines may on occasions affect or compromise (...) Julio A. Roca, Osvaldo Magnasco (Diario de Sesiones, 1899:107-122).

This message has the virtue of showing the type of liberal Nineteenth Century speech, foundering of the Argentine public universities, whose notable difference in respect to the actual neoliberal doctrines, is the valuation of "scientific activity and high intellectual culture," and the recognition of its independence from all governmental control. The University as a "source of producing culture and scientific thinking" must respond to the liberty of the discipline itself. It was with this emancipating spirit that the disciplines that "encourage the progress of the sciences, of applied sciences or just the delight of the spirit" historically enjoyed a real autonomy only interrupted by the coups d'etat and the authoritarian governments. Together with culture and science, the public universities also had as objective, to form "professionals" who will be looked after by the State.

Luis Scherz (1968) characterized the "professional university" by using three dominant adjectives: secular, pragmatic and state. Consequently, he undertook the task of forming citizens, professionals and administrators. This model would have surged together with the Napoleonic idea of the university. It adapted to relatively static social systems, it maintained a close relationship with the State, which acknowledges forums and rights and finances them. That way, the post-colonial universities went consolidating themselves, particularly the two most traditional Argentine universities: the National University of Cordoba and the National University of Buenos Aires. These turned into public national institutions towards the end of the nineteenth century century, subject to the "teacher state," which, as such, was the administrator and inspector of all the educational system: exclusive sovereign of all educational matters (Scherz, 1968:107; Martinez Paz, 1980). These were elite universities which opened their doors to a minimum percentage of youngsters with the corresponding age.

On the other hand, Law and Medicine were the most popular and most prestigious careers because of the professional development they offered. Hence, the possibility of introducing careers linked to a scientific and/or technological production was restricted.

Another aspect that identifies them, refers to its "professorial" conformation and its organization in chairs of a more teaching rather than scientific orientation. This feature had its influence hindering the development of innovations coming from disciplinary fields, or in the development of the scientific knowledge of the specialty (Mollis, 1990). The lawyers who graduated from these institutions were professionally or ideologically related to the agrarian property, and as statement or public employees they created the instruments for political control within the State institutions such as the courts, prosecutor offices and police departments. Through the schools and the press, they managed other activities that allowed them to broaden the expression of the class hegemonies as writers, poets or educators.

> This group generated a bureaucratic elite and a political class with a formalist and flamboyant style that adequated itself perfectly to the interests of the dominating class (Canton, 1966:37-49; Allub, 1989:130).

One of the constitutive characteristics of this type of university is the academic and administrative autonomy to organize its institutional offers. What appears as the main task of the "university for lawyers" is its professional preparation. For this reason it attends to the demands of a political and cultural social class which shares or controls the political power, exerts a significant influence in the field of ideas and has a growing weight in the system of cultural institutions (Brunner, 1990:55).

When the Intervention of the Central Government Guaranteed Autonomy

Among the multiple paradoxes that condition the historical concept of autonomy is that at times the intervention of the Executive Power guaranteed and promoted university autonomy. That was the time of the University Reform, the time of the outbreak of a movement that recuperated the feudal corporative tradition of Bologna as well as giving birth to the new history of Latin American universities. The academic autonomy became a fundamental principle for the reformist institutions, since it was its purpose to break the vicious circle of the mediocre personnel (i.e., academic members for life) of the traditional government in charge of education, and it was projected in the university culture through the participation of the three collegiate bodies (professors, students and graduates) in the pedagogical, academic and scientific decision making. This meant that the selection and appointment of professors via public contest—curriculum and public class—the freedom of teaching and research of the professorship, the elaboration of syllabi, the conditions for admission and promotion, remained in the hands of the Executive Councils of each school and the Superior Councils of each university, represented by the three collegiate bodies. This movement organized the pedagogical and academic government around the university actors, just as the University of Bologna had done seven centuries before. The academic autonomy was achieved through the intervention of the Executive Power (Decreto del PE, 1919:81), the successive statutory reforms of the universities and the financial dependence of the State. The faculty searches through public contest, the alternative teaching (also called parallel courses), promoted by the renewed statutes could be implemented by a "partner"—like those public feudal powers in the past—who would finance those procedures. What better partner than the State, politically representing the middle classes, which, thanks to the "universal suffrage law," had conquered the central power?

The Autonomies, in Plural

It has been mentioned, so far, that the concept of "autonomy" presents multiple dimensions: on the one hand the academic dimension, on the other the financial dimension (legally known as autarchy). Even though both dimensions are interwoven in the concept of autonomy, they must not be confused. Another dimension connected to these two is the administrative. Since the '70s when enrollment skyrocketed, and important tension between two logics coexisting within public universities developed.

On the one hand, there is a bureaucratic—administrative logic—that is the pyramidal bureaucratic logic linked to the concept of the university as a state organism or public institution, whose administration reminds us more of a Ministry of Education than a center for intellectual activity. On the other hand, there is a corporative academic logic of the "academics" (professors, intellectuals, researchers) that intimately relates to the history of the medieval universities and even to the Humboldtian model of German university. To understand the concept of institutional autonomy it is easy to recognise that there are fields for confrontation within universities. For example, in relation to the diversity of functions and interests one can describe some antinomics pairs who embody antagonic logics: faculty members (the academic logic) versus administrative staff (the bureaucratic logic) full-time professors versus a majority of part-time professors (unionized or not); scholars versus academic officials (academic administration); student movement versus academic officials.

Each of these actors has a different institutional identity that submit him or her to the power of the State under different formulas: civil servant (part-time professors), ad honorem civil servants (university bureacracy), professionals corporation (professors, researchers), students corporation (student union groups). What intervention implies for some, may mean control for others, supervision to a few, subjugation of professorial liberty to the rest, etc. Finally, a set of truths conditioned to the practice of the different functions and the development of the institutional identities (also different) is produced around institutional autonomy, which adds more complexity to the description we have been developing.

The Policies of Higher Education of the 1990s:
From State to Central Government

The course of historic events has proved they emancicipated the classes whose special interests they represented, rather than human beings impartially. ... Fortunately it is not necessary to attempt the citation of relevant facts. Practically everyone admits there is a new social problem ... and that these problems have an economic basis (Dewey, J., 1960:271).

Argentina, like Mexico and Brazil, has been influenced and conditioned by an international agenda of the modernization of the higher education systems (Brunner: 1993b) that implies the reduction of state subsidies, the expansion of private institutions and enrollment, the promulgation of a Higher Education Law with consequences on systems of evaluation and accreditation and the traditional concept of institutional autonomy, a selective control for the distribution of financial resources, etc. From the point of view of the relation between State and university, modernization is organized mainly around the transformation of a political actor: from the liberal State of the final stages of the nineteenth century to the central government of the twentieth century. Any component of this formula is also present in other Latin American cases "modernized" before the process put in motion by the Menem administration (for instances Chile and Mexico). In Argentina, an important paradox has taken place instead. One of the disadvantages of centralization in respect to university government being in the hands of an omnipresent State, is the control that the latter has over the institutions hindering an independent and pluralist academic and scientific development (Levy, D., 1993b). However, and as a consequence of a reformist government, the academic control remained in hands of the collegiate bodies of each university, whereupon institutional autonomy is as powerful as the American models compared to the continental European model. This characteristic of the Argentine universities leads us to ask ourselves about the apparent contradiction between the proposals that claim for more control against more autonomy which "self-regulation" promotes.

The Argentine Higher Education Law:
Control or Self-Regulation?

The Argentine Higher Education Law No 24.521, was promulgated the 7th of August, 1995, and includes all institutions of higher formation, be them universities or non-universities, national, provincial or municipal, state-owned or private, all form part of the National Educational System regulated by Law No. 24.195. It comprises IV titles, subdivided into Chapters and Sections with 89 articles in all. The topics which head each part express the matters it legislates on: About Higher Education: Aims and Objectives, Structure and Articulation, Rights and Duties; about Non-University Higher Education: jurisdictional responsibility of the institutions, degrees and syllabuses, institutional evaluation, about University Higher Education: university institutions and its functions, autonomy: its reach and guarantees, conditions for its functioning—general requisites—degrees, evaluation and accreditation, about National University Institutions: creation and organizational basis, governing bodies, support, economic and financial regimes, about private university institutions about Provincial Institutions (there are no subheadings) about the Government and coordination of the University system Complementary Dispositions.

The aforementioned Law introduces substantial changes in what has to do with the historical concepts of autonomy, financing and university governing. As an example, it authorizes university institutions to establish their own system of admissions, permanence and graduation of their students in an autonomous way (in universities with more than 50.000 students the conditions for entry, permanence and promotion may be defined by each school or school; it authorizes each university to set its own scheme for scholars salaries and administration of personnel, assuring them the decentralized management of the funds they themselves generate; they can foster the constitution of societies, foundations, or any other form of civic associations destined to support the financial action and facilitate relations of the universities and/or schools with the environment; the collegiate bodies will have the task of defining policies and methods of control while the unipersonal bodies will have executive functions; it modifies the integration of the faculty of professors authorizing them (even auxiliary staff) to be elected to represent their faculty; it increases the number of bodies represented on the collegiate bodies integrating the non-teaching staff representatives and establishes as a requisite for the students representatives the attendance and approval of at least two chairs per year. Apart from introducing changes that affect traditional university methods, it also sets new evaluating processes through the establishing of organisms and actors dedicated exclusively to such thing.

The institutional evaluation is promoted at both levels, internal and external. Apart from introducing changes that affect traditional university methods, it also sets new evaluating processes through the establishing of organisms and actors dedicated exclusively to such thing. The institutional evaluation is promoted at both levels, internal and external. The internal evaluation—in the hands of the universities themselves—has the objective to analyze the achievements and difficulties in the observance of the university functions, as well as to suggest measures for its operation. The external evaluation takes place every six years, and it is made by the National Commission for University Evaluation and Accreditation. Together with this body there may also be private entities recognized for such task. In both cases, with the participation of peers of accepted competence. The National Commission for University Evaluation and Accreditation is an decentralized organ and it operates under the Ministry of Culture and Education. It is formed by 12 members designated by the National Executive Power (PEN) and proposed by the National Inter-university Council (CIN) (five members), the Private Universities Rectors' Council (CRUP) (three members), the National Academy of Education (1 member). They shall last in their posts for four years. Through accreditation any of these organisms award public recognition to the institutions, guaranteeing to society that they meet pre-established standards. The recommendations that arise from the evaluation will be made public. That "frame" spirit of the so called Avellaneda Law with its four articles (Mignone, F., 1979), is today replaced by a law with 89 articles (one referred to the universities with more than 50.000 students), that remits by comparison to a more disciplinarian spirit.

One can detect certain tensions between a type of neo-liberal view that aspires to deregulation steered by the freedom of the markets and the new type of selective financing of the central Government, and so then to institutional self-regulation, and other conservative expressions that seek control of the university institutions that rush into the described autonomies. Four public universities (University of Buenos Aires, University of Rosario, University of Mar del Plata and the University of La Plata) have interposed an appeal in court because they consider Law 24.521 to be anti-constitutional in what concerns autarchy and autonomy. The universities—as it has been endorsed by a federal judge—cannot be considered as a dependency, delegation or decentralization of the national Executive Power, as they have institutional hierarchy demarcated by the same Constitution (*La Nación*, 1995:13).

The International Scenario of the Autonomies

Institutions of higher education have been in existence now for nearly twenty-five hundred years—for the first two thousand years in the wandering scholar model under the sponsorship of students and scholars and in some places also of the church—and now for nearly five hundred years increasingly under the sponsorship and then control of the nation-states (Kerr, Clark 1994:25).

Burton Clark (1977) recognizes that, even though autonomy can be manipulated from the financial point of view, from the point of view of those dimensions that are often cast aside by the central administrators (intangible aspects of power), it is really difficult to control. When significant changes and innovations for the institutions are intended, it is indispensable to identify the organizational tradition that underlies the institutional methods. It is not enough to know the "lean facts of institutional history," it is also necessary to recognize "the organizational legend" (Brunner, J. J., 1990:53).

The universities of continental Europe—German, Dutch or Italian—characterize themselves for a type of centralized organizational tradition, dependent of the State and the government that controls and supervises the universities. In the '70s, it was the State who planned the academic activity of the universities (the designation and appointing of professors), it took part in curricular matters, in the conditions for entry and graduation, etc. (Neave, G and Van Vught, F. 1994:388-389). This idea of a planning State in the `70s conditioned European university autonomy, opposing the concept of state planning to that of institutional autonomy. The said model tends to homogenize the products and propose homogeneous policies that apply to a reality that is supposedly undifferentiated.

Today, Holland, Belgium and Sweden show the need to change the tendency of a "controlling State" for an "Evaluating State," which implies that the State ceases to intervene in the academic affairs of the university to advance towards self-regulation. In this sense, the university gains more freedom and can organize its own administration better, which was, in fact, the preoccupation since the last years of the '80s. However, the experts show certain apprehension (Van Vught, F, 1989) in respect to the strategies used by the central governments: "... Behind a facade of amply proclaimed autonomy, the traditional strategy for planning and control is perhaps as active as never before ... the renouncement of the governments to develop an interventionist policy is, in the best of cases, only partial since at the same time those governments are engaged in projecting procedures and instruments equally coercive for higher education" (Van Vught and Guy Neave, 1994:392). The preoccupation arises in the same way that Latin America by the hand of criteria that link autonomy with financing. These European universities have developed strategies to free themselves from the weight and control of the State, but at the same time the State has developed strategies that imply the reduction of funds for university financing. This way, the process of reinforcing the European academic liberty was accompanied by policies of budget reduction. The European specialists acknowledge the paradoxical situation that is generated by the need of greater autonomy together with State financing reduction.

Higher Education at the Turning Century:
The Challenge of Integrating Autonomies

The fate of an epoch that has eaten of the tree of knowledge is that it must...
recognize that general views of life and the universe can never be products of increasing empirical knowledge, and that the highest ideals, which
move us most forcefully, are always formed only in the struggle with other
ideals which are just sacred to others as ours are to us (Max Weber, in:
Harvey, D. 1995:1).

[We alumni and alumnae of the colleges] ... our motto too is noblesse oblige
and unlike them [the aristocrats] we stand for ideal interests only, for we
have no corporate selfishness and wield no powers of corruption..."Les
Intellectuals"! What prouder club-name could there be that this one which
refers to those who still retained some critical sense and judgment (William James [1907] 1995).

It has been shown how the concept of autonomy historically, became
more complex to the point of making it dependent of the public powers, of
associating it to the intervention of the Central Government and to the
interests of a certain political class, to the game of a variety of institutional
actors and, so, to the necessary reference in plural to the autonomies. The
charm of autonomy is found prisoner of the "charmer" that promotes it.

New conditions of the Latin America of the 1990s, such as market-
oriented restructuring, lead to a severe retrenchment of the public sphere's
traditional "entrepreneurial" functions and to a smaller state apparatus,
on the one hand. On the other hand, the capacity of civilian elites to impose restrictions on organized labor, strengthened the public and governmental authority significantly (O'Donnell, G., 1994; Torres, C. 1994; 1996).
These new tendences applied to the institutions of higher learning, make
the autonomies play on a stage, as complex as paradoxical: control and
self-regulation, liberalization and supervision, globalization and
regionalization, external conditionalities and institutional self-evaluation,
systematic policies and institutional cultures.

The traditional social contract between public universities and the State,
has been broken in the name of a "minimun State" with maximum market
and, at the same time, in a context of structural adjustment and regulatory
framework. The neoliberal reform may be characterized by both images of
the State: stronger and weaker. The universities'autonomies are being
constitued in a process of globalization (McGinn, N., 1995; Torres, C., 1995)
that affects the institutional culture.

Changes in the composition and strength of the State are already affecting especially public universities in Latin America. State suport for higher education is declining in some countries and in all threatened. The new doctrine of the World Bank urges a shift of public funds away from traditional forms of universities toward new kinds of post-secondary institutions, away from public institutions toward private institutions. The national State has been affected by the ascendance of supranational organizations that reduce the ability of a state to be the major influence on everything that takes place within its borders. In effect, supranational organizations contribute to reduced national sovereignty (McGinn, N. 1994:7).

The reduction of sovereignty and the notion that to govern is to manage the economy effectively are two of the most powerful regulatory policies of the plural autonomies of today. Anyway, in order to change the undesireable effects of the statu-quo oriented tradition of the universities, it is necessary to find responses to:

- who will be in charge of controlling quality in higher education: experts, technicians, academics or politicians ?;
- what must the market finance and what must the State?;
- How do the external conditionalities of globalization relate with the intrinsic "faculty" liberties of teaching and learning?

The tensions that crop up about the problem of autonomy can be summarized in two models: a) the model of governmental control or interventionist State; and b) the model of State supervision or evaluating State (Neave, G. 1994). The former conceives higher education as a homogeneous enterprise with the governmental intention of regulating and controlling all the elements of the system dynamics: admission, curriculum, requirements for awarding diplomas, personnel recruitment, quality of the offerings, etc. It does not recognize the organizational culture of higher education as "loosely coordinated" and multidimensional." The latter recognizes the need for the State to establish basic parameters for functioning but leaves in the hands of the institutions the fundamental academic decisions, shown in model 1. Clark Kerr looking into the twenty-first century claims a new meaning for the concept of autonomy given by the convergence and the construction of institutional consensus (Kerr, C. 1994). The challenges of the twentieth century for the Argentine universities—and probably for Latin American universities in general—lies in the impossibility of combining both models without affecting the different autonomies. The new role of the State minimized in the neoliberal context, expresses its new contract deals of the good citizen for the economic subject, global and rational consumer, indoctrinated by the new market religion, leaving no room for the scientific labors and the high intellectual culture which Roca spoke of at the beginning of the century. Our proposal is to reconstruct the subtle enchantment of the autonomies, on the basis of the integration of the institutional powers, the public-social powers, the political powers and the economic powers in a framework of negotiation, consensus and construction of institutional capabilities for the better of the university culture.

References

Debate Parlamentario sobre la Ley Avellaneda. 1959. Universidad de Buenos Aires, Departamento Editorial, Imprenta de la U.B.A.

Roca, Julio Argentino y Magnasco, Osvaldo. 1899. iMensaje y proyecto de ley sobre el plan de instruccion general y universitariai, en: Diario de Sesiones, Sesiones Ordinarias, Cmara de Diputados de la Nacion Canton, Daro (1966) El Parlamento Argentino en Epocas de Cambio: 1816-1916-1946, Editorial Instituto, Buenos Aires. Decreto del Poder Ejecutivo interviniendo la universidad y designando Comisionado Nacional (1919), en: La Reforma Universitaria en la Universidad de Cordoba, en la Universidad de Buenos Aires, Buenos Aires, Penitenciara Nacional.

Allub, Leopoldo. 1989. iEstado y Sociedad Civil: Patron de Emergencia y Desarrollo del Estado Argentino (1810-1930i, en: Ansaldi, W y Moreno, J. L. (1989) Estado y Sociedad en el Pensamiento Nacional, Editorial Cantaro, Buenos Aires, Boletin Oficial de las Republica Argentina (1995) Ley de Educaci, Superior 24.521, Jueves 10 de Agosto, Buenos Aires.

Brunner, J. 1990. *Educación Superior en América Latina, Cambios y Desafios*, FCE, Santiago de Chile.

Clark, Burton. 1977. *Academic Power in Italy. Bureaucracy and Oligarchy in a National University System*, The University of Chicago Press, Chicago and London.

Cunha, Luiz A. 1988. *A Universidade Reformanda*, Francisco Alves, Rio de Janeiro.

Dewey, John. 1960. *On Experience, Nature and Freedom: Representative Selections*, Ed. R. Bernstein, Bobbs-Merrill, Indianapolis.

Harvey, David. 1990. *The Condition of Posmodernity*, Blackwell Publishers, Oxford.

Hilderbrand, M. and Grindle, M. 1994. *Building Sustainable Capacity. Challenges for the Public Sector*, Harvard Institute for the International Development, Harvard University, Massachusetts.

James, Williams. 1907. "The Social Value of the College Bred Man," 21; in: Lerner R. and Nagai, A. and Rothman, S. (editors) (1995) *Molding The Good Citizen*, Prager, USA.

Kerr, Clark. 1994. *Higher Education Cannot Escape History. Issues for the Twenty-first Century*, State University of New York Press, New York.

Le Goff, Jacques. 1983. Tiempo Trabajo y Cultura en el Occidente Medieval, Taurus, Barcelona.

Levy, Daniel. 1993. "El Gobierno de los Sistemas de Educación Superior," en: Pensamiento Univeristario, No. 1, Buenos Aires.

Levy, Daniel. 1993. "The New Pluralist Agenda for Latin American Higher Education," Documento presentado en el Seminario sobre Educación Superior en América Latina, Universidad de los Andes, IDEE/World Bank, Colombia.

Levy, Daniel. 1993b. "Formas de Gobierno en la Educación Superior," en: *Pensamiento Universitario*, No. 1, Buenos Aires.

McGinn, Noel. 1994. *Options for Higher Education as Latin America Joins the World Economy*, Harvard University, December (unpublished).

McGinn, Noel. 1995. "The Implications of Globalisation for Higher Education," in: *Learning from Experience: Policy and Practice in Aid to Higher Education*, CESO Paparback, The Hague, No 24, 77-93.

Mignone, Fermón. 1979. Universidad y Poder Político en Argentina: 1613-1978, FLACSO, Buenos Aires.

Mollis, Marcela. 1990. *Universidades y Estado Nacional*, Biblios, Buenos Aires.

Mollis, Marcela. 1994. Estilos Institucionales y Saberes en: *Revista de Educación*, No 303, Ministerio de Educacion y Ciencias, Madrid.

Neave, Guy and Van Vught, Frans. 1994. *Prometeo Encadenado*, Gedisa, Barcelona.

O'Donnell, G. 1994. "The State, Democratization and Some Conceptual Problems (A Latin American View with Glances at Some Post-Communist Countries)," in: *Latin American Political Economy in the Age of Neoliberal Reform*, Smith, Acuña and Gamara (editors) North South Center, University of Miami, 157-181.

Van Vught, Frans. 1989. *Governmental Strategies and Innovation in Higher Education*, Jessica Kingsley, London.

Scherz, Luis. 1968. *El Camino de la Revolución*, Universitaria, Editorial del Pacifico, Santiago de Chile.

Torres, Carlos A. 1994. Estado, Privatización y Política Educativa. Elementos para un critica del Neoliberalismo, Ponencia presentada al Coloquio Internacional sobre Relaciones entre el Gobierno, Justica y Cultura, Embajada de Francia, Mexico, Oct 4-6 (unpublished).

Torres, Carlos A. 1995. "State and Education Revisited: Why Educational Researchers Should Think Politically about Education" in: *Review of Research in Education* 21, 255-331.

9

University Restructuring in Argentina: The Political Debate

Daniel Schugurensky

Introduction

Universities all over the world are experiencing intense pressures from governments and private organizations to change their goals, functions, and organizational structure. A review of current transformations worldwide indicates a shift from the autonomous to the heteronomous university, where the direction of the university is increasingly conditioned by external forces. Some institutions of higher education fervently endorse the proposed changes, most resign themselves and sooner or later adopt them, and a few present resistance. In the latter case, a conflict between the state and the university, and within the university itself, is inevitable. This is the situation of the University of Buenos Aires (UBA), the largest institution of higher education in Argentina.

In Argentinean society, there is general agreement that the public university is in a state of crisis. However, there is little agreement as to the nature of such a crisis, its causes and its remedies. On the one hand, the government claims that the university has become obsolete, inefficient, insensitive to societal demands, and unwilling to adapt to the new era of fiscal restraint. Challenging this view, most university representatives (led by the Universidad de Buenos Aires) contend that the state is abandoning the public university, and that, given the poor working conditions, the scarcity of resources, and the high quality of graduates and research products, the public university is one of the most efficient social institutions. In other words, whereas the government perceives the nature of the crisis as one of performance, the academic community understands it as a crisis of funding.

It is pertinent to note, however, that the conflict cannot be reduced to a simple dispute between government and university authorities. Although they are the two main contenders, the inclusion of a variety of actors in the conflict, partly due to the democratic system of university governance, and partly due to the intense politicization of the Argentinean society, has resulted in a complex network of alliances and confrontations. This chapter presents a general description of the actors involved, the main fronts of the conflict, and the differing understandings of the university crisis. It is based on the information collected through more than 60 interviews of university leaders and government authorities, and through the analysis of a great variety of secondary sources.

The Main Camps: Autonomists and Marketventionists

Two main contending parties in the present university conflict in Argentina can be observed in the early nineties: autonomists (or reformists) and modernizers (or "marketventionists," a neologism that attempts to capture the combination of laissez faire and state interventionism in university life). The former are grounded in the principles of the 1918 Córdoba Reform,[1] which emphasize internal democratization and eventually a democratization of the entire society. Presently, their major concern is to preserve the situation of autonomy, understood as a basic prerequisite for a progressive academic institution. The latter contend that autonomy has led to internal and external inefficiency, and therefore call for increasing market participation and state control, and advocate technocracy, accountability, rationalization, and depoliticization. In general terms, the autonomist movement has an overwhelming hegemony at UBA, whereas marketventionists control the state apparatus. However, autonomists have allies outside UBA, and marketventionists have supporters in some universities, and even among UBA members.

The marketventionist bloc is headed by President Menem himself,[2] and is entrenched in and consolidated through government agencies (particularly the Ministries of Economy and Education), international agencies (particularly the World Bank), some local media, powerful business associations large industry associations (such as the Unión Industrial Argentina) and some alumni societies linked to foreign universities. Within UBA, the marketventionist bloc has its base in the faculty of Medicine; it also enjoys the backing of alumni, professors and students of the neoliberal minority, as well as the hesitant support of some deans. The autonomist bloc is led by UBA authorities and the majority of representatives of students, professors and alumni, particularly the student group Franja Morada (FM), the youth branch of the Radical Party, which prevails in all Argentinean universities since the restoration of democracy in 1983. In the 1991 elections, FM obtained 49.17 percent of total votes and won the majority in eight of the 13 faculties: Law, Architecture, Psychology, Economics, Pharmacy, Dentistry, Animal Sciences and Social Sciences. In the five remaining faculties the student associations are controlled by the following groups: Humanities and Exact Sciences by the left-wing Compañeros de Base, Agronomy by an independent slate, government branch of the Peronist student movement.[3] Consequently, FM obtained three of the five seats allocated to students in the Consejo Superior (University Senate), and the remaining two seats are occupied by Compañeros de Base and UPAU (Unión para la Apertura Democrática, a student slate associated with the Unión de Centro Democrática, a neoliberal political party).

In 1992, FM increased its popularity, winning in 10 faculties. FM leaders argued that these electoral results implied a plebiscite against the government's university policy, which is "an attack against free education, co-governance and autonomy." They claim that the university model of the government is individualistic and restrictive, contrary to the model of the 1918 Reform. They proclaimed that the electoral results were a call of attention to the government "who must dialogue, and not combat, the university community."[4] Whereas the minority representatives of the left (students, professors and alumni) tend to make alliances with autonomists, the minority representatives of the right tend to support the marketventionist proposals for university restructuring. Outside UBA, autonomist have strong allies in the Consejo Interuniversitario Nacional (CIN), which is comprised of the rectors of all public universities, as well as in the Radical Party. As the conflict become more polarized, those who still remain neutral are increasingly pressured to take sides, and the chosen side depends on the inclination to resist or to adapt to the marketventionist agenda.

Present university leaders and government officials have a clear disadvantage with respect to their predecessors. While the 1918 Reform was supported, and encouraged, by the state, and therefore was based on an alliance between the students and the Radical government, the current counter-reform finds the university and the government in opposite trenches. The 1918 Reform was part of the modernization process of the Argentine society that took place between 1885 and 1930, in which the middle classes replaced the traditional oligarchy in the control of the state apparatus. The strategy of the newly arrived Yrigoyen's government to increase its political hegemony included the control of universities,[5] and the flow of the middle classes to the university during the previous decades assisted the achievement of that purpose. Today, autonomists no longer have an ally in the government but rather an adversary. Conversely, the Menemist government needs to boost supporters within a hostile university in order to build consensus for its agenda, and so far it had recruited followers among minority representatives, and was able to build a beach head in the faculty of Medicine. Additionally, whereas in 1918 the international context favored the reformist agenda, in the early 1990s it bolstered the marketventionist coalition.[6]

The relative weight of each contender is determined by its public support, but also by its power to control public resources and influence public policy. Whereas autonomists seem to hold the sympathies of the university community (particularly students) and large sectors of the middle class, marketventionists have the power of the purse and the control of the state apparatuses. As Neave (1991:78) points out, the free market model does not have a popular appeal but the political influence of its proponents inversely related to the number.

The conflict between autonomists and marketventionists is permeated by mutual distrust and threats. Marketventionists recurrently claim that the university administration is engaged in administrative corruption and disguises political activities as academic activities. On the other hand, autonomists do not trust the promises of the government, particularly in relation to evaluation and finances. Although institutional stability, autonomy and open competitions for academic positions promote the utilization of more consensually shared evaluation mechanisms than during the military period, autonomists fear that state evaluation of quality can be used— as it has been used in the past—for ideological and political discrimination. In regard to finances, although government officials constantly promise that tuition fees and other potential sources of revenue would be "complementary" and not "alternative" (and hence the state would maintain its commitment to higher education) autonomists distrust such promises.

Indeed, there is a concern on part of university actors that if the university increases its own sources of revenue, this income would replace (instead of complement) state funding. Their suspicions about government's reassurance that private sources of revenue will complement—and not replace—public funding have some basis in international experience. Interestingly, while Argentinean government officials point out that such fears are unfounded, two World Bank papers admit that there is some reason for concern. Eisemon and Salmi (1992:13), for instance, call attention to the serious constraint that any savings or income derived simply reduces government obligations to the universities, and warn that government support should not fall by a dollar for each dollar of revenue generated. Albretch and Ziderman (1993) confirm this warning, showing that in 1990, Chilean institutions received only about 60 percent of the resources forecasted in the initial plan. Moreover, UBA itself experienced this situation. Rector Schuberoff (1991:15) claimed that the 1992 budget contemplated reductions equivalent to the revenues generated by the university in the previous year.

Autonomists also indicate that they carried out certain reforms against their own will, due to the threats expressed by some government officials. These threats could be summarized as follows: "If you don't do the changes right now, we will do them for you later, and it will be much worse." In an interview with a national magazine, one professor confessed that Enrique Bullit Goñi, a Ministry of Education top official, told university rectors that at the end the 1980s adjustment policies could not be postponed any longer, and that is was preferable that they do the adjustment themselves and not the Ministry of Economy.[7] It is interesting to note that the 'grinch' pointed out by Bullit Goñi was not his own Ministry but the Ministry of Economy which, according to many interviewees, was the site where university restructuring was being designed. Not surprisingly, a World Bank document on university reform recommends that a key location for external agencies to be involved in Latin American countries is the Ministry of Finance, "as it is where funding decisions can be heavily influenced" (Carlson 1992:98).

The Conflict as Perceived by the Actors and the Media

Marketventionists and autonomists understand the university-state conflict from different perspectives. For marketventionists, particularly government officials, this conflict is rooted mainly in the university's own shortcomings. Interesting, marketventionists recognize that the existence of an educational crisis in basic education results from the low allocation of resources and the chronic deterioration of teachers' salaries (Ministerio de Cultura y Educación 1991), whereas the university crisis is usually interpreted as the result of internal deficiencies of higher education institutions.

In their view, university actors have committed a variety of sins. First, they have not understood yet that Argentina is a poor country, and that the state has a deficit problem. Second, university actors are blamed not only for the low contribution to national development but for their lack of intention to contribute to it, which was perceived as a symptom of low social solidarity and arrogance. Third, government officials accuse university authorities of mixing university affairs with the politics of the Radical Party, and of having an excess of personnel who allegedly are cadres of the Radical Party. Fourth, they claim that full-time professors do not work the number of hours that they are supposed to, that a significant proportion of support staff only show up for the payment day, and that enrollments are inflated for funding purposes. Fifth, they claim that research products are scarce and of dubious quality and that, as a result of overexpansion, the quality of graduates has been steadily declining.

For autonomists, the conflict originated in the government's poor understanding of the relationship between higher education and development, which leads it to consider universities as an expenditure rather than as an investment. For instance, in a document entitled "The University and the Future of the Nation," [8] ten rectors attributed the crisis to the failure of the state to express a clear commitment to support universities, and to the lack of understanding among politicians and civil society about the importance of higher education for national development. Therefore, according to the rectors, both the state and society must give a higher priority to higher education. Although the rectors claimed that the universities were undertaking a responsible, severe and profound self-criticism, such effort—except for a paragraph stating that universities should strengthen their links with social and economic realities, and should be prepared to modernize their structures—is not noticeable in the document. The only problem of the universities seems to be related to their public image, that is, their inability to find an adequate strategy to regain public confidence, and particularly to obtain the support of the state and industry.

The rest of the document is a passionate defense of the university and a condemnation of state politics and social apathy. In fact, the university is portrayed as performing miracles in order to overcome financial constrains and the deficiencies of secondary schools. Among the state policies criticized for "putting at risk the existence of the higher education system itself" are budget cutbacks, the reinforcement of social inequalities, the proliferation of new universities with obvious decreases in quality, and the absence of a clear system of certification (similar diplomas are granted by dissimilar institutions). According to this document, which is representative of many other documents released by university actors, the mistaken policies undertaken by the government may lead to the destruction of the higher education system.

Most observers of the conflict (e.g., the media, and university actors who are neither autonomists nor marketventionists) perceive it as a confrontation between two groups unwilling to compromise, or as a stalemate in which none of the parties are even inclined to negotiate with the other.

One student from Juventud Universitaria Peronista (JUP) summarized this generalized perception in the following way:

> Neither of the two main actors in this conflict, namely the Ministry of Education and the university, are willing to make any conciliatory movement. The university requests more money, and the government says no. Reformists are still defending a status quo that is not functional to anybody, and clashes against the logic of structural adjustment, which aims at reducing both the budget and autonomy of the university. University authorities cannot endorse the policies proposed by the Ministry of Education, like tuition fees, because its power is based on the support of Franja Morada in Particular and the Radical party in general. The situation is stagnant.

However, there was also a consensus among observers and actors that marketventionists have both the initiative and the upper hand. One member of 'Project 06' (funded by the government through a loan from the WB) was very clear in this respect:

> This is a critical moment. The university must make an effort to improve, and from that position, start to negotiate with the state. Otherwise, by confronting a very strong state, it is going to lose the battle, and that will mean the destruction of the public university.

Although the situation can be defined as a temporary stalemate, even autonomists acknowledged that the government and its allies have the upper hand because they have a proactive agenda.. One of them portrayed the situation as "a conflict between an offensive state and a defensive university," and the majority complained that this "reactive" university spends too much energy at the barricades, reacting to government's attacks at the expense of developing its own plan. Three quotes from reformist actors (two deans and one university authority) illustrate this point:

> There are two possible strategies for UBA. One is linked to the current state policies, with the private sector as an alternative source for financing, fees, quotas and so on. The other option is still unclear, because the alternative to that model does not constitute yet a homogeneous discourse. The university has not had time yet to generate this alternative policy, because it allocates all its time, energies and resources to respond to the adjustment policies (dean).

On one hand, the university is suffering a painful financial situation because of the state withdrawal from public expenditure, but on the other hand the university has not yet internalized the need for reform. Although many of the principles of the 1918 reform are still valid, it is necessary to update them to the current historical context. However, that debate is not taking place yet, because the attack by the state is so strong that the university is adopting a defensive attitude, which only aggravates the crisis (dean).

The confrontation with the government has polarized the debate, and there is a lack of space to think and dialogue about the big issues of the university. Unfortunately, not even in the GFC there is debate about the big topics (vice-president).

According to a national leader of university professors, the university sector is in a defensive position because it lacks the necessary initiative to develop a university policy and a coherent planning. In his view, the National University Council has not yet produced a unified and serious strategic plan, or any important contribution to improve the university or to develop new policies, because of internal struggles over resources and ideological differences. He notes reproachfully that its only creation was the a Protocol of agreement with the government, which in his view "leads universities to administrative rationalization and adjustment," and constitutes a mere compromise rather than an original formulation. For this leader, three reasons can explain why academics have been unable to articulate an alternative proposal to the current state policy:

Firstly, and mainly, because of the long years of [military] intervention. As a result of it, there is no history of participation in the creation of policy. Secondly, budgetary decisions, which are translated as cuts, are beyond the power of the university, and it is very difficult to develop a policy without resources. Thirdly, the university has been unable to establish links with its productive and social milieu.

Most observers also agree that the conflict between autonomists and marketventionists is influenced to a lesser or greater extent by the larger dispute between Radicalism and Peronism. For marketventionists, it is indeed a problem that university authorities and students have a political affinity with the Radical Party. In recurrent statements, marketventionists claim that Radicals confuse the university with a *comité* (in direct reference to the internal structure of that party) and that they administer UBA as if it were one more province under their control. To quote a marketventionist dean,

The university-state relation is bad, because the university has developed a political line. The current university responds to one political party, and that is inappropriate. There is no doubt that UBA is extremely politicized, and that's a big problem. The rector has recently been a candidate running for a political party, and even the council representatives respond to political parties. Likewise, student representatives respond more to the Radical Party than to students' needs. That's a disaster. If [GFC] council representatives persist in taking a partisan attitude, the university will be over.

Most autonomists tend to assert that their resistance to government's policies is related to an ethical commitment to public education rather than to party politics. A dean expressed this view in the following way:

If the model implemented by this government model continues and wins, the future is black. In such model, the university is considered either as an obstacle or as booty. This model is supported on very weak bases. It is based on a restructuring process, leaving aside crucial areas which are duties of the state. The fiscal deficit is currently covered with the selling of our patrimony, but there are no genuine foreign investment in productive areas. Our opposition to this government has nothing to do with the Radical Party, but with our academic and critical perspective.

While other autonomists admit that the university is politicized, and regard it as a positive trait, they attempt to distance this politicization from party politics. A reformist student leader stated that

The fact that its actors have clear political commitments, gives it support from several sectors of the population and prevents it from falling apart. This is what keeps the university alive. The fact that university is politicized does not mean that university leaders act according to their political parties. No, we are primarily human subjects, and our explicit ideology and action is, from a corporatist perspective, in the good sense of the word, the irrevocable defense of the university. Although opposition to government policies can be observed in many areas, as it happens in most democratic societies, there is no other public institution besides the university engaged in clear and organized opposition. We never say that the university is against the government, except when the latter attacks its fundamental principles like autonomy, or cuts its budget. In these occasions the university responds as such, and not as a political party within the university. Since the opposition is an organized one, the government cannot stand it, because of its own perverse logic that makes them feel as owners of the state.

Standing somewhat a crossroads between autonomists and marketventionists, some university actors blame both the Rectorado and the government for mixing party politics with academic affairs. For those who feel this way, like one dean, the conflictive university-state relation "has become very political, in the negative sense of the word, that is, the relationship is shaped by the active participation of political parties." This dean, who represents a minority of actors who are interested in a reform but do not agree with government policies, simultaneously condemns university authorities and government officials, the former for engaging the university in the internal political struggle of the Radical Party, and the latter for ignoring or punishing the university due to political reasons.[9] In this view, the Peronist-Radical antagonism puts the university in a dangerous situation.

The links between party politics and institutional policy have been addressed by both contenders in a confrontational way. For instance, Schuberoff accused the then Minister of Higher Education, Ignacio Palacios Hidalgo, of authoritarianism and submission to the frivolity of politics, and Palacios Hidalgo accused Schuberoff precisely of the same sin. Nevertheless, according to higher government officials, the university-state dispute has been exaggerated by the media and the public opinion. One of them, for instance, contends that this relation "is not as conflictive as many people think. There is a heated debate due to different perspectives. There is a controversial relation, but not a conflictive one. Under this government there are no interventions or any other type of authoritarianism."

This government official is correct in the sense that this government, unlike previous military regimes, does not resort to the big stick in order to influence university policy. As a matter of fact, the conflict between autonomists and marketventionists has very seldom escalated to the level of violence, and when it has (like in the case of reformist leader Daniel Petrillo, President of the Student Association of the faculty of Architecture, who was beaten and received death threats), it immediately attracted the concern of media and politicians, including President Menem.[10]

Indeed, even when the UBA-state conflict is characterized by hostility, distrust and mutual accusations, contenders never allowed the dispute to escalate beyond a degree that would breakdown the dialogue. For instance, at one peak of the confrontation UBA's central administration almost took over in the faculty of Medicine (on the grounds that it did not comply to a GFC resolution) but eventually refrained because that would have led, in turn, to a government takeover of the university. On another occasion, when an open clash seemed inevitable, the government temporarily withdrew the issues of tuition fees and performance-based salaries from the negotiation table. In exchange, university rectors (including UBA's rector,

Schuberoff), accepted external evaluations and a new governing system that gives the majority to professors. These agreements have avoided a high political cost to the government and at the same time have prevented a fracture within the National University Council.[11]

The Most Debated Issues

The core of the conflict lies in the efforts undertaken by marketventionists to implement a thorough university restructuring more in line with the heteronomous model, and the eagerness of autonomist (the majority of university actors in decision-making capacities) to remain loyal to the reformist model. The pressures to abandon the autonomist model is apparent in a variety of aspects, such as tuition fees, admission policies, student participation in governance, responsiveness to societal demands and state control.

The most controversial among them is the issue of tuition fees, which has become the flagship of the battle between autonomists and marketventionists. It is an emotional issue that creates intense debate in political life within and outside universities. Indeed, tuition fees constitute a symbol of the struggle over accessibility, usually expressed as the quality vs. equality debate.[12] In UBA, tuition fees were imposed in the period 1980-83 under the last military regime with the explicit purpose of increasing revenues. Nonetheless, the impact was much lower than what their supporters expected because they representing only 3.8 percent of the total university revenue. To avoid criticisms of social selectivity, it was decided to use a large part of the fees to help students from lower strata. However, the loans and scholarships thus dispensed benefited only 1.3 percent of the university population (Cano 1985:91, Perez Lindo 1985:184).

As a result of this experience, Cano predicted that tuition fees were very unlikely to be applied in Argentina under a democratic government, because it is emotionally associated with the militaries. Hence, he forecasted that the only alternative to face the growing demand for access was a drastic increase in the budget allocated to university.

However, in the early 1990s, under a new political and ideological climate, the issue of fees, formerly a taboo, became a topic of open discussion. Advocates of tuition fees in Argentina invoke the widely appealing redistributionist argument which has been advanced by sources as disparate as Marx and the World Bank. This argument contends that tuition fees should be understood as a basic redistributionist policy to eliminate the 'subsidy to the upper classes' implied in the free public university. In an unexpected rupture with autonomists, the leader of university professors,

Aníbal Velásquez, concurred with this redistributive view, agreeing with the government's claim that low income groups are underrepresented in higher education.[13] He declared that public universities are moving toward privatization and, although he recognizes that tuition fees are just a palliative measure for the situation of universities, he supports them in the name of equity. For him, the problem that working class youth cannot afford to study is not only a university problem, but also a broader problem that requires a political solution through intervention.

In 1991 voluntary fees were implemented in two bastions of Reformism, such as the Universidad de Córdoba and the Faculty of Architecture in UBA. Simultaneously, certain services like diplomas, certificates, transcripts, etc., have begun to be charged for in several universities. Although fees still remain a political impossibility in many public universities, the 1995 university law has removed the legal prohibition to charge fees to undergraduate students.

The debate over fees often reached the stage of electoral campaigns. A candidate to governorship of the Province of Buenos Aires for the October 1991 elections, Santiago de Estrada, considered "positive" the concern of the Ministry of Education to generate genuine resources for higher education. He labeled as "unjust socialism" the fact that funding of public universities relies on 32 million Argentines, of which one third live below the poverty line, and contended that most university students can afford the partial or even total cost of the educational service they receive."[14]

University rectors demand state support for higher education in an indirect way, using a technical language that recalls the importance of education for society. In the aforementioned *The university and the future of the nation*, the rectors pointed out that "university is the natural place for creation, renovation and dissemination of strategic knowledge." Therefore, they contend that "education, and higher education in particular, is the most strategic investments a nation can make in today's world," and reinforce their case by claiming that "the creation of new scientific and technological knowledge presents the highest aggregated value of the history, and a nation without such capacity cannot face with autonomy the challenges of today's world."[15] In his answer to the rectors, the Minister of Education acknowledged the "basic responsibility of the state in scientific and technologic research, which is mainly based in universities" but explained that, in the context of the crisis, "the exercise of such responsibility requires to access all available means and resources, without restrictions," and openly referred to tuition fees as a possible funding source. Although the Minister made it clear that the implementation of tuition fees would be left to the 29 university rectors, some months later President Menem stated that "in the future university students must pay for their education," a statement criticized by autonomists as an infringment in institutional autonomy.[16] During 1991 students' demonstrations against tuition fees began to take place, sometimes resulting in violent incidents.[17] These demonstrations continued to this date, cautioning both government officials and university authorities of the political costs of imposing fees.

Among the 29 rectors, it is difficult to identify who were in favor of fees because, with a few exceptions, they preferred to maintain a low profile on the issue. Those who opposed them are generally more vocal, standing out among them Oscar Schuberoff (UBA), Ricardo Biazzi (Misiones), Martín Campero (Tucumán) and Fortunato Daher (Jujuy), who publicly claimed that such a policy was a form of discrimination against poor students, and the "it constitutes an affront in the context of the socio-economic situation of many families because, in addition to already existing difficulties in attaining an adequate standard of living, there are now additional difficulties to access education."[18] Likewise, the rectors of the universities of Catamarca and La Pampa made public declarations against imposing tuition fees in their institutions, arguing that they reinforce existing inequalities.[19] Although in 1990 and 1991 politicians of the ruling party were reluctant to publicly promote tuition fees for electoral reasons, they became more outspoken since 1992.

The Argentinean government rapidly transformed the discussion on the pertinence of tuition fees to a debate over who was going to pay, and how much. In other words, if tuition fees were to be universal or differential and, if the latter were the case, which criteria would be used to determine who pays less and who pays more? Antonio Salonia, the Minister of Education who once said that tuition fees would be left to the will of universities, later declared that "tuition fees will vary according to careers that are, or are not, of nation's interest."[20] Some rectors, like Daher (Jujuy), opposed this formula on two grounds: first, the difficulty to define what is the national interest; and second, that such a plan would be a deterrent for careers that are not of the interest of the national state. At the same time, the possibility of differential fees by careers ignited existing interfaculty struggles. On the one hand, following the rationale of the rector of UNAM (Mexico), arts and humanities students maintained that they should pay less than science and engineering students, because those programs use expensive equipment and facilities (infrastructure, labs, chemicals, instrumental, etc.). On the other hand, science and engineering students argued that they shouldn't pay at all, because their work was socially and economically relevant for national development, and contended that arts and humanities students should pay, because those were luxury activities, good for individual growth but socially irrelevant.

The other contentious issue in the marketventionist agenda relates to admission policies. For marketventionists, the public university has experienced a quality decline, and such decline has been caused by enrollment expansion. Hence, they claim, a more restrictive admission policy is imperative to restore quality. Whereas supporters of free and open access enjoyed ideological supremacy for several decades, in the 1990s they are increasingly challenged by marketventionists, who accuse them of being populists, demagogues, idealistic. In an unprecedented movement, two faculty councils at UBA (Medicine and Engineering) called for the elimination of the university-controlled introductory course (CBC) and its replacement by an admission policy controlled by the faculties, which could include the implementation of a quota system. The Dean of Medicine, Luis Ferreira, even had a target number of 700 incoming students per year. In the Faculty of Medicine of La Plata University, entrance examinations were already approved in 1991 and since implemented.[21]

Marketventionists argue that, although access to university is a legitimate aspiration of everybody, free access generates some unpredicted and undesired effects, such as the aforementioned quality decline, the devaluation of diplomas, the lack of articulation between large contingent of graduates and job opportunities, and state's difficulties to channel resources to other cultural and scientific areas or to other levels of education. They also contend that expansion resulted in low terminal efficiency (high drop out rates, extremely long careers, etc.) and brain drain. Autonomists, on the other hand, contend that there is not enough evidence to link expansion with quality decline. For them, the quality of graduates has more to do with educational practices than enrollments. This was precisely the argument raised by Rector Schuberoff in response to Dean Ferreira. Based on a study conducted by an ad hoc committee, he stated that the number of students enrolled in certain courses offered by the faculty of Medicine was the same as it had been twenty years before, during the golden age, when students received three times the lectures with one-fifth the number of professors.[22] Autonomists and marketventionists also disagree about the origins of the brain drain. Whereas marketventionists contend that the excessive number of university graduates emigrating abroad or underemployed is due to an overproduction of graduates relative to the capacity of the market to absorb them, autonomists suggest that the alleged surplus of graduates has not been created by the university, but by an obsolete economic structure, the low level of indigenous research and development, and the rigid social structure typical of conditioned capitalism.

Curiously, the third area of proposed restructuring raised by marketventionists, the increasing links with industry, has not become a contentious issue. The new wave of contracts with the private sector in the early 1990s, the clear support of them expressed by the university administration, and the almost complete absence of critical voices about their potential negative effects[23] shows that the "service university" (Newson and Buchbinder 1988) is under full implementation. In spite of the poor public image of business,[24] autonomists not only do not oppose partnerships with the private sector, but also publicly express their strong support for them. Reformist faith in the positive effects of the "service university" can be partially explained by the historical insulation of Argentinean universities from the national economy. Balán (1990:19), for instance, has pointed out that the Argentinean public university had grown out of tune from societal demands for human resources and knowledge and warned that, if the situation was not corrected, the lack of tune would only increase in the future. The scarce historical experience in university-industry partnerships explains why, in Argentina, unlike in developed countries, there is little debate about this issue.

The Four Fronts of the Conflict

The dispute over the university is fought in a variety of fronts. Prominent among them are the legislative, the institutional, the ideological and the financial.

The Legislative Front: An Indecent Proposal?

The strained relation between marketventionists and autonomists can be traced to the higher education policies of the Menemist government which assumed power in 1989. That very year, the then Minister of Education, Antonio Salonia, called for the end of the educational island, the pure science in the isolation of the laboratory, and the culture of stratosphere, faraway from the people and the concrete problems. He also claimed that resource allocation traditionally favored university at the expense of basic education, which is not only inadequate but also unjust. In an implicit reference to autonomous governance, he stated that "the current university is not the one of 1918. There are new social, technological and cultural demands. Therefore, university affairs are of interest to society as a whole, and new institutional mechanisms to include social and governmental representatives in the university should be developed." Furthermore, he contended that "university planning must constitute a technical-political instrument, coherent with national socio-economic and educational planning" (Salonia 1989).

Following these directions, a legislative proposal was prepared by the Secretary of Educational Coordination, Enrique Bulit Goñi (who was the head of the Argentine delegation to the World Conference on Education for All held in Thailand in 1990, co-sponored by the World Bank, in which an emphasis on basic education was proclaimed) to modify Law 23,569 which regulates university funding. That project attempted to eliminate the prohibition to charge fees, and to promote alternative sources of funding. Article 6 of the proposal stated that universities could not allocate to non-academic staff salaries more than 20 percent of the amount allocated to academic staff. Additionally, article 11 compelled universities to submit to the Ministry of Education information about academic, administrative and financial affairs at the times and under conditions required by the Ministry. Minister Salonia denied the existence of such a proposal stated that "there is no official project oriented to move the state away from its financial duty to universities" and attributed the misunderstanding to a rumor initiated by a newspaper. However, the newspaper alluded to by the Minister reaffirmed the existence of the project (Clarín, April 3, 1991:39). One month later, in an interview with another newspaper, Salonia acknowledged that the project indeed existed, and that it was designed "to define new, non-conventional sources of funding which could include, fees, consultories and research results" (*La Nación*, May 9, 1991:10).

Some months later, Clarín (Sept. 21:2-3) disclosed more specifics of the government's project. The main proposal was that state funding would no longer be the major source of resources. Moreover, the state would "reward" universities which comply with its educational policy, obtain their own financial resources, increase the proportion of graduates and reduce the budget allocated to support staff and administrative activities. In fact, Article 4 made it clear that the state would reward universities that charge fees as well as show greater efficiency and educational quality and that, for funding purposes, the state would take into account the correspondence of academic activities of universities with the overall government educational policy. Other administrative reforms contemplated annual external audits and a selective salary policy for academic and support staff based on performance. Universities would be granted the freedom to hire personnel and make investments. Student fees would be implemented together with fee waivers, scholarship and graduate tax.

These administrative and financial reforms proposed by Bullit Goñi were accompanied by a plan for academic reform, prepared by the then Vice-secretary of University Affairs, Luis de Imaz. Among the changes proposed was the elimination of co-governance: only full professors would form part of university government; students, assistant professors, and support staff would no longer be entitled to have representatives in university councils, although they could present specific problems related to their areas. Another intended reform was the creation of boards (with representatives of both the university and the community at large) to manage the use of non-state resources, and to pursue donations and subsidies. University products, both in terms of teaching and research, were to be subject to quality control, implemented through evaluations performed by internal and external juries. These evaluations would lead to the development of rankings by discipline. In the same plan it was proposed that the granting of professional licenses be removed from the university and allocated instead to a commission formed by representatives of the university, the state and professional corporations. In terms of hiring and salary policies, the plan stated that professors would be hired through open competition (as it is currently the case) but also through direct contracts, and that salaries could vary by universities.

The response from the university community was ardent. The National Interuniversity Council (CIN) vehemently opposed the majority of the 16 articles of the administrative-financial project, especially Article 4. Rectors argued that, although budget distribution was supposed to consider educational quality and administrative efficiency, in reality resource allocation would punish those universities that do not follow the government's agenda. They also opposed tuition fees and some of the indicators for quality and efficiency proposed by the government such as graduate/undergraduate enrollment ratios, proportion of expenditure in academic and support staff, and the procurement of additional resources. The rectors also pointed out that site control and evaluation of university activities would reduce university autonomy and lamented that the Ministry of Education perceived education as an expenditure rather than as an investment. In this regard, CIN rejected the proposal that henceforth the university budget would be allocated by the Ministry of Education and not by the Parliament. Some rectors alleged that the proposed reforms followed IMF requirements, and Schuberoff, the Rector of UBA, took a strong stand against budgetary cuts, and pointed out that the proposed reform, if implemented would limit access to the university to an elite and would mean an end to knowledge creation. He also expressed a concern about the Minister of Education's announcement that universities would not have any choice but to impose fees because of the state's unwillingness to continue taking charge of budgetary necessities that exceed the current allocation of resources (*La Nación*, May 10, 1991:9).

In a meeting held in Jujuy in March 1991, the rectors of the five North West universities (Jujuy, Tucumán, Santiago del Estero, Catamarca and Salta) opposed the project of university privatization which, according to them, originated in the Ministry of Economy. The rectors denounced the proposal, saying that its implementation would transform universities into non-state public institutions which would receive state support similar to that received by private institutions. The rectors argued that the state should not abandon its responsibility for public education, and that revenues from business or from students would be insufficient to cover operational costs of legislation, it created fertile ground for a national discussion on topics that only a few years ago were taboo in Argentina. Moreover, it pressured university authorities to recognize the shortcomings and inefficiencies of the university system, and to show a willingness to seek solutions for the problems identified by the government. For instance, the aforementioned five rectors, after criticizing the government's initiative, expressed a commitment to reduce spending and to avoid duplication of programs.

But the legislative battle was not over. By 1992, several drafts of a new education law intended to replace the Law 1420 (sanctioned more than 100 years ago, and considered the pillar of the Argentinean educational system) were ready to be discussed in the Parliament. In terms of higher education, the most contentious issue revolved around tuition fees. The character of the competing proposals and the significance of the social forces backing them made it clear to the government that it would not be an easy task to convince legislators about the benefits of privatization. When the government realized the difficulties involved in imposing direct fees, it attempted to introduce them indirectly through the tax system. Indeed, in July, 1992, the government proposed a new law according to which wealthy parents with children attending public universities would pay an extra tax of US$1,000 per annum.[25] Coincidentally, a study sponsored by the World Bank published in 1990 suggested that income tax surcharges might be more politically acceptable than a violation of the principle of zero tuition.[26] However, although the government proposal theoretically excluded people with low income or capital from its tax, autonomists rejected it. They argued that education (like health), being a public good, cannot be divided into users and non-users for forms of tax collection, and rapidly organized a massive demonstration "for the defense of public education." On July 5, 1992, 100,000 people congregated in front of the Parliament shouting the slogan "students yes, customers no." Those demonstrators demanded free public education at all levels, participation of the education community in policy formation and decision making, and respect for the principles of autonomy and co-governance. President Menem claimed that he totally agreed with these demands, because his government was never against public education. Moreover, as an attempt to gain public support, during the days before the demonstration, his government published full-page advertisements in the major national newspapers asserting its commitment to public education, free education, adequate financing and community participation (*La Prensa,* July 1, 1992:3; *La Nación,* July 6, 1992:2; and Clarín, July 31, 1992:33).

Another area in which legal concerns were raised relates to the newly created public universities. These universities are governed by their own legislative actors that do not provide for the establishment of GFCs and co-governance. Instead, government is given a leverage in the selection of university authorities. Autonomists denounced this situation saying it violates the law 23,068 (Normalización Universitaria), undermines the principles of autonomy and democracy, and constitutes one more instrument of government control over universities.[27]

The juridical battle reached its peak on Auguust 10, 1995, with the passing of a new Higher Education Law (No. 24,521). Some of its articles, such as the restrictions of student participation in the governing system or the authorization to charge fees generated legal challenges, institutional conflicts and even violent confrontations with the police. Other controversial articles related to possible causes of state intervention, the power to grant professional degrees, the provision of state funds to private universities and some regulations on access and regularity of students, and one article that included an unusual clause seemingly to respond to the specific demands of UBA's Faculty of Medicine.

The Institutional Front: The Enemy Within

Within UBA, the marketventionist agenda was advanced by the representatives of the minority in the GFC, particularly by members of the Faculty of Medicine. As a matter of fact, Medicine was the pilot site used by the government to introduce market-oriented reforms and to confront the central administration. Three concurrent elements seem to have interacted in this choice. First, the government needed to have a forceful ally within the university which would play a strategic role in shifting the university-state conflict into an intramural dispute. Second, the prestige and tradition of the Faculty of Medicine makes its case more appealing to the community at large than those of other faculties. As one student member of the minority pointed out "in this country, the image of the university, in terms of the public opinion, is focused on Medicine." Thirdly, the historical opposition of the faculty of Medicine to UBA's central administration, based on demands for autonomy and the ideological affinity of the dean to the government agenda, made this faculty a "natural" site to initiate the offensive against autonomists.

Since students are a key factor in university decision-making, it was important for marketventionists to control the Medicine Students Association. In highly controversial elections, the pro-government slate, FUNAP, won the majority of votes. Franja Morada formally issued an accusation of electoral fraud, arguing, among other charges, that CBC students were not allowed to vote. The Faculty of Medicine, invoking a recent decree issued by the government (known *as Decree 1111, or Recurso de Alzada*), bypassed the authority of the GFC and appealed to the Ministry of Education, which settled the dispute in favor of FUNAP. The decision was denounced by university authorities and student leaders as one more government assault on institutional autonomy. The connections between this slate and government officials were openly acknowledged by one of its leaders, who proudly recounted that, after electoral victory, he was personally congratulated by President Menem in the official residence. Likewise, he complained that, since university authorities were unwilling to release financial information, he gathered data on administrative inefficiencies and corruption from the Ministries of Economy and Interior.[28] Furthermore, this student leader advocated a reallocation of funding from higher to basic education, using a justification that was, in essence, a simplified version of World Bank argumentation.

The neverending confrontations between the Dean of Medicine, Luis Ferreira, and the reformist bloc, particularly the Rectorado and FM, continued in GFC meetings and in media statements. Ferreira and Schuberoff not only disagreed over university policies, but even over statistical information. For instance, Ferreira argued that in the 1992 budget his faculty was discriminated against because it received only 7.8 percent of the budget, while Rectorado allocated 19 percent to itself and 12.3 percent to the CBC. Schuberoff contended that the budget allocated to the Faculty of Medicine was close to 23 percent, whereas the CBC, which provides services to 35 percent of UBA student, only receives 9 percent.[29] During 1991 and 1992, it was very rare that in the Senate meetings (which take place twice a month) a conflictive issue related to the Faculty of Medicine was not addressed. Usually, Dean Ferreira was accused by other members of violating one or more university laws and/or resolutions. For instance, in the last meeting I attended (March 25, 1992), Ferreira was indicted with two charges that, according to the accusers, justified taking him to academic court. A professors' representative (majority) expressed his frustration with this situation, and one dean interpreted it as a larger problem related to the weakening of university autonomy:

> Professor: I'm tired of spending all our time on the faculty of Medicine. The Dean of Sciences was just telling me that he will not be able to pay salaries to his academic staff after September and the same situation is taking place in other faculties. I think that we have grave problems in this

university besides Medicine that demand our attention as GFC representatives.

Dean: It is not a problem of Medicine. It is an institutional problem of the
university. The problem is who rules in UBA. The central issue is not Medicine, but the state-university relationship in the context of autonomy. There
is a steadily increasing hegemony of the Executive Power in institutions
such as the judicial system and the university.

In the same meeting, Rector Schuberoff also linked the Faculty of Medicine issue with an attack against university autonomy orchestrated by the
government:

Only the Minister of Education knows what the next aggression will be,
and what he wants from the university. The university functioning itself
is being threatened, because autonomy is being violated, and there is no
university without autonomy.

In constant declarations to newspapers, Ferreira accused the university authorities of administrative corruption particularly in the CBC and
Rectorado, but also in other areas such as Extension, Culture, and Sports.
Some newspapers linked these allegations to the Peronist-Radical confrontation at the national level, pointing out that Ferreira's main target was an
internal group within the Radical Party known as "Coordinadora," in which
UBA's rector is an important protagonist. Dean Ferreira, during the annual
dinner of physicians of 1991, in the presence of President Menem, issued
an alert about a supposed Marxist infiltration in the CBC (he referred to
the inclusion of Althusser's work in the course on state and society), an
accusation by Domingo Cavallo, the Minister of Economy. One year later
on December 9, 1992, during a similar celebration, and again in the presence of President Menem, the Dean of Medicine criticized the links between the University of Buenos Aires and the Radical Party, as well as the
use of university autonomy to promote an island which is divorced from
the community.[30]
In certain claims, particularly the replacement of the CBC by an admission system controlled by each faculty, the Dean of Medicine has received the support of four other deans.[31] While critics of CBC argue that it
is merely a waiting room that makes students waste a full year, and that it
has no usefulness at all,[32] autonomists contend that the elimination of the
CBC (which has been proven successful on several grounds) would allow
Ferreira to control access to Medicine, imposing quotas and entrance examinations. The Rectorado also accuses Ferreira of being the founder and

former director of a private health care system in which many doctors have full-time appointments at the university, including Ferreira himself (*Página 12*, April 3, 1992).

In mid-1993, the government submitted draft legislation to Parliament imposing tuition fees in public universities. At that time, a World Bank document circulated among government officials recommending that Argentinean students should be charged a "a modest tuition of US$100 per term plus US$20 per month," and proposing that fees and tuition be combined with loans and scholarships for low-income and meritorious students (WB 1993:91). Simultaneously, the Vice-Minister of University Policy, Juan C. del Bello, stated that fees would be complementary to state monies, that part of the revenue generated would be channeled to student aid programs, and that no portion of it would be allocated to salaries. He added that the proposal induced universities to rationalize their spending. The government's argument for fees was based on the results of a survey carried out by the Faculty of Medicine under the auspices of Dean Ferreira, involving 1,800 incoming students. Based on the SES of these students, Ferreira estimated that the majority of them were able to pay a monthly fee of US$100. The national leaders of students and professors' associations (FUA and CONADU), rejected the draft arguing that only a minority were able to pay a fee, that the faculty of Medicine of Buenos Aires is not a representative sample of Argentinean universities, and that Ferreira's estimations did not consider total family expenditure per student (*La Nación*, July 19, 1993:3).

Interestingly, the eagerness on the part of the Faculty of Medicine to introduce fees and quotas is not restricted to UBA. In 1991, the faculty of Medicine at the Universidad de Tucumán imposed both fees (for a value of US$7.50 per month, the equivalent of 25 bus fares) and entrance examinations. According to the dean, Carlos Fernández, entrance examinations helped reduce the number of incoming students from 1,800 to 1,500, which still far exceeds his ideal figure of 300 incoming students per year. At UBA, although the Faculty of Medicine was the most visible opposer to Rectorado, it had the support of other faculties on specific issues such as admission policies.[33]

The Ideological Front: Manufacturing Consent

In addition to the legislative and institutional combats, a third contest took place in the realm of ideas. The aim was to persuade the contending party—and public opinion—about the adequacy and the social benefits of each agenda. The battlefield included papers presented in academic fora, articles and inserts in newspapers and magazines, press conferences, media interviews, institutional documents and the like. On most occasions the strategy was not to present the appropriateness of one's own case, but to attack the opposition on various grounds, ranging from inefficiency to corruption. For this reason, several university analysts complained that there was an absence of serious debate, and that much of the debate taking place was rather fruitless.

Ideologically speaking, the headquarters of the marketventionist bloc was in the Ministry of Economy, where a professional team was developing the government's agenda for the social arena. The coordinator of the World Bank-funded project, made it clear that the project aimed at pushing the university closer to market and state imperatives:

> University people have plenty of biases against businesspeople and politicians. They don't feel that they are part of national reality. Now, with Cavallo [the Minister of Economy] they are finally waking up. Radicals are stagnated in the 1918 Reform principles. They defend an autonomy that makes no sense. They must understand that they depend on the government, be it the Ministry of Education or the Ministry of Economy. In other words, if they don't behave as required, that is, with social responsibility, we'll cut the funding.

The specific project for university restructuring, Project 06, aimed at improving efficiency and quality through the development of administrative and academic criteria. Administrative criteria would provide the foundations for an organizational rationalization, focusing on cost reductions. Academic criteria would provide objective elements for quality evaluation In both cases, the project proposed comparative analyses across different institutions. Fees, restrictive admission policies, non-governmental sources of revenue, managerial procedures, performance-based incentives and reduction of students' participation in governance were among the broad array of policy issues addressed by Project 06 members. Although the loan provided by the World Bank for the Project 06 is not tied to any specific agenda, the similarities between World Bank recommendations and Project 06 proposals are inescapable. In their efforts to foster institutional and ideological support for university restructuring, the state and its social policy development agencies and functionaries find a reliable and resourceful ally among World Bank personnel who are responsible for promoting the Bank's own education agenda (see, for instance, the correspondance between William Experton, senior economist of the WB, and the then Secretary of University Policy, Juan Carlos del Bello published by La Nación on June 29, 1995).

Both the WB and the Project 06 staff attribute the university-state conflict to the resistance to change of a conservative institution rather than to compatible perspectives on the role and functions of university in society. Both agree that, since the university is unable to change by itself, the restructuring process should be imposed from outside, and both are aware that this imposition will lead to strife. Indeed, one member of Project 06 predicted that many conflicts were going to arise "because the university community has a resistance to change." Anticipating these situations, WB documents warned government officials about the potential difficulties of implementing university change in a hostile environment and offered advice on how to deal with specific dilemmas.

World Bank documents also tend to lament the politicization of university life in Latin America. As Winkler (1990:16) states, "the political nature of some administrative positions leads to their being filled by individuals with strong political skills rather than individuals with expertise and experience in university administration." Coincidentally, one of the most recurrent criticisms of UBA authorities by Project 06 staff, and marketventionists in general, is that the political activism of Rector Schuberoff is incompatible with the stature of his position. Curiously, the reproach has been very seldom used to target university authorities connected to the Peronist Party, or even to those who, though devoted to the Radical Party, are sympathetic to the marketventionist agenda, such as Universidad de Córdoba Rector Francisco Delich. In other words, the concern of marketventionists does not seem to lie in the fact that Schuberoff is involved in party politics but rather in his opposition to government plans. For instance, one member of Project 06 admonished that:

> Universities should not assume a confrontational attitude with the state. They have many sins and inefficiencies that they need to deal with internally before confronting the government. Schuberoff's strategy is to confront the government, probably more for political reasons, because he is concerned about his future in the Radical Party, than for academic ones. A possible outcome of that strategy is that the government let the public university die.

By and large, autonomists firmly oppose the World Bank's social and educational policies. They identify them as a new version of the modernization project attempted by the Atcon Plan a few decades ago:

> Today, the second wave of external influence is led by the World Bank whose staff are mainly economists and technocrats. This inhibits Latin America to carry out its own reform. It's a cut throat environment. The

university of the 1918 Reform is more democratic than any alternative model proposed by the WB or the government (professor).

The WB, in the economic area, uses the spillover theory, but in the social area is the other way around. It says: "those who can pay, must pay," and this applies to all social areas, such as education, health, housing, etc. (Vice President).

The ideological battle is also expressed through the media. During the early nineties, almost no week went by in which the mutual accusations between autonomists and marketventionists were not displayed by local media, particularly newspapers. Some newspapers, such as *La Prensa*,[34] recurrently criticize the UBA administration, publishing alleged administrative irregularities in the Rectorado, sometimes on the front page.[35] Other newspapers, like *Página 12*, tend to give more coverage to the reformist viewpoint which emphasizes university achievement in spite of government cutbacks. Between them, *La Nación* attempts to provide a more balanced view, yet in its editorials it tends to show more sympathy for the government's position, arguing that "nobody ignores the reality that the state's ability to pay for everything is disappearing, and that public resources are increasingly insufficient."[36] Sometimes, government officials anonymously release information to the media about internal and external inefficiencies of universities, in order to justify the need for university restructuring.[37]

Another social actor actively using the newspapers is the Club de Harvard (formed by Harvard Alumni), which regularly conducts studies, releases reports and organizes press conferences to divulge its findings and to propose university reforms.[38] The main targets of the Club de Harvard are the CBC (on inefficiency grounds), the Rectorado (which supposedly manages resources which should be managed by the faculties), open admission policies and tuition-free education (which allegedly lead to irrational planning and wastage).[39] The arguments advanced by the Club de Harvard are similar to those advanced by government officials, by deans of professional faculties (particularly Engineering and Medicine) and by Project 06. Coincidentally, the Minister of Economy, Domingo Cavallo, is a Harvard graduate. Some university authorities complain that the government has implemented a media campaign to devalue the university, while other autonomists disagree, arguing that such a strategy is unnecessary. For instance, a reformist student leader said that:

I don't think that there is a campaign against the university orchestrated by the dominant sectors, as Alicia Camilloni [Academic Vice-President] says,[40] because the university is not as important for the public opinion, partly due to its own shortcomings. If the university is unable to implement a campaign to promote itself, because it lacks the necessary resources to do so, I don't see why the government will need to erode its image. Having said that, we cannot ignore that there are systematic mechanisms implemented by the sate to destroy the public university.

Beyond the accuracy of this analysis, both parties know that access to the media plays an important role in developing pubic image. Hence, although the government may not be interested in negative campaigning, it can erode the university's prestige by reducing its exposure to the public. Indeed, as part of the ideological battle, the government increasingly restricted UBA's access to the media. While, until the early 1990s, UBA had programs on the official TV station and two public radio stations, the government gradually removed all of them.[41] Most of the programs broadcasted consisted of distance education.

The Financial Front: The Color of Money

Whereas in the legislative, institutional and ideological battlefronts both contenders have a relative balance of power, on the financial front the control is almost exclusively in the hands of marketventionists. Autonomists claim that the budget is insufficient, and that it discourages teaching and research, while marketventionists argue that the public university is obsolete and inefficient, and that is not accountable for the funding it receives.

Autonomists recurrently complain that the state punishes the university through the power of the purse, and that the budgets of the 1990s have been even lower than those of the military regimes. However, there is no agreement between the two contending parties on this particular issue. Whereas UBA's Rector Schuberoff claims that, between 1987 and 1991, the university budget had declined by one-half, government authorities argued that the budget had increased. Each one accused the other of falsifying information and manipulating data. As a matter of fact, it is very difficult to assess the evolution of the university budget, because high inflation rates and changes in the dollar-peso parity complicate the analysis.

Nevertheless, government officials acknowledged that, at least for the period 1990-1991, although the total sum was the same for both years, there was a budget reduction in real terms of 20 percent due to inflation. Moreover, in 1991 the direct subsidies for university research assigned in the budget (known as Item 08) were eliminated and allocated instead to the Ministry of Education, which distributed the resources according to its own criteria. After an intense political campaign and lobbying, the universities pressured the government to distribute research funds according to historical patterns. For most autonomists, the financial front is, in comparison to the other three, the one most effectively used by the government to influence university policy. In their view, budget cutbacks have more power to sway the direction of the university than legislative means, institutional alliances, ideological persuasion or even direct intervention in university affairs:

> I have no doubt in my mind that many state bureaucracies are thinking of suppressing universities, but they plan to do it by strangling them through budget cutbacks. For that reason, when representatives of Franja Morada at the GFC talk about a possible intervention, I tell them that the government is smart enough to avoid an intervention, because they are aware of the political cost that such a policy may imply. Instead, they know that it is much more effective financially to strangle the university until it practically vanishes (dean).

The most common tool used by the autonomists to protest funding cuts was the call to strikes, usually in conjunction with other sectors of the education system. Between January 1, 1985 and June 26, 1992, teachers and professors engaged in 1,062 strikes, one-fifth of all the 5,034 labor strikes undertaken in Argentina in that period.[42]

Internal Conflicts

As mentioned above, neither the university nor the government constitutes a homogeneous bloc. In an intricate network of sectorial and corporate disputes, both contenders suffer a multiplicity of internal conflicts, to the extent that some individual or collective actors occasionally switch constituencies. Although the government bloc is relatively more homogeneous than the university one, the internal disputes between the Ministries of Economy and Education were not only mentioned in the interviews, but also in the media. Most descriptions agree that in this battle Economy has enjoyed a clear superiority over the Education portfolio. University actors are aware of these intra-state disputes, and alluded to them on different occasions. What follows are three examples of these references:

> The traditional scenario of the Argentine university life is changing rapidly. The state as a master of higher educational policy through its educational Ministry is now absent, and the leverage of the Ministry of Economy is increasing day by day (dean).

The government lacks an educational policy, partly because of lack of technical competence, and partly because of lack of political will. The Ministry of Education follows the orders of the Ministry of Economy, and the latter is only concerned about reduction of public expenditure. Hence, the main thing that they demand from the university is that it spends less resources; however, it is very little what universities can really save, and therefore the government is not very keen in promoting a big political confrontation (university authority).

For the time being, the only university policy of this government is adjustment, which means basically budget cutbacks. The Ministry of Education is a devaluated Ministry; it has not taken any important decision in regards to education. The most important issue is the fiscal policy of the Minister of Economy. This Ministry thinks that no substantive problem of the economic area is related to the university. This implies that science and technology are not considered a priority (student leader).

In the Ministry of Economy itself, the sympathies towards their Education colleagues are not very high. The following quotation illustrates such dismissive and derisive postures:

The Minister of Education spends the money on candies, and they request more money again and again. Until now, budgets were done in a very haphazard manner, and at the end of the year they executed the budget in a rush, regardless of the relevance of the activity. As of this year budgets are going to be elaborated by program. Likewise, there will be no more double appointments and 'ñoquis' (ghost employees). The Ministry of education has a great deal of irrationality; a profound rationalization is needed (high official at the Ministry of Economy).

High government officials in the MInistry of Economy were also concerned about the presence in the state apparatus of bureaucrats who were not completely loyal to the marketventionist agenda. One of them openly stressed that:

Those public functionaries who are in disagreement with the state's current policies should resign. If they agree, they should thoroughly support them. There is no space for sitting on the fence.[43]

Within the Ministry of Economy, there were also conflicts between staff and management of Project 06. The former, composed of educational experts, complained that the political rationality of the project coordinators has sometimes undermined technical rationality. In the same vein, they objected to the criteria used for resource allocation, arguing that project funds were used to reward personnel at the Ministry of Economy who were not directly involved in the project, but were performing political duties for the government. Finally, another internal conflict within the government has been the dispute between the legislative and the executive wings. For instance, at the end of 1993 President Menem vetoed a Congress resolution to increase the 1994 university budget by US$120 million.[44] Since that resolution had been approved by both Radicals and Peronist legislators, as a consequence of an agreement signed two weeks before between university rectors and the Secretary of University Affairs, the veto created confusion among leaders of the governing party and further exacerbated the contradictions between the Ministries of Education and Economy.

The university has not been immune to internal discord either. A number of intramural conflicts, some of them originating a long time ago, are being exacerbated by the current confrontation with the government. A first conflict manifesting through institutional and formal channels, relates to the internal disagreements in the GFC between minority and majority representatives. A second conflict corresponds to the confrontations between some traditional professional faculties and the Rectorado over issues such as fees, admission policies and budget distribution. For instance, the Faculty of Architecture imposed in 1991 a "voluntary" tuition fee like the one implemented by Delich in Córdoba. Likewise, in 1992 the faculty councils of the faculties of Engineering and Medicine denounced "administrative irregularities" (an euphemism for corruption) in the central administration, and demanded the elimination of the CBC and its replacement by an admission system controlled by each faculty. The most noticeable aspect of this conflict, as expressed in the local media, was the battle between the central administration and the Dean of Medicine describe above.

A third conflict has been the internal disagreement among autonomists as to what is the most adequate response to the pressures for university restructuring. Within the university, autonomists have to combat not only marketventionist forces allied with the government, but even some well-recognized reformist leaders and militants of the Radical party such as Rector Francisco Delich of the Universidad Nacional de Córdoba. The mutual accusations between Delich, on the one hand, and Schuberoff and Borón (President and Vice-President of UBA, respectively), on the other, were displayed in the local media, and almost ended up in Court.[45] This duel was the public expression of an increasing division of autonomist forces throughout the country into two parties: those loyal to the 1918 Reform, and those calling for its partial or total adaptation. Both groups are aware of this fracture within the autonomist movement, and refer to it using different terminology. Those loyal to the 1918 Reform consider themselves "principistas" (consistent with the 1918 principles) and accuse the other group of having an acquiescent position. On the other hand, those calling for adaptation call themselves "modernizing reformists," and refer to others as "populist reformists." It can be observed in the taxonomies advanced by the two contenders a deliberate intent to express a positive connotation for themselves and a negative connotation for their intellectual adversaries. Likewise, terms like "principismo" (consistency), "pragmatism," "state interventionism" or "market logic" were used as positive or negative, according to the ideological perspective and the intention of the interviewee.

Another internal conflict, very important for the influence of its actors in university decision-making, has taken place in the arena of student politics. Pérez Lindo (1989) argues that, in the context of the deep economic crisis and the many problems that universities are facing, the students constitute the only university group that is seriously addressing this dilemma. Regardless of the accuracy of this statement, it can't be ignored that the student movement in Argentina is very active. Cano (1985) identified four main visions or models for the university, each one supported by competing forces within the student movement: democratic-reformist, national-popular, sanitary and revolutionary island. The democratic-reformist model, based on the principles of the 1918 reform, emphasizes the function of university as an agent of social change responsive to the demands of popular sectors. It advocates institutional autonomy, democratic governance with student's participation, pluralism, quality of teaching and a linkage or research and teaching topics with national reality. The main groups supporting this model are Franja Morada (the students' organization of the Radical Party) and some moderate socialist and Marxist groups.

The national-popular model criticizes the historic divorce between the university culture (elitist and foreign-oriented) and the "popular culture," and proposes to integrate the university with the people. In terms of university policy, it agrees with many of the postulates of the previous model, although it emphasizes academic freedom and the education of non-academic staff in governance, and rejects the concept of institutional autonomy. This model is sponsored by the Juventud Universitaria Peronista (JUP), linked to a progressive branch of the Peronist Party.

The "sanitary" university model rejects the idea that universities are a site appropriate to engage in disputes over broader national political conflicts. In this view, the university must confine itself to a scientific analysis of the national problems, offering objective, academic and dispassionate solutions. This model, which also opposes politicalization, is usually supported by the independent slates.

Finally, the fourth model is the revolutionary island. It perceives university autonomy as a means to create a space of power to confront the state, which is perceived as a mere instrument of the dominant classes. Groups supporting this model, usually at the left of the political spectrum, favor the exacerbation of the contradiction between the university and the state.

Although Cano's description accurately represents the situation of the 1970s and early 1980s, during the mid 1980s a student group called UPAU emerged in the university scene. UPAU is the university branch of the UCD, a right-wing political party which endorses the privatization policies of the Menemist government. As a matter of fact, during the first years of the Menem's administration UPAU leaders received instructions on policy and strategy from high government officials at the Ministry of Education 46, who subsequently selected FUNAP as the key ally within the student movement. Although Franja Morada was recurrently attacked from the right by UPAU and FUNAP, and sporadically from the left by a variety of groups, during the early 1990s its leadership among students was practically uncontested.

In addition to these areas of dispute, the university was afflicted by other conflicts which, although not necessarily political, were influenced by (and in turn influenced) the political battles. Among these conflicts, three were particularly noticeable: inter-faculty rivalry, generational clashes, and competition between academic and administrative staff. The competition and distrust among faculties could be observed in the resistance to efforts geared towards departmentalization and even cooperation. For instance, in relation to a probable creation of one department of mathematics for the entire university, one dean argued that the specificity of mathematics in each discipline (i.e., Engineering, Exact Sciences, Architecture), should be preserved through the control of each faculty. Similar views were present in the area of health, where each faculty (i.e., Economics, Law, Social Sciences) offer similar courses, each one believing that the others are doing a poorer job. Additionally, disciplinary training also affected the attitude of university actors towards the conflict. The "two cultures" examined by Snow (1950) come to mind in the following opinion advanced by one dean:

> As a scientist, I am more pragmatic and less tied to principles ("memos principista") than other colleagues of mine, particularly deans from the humanities. I do not question if shifting from a protectionist state to a free-market state is positive or negative. For me, that is a fact.

The generational conflict is more evident in the professional faculties, where senior and junior professors are guided by a different logic, mainly due to their class origin. One professor summarized this situation in the following terms:

> Some decades ago, the university, and particularly the faculty of Medicine, used to be the place in which the upper classes did charity or gained prestige, but that time is over. Today, the rich seclude themselves in the private practice. Nowadays this is the university of the middle classes and the middle classes cannot afford charity. There is an encounter of two generations: the rich professors who earn their living from their professions and oppose the concept of full-time, and the middle class professors who earn their living from the university. Those who have simple dedication are here (in the professional faculties) either for prestige, or to avoid being totally unemployed and have some income. As a remnant of old traditions, university teaching is still perceived by many as an honor, and that perception does not correspond to the present situation. The university is still functioning with criteria from the beginning of the century, such as glory, honor and the like, and not as a daily workplace which deserves as remuneration. However, the academic work should be considered a work as any other.

This description suggests that, although the shift from the oligarchy to the middle class in the control of university policies that took place in 1918 was a relatively expeditious process, a complete change in attitudes and behavior has not occurred. Remnants of the old persist to this day. With a few exceptions, the emerging middle class has been unable to radically change the conception of the university (held both inside and outside campus) from that of being a sacred place dedicated to intellectual energy to that of being a workplace. This may explain the fact that almost one out of four UBA professors works ad honorem. This also explains why younger professors are more likely to engage in an organized union. As a matter of fact, UBA's senior professors seldom participate in the Coordinadora nacional de Docentes Universitarios (CONADU), which has a militant stance and recurrently accuses the government of "the destruction of the public university system."[47] CONADU leaders and student leaders tend to express similar viewpoints, and this affinity results in joint demonstrations and press releases.

Finally, the conflict between academic and non-academic staff has been escalating in direct proportion to resource reductions.[48] Academic staff feel at a disadvantage with respect to the unionization of support staff and the privileges enjoyed by the administrative staff. In addition to the aforementioned conflicts, university actors engage in disputes originating in factors such as political ideologies, party affiliations or disciplinary orientations. The combination of all these variables creates an intricate and fluid network of enmities and friendships, antagonisms and alliances.

The absence of internal homogeneity is not exclusive to the government and university. Within the national industry as well, an internal division can be observed. The distinct interests of large and small industry are reflected in different attitudes towards the public university. Large industry, allied with MNCs and the rural oligarchy, calls for a lean state, and is not very keen on supporting the public university. For UIA (Unión Industrial Argentina, the organization that represents the interests of large industry), the main problems of the public university are the bureaucratism and centralization typical of state agencies, and its open admission policies. In relation to the former, UIA contends that increasing state interventionism has resulted in an undesirable control and the restriction of choice, and therefore call for the urgent deregulation and decentralization of Argentinean education, for the supervision and control of public education by parents, community members and students, for the total or partial privatization of public universities, and for the separation for the academic diploma and the professional license through a system which excludes state participation.

In relation to admission policies, UIA points out that open admission has resulted not only in low quality graduates, but also "in an excess of graduates for a country whose capacity to offer a job according to the years of studies grows at a very low pace," a situation that leads to the conclusion that "the community is badly allocating an enormous amount of resources" (UIA 1988:2).[49] Given this diagnosis, the UIA recommends elimination of open admission policies in public universities and its replacement by a rigorous entrance system based on intellectual and academic merit, which should be complemented by tuition fees. According to local sources, one leader of UIA has declared that it is cheaper to import technology than to invest in R&D, and another has stated that universities should undertake only applied research.

These statements have been criticized by the scientific community, who argue that they reveal a complete ignorance about the dynamic relationship between basic and applied research (Pichel 1991). The small and middle industry representatives (organized in the Confederación General de la Industria, or CGI), instead, seem to realize their own vulnerability in the absence of an expanding internal market and an alliance with a protectionist state. They express a concern about the deterioration of the public university, and the limited relationship between university outcomes (graduates and research products) and industrial needs. Their support to the public university is not based on benevolence, but on perceptions of their own interests. They wish a betterment of the university, but such improvement should be accompanied by an increasing adaptation to the demands of small and middle enterprise.

Main Patterns in the Diagnosis and Interpretation of the Crisis

In this section, the main trends of the actors' perceptions of the situation of the Universidad de Buenos Aires are presented. The diagnosis advanced by autonomists and marketventionists has resulted in different (often conflicting) descriptions, understandings and explanations of what they referred to as "the university crisis." Though there was consensus in the description of the manifestations, discrepancies were evident at the level of interpretation: autonomists tended to emphasize the external origins of the crisis whereas marketventionists (both government officials and minority representatives within the university) stressed internal factors. Between them, it was also possible to identify the existence of smaller groups of people ("soft" marketventionists) who took some distance, pointing out relational factors. Seven general conclusions can be summarized from the main patterns observed.

The Debate on the University Crisis Was Highly Polarized

In the context of a high level of hostility between the university and the state, most of the actors approached the analysis of the university crisis from a political rationale, aligning themselves either with the university administration or with government officials. As it was possible to observe in the previous pages, contrasting appraisals were present in almost all aspects of the diagnosis, from the identification of the crisis, to its description, to the interpretation of its origins. Moreover, discrepant views were held across a broad spectrum of issues. Not only the description of the situation and the reasons advanced to account for the situation, but also the basic data: from enrollment to budget, figures provided by autonomists and marketventionists were seldom consistent. This can be partly attributable to the deficient system of statistical information,[50] but also to the manipulation of data for political purposes. In general, the relation between advocates and critics of restructuring proposals was highly confrontational, and the discussion very seldom addressed academic issues or the functions of the university in a developing society.

There Was No Agreement Regarding the
Real Extent of the Financial Crisis

First, while the university claims that the budget has suffered a drastic decline in recent years, government officials contend that this is not the case. The discrepancy seems to lie in the year of reference used as the base to compare the current budget. Second, the university administration claims that funding is insufficient, whereas the government claims that the problem is not the amount of resources, but their inefficient use. The university responds to this accusation arguing that 90 percent of the budget is directed to salaries which are determined by the state, and that there is no room for misallocation of resources. The government counters that inefficiency in resource allocation also includes staff policies. Finally, the university claims that the Argentine society and the state have sufficient financial resources to increase the university budget, but that these resources are allocated to non-priority areas or not collected due to tax evasion, loopholes and corruption. In contrast, the government contends that it is indeed suffering a real financial crisis, and that priorities in resource allocation are clear, sensible and sensitive to social problems.

In Relation to the Origins of the University Crisis,
There Was a Tendency to Assume a "Blame the Other" Attitude

The antagonistic nature of the debate is manifested in the trend to locate the roots of the problem almost exclusively in external or internal causes. In general terms, actors tended to behave according to their relative position in the system. Therefore, the academic community was more likely to identify external causes (state attack, expansion of demand, societal indifference, quality of previous educational levels, etc.), whereas government actors were more likely to identify the roots of the crisis in the internal deficiencies of the university (inefficiency, mismanagement, politics, etc.). Only a minority of academics took distance from this polarization and understood the crisis as "relational."[51]

The State Presented a More Cohesive Discourse than the University

Indeed, although in general terms university and state actors tended to blame each other for the crisis, the government presented a much more monolithic bloc, whereas the university was more fragmented. In fact, while governmental actors advanced a unified discourse, among university actors a number of conflicts and contradictions were present, with some actors defending the government position. One marketventionist idea, regularly exposed in the media, was the most clear and public example in this regard, but similarities with government diagnosis were also found among students, professors and alumni who represent minority slates. This suggests the existence of political alliances between the state and some university actors. Although these contacts were usually "underground" (in order to avoid criticism regarding state violation of university autonomy), sometimes they were reflected in the press. For some observers, the state rationale behind this strategy was to promote an internal opposition to the university administration, and to shift the public image of the university-state confrontation to a conflict within the university.

The State Presented a More Consistent Discourse (Public-Private) than the University Community

The state had not only managed to give a more monolithic structure to its position on university restructuring, but it also had a greater consistency in terms of public and private speech. While government officials usually advanced the same diagnosis in public and in private, university actors were less reluctant to engage in exercises of self-criticism in the interviews. Without considering the minority of university actors who criticized the university in public, there was a good number of university leaders who had a confrontational public discourse against the state, but a more temperate attitude in private. The self-criticisms expressed by university authorities in the interviews are practically absent in their public discourse. The greater discrepancy between public and private discourse within the university community can be explained on various grounds. First, the nature of the conflict puts the university in such a defensive position that it feels constrained to permanently publicize its achievements in terms of quality and efficiency. In this context, the university community feels that, if it publicly acknowledges inefficiencies, this may be used as justification for further cuts and would lead public opinion to transfer its sympathies to the government. Second, the confidential nature of the interviews allowed actors to express their genuine ideas without fear of political consequences. In fact, given the distinct institutional character of the state on the one hand and the university on the other, discussion, debate and internal disagreement are more likely to be present in the academia than in the state. While government officials are more inclined to appeal to instrumental rationality,[52] the nature of academic work is more likely to promote critical thinking. Therefore, university actors were more willing to criticize their shortcomings than state officials. Furthermore, it is also possible that by identifying me as a "colleague" coming from a similar institution, they felt more inclined to speak as academics than as political representatives of a particular interest group in society, and therefore, were more inclined to present a critical, "objective" diagnosis of the crisis than a passionate political apologia. This view, in which external and internal factors are seen as "objective" elements has a greater purchase among academics generally, and it is well-illustrated in the interviews by one dean who interpreted the crisis as the result of the simultaneous and contradictory developments of expansion and cutbacks, on the one hand, and inappropriate managerial procedures in the administration of the university, on the other.

In Order to Garner and Consolidate Public Support, the Two Main Actors of the Conflict are Attempting to Build a Different Concept of Crisis

Subjective factors constitute an important element of a crisis. In this sense, "crises" are partially constructed by social actors who aspire to draw societal attention to particular problems which may or may not exist. From the examination of public statements as expressed to the media, and to some extent private statements made in the interviews, it may be suggested that autonomists are attempting to build the notion of "financial crisis," whereas marketventionists are attempting to create consent around the idea of an "institutional crisis." While the university emphasizes the miraculous achievements accomplished in totally unfavorable conditions, the government stresses the inefficiency, obsolescence and social irrelevance of the university. The university debate therefore consists of a struggle for consent over the meaning of crisis. For autonomists and marketventionists, the university crisis must be interpreted as a crisis of underfunding or as a crisis of efficiency, respectively, as if they were exclusive categories. Both sets of actors of the conflict seem to be most concerned about convincing the pubic opinion of the accuracy of their perception of the crisis than in engaging in a genuine debate on the values, purposes and functions of the university.

The Debate on Diagnosis Is Being Increasingly Framed Within the "Service University" Vision

Considering the three visions of the university proposed by Newson and Buchbinder (1988), that is, social transformation, academic haven, and service university, the description provided in this paper suggests that in Argentina the debate was framed within the third vision. While very few actors diagnosed the university using as a criterion for assessment of its success its contribution to social change or its need to protect its academic environment from external interference, the majority confined the discussion within the parameters of the service model advanced by the government. In this new discussion, principles and ideas that have remained unchallenged for decades are being questioned. For instance, the once sacred principle of autonomy has moved into a discussion of accountability, in which the state accuses and the university defends itself. Likewise, academic institutions have traditionally contended that they cannot be measured with indicators that may apply to other types of institutions, such as corporate businesses. However, in their diagnosis university actors seem to be compelled to accept that the university can be considered a factory, in which input-output models and economic indicators of efficiency can be applied, and attempt to justify their social function on those grounds.

The Main Patterns in the Debate
on the Direction of the University

The different perceptions of the university crisis as described previously led to a variety of proposals about the preferred direction of the university. Whereas marketventionists have an agenda for university restructuring similar to the one undertaken by other Latin American governments, reformists are keen on defending the status quo adopted in 1918. As expected, the proposals advanced by the different actors were generally consistent with their diagnoses of university problems. Marketventionists' proposals focused on adapting the university to the needs of the economy, establishing more government control over university activities, reducing expenditures and increasing efficiency.

The main areas of dispute and agreement can be summarized in seven areas. The first area, administrative rationalization, presents the actors' views on the need for university reform, and their proposals on changes related to its organizational structure, including the possibilities of departmentalization. The second area deals with financing, the most controversial issue of the university-state conflict. The debate on financing included the topics of subsidies, resource allocation, and complementary-alternative sources of revenue, such as sale of services to the private sector and tuition fees. The third issue of debate was the function of the public university in the context of the higher education system. The discussion encompassed the role of the public university vis-a-vis the private one, and the three main functions of a university (teaching, research, extension), including topics such as the type of human resources to be developed and the clientele to be served. The fourth area deals with the debate on university governance. Salient topics in this regard were the distribution of power in decision making, the role of different constituencies in the GFC, the appropriateness of the three-party system, and the intramural struggle between the central administration and certain faculties for decision-making.

A fifth axis of debate is related to admission policies. The main disagreements here were in relation to the adequacy of quotas in terms of accessibility and market demands, the impact of massive enrollment on educational quality, and the pertinence of the introductory course known as CBC. Area six picks up the debate on research and development, and includes issues such as the role of science and technology in a developing country, the appropriateness of the Napoleonic university, partnerships with industry, the national research system and the mission of graduate programs. Finally, the last area describes the different viewpoints on the role of the state in the higher education system. Controversies arose in relation to the conflict between autonomy and accountability, evaluation of performance, differential funding policies and creation of new universities.

These goals are expected to be achieved through the implementation of stricter admission policies, tuition fees, accountability mechanisms and conditional funding. In order to remove political obstacles for the implementation of this agenda, marketventionists propose reforms that would diminish the power of students and Rectorado, and eventually lessen institutional autonomy. Confronted by this battery of proposals, distressed by cutbacks, and conscious that the university requires some urgent changes, autonomists are generally on the defensive, and unable to outline a coherent alternative. Autonomists justify their incapacity to formulate a coherent project because they are too busy responding to government pressure. In their view, a genuine reform should not be a mere response to external pressures, but the result of an internal, democratic, collegial process in which different alternatives are discussed in an open debate. For marketventionists external pressure is indispensable to provoke changes, given the conservative nature of the university.

Taking into account the patterns of proposal, it is possible to infer an informal alliance between the government, the conservative slates among professors, alumni and students, and the deans of some professional faculties, the Rectorado and the partisans of the 1918 Reform who are the majority. Although autonomists have been able to resist many of the proposals so that they are conscious that they are in a disadvantaged position and that the government has leverage in influencing the direction of the university through the power of the purse. It was also clear in the interviews that the key government agency in determining the direction is not the Ministry of Education but the Ministry of Economy, and that the proposals emanating from this Ministry and the recommendations formulated by the WB are astonishingly similar.

Institutional Structure

In relation to changes to UBAs internal institutional structure, marketventionists proposed a variety of alternatives aiming at the reduction of Rectorado power. These alternatives range from the elimination of particular units controlled by the central administration (i.e., CEA, CBC), to a fragmentation of UBA into smaller semi-autonomous units like in the Californian system. Autonomists, instead, seek administrative reforms that promote more infraction among individual faculties and reduce duplication, with the probate collateral effect of limiting the power of professional faculties. The issue of departmentalization was still a marginal topic in the debate, and not well understood by many actors. As was pointed out over departmentalization is sometimes perceived as the mobilization of professors (and not students) from one faculty to another. This misconception leads some deans to fear that their faculty may lose in the arrangement. Deans of professional faculties were also blamed for the resistance to departmentalization, and they, in turn, blamed each other for not engaging in collaborative efforts. Finally, another aspect of institutional reform stressed by marketventionists was the need to promote efficiency by including rewards for better performance.

Financing

Proposals related to financing were the ones that received the most attention in the debate. Autonomists recurrently blamed marketventionists arguing that the problems to be corrected were waste, inefficiency and mismanagement, as well as the inequities of free education. Thus, marketventionists' proposals focused on conditional funding (contingent upon outcomes and the fulfillment of certain performance indicators), and private sources of revenue, particularly through contracts with industry and tuition fees. Autonomists expressed concerns about the academic pertinence of performance indicators developed unilaterally by the government. They also feared that the high degree of discretionary power enjoyed by the government could lead to situations in which universities are financially rewarded or punished for non-academic reasons. A related concern is that the new sources of revenue become alternative, and not complementary, to state subsidies, resulting in a de-facto privatization. Increasing contracts with business, however, do not represent a contentious issue for most autonomists.

With a few exceptions, autonomists did not perceive potential risks of linking research activities. While in developed countries this topic produces a heated debate and receives substantial attention in the literature, in Argentina, probably due to the lack of experience in this regard, almost everyone anticipated that closer links with industry would bring only benefits to the university. Nonetheless, the establishment of tuition and fees was the most controversial proposal. It is the one that probably occupies the most energy in university debate, and a variety of academic, economic, and social arguments have been developed to both justify and reject fees. The dispute on fees is so emotional and intense that it seems that all contenders are taking it as the battle that can decide the outcome of the war.

Function

Partly because of the great amount of energy spent on the discussion on fees, the debate on function was almost negligible. In relation to the higher education system, UBA's autonomists criticized the recent proliferation of public universities as a waste of resources because these universities—contrary to the government's claim—have no possibilities of becoming serious academic enterprises. They also contended that UBA is not challenged by private universities because of their shortcomings in terms of accessibility, their lack of research, their low quality teaching, and their failure to offer programs in a broad variety of areas, and not only the profitable ones. Although autonomists admitted that the newly created elite private universities offer high quality programs, they claim that these universities are far removed from national reality, and provide cadres for management and not for production. Marketventionists, on the other hand, argue that private universities save public funds and that open competition elevates the standards of public universities.

At the institutional level, marketventionists contend that UBA should abandon dispensable units such as the CBC, CEA, extension hospitals and secondary schools. Not surprisingly, most of these areas are under the jurisdiction of Rectorado. Marketventionists also claim that research should be more "relevant" or applied, and that the university should be more responsive to the market and to the national economy, particularly in the context of the South American common market (MERCOSUR). Although not all these recommendations are shared by autonomists, extension is already moving towards cost-recovery services, and the commercial university is taking place in the form of research and consultations for industry even in traditionally anti-business faculties like Arts and Humanities, and Social Sciences. The transformer university model, once the hegemonic project in these two faculties and even in the whole university, has been practically absent in the debate on function; only a few representatives from the left slates (mainly student) advanced the vision that the university should be an active agent of radical social transformation.

In terms of government, the discussion focused on the ideal representation of the university community in decision-making bodies. The issues
at stake were the internal balance of power among the three parties currently represented (professors, students and alumni), and the appropriateness of including two new constituencies (assistant professors and non-
academic staff). Marketventionists tend to complain about the excessive
politicalization of the GFC, and perceive students as one of the main obstacles to the implementation of the heteronomous agenda. In this particular situation marketventionists have clear allies among a broad range of
autonomist deans and professors who would like to see a reduction of
alumni and student power, and an increase of academic power.

Admission Policies

Admission policies were, after fees, the second most contentious issue
in relation to future policies. At an abstract level, autonomists and
marketventionists advanced academic, social and economic arguments for
open admission policies, and for selective admission policies. At a more
concrete level, the original consensus on the CBC is dissipating, and even a
significant number of autonomists are accepting that the CBC has serious
administrative problems. Two professional faculties (Medicine and Engineering) are in the forefront of the battle against the CBC, claiming that it
should be replaced by an admission system controlled by each individual
faculty, which should have the prerogative to set quotas. The main criticisms to the CBC were justified on administrative, academic, political and
ideological bases. Indeed, marketventionists claim that the CBC is an inefficient and expensive mechanism to select students, that its academic standards are deplorable, that it delays student entrance into their faculties for
one year, that it promotes Marxist indoctrination, and that is a political tool
of the Rectorado to accumulate power. From an opposite perspective, autonomists contend that the CBC facilitates the transition between high
school and the university, that it allows for career changes at an early stage,
that it bridges the vacuum among separate faculties and last, but not least,
that it promotes greater accessibility. Beyond the validity of each specific
argument, the debate over the CBC cannot be isolated from the battle between the Rectorado and certain professional faculties, and the overriding
conflict between autonomists and marketventionists.

Research and Development

In the marketventionist agenda, R&D activities should be more responsive to the market, and eventually undertaken privately. Moreover, in tune

with WB recommendations, the government attempted once—in that case unsuccessfully—to privatize the national research system (CONICET). The WB has also recommended a progressive privatization of CNEA (Atomic Energy Commission). In the context of gradual reduction of state subsidies to national research centers such as INTI, INTA, and CONICET,[53] researchers are increasingly looking at the market for research opportunities.

In relation to industry's position on R&D, it is interesting to note a difference between the interests of large enterprises, on the one hand, and the small and medium enterprises, on the other. While the leaders of large enterprises, closely linked with MNCs, express concern for research at the national level and are strong advocates of privatizing the system, leaders of small and medium enterprises clearly understand the importance of the active role of the state and the university in scientific-technological development for their own survival. In spite of the traditional mutual distrust between university and industry, the links between them are increasing yearly through UBATEC. As mentioned above, very few interviewees expressed the type of concerns present in developed countries about the potential risks of these links. This indicates that whereas one of the elements of the heteronomous university (government control) is highly resisted, the second element (the commercial university) is being implemented with the appease of most autonomists.

Final Remarks

In summary, although marketventionists control the state apparatus, and autonomists steer university decision-making, both have allies outside their institutions. The debate is full of condemnations, accusations, threats and distrust. The conflict takes place on four major fronts (legal, institutional, ideological, and financial) and the influence of national politics (the Peronist-Radical dispute) is inescapable. This context may contribute to understanding who are the main actors of the university restructuring, and what are their agendas. As was advanced before, marketventionists and autonomists disagree in their diagnosis of the university problems, and thus in the pertinent intervention strategies to solve them. This chapter analyzed a conflict between two university models, a conflict that is part of a larger conflict between two societal models. Although this conflict is taking place in all regions of the world, and the two models have universal, generic characteristics, both the intensity of the conflict and the specific features of the models under dispute vary according to the social structure of each national formation and the historic development of its higher education system.

In Argentina, no one denies that the university must undertake important transformations. Government officials and universities actors alike perceive the depth of the current university crisis, and the need for change. However, since there is no consensus as to the nature of the crisis, there is no consensus about the direction and pace of change either. Although technical elements are—and should be—present in this definition, the preceding sections have shown that the process of university restructuring is essentially political. Indeed, issues like who makes the decisions, what are the criteria for making these decisions, and who are going to benefit from these decisions are not just technical matters.

The worldwide conflict between the autonomous and heteronomous university also takes place in Argentina but, due to specific historical conditions, it assumes particular expressions. As in other countries, the autonomous model is characterized by expansion, that is, availability of public funding and high accessibility, while the heteronomous model is characterized by contraction, which means declining public funding and low accessibility. The autonomous model is characterized by a high degree of publicness and homogeneity, whereas the heteronomous model is shaped by increasing government control and a market rationale that encourages privatization, cost-recovery programs, user fees, partnerships with business, competition among unity and economies of scale. In Argentina, the conflict between these two models assumes distinct features which derive from the particular developments analyzed at the beginning of this paper.

In this country, the model based on the reformist tradition is being challenged by an alternative model which has its most clear expression in the reforms institutionalized in Chile in 1981. The difference between 1918 and 1981 is more than a numerical alteration; it represents two distinct approaches to the university in particular and to society in general. These two sets of contending social actors have been identified as autonomists and marketventionists. Table 1 summarizes the main features of the competing models.

Although defenders of both models identify a university crisis, they have a different interpretation as to the causes of the crisis. For marketventionists, it is the natural result of the university's own shortcomings: inefficiency, social irrelevance, excessive expansion, politicization, and inappropriate use of institutional autonomy. For autonomists, the crisis has a clear external origin, particularly government cuts in funding. The two positions can be found in public statements made by Juan Carlos del Bello, the current Secretary of Higher Education in Argentina, and Oscar Schuberoff, the Rector of Universidad de Buenos Aires. The former contends that the profound crisis experienced by UBA is the result of inadequate allocation of internal resources and "important pockets of ineffi-

equate allocation of internal resources and "important pockets of inefficiency," whereas the latter maintains that the problems affecting UBA are "clearly budgetary."[55]

Expectedly, the disagreement in the diagnosis leads to disagreements on solutions. While autonomists maintain that the essential elements of the 1918 model should be preserved, marketventionists call for a drastic restructuring that combines market dynamics and state controls. As could be inferred from the debate on policies described in the last section, there is a high degree of correspondence between the conceptions held by each group, their diagnosis of the situation and the strategies adopted for political and institutional action. Like Persephone, the public university is being forced to live in three worlds, each one having its own rules. How each institution is going to combine the world of institutional autonomy with market dynamics and state regulations is still to be seen, as remains to be seen the way knowledge is going to be produced and distributed, and the impact of the new arrangement on national development and democracy.

TABLE 1 The Public University as Perceived by Autonomists and Marketventionists

	Autonomists	*Marketventionists*
Diagnosis	crisis of funding	crisis of efficiency
HES organization		
institutional diversification	homogeneity (equality)	heterogeneity (choice)
institutional interaction	self-regulation	competition and regulation
public-private interaction	public-private distinctiveness	public-private mix
Finance		
public sources	"historical" funding	conditional funding
private sources	almost nonexistent	cost-recovery, entrepreneurship
Functions		
research	focus on basic research	focus on applied research
teaching	public, free	commodified knowledge
extension	community service	cost-recovery activities

(continues)

TABLE 1 (continued)

	Autonomists	*Marketventionists*
Governance		
main principle	autonomy	accountability
representation	only university actors	inclusion of external actors
decision-making process	co-governance	professional managerialism
Internal organization	faculty and chatedra	departmentalization and amalgamation
Admission policies		
main rationale	entitlement rights, public investment	privilege, individual investment
entrance requirements	open access	restricted access
Employment conditions		
academic staff	tenure	"hire and fire"
non-academic staff	unionization	flexibility
remuneration policy	isonomy	individual performance
Relation with outside world		
state	financial accountability	performance evaluation
industry	research and service contracts	research and service contracts
Declared values	equity, excellence accessibility	equity, excellence efficiency

Notes

1.   The 1918 Reform, the result of an original student movement for university and societal democratization has been characterized as an historic legend, and as a grand emancipatory epic that opened a heroic cycle in the development of Latin American university (Mariátegui 1928, Brunner 1990). Student leaders of the

1918 Reform asserted that the solution of educational problems should be related to the solution of the entire national problem, which implies a profound economic and political reform of society and state. They were explicit about the ideal relationship between the university, the state and the national society, and allied themselves with workers' organizations. As a matter of fact, the Córdoba movement was endorsed by labor unions, leftist political parties, liberal groups and important newspapers, while opposition was based on the church and conservative institutions (Del Mazo 1957, Liebman et al. 1972). The most important features of the Reform can be summarized as follows:

a. institutionalization of student participation in university councils, in a three-party system including professors and alumni (co-governance);

b. a linkage between student politics and national politics, to mobilize the university toward the solution of economic, social and political problems;

c. a concern for university extension, particularly to courses for workers leading to the development of fraternal bonds with the proletariat;

d. tuition-free education, conceived as an instrument to achieve democratization of access, expanding enrollments to include all academically qualified applicants and replacing the elitist, oligarchic and archaic 19th century university by a mass university;

e. a defense of institutional autonomy with respect to the state;

f. institutionalization of mechanisms to protect academic freedom, including the implementation of "free teaching" (docencia libre) to ensure academic pluralism and to break the monopoly of teaching enjoyed by positivist disciplines;

g. promotion of new ideas, innovative methods of teaching, changes in exam systems, optional classroom attendance, original research, and a rejection of dogmatism, all leading to the replacement of theology by positivist disciplines;

h. selection of faculty through open, competitive examinations in order to counteract nepotism and patronage, and promotion of professors on the basis of merit and achievement rather than seniority;

i. the enlargement and diversification of professional training through the establishment of new professional schools;

j. an understanding of university life as a truly communitarian experience, therefore encouraging the development of a population of full-time professors and full time students.

The objectives of the 1918 Córdoba Reform were promptly endorsed by the International Student Congress on University Reform held in Mexico City in 1921, with the participation of delegates from Latin America, United States, Europe, and Asia. European and US student leaders of the 1960s movement also used the ideas which emanated from the Córdoba Reform to build their university and social projects (Ribeiro 1971, Liebman et al. 1972, Cúneo 1974, Levy 1986, Delich 1988, Pérez Lindo 1991, Brunner 1990, Tunnermann 1990, Torres 1993).

2.   For instance, in a press conference held in Santa Fe, President Menem stated the need to transform the Argentinean university. He claimed that government economic policies "do not accept a university like the current one," and argued for closer links between the university and the business sector, and for tuition fees (*La Nación*, October 18, 1991:2). At the same time that Menem pressure public universities to engage in the restructuring process recommended by the government, he publicly expressed his support to private universities. When reformists denounced in the local media that the government benefited the private Universidad de Belgrano with a tax exemption (decree 80/90 of the Ministry of Economy) for the importation of elevators installed in the new building of that institution, Menem presided the opening ceremony of that building. The rector and owner of Universidad de Belgrano, Avelino Porto, was a Minister in Menem's Cabinet. At that time, the Secretary of Education, Scientific and Cultural Co-ordination (the most powerful position in the Minister of Education after the Minister) was José Aromando, who was the Dean of Economics in the Universidad de Belgrano. Moreover, the meeting held in the presidential residency by Menem and Dean Ferreira to plan the marketventionist strategy were constantly denounced in GFC meeting by reformist actors, and referred to in newspapers (see *Página* 12 (February 25 and March 24, 1992), *La Nación* (March 22, 1992) and Clarín (July 15, 1992:18). In a personal interview, Patricio Downes, the educational columnist of Clarín, ratified to me the existence of these encounters.

3.   Another student movement called Juventud Universiatris Peronista (JUP), which represents the left branch of Peronism, maintains a more critical position to the government than FUNAP. Although JUP was the hegemonic student movement during the early 1970s, in the early 1990s it does not hold the majority in any of the 13 faculties.

4.   *La Nación*, Nov. 2 and Nov. 9, 1992:3.

5.   However, since the state is not a monolithic structure, this process was not absent of internal conflict. The polemic between the Minster of Interior and the Premier of the Province of Buenos Aires about the intentions of the student movement describe by Mollis (1990:92-93) is a good example of contradictions within the state apparatus during the 1918 Reform.

6.   The most evoked symbol of this shift is the rise and fall of the Bolshevik Revolution.

7.   *Gente*, October 16, 1990: 51.

8.   Reprinted in the "Boletín de la Academia Nacional de Educación," Buenos Aires, September 1991:7 and 8.

9.   Several university actors mentioned that the only government officials who could be interested in supporting the university because they understand its importance for national development were those working in the team of Domingo

Cavallo (the Minister of Economy, a Harvard Graduate), who was recognized basically as an intellectual. In an attempt to explain Cavallo's alleged aspiration to run in the 1995 Presidential elections, a rumor that circulated among political circles during the period of interviews.

10. See *La Nación*, July 12, 1993:3.

11. See *Página* 12, December 16, 1993:8.

12. The quality vs. equality dilemma is permanently present in debates about university policies, and the challenge of every higher education institution is how to achieve an adequate balance between them. For a discussion on this debate see Schugerensky (1994: 68-70).

13. See *La Prensa*, June 12, 1991. Velásquez argues that 35 percent of the "rich" and "very rich" benefit from public universities, in comparison to only 7 percent of lower-middle class. According to the statistics referred to by Franja Morada, however, lower and middle income groups are the one that benefit the most from higher education. As pointed out above, the indicators used to define these categories are not necessarily the same.

14. See *La Prensa*, June 11, 1991, p. 7. Estrada was the candidate of the Frente Independiente, and lost.

15. See *La Prensa*, May 10:1991:6.

16. For the Minister's statements, see *La Prensa*, May 29, 1991:4 and 6. For Menem's statement and the reactions to it from the university community, see *La Nación*, October 18, 1991.

17. *La Prensa*, June 7 1991:4.

18. *La Prensa*, May 11, 1991:5.

19. *La Prensa*, May 12, 1991:3.

20. *La Prensa*, May 29, 1991:4 and 6.

21. *La Prensa*, June 10, 1991:5.

22. See *Página* 12, February 15, 1991:6.

23. One of few voices of disagreement was observed among some groups in the faculty of Humanities (Filosofía y letras). In a document published in 1992, they complained that "la crisis por la que atraviesa la universidad argentina, resultado de una política nada favorable al desarrollo sostenido de las instituciones del estado en desmedro de la furia privatista, la hieren demuerte. A menos que salga a vender servicios y objetos varios para solventar desde sus gastos menores hasta los gastos mayores, la autonomía, la autarquía, el prestigio y la calidad académica de poco han de servir" (Boletín del Instituto de Investigaciones en Ciencias de la Educación; Faultad de Filosofía y Letras de la UBA, Vol. 1, No. 1, April 1992:1). Curiously, the objection is not about the potential negative implications of the involvement with industry, but about the inappropriateness of demanding an academic institution to look for its own sources of funding. Even more curious is the fact that the faculty of humanities receives one of the highest revenues from contracts.

24. A poll on the image of the Argentinean big-business people carried out in Buenos Aires showed the following results:

Bad	63.2%
Regular	21.3%
Good	13.7%
Very Good	0.9%
No answer	0.9%

Source: *Noticias*, February 10, 1991

25. The definition of "wealthy" was not very clear, and varied depending on the government spokesperson. According to one of the versions, parents with properties over US $100,000 were to contribute with that special text. According to another version, that sum referred only to liquid assets (see Clarín, July 29, 1992:1, 2 and 3).

26. See Winkler, 1990:84.

27. See *La Nación*, July 12, 1993:3.

28. Personal interview, March 17, 1992.

29. Clarín, March 19, 1992.

30. *Página* 12, January 7, 1992:12, and *La Prensa*, December 1-, 1992:1 and 6.

31. In addition to ferreira, four other deans are openly against CBC: Dentistry, Exact and Natural Sciences, Animal Sciences and Agriculture. The last two deans are actively linked to a dissident branch of Peronism.

32. See *La Prensa*, November 12, 1992:7)

33. The most visible ally was the Faculty of Engineering. See *La Nación*, April 2, 1992, and *Página* 12, April 3, 1992.

34. *La Prensa* is an old, conservative newspaper which represents the interests of the rural oligarchy. In its editorial columns occasionally write militaries condemned by human rights violations (i.e., Gral. Ramón Camps). Although it was severely censored during the first and second Peronist regimes, it presently supports Menem's policies.

35. See, for instance, *La Prensa*, December 10, 1992:1.

References

Albretch, D. and A. Ziderman Funding mechanisms for higher education: financing for stability, efficiency and responsiveness. Washington, DC, World Bank, 1992.

Balán, Jorge *Private universities within the Argentine higher educational system: trends and prospects*. CEDES, Buenos Aires, 1990.

Brunner, José J. *Educación superior en América Latina: cambios y desafios*. FCE, Chile, 1990.

Cano, Daniel *La educación superior en la Argentina*. Flasco, Cresalc/Unesco, 1985.

Carlson, Sam Private financing of higher education in Latin America and the Caribbean. Washington, DC, World Bank, 1992.

Cúneo, Dardo *La Reforma Universitaria 1918-1930*. Biblioteca Ayacucho, Perú, 1974.

Del Mazo, Gabriel (ed.) *La Reforma Universitaria y la Universidad Latinoamericana*. Universidad Nacional del Nordeste, 1957.

Delich, Francisco *La invención de la universidad*. Buenos Aires, 1988.

Douglas and Ziderman (1993)

Eisemon, Thomas and Jamil Salmi *African universities and the State: prospects for reform in Senegal and Uganda*. The World Bank, mimeo, 1992.

Levy, Daniel *Higher education and the state in Latin America. Private challenges to public dominance*. The University of Chicago Press. Chicago and London, 1986.

Liebman, A., et al. *Latin American university students: a six nation study*. Harvard University Press, 1972.

Mariátegui, Juan C. Siete ensayos de interpretación de la realidad peruana. *Editorial Crítica*, Barcelona, 1976.

Ministerio de Cultura y Educación *Transformacion de la Educacion Natinal*. Buenos Aires, 1991.

Neave, Guy and Frans Van Vught, "Introduction." In G. Neave and F. Van Vught (eds.), *op. cit.*, 1991.

Newson, Janice and Howard Buchbinder *The university means business. Universities, corporations and academic work*. Garamond Press, Ontario, 1988.

Pérez Lindo, Augusto El rechazo al saber y el fracaso argentino. *Página 12*, July 6, p. 2, 1991.

Pérez Lindo, Augusto *La batalla de la inteligencia. Ciencia, universidad y crecimiento*. Cántaro, 1989.

Pichel, Ricardo *Desarrollo sin ciencia: otra fantasía argentina*. Fundación Favaloro and Torres Agüero, Argentina, 1991.

Ribeiro, Darcy *La universidad latinoamericana*. Editorial Universitaria, Santiago de Chile, 1971.

Salonia, Antonio "Universidad inserta en el sistema educativo y en la sociedad nacional." Speech at the Universidad de Cuyo, August 9, 1989.

Schuberoff, Oscar Un compromiso de transformación. *Gaceta de la UBA* No. 1, October 1991:15.

Schugurensky, Daniel. *Global Economic Restructuring and University Change: The Case of Universidad de Buenos Aires*. Ph.D. Thesis, University of Alberta, 1994.

Snow, C.P. *The two cultures and the scientific revolution*. Cambridge University Press, Cambridge, 1959.

Torres, Carlos A. "The Latin American University: From the Reform of 1918 to Structural Adjustment in the 1990s. Unpublished manuscript, 1993.

Tunnermann, Carlos *La universidad lationoamericana*. UCA, 1990.

UIA *Estadio sobre la oferta y demanda laboral de graduados universitarios en la Argentina.* Estudio realizado para la UIA por el instituto Gallup de la Argentina, November 1988.

Winkler, Donald Higher Education in Latin America. *Issues of efficiency and equity.* World Bank Discussion Papers. Washington, DC, 1990.

10

Women, Education, and the State in Cuba

Sheryl L. Lutjens

The performance of the Cuban educational system offers valuable insight into the objectives, achievements, and difficulties of three decades of socialist development. While a paucity of scholarship on Cuban education after the 1970s justifies an examination of recent policies and outcomes,[1] it is the widespread speculation about Cuba's future in the dramatically altered international context of the 1990s that recommends why and where insight is indeed needed. For example, in assessing Cuba's economic prospects given the disappearance of the Soviet bloc and the tightening of an ongoing U.S. embargo, the technical and scientific capacity created by the educational system is a critical issue. Similarly, in evaluating the legitimacy of the role and rule of Castro or the Partido Comunista de Cuba (PCC) 55—key disputes in the internationalized debates about Cuban politics, the effectiveness of socialization through the schooling process is a crucial question. The purpose of this essay is to use educational policy to look at Cuban socialism and the current reform process called *rectificación* (rectification), focusing specifically on women and the socialist state.

The results of educational policies for Cuban women provide striking evidence of the accomplishments of a revolution that stubbornly refuses to abandon socialism or to collapse. Beginning with the quantifiable outcomes of formal education, progress—and problems—in women's education can be traced through three phases of post-revolutionary policy: the democratization of schooling in the 1960s; the *perfeccionamiento* [improvement] phase of qualitative improvements initiated in the 1970s; and the present phase of *perfeccionamiento continuo* [continuous improvement] associated with the

rectification process that began in the mid-1980s. Each of these phases reflects the prominent role of education within the goals of the revolution, a
role defined by nationalism, changing development strategies, and a socialist vision of economic, political, and social transformation. Gauged by
the traditional measures of access and employment, formal schooling organized by Cuba's socialist state has facilitated significant movement toward equality for women. Women's gains help map the scope of post-revolutionary change, a necessary foundation for seeing how educational policy
contributes to the process and prospects of Cuba's survival in the 1990s.

Contemporary feminist theories caution, however, that such a map-
ping must move beyond traditional measures of progress to acknowledge
the deeper dynamics of the gendered inequalities that inform the experiences of women in all societies.[2] Feminist impulses in the literature thus
offer a critical position for analyzing the more obvious inequalities in education, as well as the biases that remain hidden in our theories and educational practices.[3] In a recent essay on China, for instance, Beverley Hooper
begins by asserting gender as a variable in enrollments, areas of study, and
post-school earnings "in both capitalist and socialist countries, whether
developing or industrialized." She claims that erosion of the "gender variable" in education has been greater in Western socialist societies, that the
socialist guarantee of equal education is a necessary but not sufficient condition for women's equality in the public sphere, and that impediments in
the case of China are personal, familial, and institutional.[4] Gail Kelly argued in 1989 that work on education and third world women tended still
to "study women as if they were men and assume the schools, institutions
like the family, the political system and the work place are neutral and
devoid of [sic] attachment to sex gender systems." With praise for emerging "women-centric studies," Kelly noted that only a few consider
education's relationship to power in the family and "even rarer are those
studies which look at how education affects women's access to power and
authority in society."[5] A feminist perspective reveals more about women
and change by turning attention to the less-measurable gender realities
associated with education *and* the socialist state.

Accepting feminist assumptions about universal gender subordination,
women themselves become a useful measure of education and its contribution to post-revolutionary development in Cuba. Indeed, women have a
crucial place in the transformation of social relations promised with socialist educational policies, a place defined by the purposes, principles, and
organization of Cuban education, as well as the gendered division of labor
in public and private life. Yet feminist debates also contest the epistemological status of universal claims and categories, suggesting that *Cuban*
women must be the focus for exploring the historically and culturally spe-

cific expression of the "gender variable" in Cuban education.[6] The challenge of locating Cuban women in the process and practices of education is indeed a matter of focus. Seeing more clearly the complex location of women within the dynamics of education, as well as the participation of women in making change, a challenge is mounted, in turn, against the categorical claims about socialism that confound the understanding of the past and present needed for forecasting Cuba's future.

It is possible to use Cuba's distinctive commitment to education to think more carefully about Cuba, about reforms that still reject capitalism and liberal democracy, and about a future that will undoubtedly be shaped by economic crisis and the centralized authority of a socialist state. Critics who find only failure in the persistence of planning, a vanguard party, or Fidel Castro have erred time and again in announcing Cuba's collapse. Moving from traditional measures to newer feminist concerns to frame an examination of women, education, and the state, this essay argues that uncovering the perplexities of gender can provide vital clues to the societal dynamics of socialism *and* crisis in the 1990s.

Women and Formal Education

The educational policies of the Cuban revolution increased women's access to education in important ways. Women elsewhere in Latin America and the Caribbean made gains in this period, too, as global trends between 1950 and 1980 included a marked regional movement toward gender equality in enrollments.[7] Still, Cuban history and socialist goals warrant special attention in reviewing the outcomes for women of better access to formal schooling after 1959. The long-standing feminist concern with exclusion of women from public life can be explored, using enrollments and employment to show where the gendered division of labor has been affected by the changing educational policies of Cuba's socialist state.

Education in pre-revolutionary Cuba is a necessary backdrop for reviewing women's advances after 1959. With illiteracy at 63.9 percent at the end of Spanish colonial rule, the functioning of the educational system created during the U.S. occupation reflected the structural conditions and social dynamics of the dependent 20th-century Cuban republic.[8] Recording relatively good performance as a Latin American country along some indicators—including women's education, by 1953 the average level of education was 2.4 years and nearly half of Cuban children aged 6-14 were not enrolled in school.[9] The constitutional promise of public schooling went unfulfilled as education was caught up in the politics of patronage, private schools prospered, and disparities between rural and urban Cuba accentuated class differences.[10] Educational opportunities illustrated the complex intersections of class, race, and gender inequalities in pre-revolutionary Cuba.

Cuban women were the first in Latin America to benefit from secular public education "with full access to all levels in coeducational institutions," according to Miller.[11] By the 1930s and 1940s the rate of female literacy outpaced that of males, while in the 1950s, female enrollments were 51 percent at the primary level, 41 percent at the secondary level, and 46 percent in higher education.[12] Nevertheless, figures from the 1953 census show 21.21 percent of females aged ten or over were illiterate; in 1952-53, 22 percent of women over 14 were enrolled in all levels of schooling, with 0.48 percent studying at the university level where women clustered in the areas of pedagogy, pharmacology, and philosophy and letters.[13] The limited availability of secondary schooling for both women and men and the patterns of enrollment in advanced studies reflected the disjuncture between formal education and the Cuban economy.[14] Women's employment, moreover, shows that comparatively good access to education and professional training was disciplined by a traditional division of labor. Thus, in 1953 only about 17 percent of Cuban women worked outside the home, while women constituted 84.4 percent of primary and 89.8 percent of secondary teachers.[15]

Compared with the constrained opportunities and outcomes of public education before 1959, the extension of schooling to all Cubans regardless of gender, race, class or region is the most prominent characteristic of the first decade of post-revolutionary educational policy. The spread of education began quickly with the creation of thousands of new classrooms, a call for teachers, and the Literacy Campaign of 1961 that carried basic skills to some 700,000 Cubans. Educational policies demonstrated a nationalist reinterpretation of the role of formal schooling in economic and social development, and the revolution officially embraced socialism in 1961. Private schools were closed, while adult education, the combination of work and study, access for rural Cubans, and the pursuit of Che Guevara's "New Man" became principles of education within the atypical socialist strategy of the 1960s. In 1958-59 there were some 811,300 students at all levels in Cuba; by 1970-71, there were 2,392,500, with 47,400 in day care, 1,664,600 primary students (counting the pre-school year), 272,500 secondary students, and 35,100 in higher education.[16]

Women's better access to formal schooling is measured by their share in the expanding enrollments at all levels. In 1967, the female percentage of enrollments was 49 in primary schools, 55 in secondary, and 40 at the university level.[17] Specific attention to women's opportunities and educational achievements was also apparent. In 1961, for example, 14,000 girls traveled to Havana for the first course of the Ana Betancourt Schools for Peasant Women, a program that emphasized sewing, but eventually provided a broader education for some 10,000 girls each year. Reeducation of prostitutes was an immediate objective and a program for Cuba's nearly 70,000 domestic servants lasted until 1967. In the 1961 Literacy Campaign women constituted 59 percent of those who taught and 55 percent of the new literates.[18] Efforts to close the gap between rural and urban Cuba benefited women, much as the rejection of class privileges did.

A second phase of educational policy began in the 1970s, aiming for qualitative improvement in the system created in the 1960s. *Perfeccionamiento* policies emphasized reform in the content and organization of formal education, while the introduction of planning to better orient education to the economy reflected the more orthodox development strategy of the second decade of Cuban socialism. *Perfeccionamiento* emphasized technical and professional education, as well as expansion of secondary and higher education. By 1980-81, the number of students at the secondary level was 1,146,500. Increasing from four centers in 1970 to 47 by 1991, higher education's share of all enrollments grew from 2.4 percent in 1959-60 to 12.2 percent in 1989-90—with more than 270,000 students.[19]

Women's access continued to improve within the policies of *perfeccionamiento* and the growth in higher levels of education. In 1976-77, female enrollments were 44.7 percent of the total; in 1988-89, they were 50 percent, counting for 48.5 percent of preschool, 47.4 percent of primary, 48.9 percent of basic secondary (grades 7-9), 61 percent of pre-university (grades 10-12), 46.5 percent of technical and professional (preparation of qualified workers and mid-level technicians after ninth grade), 77.8 percent of teacher training (intermediary level); 17.2 percent of trade schools, 31.4 percent of special education, and 56.8 percent of adult education.[20] Several avenues existed for entering post-secondary education, including courses for workers and by 1979, directed study. In 1988-89 women counted for 57.1 percent of all university-level enrollments. In the formal day-time track, women were 42.8 percent of enrollments in 1974-75 and 56.9 percent in 1988-89; in courses for workers, they were 29.2 percent in 1974-75 and 56.6 percent in 1988-89. Using graduates as another measure of progress, more women than men graduated at the secondary levels in each year between 1977-78 and 1988-89 (except 1983-84), and in higher education, more women than men were graduating in the second part of the 1980s.[21]

If gains in primary and secondary education are shared with other Latin American societies, only a handful see a similar proportion of women in higher education. Women's specializations in Cuban higher education demonstrate other significant changes in access and what Miller calls a "critical difference"; compared with others in Latin America, Cuban women are "more likely to pursue studies in the hard sciences and technology."[22] In 1985, women were 32 percent of enrollments in engineering, 52 percent in natural sciences, and 63 percent in pedagogy. Figures for Argentina, where women were 53 percent of all enrollments, were 12 percent in engineering, 62 percent in natural sciences, and 92 percent in pedagogy—and in the GDR women were 53 percent of all enrollments, 27 percent of engineering students, 78 percent in pedagogy, and 43 percent in natural sciences.[23] Although almost 50 percent of women's enrollments were in pedagogical sciences in 1984-85, the successful integration of women in medical education led to "affirmative action" for Cuban men (women were 68.5 percent of enrollments in 1993-94).[24]

The better distribution of educational opportunities since 1959 has facilitated women's entry into the work force, a commonly-used measure of the outcomes of education. The relationship of women's traditional, unpaid work as housewife and mother with paid activity outside the home is almost always used to assess women's economic and social status in societies of different types, although the historic Marxist strategy for the emancipation of women makes participation in production a crucial goal and measure. In Cuba, women's movement into the work force has been encouraged by egalitarian educational policies, as well as by the official socialist strategy for women's equality. As the 1990s began, women were 38.6 percent of the national labor force, compared to approximately 10 percent in 1953.[25]

The characteristics of women's work show the progress associated with changing qualifications, as well as occupational inequalities that are part of a traditional gendered division of labor. At the start of the 1990s, women were 58.3 percent of the technical workforce in Cuba, for example, and 40 percent of scientists. Despite the significant access of women to the "male" world of science, women were also 62.5 percent of service sector workers and 84.7 percent of administrative (clerical) employees, and only 18.9 percent of "workers" and 26.5 percent of managers.[26] A similar blend of change and the persistence of old patterns is found in the rapid growth in women's employment, a lower overall rate of labor force activity in Cuba than in many other socialist societies, and differences in rate of activity of rural and urban Cuban women.[27]

The relationship of formal education to women's work in Cuba reveals more about change in the public division of labor. First, the location of women in the teaching profession remains an obvious feature of the public division of labor. At the beginning of the 1989-90 term, 61 percent of the 204,508 teaching personnel were women; women were 99.8 percent of day care and 73.5 percent of primary school teachers, 58.7 percent of teachers in basic secondary schools, 46.8 percent in pre-universities, and 28.4 percent in trade schools.[28] The presence of women and absence of men is most noticeable at the lower levels. According to the principal of a primary school with a staff of 48 that included two male gardeners and two male teachers, "[i]t is apparent right now that a better incorporation of men is coming, but the percentage of women prevails, above all at this level of education."[29] "Almost all my teachers are women, very young and with small children," noted another principal in La Habana province as she described the functioning of her primary school.[30] The pattern in primary and secondary teaching is one typical of many societies, yet Cuba stands out with the large share of women faculty in higher education. In 1985, Cuba was among the top four internationally, while women counted for 45 percent of those teaching at the post-secondary level in 1991-92.[31]

Related to their numbers in the teaching profession is the comparatively high proportion of women in the National Union of Education, Science, and Sports Workers (SNTECD). In 1989, 68 percent of union membership was female (of 398,181 members—99.5 percent of all workers). The percentage of women in leadership roles in the union structure in 1989 was above the national averages, except at the municipal level. Women were 41.6 percent of national leadership, 35.7 percent of provincial, 30.0 of municipal, and 53.1 percent of bureau-level leadership, and in the base-level sections, 64.6 percent.[32] Within formal education, 20,000 of the 40,500 "management" posts were occupied by women in 1985 (49.4 percent), while in 1990 women constituted 31 percent of management in the central Ministry of Education and 37 percent at provincial and municipal levels.[33] Despite their numerical weight, women are not found in equal numbers in the ranks of union or educational leadership, a characteristic of other areas of public life, including the PCC and the representative system of Poder Popular.[34]

Second, despite the occupational segregation associated with a gendered division of labor, the emphasis on technical training beginning with *perfeccionamiento* did not exclude women. In the 1981 census, women comprised 51.6 percent of the category of "intellectual work"; in 1988, they were 47 percent of those conducting research in science and technology units.[35] Along with the stress on technical expertise and meritocratic performance standards, the reforms begun in the 1970s led to selective provincial high schools for the study of the exact sciences—beginning with the Lenin School in Havana City. Despite observers' suspicions about emergent educational hierarchies or tracking, gender does not seem to be at issue. At the start of the 1989-90 school year, 64.2 percent of the 16,776 students enrolled in these 15 "elite" boarding schools in the countryside were girls. Female enrollment in the 300 pre-universities in the countryside was 61.2 percent.[36]

Third, the formal arrangements for ongoing adult education after the Literacy Campaign have maintained educational opportunities for all women, whether they work outside the home or not. The proportion of women has increased within the declining enrollments in adult education, a decline related to the achievements of the Battles for the 6th Grade (1975-1980) and the ninth grade (1980-1985). In 1976-77, 37.2 percent of students in adult education were female and by 1988-1989, the figure was 56.8 percent. There were 42,504 housewives studying in adult education in 1989-90.[37]

Finally, if women's opportunities have increased decidedly within the expansion of Cuban education, the shape of the public division of labor is related to the distribution and redistribution of the skills and knowledge that link access to formal education to outcomes. The content of education is therefore important for determining where change has—and hasn't—occurred. In terms of a formal curriculum that has explicitly sought to educate toward socialist goals, observers have noted the strong emphasis on math and science from primary through pre-university education, the conspicuous absence of gender segregation in subjects studied or the organization of school activities, and such seemingly insignificant facts as the smocks provided both girls and boys attending day care centers.[38] The exceptional egalitarianism in formal education has not been monolithic, however. Traditional gender patterns have found expression in Cuban education, from a reading text that stresses women's new roles more than men's to the choice of toys, the absence of men in the study of early childhood education and nursing, or the laundress role sometimes assumed by young women in boarding schools.[39]

The relationship of educational opportunities to women's public activities cannot be explained without a recognition of other state policies, including those dedicated specifically to the pursuit of equality. The incorporation of women into the labor force was not an immediate priority, for example, though Cuba's socialist strategy for the emancipation of women has stressed infrastructural supports for working women. Among the provisions for working mothers are day care centers and semi-boarding schools, both important parts of the national system of education. In 1988-89, 35.2 percent of primary students were in semi-boarding schools (offering meals and extended hours).[40] As the literature on Cuban women suggests, the realization of equality is affected by material conditions, as well as by the choices reflected in socialist development strategies. Women in Cuba are not pushed into the work force by necessity, explained the Education Secretary of the Federation of Cuban Women in 1990, though more would work if the conditions for doing so were in place.[41]

History and ideology have both contributed to educational policies that have improved women's access and altered the public division of labor. Cuban assessments recognize the progress made in better distributing education, although they also admit problems, including ongoing differences between rural and urban Cuba.[42] The issues of formal education and gender can be further addressed by exploring women's place in the process of change.

Nonformal Education and the Public Sphere

Centralized state control of education characterizes the goals and structure of the system of formal education created in post-revolutionary Cuba. Though few are excluded from the education provided by the socialist state, opportunities for women have not been limited to formal schooling. To understand women and the less-formal avenues of education after 1959, it is necessary to look at the distinctive features of a socialist organization of formal schooling, the process of education, and the issues of participation that are important in discussing formal and nonformal education in other settings.[43] Traditional measures of women's roles and the public division of labor tap only the most visible parts of their experiences. Discussing the ideological and material conditions of women's subordination, Nelly Stromquist explains that "[t]he reality of gender is such that people do not simply play roles but are made to live identities—a more pervasive and unavoidable social feature."[44] Women's participation in the process of education is crucial for pursuing further the feminist concern with inequalities and their transformation.

Official definitions published in 1989 in *Pedagogía Cubana*, the Ministry of Education's new journal, provide a starting point for examining women and the process of education centered by the centralization of the formal system. Formal education is defined as "regular education that is pursued in educational centers through official enrollment." Nonformal education is "education imparted outside the school system in regular or intermittent form. It can be considered an ensemble of nonschool environments that permit the acquisition of general knowledge or professional qualifications." Informal education is "that received through life, from the family and social setting, apparently without systematic educational purposes. It is also a continuous process of acquiring knowledge and competencies that are not located within an institutional framework."[45] The extensive reach of formal education in post-revolutionary Cuba means that the circumstances of nonformal or informal education are different from those in other (nonsocialist) settings.

While the interplay of formal and nonformal education in Cuba is clearly demonstrated by policies for adult education, the 1961 Literacy Campaign demonstrated two enduring features of the less formal process of education after 1959. First, the mobilizational techniques used to organize the campaign have marked the subsequent development of educational policy. Popular mobilization involves the unions, as well as the mass organizations created in the early 1960s to structure participation, including the Committees for the Defense of the Revolution, student organizations at each level of education (that for secondary students was created in the early 1970s), and the Federation of Cuban Women (Federación de Mujeres Cubanas, FMC). Second, the mass organizations have conducted ongoing educational programs for their membership. The role of the mass organizations in education is thus two-fold; they contribute to the implementation of educational policies and complement the official goals of formal schooling. The centralization of Cuba's socialist state has authorized the role and goals of mass organizations through the programmatic control of the PCC, national planning, and the critical capacity of state ministries in every policy area.

In this context, the organization and activities of the Federation of Cuban Women reveal some of the dynamics of education in general, and of the process of improving women's education specifically. Created in August 1960 and counting a membership of more than 3.3 million in 1989, the FMC has been deeply involved in the implementation of special programs for women, as well as in the functioning of the formal system of schooling. The explicit mission of the FMC has been to organize women to participate in the pursuit of the goals of the revolution. Yet, as FMC President Vilma Espín explained in her report to the II Congress of the FMC in 1974, "from the beginning we have pursued a dual purpose: to create consciousness to accomplish tasks through ideological education; to educate ideologically through the tasks."[46] The responsibility of the FMC in achieving the educational goals of the revolution and for the education of women has been great, though it has evolved in accord with the educational policies of the state.

The FMC was instrumental in many of the early programs geared to the education or reeducation of women. The Ana Betancourt schools and the schools for retraining domestics as bank employees or taxi drivers fell in the province of the FMC, for example. And more than 91,000 FMC members assumed responsibilities in the Literacy Campaign—caring for the 100,000 students in the "Conrado Benítez" brigades, acting as literacy workers, or participating in the Literacy Councils that structured the campaign; "[t]he women's organization got bigger and stronger in order to carry out the missions which had been assigned to it...," according to an article in the

FMC's *Boletín*.[47] By the end of the 1960s, the Federation had organized 2,000 family reading circles as follow-ups to the Literacy Campaign and some 700,000 women participated in the health and hygiene courses of the Federation; 24,470 of the organization's *dirigentes* were studying and 3,309 finished courses of technical self-improvement in 1970.[48] The FMC has emphasized the education of its members through study circles and also has a national school for cadres. Working with other organizations and the state, the Federation has participated in health education for women, as well as in sexual education.

Remarkable among the responsibilities of the FMC in the 1960s and 1970s was the creation and staffing of day care centers. The first three day care centers were opened in Havana in 1961; the Mariana Grajales school for directors was created, followed by the Marina Azcuy school for assistants. In 1971, the Children's Institute was created to "direct, orient, supervise, and evaluate all activities geared to the education and attention of children under six years," with Vilma Espín as president, while formal supervision of day care education passed to the Ministry of Education in the 1980s.[49] Besides providing early childhood education, the expansion of day care has been viewed as essential in bringing Cuban women into the work force. The number of day care centers grew from 37 in 1961 to 832 in 1980-81, 1,071 in 1989-90, and 1,157 in 1992-93; the corresponding enrollments were 2,145 in 1961, 91,736 in 1980-81, 149,300 in 1989-90, and 152,00 in 1992-93.[50] The rate of growth in facilities quickened during the second part of the 1980s, although in addition to the 145,500 women with children in day care in 1989-90, there were 81,500 unfulfilled requests.[51] The training of day care personnel has been improved with a program of university studies in pre-school education. According to Leahy, day care assistants entered paid employment at the lowest starting salary of all workers in 1973.[52]

Because the Federation is the state-sanctioned organization of and for women—Randall referred to it as the "female arm of the party"[53]—its educational responsibilities and mobilizational efforts permanently blur any neat distinction between the formal and the nonformal in education. If the oversight of day care, or of scholarship programs in the 1960s, illustrates that the tasks of the FMC have been weighty ones, the FMC also reveals more about the process and practices of education within the centralization characteristic of both official policy-making and the functioning of mass organizations.[54] Women's participation in and through the FMC creates places for them in the process of education that differ from their positions as students, teachers, or administrators. Looking for the existence and content of these places within the socialist state and its comprehensive system of formal education, women's activities reveal the range and possibilities of nonformal or informal education.

More specifically, by the early 1980s one of the priorities in the work of the FMC was the Movement of Militant Mothers for Education (Movimiento de Madres Combatientes por la Educación). Beginning with the activities of mothers in a rural school in Camagüey province in the 1968-69 term, the movement spread throughout Cuba as part of the Federation's efforts in education. In 1970 there were 2,681 Madres Combatientes, with membership growing to 430,000 by 1974 and 1,700,000 by 1985; in 1990, there were more than 1,400,000 Madres.[55]

National educational policy oriented the work of the Madres Combatientes as part of the FMC. Thus, among the movement's specific goals by the 1980s were improving student attendance, retention and promotion, as well as assisting with the activities of student organizations, resolving the special problems of individual students, and supporting the educational work of teachers and the school in general. The Madres Combatientes helped organize school parties, sometimes served as substitute teachers, and provided materials and labor needed to arrange cultural and other events scheduled by the schools. Present in both primary and secondary schools, a delegate of the Madres movement represented the FMC in the council that gathered representatives of the school's administration, party, union, and student organizations. The work of the Madres was "recognized by teachers, principals, and the top leaders of the Ministry of Education," according to Espín's comments in a 1980 interview.[56]

If official recognition means that participation organized through the Movement of Madres Combatientes was integrated into the workings of the formal system, it also reflects an educational process that had long since called for a link between homes and schools. Yet there is another, more complex face to women's participation. While the Madres movement did not invent the relationship between home and schools that is animated with parent participation, it did organize the participation of Cuban women as mothers. And the problem-solving efforts that launched the Madres movement continued to characterize their work as it was formally incorporated into educational policy. Though the Madres have been described as "kind of a voluntary service guild of otherwise unemployed mothers,"[57] participation was not limited to housewives or mothers. There were "militant grandmothers" and "militant aunts," for instance, women who were active in boarding schools too distant for the regular participation of mother/Madres. Working mother were also encouraged to participate in the day-to-day life of the schools. The participation of mothers was joined by the efforts of other mass organizations, including the union-organized "adoption" of schools by individual work centers. Such participation matters because the purposes and principles of socialist education called for a transformation of values that could not be imposed by a ministerial resolution, nor fully accomplished through the practices of formal schooling.

The notion of parental participation is, of course, not unique to Cuba, where the relationship between home and school is indeed organized through the Ministry of Education's Office of Extracurricular Education and Scholarships, the school council system, and the ample programs and activities of mass organizations. The participation of women as mothers is different, however. It is motivated by interests that are not reducible to state policies, to women's access to education, or to the gendered shape of the public division of labor, though all of these have contributed to the realities of motherhood—and mothers' participation—in Cuba.

Policies for formal education, the work and responsibilities of the FMC, and the socialist state itself have all changed over time. Preparations for the 5th National Congress of the Federation in 1990 included serious, bottom-up discussion of women's gains in education and other areas of public life, of old and newer problems, and of the organization's role and activities. The *Draft Thesis* that oriented base-level discussions leading to the Congress distinguished the formal and nonformal dimensions of women's education, stating "[f]inally, we want to point out that the educational process is frequently associated only with classrooms and curricula, and we tend to forget that it has a much wider meaning: it is constant learning that enriches life."[58] An official view of this wider meaning and women's "integral development as human beings" is found in the preliminary version of the Central Report for the Congress: In this sense, we understand that the educational process is extremely rich and complex, that it is not limited to the classroom route, but that its objective is the acquisition of knowledge, of norms of conduct, of relations with others, of making good use of diverse cultural options, all with the purpose of not only finding a job, but of the fruits promised by the incorporation of greater knowledge into life.[59]

The organizational arrangements of the socialist state and Cuban educational policy do determine where the formal and the nonformal meet and mesh. Yet as the Madres Combatientes suggest, this intersection is created by the interests and activities of mothers, fathers, and other participants; it cannot be decreed or imposed. In her study of parental participation in the very different conditions of Buenos Aires, Schmukler uses the notion of a "public-private border zone" to discuss the family-school relations that locate mothers in terms of the state.[60] What places at the intersection of formal and less formal, public and private, mean for Cuban women and their educational gains can be examined further by turning to the particular conditions within which the revolution that secured those gains is now being challenged.

Education and Women's Private Lives

The current period of reform in Cuba offers a different vantage for assessing education's role in the transformation of gendered inequality. Clearly, the public division of labor and the organizational relationships of the formal and less formal in education are associated with the fact and actions of Cuba's socialist state. And the *rectificación* process launched in 1986 reaffirmed Cuba's socialist goals and the institutional foundations of a socialist state, including a single vanguard party and economic planning. Beginning with remedies for poor economic and organizational performance more akin to the Cuba of the 1960s than to the markets and electoral politics pursued by reformers elsewhere, by 1990 escalating difficulties resulted in the severe austerity of what is called the "Special Period in a Time of Peace." *Rectificación* also ushered in a new phase of educational policy. The educational reforms called *perfeccionamiento continuo* can be surveyed with a distinctly feminist focus on the relationship of education to the private sphere of social life. Indeed, the role of education in reproducing or recasting the gendered patterns of authority that join public and private in a single sexual division of labor provokes demanding questions about women, equality, and education. Using women's place to search for answers will reveal more about ideological commitments, economic realities, and the authority of the socialist state.

The crisis conditions of the Special Period have disrupted both public and private life as survival has become the compelling goal of policy-making in the Special Period. With the loss of the socialist bloc and an ongoing U.S. embargo defining Cuba's precarious position in the New World Order, survival strategy has stressed both import substitution and export promotion, tourism, agricultural production for domestic consumption, and foreign investment. Committed still to socialism, recent reforms include the 1992 modification of the Constitution, direct elections for provincial and national representatives, the legalization of foreign currency holding, and limited individual enterprise in 1993. Education remains a priority within a Special Period characterized by the scarcity associated with a dramatic contraction of the economy. There were 2,206,400 students and 247,400 personnel in the educational centers of the formal system in 1993-94, and preserving this system has joined the other crucial issues of survival.[61] All of the reforms of *perfeccionamiento continuo* address the quality of formal schooling, each bearing on women and the public and private dynamics that create their place in the process of education.

Curricular changes studied and initiated in the rectification period have refined the content at each level of education, reducing content while adding new subjects. Among the additions in general education are more study of Cuban history, civic education, and an improved and better integrated program of sexual education. The emphasis on Cuban history and civic education shows official concern with political socialization and a revitalization of the domestic sources of Cuban socialism, while current attention to sexual education suggests some change in the official perspective on gender socialization. Sexual education became part of the official understanding of "integral education" in the 1970s, supported by party resolutions and the creation in 1977 of a National Group of Sexual Education with the participation of the FMC and the Ministries of Education and Public Health, among others. Criticism of the "insufficient and fragmented content" of sexual education informed the approach that now guides formal instruction in the schools.[62] Starting in 1988-89, primary students receive sexual education through the study of natural sciences and civic education; in seventh and eighth grades, "workshops will examine and debate relations between a couple, their moral and emotional elements, the generation gap, questions about sexual issues, and other topics"; and students in preuniversities pursue further study in biology courses in the eleventh and twelfth grades.[63]

Sexual education is not new and the reasons for its reform lie with official ideals and perceived problems of post-revolutionary change in social practices. Cuba has had no formal population policy, though problems of teen pregnancy, early marriage, single motherhood, and high rates of abortion have been recognized and investigated. A press report of the first major study of the family and youth addressing these problems noted such causal factors as a poor intergenerational communication and inadequate knowledge of birth control. Among the negative consequences identified were "special programs for unwed mothers and abortion services"; as the article explained, "there is common agreement that teenage mothers give up their studies, become marginalized from others their age and generally lose a lot of the pleasures of being young."[64]

Drop-outs have long been viewed as one of the challenges of formal education, a concern apparent in the work of the FMC. Materials from the FMC Congress in 1990 note a relative decline in the enrollment of girls aged 13 to 16 in some locales, particularly rural areas.[65] As *the Proyecto de informe central* points out, the comprehensive Turquino Plan for improving conditions in Cuba's mountain zones includes attention to the difficulties confronting the education of girls. For example, if students have to travel to other municipalities or provinces to study, as they must when population dispersion or growth require it, their families may disapprove. And as the report explains, inherited values can limit the opportunities of teenage girls.

Prejudices and stereotypes that restrict the role of women to the sole function of housewife still persist in these rural areas, which naturally discourages and limits the training and development of some young girls and contributes to an increase in cases of early marriage and earlypregnancy, which also still occur in urban zones.[66] In Cuba, sexual education is carried out by the schools, the media, the Federation, and other organizations, though expectations about the family's responsibility remain in place.

The modification of teaching methods is a vital part of *perfeccionamiento continuo*, one related to improving the curriculum and change in the procedures for evaluating students. There is renewed interest in the legacy of Cuba's own educators for a distinctively Cuban pedagogy—including the contribution of José Martí and other pre-revolutionary figures, as well as an official recognition of the problems of authoritarian relations within the school. Role-playing, questioning strategies, and methods of discussion and debate are all emphasized as current policies turn to active and participatory learning. According to the Vice-Rector of the National Institute of Educational Improvement, what is required is letting go of "rigid schemas"; the *formalismo* of teaching a curriculum that the Vice-Rector termed "*enciclopedismo*" would be replaced with active students and the training of teaching personnel.[67] Altering methods in formal education also entails relaxing rules governing student behavior in the schools.

An official concern with the relationship of teaching styles to student development informs efforts to transform the formal pedagogy and real practices of the Cuban schools. Research and experimentation is underway in the areas of active learning, creativity, and the development of intelligence, and gender has also been considered within Cuban research. The results of a study of sexual/gender stereotypes and the knowledge of first and fifth grade students appeared in the Ministry's journal *Educación* in 1994, for example. As the authors explain, their findings demonstrate the "strongly sexist character of the sexual education offered children in the home and the school."[68] The perception of two SNTECD officials that young girls are better controlled by their families and, therefore, better organized and "much more dedicated" is one widely accepted view of gendered behavior and its relationship to education.[69] As Núñez Aragón explained in a 1988 article on adolescence that noted the differential development of boys and girls, the tendency of girls toward self-discipline at an earlier age could represent advantages for them. Such advantages might include election to leadership posts in student organizations or greater participation in extracurricular activities that can then result in the further development of those qualities specific to girls.[70] In 1984 girls did constitute 66.3 percent of the leadership of the Pioneers organization (primary and junior high), 61.1 percent in the secondary student organization, and

48.2 percent in the Federation of University Students.[71] And girls were in the majority at the first-ever national congress of the Pioneers organization in 1991, a fact explained as a "reflection of family organization and discipline."[72]

Improving the relationship of home and school is a third significant dimension of the reforms pursued in *perfeccionamiento continuo*. Innovations in this area center in the program of "Family Education," though as with other changes the foundation lies in previous policies and practices. Called School for Parents in the past, renaming reflects some of the realities of the Cuban family. According to the principal of Guerrillero Heroíco primary, "The belief was that it wasn't really a school for parents, that we had to orient the family in general, not just parents, because often a child has no father, but lives with a grandmother or with more people inside the home. And the framework of orientation has been widened a little."[73] Among the themes of family education is sexual education. Family education, moreover, stresses the use of the innovative teaching methods; methods associated with *perfeccionamiento continuo*. The objectives of family education are several, including strengthening the link between the home and the school and eliminating confusions about the responsibilities of each in the education of children.

The nuclear family has been viewed officially as the basic unit of Cuban society, despite the alteration of generational—or gender—patterns.[74] High rates of divorce, extended families, or consensual unions might chip away at the ideal of a nuclear family, while the Family Code that legalized equality within the home in 1974 officially promised an erosion of the patriarchal interior of that ideal. Cuban studies show, however, that the practices of family life do not conform to a vision of shared responsibilities; women remain in charge of the home and the children, whether they work or not.[75] Attacked since the 1970s, this double or triple burden has various expressions in private life. The current focus on the family, for instance, worries that parent-child relations still maintain "facets of the past that enter into contradiction with the new values and requirements of the contemporary family," including the example set by parents, mainly mothers, who assume their child's tasks and thus reinforce the concept of the "self-sacrificing mother."[76] Overprotection or inattention to children's needs are related issues raised in official discussion of parenting and family life.

Helping parents understand their role and responsibilities in the education of their children is also part of family education. In the words of the FMC National Secretary of Education, "It's family education that shares the burden of the child's problems in adapting to school."[77] Most often organized as topical discussions occurring in meetings of parents throughout the school year, family education emphasizes flexibility in addressing the needs and interests of parents. An important aspect of the preferred approach in family education is creating a welcoming environment. Another is creativity within the policy guidelines for strengthening the ties between families and schools; the program called "Teacher of the 10 Families" is one example of how local schools have responded. The Federation of Cuban Women has also coordinated with the Ministry of Education in the formation of a National Group of Family Orientation and Education, participating as well in the creation of the National Commission of Prevention and Attention to Minors in 1986 (and similar provincial and municipal commissions). These commissions are intended to help prevent anti-social conduct or delinquency and to determine appropriate remedial action.

Finally, *perfeccionamiento continuo* demonstrates the response of the educational system to the increasingly harsh conditions of the Special Period and Cuba's strategy for survival. The urgent call for efficiency has meant the better use of ever scarcer resources, ranging from electricity, light bulbs, and notebooks to the imports required for the study of art or science. How schools might cope creatively with resource constraints has been included in the pages of *Educación*; school gardens for producing the food consumed by students are emphasized from the level of the National Institute for Educational Improvement to day care centers. Much remains constant, however, despite the crisis. The Ministry of Education's budget grew through 1990, when it reached 1,853.9 million; it declined to 1,443.4 in 1993.[78] The construction of new educational facilities has slowed dramatically, though it has not ended; thousands of foreign students remained in Cuba in 1993; and while enrollments in schools-in-the-countryside have declined, boarding and semi-boarding facilities were available for more than 900,000 students at the start of the 1993-94 term.

Scarcity affects Cuban homes, schools, and workplaces, however, and past priorities and policies have been affected by the struggle to survive. Strategies for survival surface in current educational policy in several ways. The emphasis on the production of food means a renewed importance for students' participation in the schools-to-the-countryside program. Given fuel shortages, transportation problems rank high among the trials of this and other programs, of teachers and students who must arrive at school, and of the Special Period in general. The 43 new agricultural polytechnical schools created in 1991-92—and the many others since—indicate a larger shift within educational policy. According to the Director of Technical and Professional Education of the Ministry, these schools represent "an important contribution to the support needed by the Food Program," at the same time mirroring decreasing enrollments in the preuniversity track "because a high percentage of these youth would not be able to continue studies in higher education."[79] A promised reversal of the shares of technical and pre-university enrollments has been achieved, such that less than 40 percent of ninth grade graduates proceed on the university track. Educational planning still supports post-secondary study; despite a decline in enrollments of some 96,000 after 1989-90, there were still 176,000 students in higher education in the 1993-94.[80]

The relationship of past educational achievements to current problem-solving strategies is also evident. The emphasis on science and technology is associated with efforts to substitute missing imports, to export of Cuban health technologies and medical discoveries, and to improve agricultural production for both export and domestic consumption. Teacher training similarly reflects the relationship of past accomplishments to present possibilities. Ample progress has been made in improving the qualifications of those whose careers began with the exigencies of massificiation in the first phases of educational policy, though the upgrading of skills and formation of new teachers continues. In 1991-92, some 21,000 teachers were released for full-time, paid study; in 1992-93, the number declined to 14,000 and has dropped further. With nearly 300,000 educators in 1990, the aggregate student/teacher ratio was 9.2, and in 1992, the Cuban press proudly pointed out that Cuba's 1/37 teacher per capita ratio was the best in the world.[81] The student/teacher ratio is now 1/14 and this and other matters of educational efficiency are caught between constrained resources and popular expectations about access to schooling at all levels.[82]

In refocusing the issues of women's education in the changing terms of public and private life in rectification and the Special Period, other critical dimensions of *perfeccionamiento continuo* must be considered. In 1991, for example, an adjustment was made in the day care system, raising the age of entrance from 45 days to six months—a change explained in terms of both pedagogy and the costliness of caring for young infants. By December 1993, however, approximately 500,000 preschoolers were receiving education, some 200,000 in a "noninstitutional" form; Cuba's National Plan of Action had accomplished early the 50 percent coverage promised in accord with the World Summit in Favor of Childhood, demonstrating the new stress on community education that has emerged in the current period.[83] The alteration of the design of formal day care clearly affects women as workers and mothers, while the concerted implementation of nonformal preschool education calls for more participation by women and others. A similar emphasis on nonformal or community education has also emerged with experimentation in adult education, where there are some 25,000 participants in activities of family and sexual orientation, local history, green medicine, or artisanry, explained in terms of helping people respond to the conditions of the Special Period.[84]

Cuban women still hold a measurable place in formal education and public production. In 1992-93, female enrollments in preuniversities were 66 percent; and women counted for 56.8 percent of university enrollments, including 32.4 percent in technological sciences, 43.5 percent in agriculture, 68.5 percent in medicine, and 61.1 percent in natural sciences and mathematics.[85] If the material contingencies of the Special Period are reflected in the call for more participation, they are also apparent in the official recognition that shortages of transportation, food, and other necessities have mounted a challenge for mothers, wives, and families, as well as for teachers, students, and the schools in general. Any conclusive assessment of both challenges and change in educational policy and practices in Cuba, however, must be grounded in an understanding of the genuine accomplishments of the revolution in organizing the education of women.

Conclusions

The educational experiences of Cuban women since 1959 reflect the state's commitment to formal education, equality, and socialist development. As a group, women have obtained more education and have entered the work force in increasing numbers. The public division of labor has changed, most notably where formal education has facilitated a more equal distribution of occupations—and knowledge. And the educational policy of the socialist state has joined mass organizations to the process of education, making women's participation important in practice and in theory. The Cuban state and a socialist centralization have established the parameters of progress, though change in women's public lives has not been dictated by the ideological or economic imperatives of socialism and its international context. Ultimately, as feminist theories suggest, it is the relationship of the home and domestic life to the measurable achievements of Cuban women that explains progress in altering the "gender variable" in Cuban education. The roots of the gendered division of labor and of education's power to make change are in the private sphere of family life.

It is thus both easy and accurate to conclude that post-revolutionary educational policies have contributed to significant advances for Cuban women. How educational outcomes are reciprocally related to the patterns of private life is less easily measured, however. The transformation of gendered inequalities in the public sphere *and* in the home is everywhere a slow and uneven process in which formal education is intimately involved. "If the society is seriously committed to its revolutionary ideology," argues MacDonald, "it cannot allow the schools to acquiesce to behavior patterns at variance with the Family Code."[86] Neither formal education nor legal codes, however, can guarantee the transformation of the imbedded social and cultural patterns that sustain traditional or newer forms of gender inequality. In fact, Cuban women's customary roles as mothers or teachers remain central in the interactions of families, mass organizations, and the state. The less formal, though often no less organized, educational process which joins the home to formal education spotlights the complex location of Cuban women in the post-revolutionary transformation of social relations.

The Federation of Cuban Women remains a useful focus for a speculative summary about the state, the process of education, and women in contemporary Cuba. Like other mass organizations, the FMC is concerned with improving its functioning by altering top-heavy traditions with more participation and listening better to the different needs and interests of Cuban women. This intended "opening" is joined by other specific developments in the FMC's work with women and education, efforts that are meaningful signals of less-visible changes within the organizational arrangements of the socialist state.

First, the current attention to the relationship between home and school extends official responsibility for the intersection of the formal and less formal dimensions of the educational process. On the one hand, family education is prominent, prioritized, and further formalized within *perfeccionamiento continuo*, stretching the scope of the state and state policies. On the other hand, *perfeccionamiento continuo* also accents responsibilities *within* the family, promoting an official perspective on gender equality that stresses men's obligations in the home and in child care, as well as the unburdening of women as sole custodians of family life.[87] In organizational terms, the shifting of responsibilities is demonstrated in the changing vantage on the FMC's Madres Combatientes.

Official attention to the Madres has diminished within the problem-solving of the present period, explained by one national FMC official in terms of the inclusion of *padres* [fathers],[88] a "degendering" that might be applauded by foreign feminists wary of categorizing women and their activities with the ascriptive interests of motherhood. Another explanation offered by a Ministry official is that the movement had become "formalized."[89] Both readings culminate with the family and larger community as the necessary remedy, a shift in emphasis fixed with the constitutional reforms of summer 1992. New Article 35 places more responsibility for education with the family, though that responsibility is still shared with the state, as explained by a published summary of Castro's intervention in the legislative debate.

Fidel reflected on the importance of not renouncing the essential obligations held by society, nor the responsibility of parents and the family. It would have to be said, he indicated, that the family has the maximum responsibility for educating its children and the State has the maximum responsibility for educating the family.[90]

The FMC's participation in establishing the formal study of women in selected institutions of higher education throughout the island is a second significant innovation in the Special Period.[91] Besides auguring important curricular change, this development suggests an official appreciation of the specificity of women's interests and experiences within the strategies and plans of socialist development. The first of these faculties was created in late 1989 at the Félix Varela Higher Pedagogical Institute in Villa Clara province; by the end of 1993 there were 12, comprised of doctors, psychologists, sociologists, and legal and other specialists, including the leaders of the FMC. Women's Studies was instituted in the University of Havana in early 1991, with Espín as honorary president and a coordinating body composed of representatives from different academic disciplines, organizations, and institutions. The purpose of the organized study of Cuban women is to investigate their lives, experiences, and problems, in relation to the other critical issues of development in Cuba.[92] In addition, by 1993 some 100 *casas de la mujer* [women's houses] had been created through the FMC to offer cultural and educational activities, problem-solving, and professional services to local women and their families.

The emergence of Women's Studies is a signal of the state's concern for women, while the less noticeable turn within the Cuban perspective on the link between home and school marks the terrain where the meaning of women's educational experiences is often concealed. As part of official educational policy in the *rectificación* period, these developments together suggest how to understand the outcomes of education for Cuban women. Official policies in education and for women have facilitated marked gains, while progress in eradicating the "gender variable" in Cuban education is best discovered by locating women within the organizational context where socialist strategies meet cultural and social traditions.

Using Cuban women to explore progress in post-revolutionary education, it is possible to move beyond traditional, quantitative, and universalizing indicators of the outcomes of formal education toward a better understanding of the range *and* significance of current reforms. Indicators of women's education suggest that acquired training and expertise make women valuable and quite visible participants in efforts to secure the survival of Cuban socialism. Women are present in science, technology, and workplaces in general; they are therefore part of the many who continue to work in the face of private and public difficulties. In 1994 a department for women was created in the National Association of Innovators and Rationalizers, making Cuba the seventh country to establish an organization for women inventors, according to the *Granma* report.[93] The 1993 election results show some decline in women representatives, though women have also moved into new leadership positions. Twenty-five-year-old Enith Alerm Prieto—the president of the Pioneers Organization—joined the Council of State in 1993; for the first time, women have been elected to head party organizations in two provinces, as well as the party youth branch. The advances in formal equality since 1959, surely related to educational opportunities and attainments, are gains that figure importantly in Cuba's attempts to preserve the revolution and its accomplishments. Indeed, achievements in education have become an important landmark of the revolution's gains and goals as the ever more critical conditions of the Special Period prod the adjustment of the Cuban economy to global competition and foreign investors.

Cuban women become an even more telling measure by finding their place in the process of education. Finding the places that women themselves have made and remade with their participation as students, teachers, mothers, and workers entails a close and careful look at the relationships underlying formal schooling, the public division of labor, and the organizational arrangements of the socialist state. Ultimately, a focus on women that takes seriously feminist concerns with these relationships facilitates insight into the pressing economic and ideological issues of rectification and survival through the Special Period. What is needed as reforms continue to unfold in Cuba, but only started here, is careful scrutiny of the transformation of the deeper, gendered dynamics of authority that connect the home, the schools, and the socialist state.

Notes

1. See the essay and annotated bibliography in Sheryl L. Lutjens, "Education," in *Cuba Resource Guide*, ed. Joel C. Edelstein (Perian Press, forthcoming).

2. Feminist theorizing is distinguished from other modes of theory by the central place granted the subordination of women; by definition, feminist theories will *all* recognize sex-specific inequalities, though methodological and epistemological differences lead to variety in explanations and prescriptions for change. One useful overview is Alison M. Jaggar, *Feminist Politics and Human Nature* (Totowa, New Jersey: Rowman & Littlefield Publishers, Inc., 1988 [reprinted]).

3. See as examples, Gail P. Kelly, "Achieving Equality in Education—Prospects and Realities," in *International Handbook of Women's Education*, ed. Gail P. Kelly (New York: Greenwood Press, 1989), 547-569; Mary O'Brien, "Education and Patriarchy," in *Critical Pedagogy and Cultural Power*, ed. David W. Livingstone (South Hadley, MA: Bergin & Garvey Publishers, Inc., 1987), 41-54; or Lynda Stone, ed. *The Education Feminism Reader* (New York: Routledge, 1994).

4.   Beverley Hooper, "Gender and Education," in *Chinese Education: Problems, Policies, and Prospects*, ed. Irving Epstein (New York: Garland Publishing, Inc., 1991), 352-374, esp. 352-353, 365. See also Maxine Molyneux, "Strategies for the Emancipation of Women in Third World Socialist Societies," in *World Yearbook of Education 1984: Women and Education*, ed. Sandra Acker (London: Kogan Page, 1984), 268-278.

5.   Gail P. Kelly, "New Directions in Research on Women's Education in the Third World: The Development of Women-Centric Approaches," in *Women's Education in the Third World: An Annotated Bibliography*, ed. David H. Kelly and Gail P. Kelly (New York: Garland Publishing, Inc., 1989), 15-37, esp. 25, 26. See also Nelly P. Stromquist, ed., *Women and Education in Latin America: Knowledge, Power, and Change* (Boulder: Lynne Rienner Publishers, 1991).

6.   The debates about and within feminist theorizing are lively, especially as they contend with the challenge of a post-modern feminism. Examples include Jane Flax, "Postmodernism and Gender Relations in Feminist Theory," in *Feminist Theory in Practice and Process*, ed. Micheline R. Malson et al. (Chicago: The University of Chicago Press, 1989), 51-74 or Linda Alcoff and Elizabeth Potters, eds. *Feminist Epistemologies* (New York: Routledge, 1993). The Cuban perspective on gender will not be treated directly, though official positions will be noted as relevant. See the speeches and ideas expressed by the president of Cuba's women's organization, Vilma Espín Guillois, *La Mujer en Cuba, familia y sociedad: Discursos, entrevistas, documentos* (Havana: Imprenta Central de las FAR, 1990) and Vilma Espín, *La Mujer en Cuba* (Havana: Editora Política, 1990), or the review in Carolee Benglesdorf, "On the Problem of Studying Women in Cuba," in *Cuban Political Economy*, ed. Andrew Zimbalist (Boulder: Westview Press, 1988). For recent changes, see Sheryl L. Lutjens, "Reading Between the Lines: Women, the State, and Rectification in Cuba," forthcoming, or "Remaking the Public Sphere: Women and Revolution in Cuba," in *Women and Revolution: Africa, Asia, and the New World*, ed. Mary Ann Tétrault (Columbia, South Carolina: University of South Carolina Press, 1994).

7.   See the summary in United Nations, *The World's Women Today: Trends and Statistics 1970-1990* (New York: United Nations, 1991), 45-49, as well as country figures on literacy and enrollment ratios, 50-52. Frances Miller briefly discusses the causes of expansion at all levels of education, *Latin American Women and the Search for Social Justice* (Hanover: University Press of New England, 1991), 59-67, and also describes UNESCO statistics—the widely-used source of data on education and gender since 1950. UNESCO figures for the region show that the female percentage of enrollments in 1975 was 49 percent in primary, 48 percent in secondary, and 42 percent in higher education; in 1990, they were 49 percent, 52 percent, and 47 percent respectively, *Statistical Yearbook 1992* (Paris: UNESCO, 1992), 2-12.

8.   The figure on illiteracy is a "very optimistic" result of the 1899 census, according to Gaspar Jorge García Galló's historical survey, *Bosquejo Histórico de la Educación en Cuba* (Havana: Editorial de Libros para la Educación, 1978), 49.

9. Ministerio de Educación, *Breve Información Sobre la Educación en Cuba* (Havana, [1990]), 112. Cuba's ranking among Latin American countries in the 1950s was much better for secondary and higher education than for primary schooling, Richard Jolly, "Education," Chs. IV-VIII in *Cuba: The Economic and Social Revolution*, ed. Dudley Seers (Chapel Hill, North Carolina: The University of North Carolina Press, 1964), 170, 173.

10. The difference in the conditions of rural and urban life are indicated by literacy rates and the fact that non-attendance in rural Cuba was over 50 percent compared to less than 20 percent in urban areas, Jolly, "Education," 170.

11. *Latin American Women*, 51.

12. K. Lynn Stoner, *From the House to the Streets: The Cuban Woman's Movement for Legal Reform, 1898-1940* (Durham, North Carolina: Duke University Press, 1991), 132; Miller, *Latin American Women*, 61.

13. María A. Martínez Guayanes, "La Situación de la mujer en cuba en 1953," *Santiago* no. 15 (June-September 1974): 195-226, esp. 223, 224 (and 65 percent of illiterate women were rural). Percentages for enrollment in higher education were 51 in pedagogy, 12 in pharmacology, and seven in philosophy and letters, though women accounted for 80 percent or more of the enrollments in each area. See also Maria Dolores Ortiz, *La Mujer en la Educación Superior* (Havana: Editorial Letras Cubanas, 1985).

14. Secondary enrollment was only 12 percent of the relevant age group, both female and male, Jolly, "Education," 173.

15. Martínez Guayanes, "La Situación," 208-211, 224. The most remarked features of women's work include the number of domestics, the proliferation of prostitution in Havana and other cities, and the limited place of rural women in agricultural production.

16. *Breve Información*, 114.

17. Margaret E. Leahy, *Development Strategies and the Status of Women: A Comparative Study of the United States, Mexico, the Soviet Union, and Cuba* (Boulder: Lynne Rienner Publishers, 1986), 107.

18. See Elena Gil Izquierdo, "Sharpening the Class Struggle: The Education of Domestic Workers in Cuba," in *Muchachas No More: Household Workers in Latin America and the Caribbean*, ed. Elsa M. Chaney and Mary Garcia Castro (Philadelphia: Temple University Press, 1989), 351-359; "A Revolution Within Another Revolution," *Boletín FMC*, special edition (1982): 14-23, esp. 18; Luisa Eng, *La Mujer en la Revolución Educacional* (Havana: Editorial Letras Cubanas, 1985), 22-23; and Margaret Randall, *Women in Cuba: Twenty Years Later* (New York: Smyrna Press, 1981), 56-58.

19. *Breve Información*, 114, 115.

20. *Mujer y Sociedad en Cifras, 1975-1988* (Havana: Editorial de la Mujer, 1990), 53. Corresponding figures for 1976-77 were 48.9 percent in preschool; 47.8 percent in primary; 53.2 percent in basic secondary; 53.9 percent in pre-university; 31.9

percent in technical and professional; 25.7 percent in teacher training; 16.4 percent in trade schools; 37.2 percent in adult; 32.4 percent in special education; and 40.4 percent in higher education.

21. *Mujer y Sociedad en Cifras* 56, 57, 59.

22. Miller points to Costa Rica, Chile, Uruguay, and Argentina, "nations that share with Cuba a historical commitment to higher education for women," *Latin American Women*, 63. The U.N. report lists 33 countries in the world where women outnumber men in higher education, including four in Latin American, ten in the Caribbean, and three once-socialist countries, *The World's Women*, 48.

23. Gail P. Kelly, "Women and Higher Education," in *International Higher Education: An Encyclopedia*, Vol. I, ed. Philip G. Altbach (New York: Garland Publishing, Inc., 1991), 297-323, esp. 312, citing *UNESCO Statistical Yearbook*, 1988.

24. Calculated from Ortiz, *La Mujer en la Educación Superior*, 23.

25. *Proyecto de Informe Central; V Congreso FMC, 5 al 8 Marzo 1990* ([Havana], n.d.), 8.

26. *Proyecto de Informe*, 8, 9.

27. The rural/urban difference was 20 percent compared to 30.5 percent in urban areas, Ravenet Ramirez et al., *La Mujer Rural y Urbana*, 29. For comparisons, see U.N., *The World's Women*.

28. Calculated from Dirección de Estadísticas de Nivel de Vida, Comité Estatal de Estadísticas, *Boletín de Inicio del Año Escolar 1989-1990* (Havana: Editorial Estadística, 1990), 37, 58. In urban primaries, 81 percent of teachers are women, while in rural schools the figure was 61 percent, 37.

29. Interview, Principal, Guerrillero Heroíco Primary, Cojímar, Ciudad de La Habana province, June 1, 1990.

30. Interview, Principal, Matilde Varona Primary, Bejucal, La Habana province, June 6, 1990.

31. The four include Cuba with 43 percent women, the Philippines (53 percent), and Argentina (47 percent), Kelly, "Women and Higher Education," 315, using UNESCO figures for 1985. For regional patterns and other comparisons, U.N, *The World's Women*, 48.

32. Eugenia López Villeda, *Los Trabajadores Exponemos Nuestra Obra de 30 Años* (Havana: Editorial Científico-Técnica, 1989), 53. Comparable percentages in the all-union average were: national, 22.9 percent; provincial, 29.4 percent; municipal, 34.5 percent; bureaus, 45.2 percent; and base organizations, 49.9 percent, 83.

33. *Integración de la Mujer Cubana a las Actividades Socio-económicas y Políticas* ([Havana: Editorial de la Mujer, n.d.]), 29 and *Proyecto de Informe*, 18; in 1987, two of 15 provincial directors of education and 33 of 160 municipal directors were women.

34. In the three levels of Poder Popular [People's Power], women have had a greater presence at the national level, with over a third of the indirectly elected deputies and 16.7 percent of those directly elected at the local level in 1989. In 1988, women were 23.9 percent of party membership, 25.5 percent of municipal leader-

ship, 24.5 percent of provincial leadership, and 12.5 percent of the PCC's Political Bureau, *Mujer y Sociedad*, 90, 91, 94.

35. *Integración*, 30, 39.

36. Their enrollment in the junior high boarding schools was a lower 46.6 percent, *Boletín de Inicio*, 14.

37. *Mujer y Sociedad*, 54, 58.

38. Theodore MacDonald, *Making a New People: Education in Revolutionary Cuba* (Vancouver: New Star Books, 1985), 214, 197; and Karen Wald, *Children of Che: Childcare and Education in Cuba* (Palo Alto, California: Ramparts Press, 1978), 170.

39. Rex Hutchens, "Women in Cuba: Education and Directed Culture Change," Ph.D. Dissertation, University of Arizona, 1984, 125-126; Wald, *Children of Che*, 126, 337; and MacDonald, *Making a New People*, 158. Labor education has tended to be similar for girls and boys, though in 1990 one principal explained how her school had added instruction in cooking, sewing, and other home skills to the manual arts education of secondary-age girls—"not to make our girls seamstresses or anything like that," but because this preparation for future homelife was sometimes neglected in the busy schedules of schools and families, Principal, Pedro Ortiz Cabrera Basic Secondary, Artemisa, La Habana province, June 7, 1990.

40. And 44.0 percent of secondary students were in boarding schools, reflecting the principle of combining work and study, *La Mujer y Sociedad*, 51. Other supports for women workers include a special shopping plan.

41. Interview, National Secretary of Education, Federation of Cuban Women, Havana, June 8, 1990.

42. A demographic study of women in three provinces conducted in the first part of the 1980s showed regional differences despite overall progress. With regard to education, the average level of schooling in Ciudad de La Habana province was 8.3 years (compared to 4.8 in 1953), in contrast to the two more rural provinces where average years of study were 6.6 (Cienfuegos, compared to 3.2 in 1953) and 5.5 (Guantánamo, compared to 2.1 in 1953). There were also more women studying and more facilities and resources available in Cienfuegos and Guantánamo, S. Catasús et al., *Cuban Women: Changing Roles and Population Trends* (Geneva: International Labor Office, 1988), 11-14.

43. On nonformal schooling in Latin America, see Thomas J. LaBelle, *Nonformal Education and Social Change in Latin America* (Los Angeles: Latin American Center Publications, UCLA, 1976) and Carlos Alberto Torres, *The Politics of Nonformal Education in Latin America* (New York: Praeger, 1990). See also Marcy Fink, "Women and Popular Education in Latin America," in *Women and Education in Latin America*, ed. Nelly P. Stromquist, 171-193.

44. Nelly P. Stromquist, "Introduction," in *Women and Education in Latin America*, ed. Stromquist, 1-15, esp. 6.

45. "Glosario de algunos terminos," *Pedagogía Cubana* 1 (October-December 1989): 102-111, esp. 107.

46. Vilma Espín, "Informe Central de la II Congreso de la Federación de Mujeres Cubanas," in *La Mujer en Cuba Socialista* (Havana: Ministerio de Justicia, 1977), 223-280, esp. 228.

47. "A Revolution Within Another Revolution," 20.

48. Max Azicri, "Women's Development through Revolutionary Mobilization: A Study of the Federation of Cuban Women," *International Journal of Women's Studies* 2 (January-February 1979): 27-50, esp. 37; "8va Plenaria Nacional de la FMC," *Mujeres* 11 (January 1971): 4-17, esp. 10. There were also 2,064 sewing academies (corte y costura) with 42,066 women. See the figure for the educational level of the FMC's professional cadres in 1984, *Memorias del IV Congreso de la Federación de Mujeres Cubanas* (Havana; Editora Política, 1987), 122.

49. Espín, "Informe Central," 238. The decision about formal responsibility for the Institute is discussed in Marvin Leiner, *Children Are the Revolution: Day Care in Cuba* (New York: Penguin Books, 1978), 170.

50. Ministry of Education, *La Educación en Cuba* (Havana: Pedagogía '86, Ministry of Education, 1986), 15; *Cuba, Organization of Education 1989-1992; Report of the Republic of Cuba to the 43rd. International Conference on Public Education* (Havana: Ministry of Education, 1992), 38, 40; and *Cuba, Organization of Education 1992-1994; Report of the Republic of Cuba to the 44th. International Conference on Public Education* (Havana: Ministry of Education, 1994), 31.

51. *Granma*, 7 August 1990, p. 1.

52. Leahy, *Development Strategies*, 105-106.

53. Margaret Randall, *La Mujer Cubana Ahora* (Havana: Instituto Cubano del Libro, 1972), 103.

54. An argument about community participation and education in Cuba that treats the Madres in more detail is developed in Sheryl L. Lutjens, *The State, Bureaucracy, and the Cuban Schools: Power and Participation*, in preparation.

55. Sara González and Carmen Gómez, "La FMC y la educación: diez años de trabajo," *Mujeres* 10 (August 1970), 26; "Las Madres en la vida de la escuela," *Mujeres* 16 (August 1976), 50; *Granma*, 7 August 1985, p. 1; and Interview, National Secretary of Education, Federation of Cuban Women, Havana, June 8, 1990. The decline in membership can be explained in terms of demographic changes affecting enrollments, since the movement was structured around the mother-child-school relationship. Other causal factors are not precluded by suggesting the association between enrollments and membership decline, however, as will become clear below.

56. "La Mujer y su papel en la sociedad, entrevista con Vilma Espín," *Bohemia* 72 (March 7, 1980), 54.

57. MacDonald, *Making a New People*, 137.

58. Federación de Mujeres Cubanas, *Draft Thesis; V Congreso FMC, 5 al 8 de Marzo de 1990* ([Havana]: n.d.), 15.

59. *Proyecto de Informe*, 43.

60. Beatriz Schmukler, "Women and the Microsocial Democratization of Everyday Life," in *Women and Education in Latin America*, ed. Stromquist, 251-276, esp. 253.

61. *Organization of Education 1992-1994*, 33.

62. Alberta Durán Gondar, "El Enfoque de la educación sexual en el sistema nacional de educación," Pedagogía '90, February 5-9, 1990, Havana, 8.

63. "Teenage Pregnancy: Social Issue Under Debate," *Granma International*, 19 May 1991, p. 2; Jose Zilberstein Toruncha and Esther Miedes Diaz, "La Educación sexual: parte de la formación político-ideológica de las nuevas generaciones," *Educación* 20 (January-March 1990): 11-18, esp. 17; and Durán Gondar, "El Enfoque." See also the discussion of training teachers for sexual education, Ann Froines, "Women's Studies in Cuba," *NWSA Journal* 5 (Summer 1993): 233-245, esp. 240-242.

64. "Teenage Pregnancy," 2. See also Marguerite G. Rosenthal, "The Problems of Single Motherhood in Cuba," in *Cuba in Transition: Crisis and Transformation*, eds. Sandor Halebsky and John M. Kirk (Boulder: Westview Press, 1992), 161-176 and Lois M. Smith, "Sexuality and Socialism in Cuba," in *Cuba in Transition*, eds. Halebsky and Kirk, 177-192.

65. *Proyecto de Informe*, 40. In 1987, marriage accounted for 31.1 percent of female dropouts of basic secondary, 22 percent in teacher training, and 13 percent in technical and professional education, "El Amor en las becas," *Mujeres* 28 (June 1989): 4-9, esp. 6.

66. *Proyecto de Informe*, 41.

67. Interview, Vice-Rector, Instituto de Perfeccionamiento Educacional, Cojímar, Havana province, May 31, 1990.

68. Alicia González, et. al, "Estereotipos sexuales: masculinidad y femineidad en la edad escolar," *Educación*, no. 82, second epoch (May-August 1994): 12-19, esp. 19.

69. Interview, representative of Department of International Relations, and Second Secretary, Sindicato Nacional de Trabajadores de Educación, Ciencia, y Deportes, Havana, June 7, 1990.

70. Elsa Núñez Aragón, "La Adolescencia: breves consideraciones," *Educación* 18 (July-September 1988): 40-43, esp. 41-42. See also "Adolescentes ¿cómo entendemos con ellos?," *Mujeres* 30 (August-September 1991): 4-6, where the results of family and school "education differentiated by sex" are extended to competition for university studies and greater social responsibility.

71. From *Memorias del IV Congreso*, 146. In 1991, five of the seven members of the national secretariat of the Federation of Secondary Students were female, including the president, "Bárbarita la presidenta," *Mujeres* 30 (February/March 1991): 2-3, esp. 3. In terms of female performance and a possible gender privilege, the percentages of vanguard students are useful. In the Pioneers, girls were 82.5 percent of the vanguards, in the FEEM young women were 57.3 percent, and in the FEU, they were 55.2 percent, *Memorias del IV Congreso*, 14.

72. Aloyma Ravela, "Nosotros, los de la Edad Dorada," *Mujeres* 30:6 (December 1991): 12-13, esp. 13.

73. Interview, Principal, Guerrillero Heroíco Primary, Cojímar, Havana province, June 1, 1990.

74. See the summary in "La Evolución demográfica de la población," in *Cuba: Informe Sobre la Evolución de su Población y la Interrelación con el Desarrollo; Conferencia Internacional Sobre la Población y el Desarrollo, El Cairo, 1994* (Havana, February 1994).

75. Findings from several nationwide studies were cited in the materials from the 5th Congress of the FMC, *Proyecto de Informe*, 24-25.

76. Elsa Núñez Aragón, "Las Escuelas de educación familiar," *Pedagogía Cubana* 2 (January-March 1990): 4-11, esp. 5. See also Julián Rodríguez Rodríguez et al., "La Educación familiar en Cuba. Experiencias y posibilidades," Pedagogía '90, February 5-9, 1990, Havana.

77. Interview, National Secretary of Education, Federation of Cuban Women, Havana, June 8, 1990.

78. *Organization of Education 1992-1994*, 10.

79. "Nuevos politécnicos agropecuarios [Interview with Aker Aragón Castro, Director of Educación Técnica y Profesional, Mined]," *Educación* 21: (January-June 1991): 11-17, esp. 11.

80. *Organizacion de educacion 1989-1992*, 44 and *Organization of Education 1992-1994*, 28.

81. *Granma*, 4 August 1990, p. 2 and *Granma*, 18 June 1992, p. 1.

82. *Granma*, 1 October 1994, p. 2.

83. *Granma*, 4 December 1993, p. 3. About 20 percent of demand was being met in 1992 (with a population aged 0-5 years of about a million) and annual cost per child was 800 pesos, Interview, Director, Central Institute of Pedagogical Science, Ministry of Education, Havana, August 11, 1992. See also "Las Vías no formales de la educación prescolar. Perspectivas de aplicación," *Simientes* 30 (May-December 1992): 2-4.

84. *Granma*, 17 March 1994, p. 2.

85. Calculated from "Anexo: información estadística sobre el curso 1992-93," Ministry of Education, anexo no. 1 and *Organization of Education 1992-1994*, 28.

86. MacDonald, *Making a New People*, 143.

87. See the more recent speeches of Vilma Espín in *La Mujer en Cuba, Familia y Sociedad* and *La Mujer en Cuba*.

88. Interview, Federation of Cuban Women, Havana, August 6, 1992.

89. Interview, Director, Central Institute of Pedagogical Science, Ministry of Education, Havana, August 11, 1992.

90. *Asamblea Nacional del Poder Popular; Debates en el Parlamento Cubano; XI Período de Sesiones 10-12 de Julio de 1992* (Havana: Editora Política, 1992), 25-26.

91. See Mirta Rodríguez Calderón, "Desde el espacio que nos ganamos," *Fempress*, no. 139 (May 1993): 8; and the tentative—and repectful—judgment that

there has been a "significant shift in thinking about women's problems," Froines, "Women's Studies in Cuba," 234.

92. See, for example, the explanation of the comprehensive first project in Santiago which included the objective of "putting equality into practice," *Granma*, 18 December 1991, p. 2.

93. *Granma*, 6 May 1994, p. 2.

PART FOUR

Popular Education in Latin America: Old and New Dreams

11

Freire, Frei, and Literacy Texts in Chile, 1964–1970[1]

Robert Austin

Introduction

As with the period of the UNESCO-backed literacy campaign in Cuba before it, the period 1964-1970 in Chile is arguably one of the few great watersheds in 20th century history of education. Responding to popular education debates reaching back to the latter decades of the 19th century, the Frei Montalva administration sponsored a literacy program which was linked to its Chilenisation reform project, intended to incorporate the popular sectors in the Christian Democrat modernisation project without fundamentally altering Chilean society, whilst *reinvigorating* the dominant mode of production. The links between the shifting ideological subtexts of adult education and popular rejection of liberal capitalism in Chile were not insignificant. And there remain wide-ranging influences in global educational discourse today of the interplay between a Chilean pedagogy of the left and Freire's development, however underacknowledged.

Here I analyse the socio-economic and cultural context of the period, and situate literacy within that context. Inter alia, it is argued that the standardised centrality accorded the early work of Freire in the Chilean literacy process has tended to marginalise the contribution of co-workers: for instance, no English edition of *Cultural Action for Freedom* carries reference to its Chilean editor Marcela Gajardo. There also remain unresolved contradictions between the stage of Freireian theoretical development applicable, and the textual representations of that theory.

The reconstitution of events which configured the politics of adult education and adult literacy in what we shall simply term the Frei period depends in large measure on three sources: official literacy texts, actors directing the programs, and others who whilst not directing from above were advisers and/or senior educators. Our investigation will heed the caution urged by Tosh with oral sources, particularly those re-constituting official discourse, whilst remaining conscious of a counterbalancing argument: that the so-often illiterate popular sectors retain through oral history a rich reserve of culture and a tool for democratising history itself.[2]

Prevailing accounts of Paulo Freire's work in Chile from 1965-1969 privilege Freire's contribution to the agrarian reform adult literacy project and pyramid-like extension into education debates North and South, derivative of this work in that period. Here we approach the era with an antiethical lens: the arguably under-recognized contribution made by Chilean intellectuals to the development of Freirian philosophy of education. Freire himself, in a recent piece entitled *I Became "Almost Chilean"* reminds us of how he "learned to learn" in Chile, and of the necessary effect on his work of Raúl Veloso's theory of the intentionality of consciousness, "the possibility that consciousness had of capturing, apprehending reality."[3]

It may be unreasonable to characterise Freire's post 1970 writings as a series of elaborate footnotes to the complex theoretical and methodological legacy of his Chilean experience. Certainly a recent engagement with postmodernism[4] and earlier abandonment of conscientisation[5] delineate apparently fresh stages of Freire's intellectual development. However, sandwiched between embryonic work in Goulart's Brazil from 1959-1964 and his later Guinea -Bissau and occidental work, the turbulent Chile of the ultimately conservative Christian Democrat Frei Montalva government endures as the engine room of Freireian intellectual history.

Definitional Matters: Interpreting Freire's Pedagogy

Before focusing more closely on the Frei era, some definitions are required. Notwithstanding involvement in revolutionary literacy campaigns in Grenada,[6] Cuba[7] and Nicaragua,[8] as well as Chile during the Frei Montalva and Allende administrations, UNESCO has persisted with its traditional definitions of literacy and functional literacy. A literate person is "one who can with understanding both read and write a short simple statement on his everyday life."[9] To be functionally literate a person must be able to:

> engage in all those activites in which literacy is requried for effective functioning of his group and community and also for enabling him to continue to use reading, writing and calucualtion for his own and the community's development.[10]

Whilst this form of words may leave open the debate as to what constitutes development, there is no contextual hint that a hybrid Freireian/feminist lexicon, for instance, might take its place; the male referent is used exclusively throughout the text.[11] Further, this blanket assumption of an apparently undifferentiated *imagined community* obscures the social and productive relationships between assumed members of the community.[12]

"Fundamental Education" was UNESCO's initial education project, persisting with the functionalist theses of failed mass literacy campaigns in Ecuador [1942], the Dominican Republic [1943], Mexico [1944], Honduras and Guatemala [1945] and Perú [1946]. Those campaigns had been linked to the US Good Neighbour program and to penetration of transnational capital.[13] In contrast, however:

> [fundamental education] to be creative "had to be responsible for the progress of the entire country" ... proposing that the economic, political and social formation of adults should be developed from their daily activities and basic concerns. Thus to the tasks of literacy work were added programs for health improvement and for development of work skills and family life, in a paternalistic and welfare mode.[14]

Fundamental Education [1951-1960] was replaced by UNESCO's human capital face, Community Development [1960-1969], firmly tied to Alliance for Progress policy and reaffirmed at UNESCO's 1960 Montreal Conference. Both programs were boosted through the collaboration of CREFAL [Regional Centre for Functional Education in Latin America] based in Mexico, which was a joint Organisation of American States, UNESCO and Mexican government exercise anticipating postwar hemispherical contests and determined to contain their Latin American manifestations through modernisation based on the dominant economic paradigm.[15] The theoretical discourse—with Deweyan and Durkheimian residues—proposed to: achieve social and economic progress in communities through the voluntary and active participation of its members, on the hypothesis that a change of values, attitudes and so forth on the individual level achieved through pedagogical activity would provoke continuous and permanent development of the community.[16]

Programs thus founded relied on foreign experts who promoted the vertical transmission of given material which was assessed externally, functionalist and based on the premise that all was resolvable within the logic of capitalism. Disarticulated and mechanically implemented, such programs ultimately sharpened divisions within communities and favoured already privileged groups.[17]

Illiteracy on this 1960s UNESCO paradigm becomes a cause of under-production and under-consumption, a "human resources" problem to be addressed as such, and linked to the UNESCO-CREFAL and subsequently [in the case of Chile] Christian Democrat development paradigm. In a UNESCO publication José Gimeno encapsulates UNESCO's concern thus:

> The amount of illiteracy constitutes a very important retarding factor in the development of the region, as much in the area of productivity as consumption ... [in diagram 4] the illiteracy situation can be appreciated as can the connection between illiteracy and per capita profit in the countries of the region.[18]

The concept of development entailed in this account of illiteracy is, like the concept of literacy itself, functionalist vis a vis the dominant mode of production: dependent capitalism and its adjunct, underdevelopment.[19] The role of literacy programs becomes the integration of the newly literate sectors into the dominant economy insofar as the predetermined division of labour allocates roles to the technically competent and thus functional worker or peasant. But as Mackie observes the achilles' heel of most functional analyses of literacy

> lies precisely in the failure to examine the context in which literacy actually functions. Thus literacy comes to be portrayed, in abstract and reified terms, as something which exists in a vacuum, remote and removed from other social relations.[20]

Freire's early work is liberal-democratic in nature, *Education as the Practice of Freedom* reflecting the progressive theology of the Brazilian Bishops declaration of 1963 and the influence of Teilhard de Chardin, Karl Mannheim, Eric Fromm, Reinhold Niebuhr, and Emanuel Mounier.[21] His arrival in Chile in 1965 shortly after its catholic bishops and run a pro-Frei Montalva campaign suggests the theological climate in which he was to operate.[22] Literacy programs were often run in conjunction with the church.

But Freire's experience with the ailing Christian Democrat "Revolution in Liberty"[23] in Chile after 1965 stimulated a radical shift in ideological groundings. Immersed in the growing momentum of a multi-faceted grass roots political activism as the country moved towards the 1970 polls, and perceiving liberalism as anachronistic, Freire moved to synthesise the traditions of Hegelian dialectics, then later Marxism and Liberation Theology.[24] He argued that the psycho-social method of literacy acquisition transforms the process from an act of simply knowing to an act of intervention. Literacy transformed into political consciousness—*conscientización*—becomes a catalyst for political intervention by the subject in contrast to the inertia distilled through functional literacy programs. Pedagogically a dia-

logic relationship is implied between teacher and student, promoting critical reflection "on the process of reading itself, and on the profound significance of language."[25] Dialogic education mediates between the dependent
present and the independent future.[26]

Generative Words as Ideological Codes

Freire employs generative words to form the initial text for the literacy
class, being words which represent situations or problems said to be germane to daily existence. The group reflects upon the implicit semantics,
moving from micro to macro analysis and synthesis. Simultaneously syl-
labic families process is repeated for all generative words. Phonemics and
semantics are seen to link in the socialized processes of language; echoing
Marx or Feuerbach, participants begin to "name the world" as a step toward changing it.[27]

Using the comparative window of official tests from presidents Frei
Montalva in the sixties to his son Frei Ruiz Tagle in the nineties highlights
the distinctive ideological codes of the Christian Democrat functionalist
project.

The only generative word common to texts in all four eras [Christian
Democrat, Popular Unity, Dictatorship, and Transitional] is *guitarra*, a cultural symbol of enhanced significance in the Chile of Frei Montalva and
Allende given the distillation of much popular sentiment in the rhythms
and lyrics—the popular cultural literacy, if you like—of the New Song
Movement. The stated objectives of conscientisation attaching to the word
in each era reveal much about the political objectives of each program, or
campaign as they were sometimes classified.

In the Frei Montalva primer, the stated objectives are:

1. reflection on the guitar and other musical instruments
2. reflection on folkloric and other types of music
3. reflection on musical and other forms of recreation[28]

By contrast in the Allende primer, the objectives are:

1. reflection of the role played by the instrument in the musical expression of the people of Chile
2. reflection on the participation of the people in the creation of liberated art[29]

The junta text repeats the Frei Montalva objectives verbatim.[30] The generative word *casa* appears in the Frei Montalva, Allende and Pinochet texts.
The Frei Montalva texts approach the implicit issues in a way in which

provokes discussion and reflection around most domestic issues *except* who is domesticated, and what the division of labour in who is domesticated, and what the division of labour in society at large means for that person, the woman. The Pinochet text of 1976 is again all but identical. The military administration's later *Yo en la Familia* characterises the making of a family as "Designio Creador" [heavenly intention] and the woman-mother as "made for maternity" and having "a capacity for tenderness which the man lacks."[31]

From 1963 to around 1985 Freire's epistemology remains impervious to systems of oppression not based on class, in particular gender and race. Latin American Women's movements were emerging belatedly elsewhere, but in Chile there had been a prominent eclectic movement since the turn of the century.[32] Terms such as *humanisation* do not differentiate men and women, black and white, or other dimensions. *Pedagogy of the Oppressed* is highly susceptible of this criticism, employing the male referent throughout and appearing not to countenance men's oppression of women once boss-worker relationships have been abolished. What is not addressed is the possibility of simultaneously contradictory positions of oppression and dominance: the man oppressed by his boss could at the same time oppress his wife, for example, or the White woman oppressed by sexism could exploit the Black woman. By framing his discussion in such abstract terms, Freire slides over the contradictions and tensions within social settings in which overlapping forms of oppression exist.[33]

Given Chile's highly stratified and class conscious social practices, middle class women traditionally exploit working class *mestiza* women as cheap domestic labour devoid of work contracts, compensation or insurance, or the limited rights which had been won for the broader labour force. It is only a single post-dictatorship official primer which has engaged the differentiation of women on this level.[34] The questions of gender and race were key blindspots in the ideological discourse of the Frei campaign, finally contributing to limitations on the otherwise feverish and well-coordinated work of teams from the agriculture and education ministries.[35]

The penetration of civil society by patriarchal discourse exerted an imposing force on the social practices of monitors and participants alike: one senior Ministry of Education intellectual involved in the campaign recalls being expected to take minutes at the otherwise all male coordinating meetings.[36] As if to underline the curious commonalitites between the sixties liberal era and authoritarian capitalism, the program texts of the Frei Montalva and Pinochet administrations claim to employ Paulo Freire's psycho-social method.

The Christian Democrat Program in Context: 1964-1970

Mainstream analyses of the history of literacy in Chile distinguish three *moments* relative to the fluctuations in the official rate of illiteracy since 1865:

The first *moment* comprises the period 1865-1920 and is characterised by a slow but permanent decrease in the rate of illiteracy from 83 percent to 49.7 percent, with a mean annual rate of decrease of a little over 0.5 percent.

The second *moment* ... extends from 1920-1930 ... and is the period in which there occurs the most important cultural leap in the transformation of [Chile's] population from an illiterate to a literate one. The percentage of illiterates in Chile's population dropped abruptly from 49.7 percent in 1920 to 25.6 percent in 1930.

The third *moment* is of relative stagnation. The rate of illiteracy climbed in 1940 to 27.3 percent ... only to drop to 19.8 percent in 1952.[37]

Disregarding the analysis of statistics in the interim, here we add a fourth *moment* from 1964 to 1970, when the rate of illiteracy again declined but was overshadowed by the transformational social structures implied and initiated during the National Literacy Campaign of the Frei Montalva administration, Freire's work being germane. This is not to stake out an excessive claim for the program, given its organic links with educational reform in the wider sense—notably university reform—which came to acquire fundamental influence in the displacement of Chilenisation by nationalisation during the Frei presidency.

Formal education in Chile had traditionally been an enclave for the central valley economic elites, congruent with the organisation of broader society. The great educational reforms instigated by teacher organisations during the 1939-1942 Popular Front government of Pedro Aguirre Cerda[38] — including an attack on illiteracy via compulsory secular primary schooling — were anaesthetised during subsequent regimes, notably those of Ibañez del Campo [1946-52] and Alessandri [1956-64]. It was not until the advent of the Frei Montalva regime in 1964 that serious attention was given to implementing the Compulsory Basic Schooling act of 1920.[39]

The situation of the indentured labour [*inquilinos*] and peasants [*campesinos*] upon which the vast agricultural estates were constructed, and depended, had ossified since decolonisation. An observer's description of 1820s Chile remained eerily appropriate one and a half centuries later:

> The peasant's station in society had not been materially changed by the subversion of the Spanish authority; while that of his landlord was essentially altered in almost every point ... while the peasant remains nearly as before, his superior has gained many advantages. He has obtained politi-

cal independence, he is free , and secure in his person and property; for the first time in his life, he has a share in the government of his country; he may aspire to the highest offices of profit or distinction; the value of his property is enhanced by the market which has been opened to carry off its produce; and he feels no reserve in displaying his wealth, or in expressing his opinions; in short, he is in possession of civil liberty.[40]

The Christian Democrat agrarian reform program responded in part to modernisation pressures from several sources but particularly international capital, and in part to increasingly-focused agitation among the permanently dispossessed peasant class amid establishment fears that it would unite with the industrial working class. This it would presently do through the political organisations MAPU [Movement for Unified Popular Action] and MIR [Left Revolutionary Movement], the former soon to join the Popular Unity government of Salvador Allende and the latter to retain influence within popular sectors of rural society.[41]

The state as embodiment of the interests of dominant elites had since the previous century fostered a dual system of formal education, primary [*básica*] being the common aspiration with secondary [*media*] and beyond the preserve of the chosen few. State formation was interdependent along three axes in education: the maintenance of the binary unevenness in the formal sector mentioned above [with an added layer of rural disadvantage], dependency on Herbartian and similar outmoded occidental theories as the standard pedagogy of classroom practice, and an entrenched gender and racial division of educational production. To a significant extent these mirrored the class divisions of the broader society, notwithstanding the postwar emergence of a substantial petit bourgeoisie or middle class to which Frei had broad political appeal and was in turn to devote considerable economic and political energy.

Official illiteracy rates for the Frei Montalva era hovered around the twelve to fifteen percent locus, based on the UNESCO definition of literacy.[42] If in contrast we take Letelier's critique of contemporary formal statistics and apply it retrospectively, the officialist and UNESCO estimations appear markedly understated. The Letelier model of years of schooling yields an average rate of illiteracy for the period of around fifty percent, unevenly distributed on gender lines and worse in rural areas.[43]

It was this chronic rural rate which first attracted the attention of Freire's team in the Ministry of Agriculture, and which when coupled with traditional nuances led to the program's being embedded in campaign mode, an almost mystical tendency in a country long the focus of campaigns: from the liberation campaign by O'Higgins and San Martín, the Atacama Desert campaign against Peru and Bolivia [1879-83],[44] the postw·ar cholera elimination campaign and numerous volatile, well-funded electoral campaigns.

The campaign tradition has a sense of illusion around it, a veil masking unaddressed core realities and incomplete analyses.

The campaign ethos is here viewed as a deficit, constructing as it does the sense of finality once a campaign finishes [as it duly did under Frei], leaving nevertheless much unaddressed terrain. The metaphor of a virus being, as Freire and Bhola have separately noted, "eradicated," is not entirely out of place.[45]

The naive construction of illiteracy confronts it as if it were an "absolute in itself," or a "dangerous plant" needing to be "eradicated": hence the current expression "eradication of illiteracy." This deformed conception of illiteracy as illness we ironically call the 'bacteriological conception' of illiteracy, wherein illiteracy appears as a wound or leprosy requiring a cure.[46]

Nevertheless, to claim for Freire the alerting of Chilean educators to the perils of the prevailing school and social systems is to marginalise the centrality of education to the social question for much of the preceding part of the century. Indeed the notion that literacy implies development, and that both are desirable, have been constants on the Chilean political landscape virtually from birth of the republic in 1810. Various 1901 editions of the daily *El Mercurio* in Valparaiso carried columns of letters debating the importance of literacy to workers in the port economy;[47] in 1917 a public forum on literacy in the capital featured prominent intellectuals, among them Pedro Aguiree Cerda, later president of the republic.[48]

The Popular Front government led by Cerda instigated a National Literacy Campaign in 1938-39 at the insistence of the Communist Party [PC], a member of the governing coalition.[49] The detailed proposal of the PC included a Department of Literacy and Popular Culture in the Education ministry, a national literacy crusade, and the establishment of literacy schools and popular libraries throughout Chile. There would be a vast coverage of cultural activity by the ministry: mobile artistic, cultural and health expositions; publication of literary works; amateur theatre; the creation of evening and night schools and universities; formation of choral and instrumental groups; creation of fixed and mobile libraries; art exhibitions; and educational cinema, inter alia.[50]

In 1941, by way of further example, the Chilean Teachers Union proposed a new educational system which would translate in a "cultural action which is truly civilising a democratic ... requiring other means of reaching the whole population, other institutions of the country which are connected with *cultural diffusion*."[51] Concern among Chilean intellectuals and state school teachers over cultural autonomy in the postwar period was eloquently expressed in the policies of both major teacher unions, the General Association of Teachers and the Chilean Teachers Union.[52] Both proposed major state intervention to democratise and universalise primary and secondary education, with programs to eradicate the 27.3 percent official illiteracy rate of 1952, the year in which Ibañez del Campo regained the presidency with a support group of teachers campaigning on his behalf on the understanding that a significant popular education reform would eventuate. They were to be disappointed.

Christian Democrat [PDC] support in the 1964 election was strongest in the sector having least to gain by reform: the Liberal and Conservative parties who avidly feared Salvador Allende's *Popular Action Front [FRAP]*,[53] capitalists who favoured a state-capital alliance to modernise key industries, and significant elements of the national bourgeoisie.[54] PDC policy was presented as a moderate version of the PRAP platform, "chilenisation" of industry supplanting FRAP's nationalisation, and a "revolution in liberty" replacing a socialist revolution [the latter nevertheless through the electoral rather than classical Leninist road]. Massive US funding of the PDC campaign promoted Frei's as a showcase Alliance for Progress state, whilst preparing the way for the generous terms subsequently granted to US companies "chilenised" during the PDC government.[55]

Given occidental domination of Chilean educational discourse for much of the present century, set against the merging momentum of revolutionary and nationalist struggle in the first postwar decade, the receptiveness of Chile to a Latin American voice of liberation follows an intelligible logic.[56] The two largest teacher organisations had since the thirties decried occidentalism and drawn heavily on the reforms of Mexican president Lázaro Cárdenas, whose policies embraced a major adult education program incorporating a mass literacy campaign.

Frei Montalva successfully promoted the "neutral state" thesis for the first two years of his presidency. The claim to neutrality meant in practice that the more radical sectors of Christian Democracy were in the ascendancy for a time; after a mid-term re-alignment, however, the right led by Frei reasserted its dominance and began an offensive [including military attacks] on organised labour and left political opposition. The rhetorical elevation of pluralist discourse in adult education was a further and for our purposes key manifestation of the neutral state thesis. The reconstitution of the period by Frei's adult education director abounds with such discourses, eliding the dominant and subaltern realities of the distribution of power in the modernising capitalist state and social formations of the period.[57]

Literacy programs under the Christian Democrat administration were predicated on conditions set down by the International Monetary Fund and World Bank, having to do with modernisation of the agricultural sector and preparation of peasants to be more efficient within it; that is, to increase productivity through higher levels of functional literacy and hence increase profits for the elites whose traditional landholdings were less competitive on international markets than required by their international financiers. Indeed the IMF had been established after World War II specifically for the purpose of controlling the conditions under which economic development would take place, on behalf of the industrialised nations and transnational capital.[58]

This so-called *Chilenisation* process, particularly concerned with modernisation of the productive apparatus and the agricultural export model, implied no fundamental change in the mode of production or distribution. Because there was to be no basic change in the political economy, there arose a tension between the reforming Freireian paradigm and that of the functionalists—best represented by UNESCO—which was uneasily resolved in the short term by the former's ascendancy, particularly though not exclusively through ICIRA [The Institute for Capacitation and Research in Agrarian Reform] based in Santiago.[59]

Freire worked in two teams in ICIRA, taking advice on political matters from both but relying heavily on the un-officialist and more radical team led by Rolando Pinto, the other having less policy and more implementational emphasis. In 1968, it was this team which advised Freire to break with the reformist project and link instead to the traditions of the popular education struggle dating back to the previous century in Chile.[60] When Freire realised in 1968 that his developing paradigm was being coopted by the Chilenisation project, he fell into conflict with the officialist sector and inclined toward the Popular Unity group within ICIRA and the government.

The Christian Democrat Texts

In its 1966 primer *Manual del Método Psico-social para la Enseñanza de Adultos* two aims are advanced by Waldemar Cortés, Frei Montalva's Director of Adult Education, in the name of the method, namely:

1. to have illiterates rapidly learn to read and write and
2. to facilitate their shedding their low self-esteem in favour of full recognition of their value as human beings.[61]

The manual explains that cultural and social transformation arise through Freireian *conscientización*, a process of engagement with reality via literacy intended to replace the student's magical consciousness with critical consciousness, the former contingent upon pseudo-knowledge and the latter upon critical engagement with it.

Broad reference is made to the [constitutional] democracy of the republic, with the interplay between introduction and text around generative words limiting the objectives of concientisation to discussion of ways one might better exercise one's rights within the confines of that system.

The manual explains that cultural and social transformation arise through Freireian *conscientización*, describing it [accurately enough] as a process of engagement with reality via literacy intended to replace the student's magical consciousness with critical consciousness, the former contingent upon pseudo-knowledge and the latter upon critical engagement with it.

In a parallel text *Manual de Alfabetización para Adultos*[62] "coordinator" replaces all reference to "literacy teacher," while "participant" replaces all reference to the illiterate person. This was consistent with the emerging egalitarian ethos of Freirian pedagogy, however opaque gender and race may have been to its perception at the time.

There are, nevertheless, totalising tendencies within sections of this text: one of the objectives of the exercises with the generative words *casa, pala* and *camino* is "comprender el significado de las palabras" [to comprehend the meaning of the words],[63] suggesting a unique meaning for, in this case, each word syllabically generated by *casa, pala* and *camino*. In the absence of explanatory notes as to the meaning of the words, it must be assumed that dominant linguistic discourse settles the matter. As has been suggested elsewhere, such a codification of language is gendered, classed and ethnicised.[64] Freirian analysis of this period incorporates Chomsky's deep and surface structure in explaining how theoretical abstractions from concrete reality are performed by codification, alternatively imaging or the image itself of the learner's concrete reality. This analytical element is asynchronically advanced on much of Freire's theory of the period.[65]

Without evidence as to what words were generated [though in Brazil *tijollo* generated around 30][66] *casa* will serve to make the point. As Fisher and others have noted, the position of women in Chilean domestic life has been historically subordinate, parallel with and complimentary to wide-ranging subaltern patterns of economic, political and social life.[67] The representations of Chilean patriarchy vary according to class and contain internally contradictory elements. As noted earlier, for instance, single bourgeois women employ underpaid female domestic *mestiza* labour, and exploit secretarial labour in entrepreneurial contexts. [The added layer of direct patriarchy has obtained historically where a husband is present.] Such dominant women have themselves been the object of discriminatory employment and education practices but without the same intensity of economic effect as that experienced by working class *pobladoras*, unable to so much as enter that terrain, let alone contest it.

Rural Chile magnifies this scenario, where peasant women represent the least educated in the nation. The durable Mapuche culture in the south has only partially resisted hispanic patriarchal intrusions, with the cultural effects of postcolonisation recasting indigenous children as national republican subjects and often separating them from their roots only to be subsumed by macho practices.

Thus *casa* encodes rather more complex meanings than some simplistic assertion around love and marriage. When Pablo Milanés speaks of the Latin American peoples who like Puerto Ricans "aún están en el *camino* de la libertad" ["are still on the way to freedom"] he echoes a codification applicable to Frei's Chile: a society where the *camino* is in dispute, where its very meaning is appropriated at that moment by the Chilenisation project but whose opponents ascribe a different, socialised meaning to it—or a corporate, facistoid one.

Official Discourse

Frei's program director Waldemar Cortés argues that women were included in the literacy program through courses at 'Mothers' Centres and Neighbourhood Centres, and in the workplace; but concedes the gender bias of teaching materials.[68] Community programs were coordinated through CEDECO [Centre of Community Education]. He portrays the programs as non-Marxist and pluralist in nature, and not determined by the Christian Democrat government.[69]

In view of the orthodox content of literacy texts issued by various of the Frei Montalva ministries, however, this claim is somewhat difficult to sustain. Any divergence in a more radical direction appears to have come in the practices employed by Freire's teams of literacy monitors, rather than from centralised administrations.

Alberto Silva draws attention to the absence of some key concepts from the official texts—struggle, class, party, power—such as to dilute or subvert the revolutionary potential of the method, transforming it into an integrationist or at best reformist strategy. He argues further that the net result of the campaign was to dissociate literacy from other social activities, and to separate technical and social preparation along with detachment of concientization from action.[70]

Given the militancy of political organisation in rural Chile, in both the agricultural south and mining north, it is curious that an officially faithful rendering of the Freirian method appears not to have produced generative words or themes going to the rapidly intensifying class consciousness of those areas as the PDC experiment with *Chilenisation* faltered. Silva's concerns are self-evident on that level.

Moreover, the discursive and practical activities generally recommended in literacy manuals were somewhat sterile, orthodox and barely resonant with Freire's evolving writings, which by that time were distancing Freire increasingly from the liberal-democratic roots of *Education as the Practice of Freedom*. For instance, the generative word "[trade]union" in the *Manual del Método Psico-social para la Enseñanza de Adultos* corrals discussion around the legalities of labour organisation and the implicit pull for workers to work within those legalities, however much the political objective may have to do with oligarchic hegemony.

By 1966 militant labour action against inflation, wage suppression and police attacks had seen a steadily rising number of factory occupations and sporadic clashes with the armed forces. Deaths of workers had resulted, the most notorious incident being the assassination of nine squatters by police at Puerto Montt in 1969.[71]

Terra Nullius had operated since the sixteenth century to progressively dispossess the 16 major indigenous nations within the boundaries of what would become in 1810 the postcolonial republic. Despite Freire's emphasis on autochthonous cultural movements, one searches in vain for appropriate material in the literacy primers. No serious effort appears to have arisen to conduct bilingual programs.

In the final months of the Frei Montalva government and after consistent pressure from popular sectors, a constitutional amendment was carried enfranchising illiterate adults. Its implementation was deferred until the next administration took office, amid conservative fears that combined with the simultaneously-granted lowering of the voting age from 21 to 18 a significant pro-Allende block would thus be created; it would take effect in the 1976 presidential elections.[72] In the view of the 1973 military coup, initially supported by Frei Montalva and the PDC, *analfabetos* were to wait another 19 years to realise their paper gain.

On the Meaning of Literacy Statistics

Since the 1920s there have been nine census collections, the last in 1992. The construction of the politically significant national profile which the census provides across wide-ranging indicators represents something more than the neutral technical picture presented by the *Instituto Nacional de Estadísticas* [National Institute of Statistics (INE)], a dependency of the Ministry for the Economy. The entire directorate of INE are traditionally political appointees of the government, appointments of *confianza* [trust].[73]

Firstly, the census form has traditionally been completed by a monitor prepared by INE, given some discretionary authority with regard to handling certain questions, including those on literacy. Probing to decide if a respondent is demonstrably literate has not been encouraged.[74] Questions and answers are verbal, with the monitor completing the form. Secondly, the question "do you know how to read and write?" is only asked if the interviewee admits to less than a certain level of completed schooling.[75] No test is applied, and the answers are taken at face value.

Thirdly, there is the grand assumption that by having completed a certain number of years of schooling the person is definitionally literate: functionally literate, albeit that the term is not used by the INE. Research has repeatedly challenged such generalisations, both inside and outside Chile. Fourthly, the possibility of even functional literacy falling into disuse and consequent illiteracy or semi-illiteracy is ignored in virtue of the absence of a "use by" date for the years of schooling.

Finally, albeit that INE employs social scientists in a permanent advisory capacity, no allowance is made for such factors as machismo, or the shame and loss of social status attaching to admission of illiteracy, on whatever definition. In the Frei period this factor was of singular significance, hence an impelling press to appear literate. The triumphalism of Chilean academic discourse on literacy belies what would appear immanent flaws in statistical processes, and this discourse combined with the subtle sociology of modernisation—the prestigious *talking up* of high literacy levels, modernisation and postmodern planning, Latin American occidentalism, and now NAFTA-driven imperatives—deliver an atmospheric in which to be illiterate is to be fossilised.[76] Impressive statistics served to embellish the Frei economic program, justifying higher World Bank loans and in effect intensifying the processes of dependent underdevelopment.

The unreality of Frei's claims of success in the *campaign* can be measured by an event thirty years later during his son's presidency, in a heavily bus and taxi dependent nineties Chile. When the Frei Ruiz-Tagle administration proposed a change in transport licensing laws requiring year 12 education levels for all public transport drivers, a near-total transport strike was held on May 3rd, 1995, its success guaranteed by the massive levels of illiteracy among the [almost exclusively male] drivers and by entrepreneurial collaboration from the privatised metropolitan bus service.

Problems with Freirian Pedagogy of the Sixties

Freire and colleagues began developing the praxis of conscientisation in literacy campaigns of the Brazilian states of Pernambuco and São Paulo in the early sixties, constructing a theoretical and methodological framework shortly to be that of president Goulart's National Literacy Campaign. Goulart's nationalist, developmentalist, modernising but dependent capitalist government was viewed by the educator as a benign laboratory for inserting radical pedagogy into an adult education system given Freire's concern to elaborate a pedagogy consistent with broadening the demands of a docile, silent and dispossessed population for a revised role in control and division of national wealth and power.

Curiously, the US government appeared untroubled by Freire's work until several months before the 1964 military coup d'etat, only then withdrawing financial support provided through USAID. Whatever else this may reflect, it tends to indicate the generally unremarkable, if not 'soft' character of Freirian methodology unto that point, capable of being pedagogically absorbed by a reforming capitalist regime and mainstreamed in the name of intensification of that process amongst the rural population.[77]

The situation prevailing in Chile from 1964 resonated closely with that of Brazil until the same year. Since 1940 the US Import-Export bank and subsequently the World Bank and International Monetary Fund had set down binding conditions under which modernisation would be effected in Chile, unfavourable to radical structural change.[78] Nevertheless, the Charter of Punta del Este committed all Latin American countries except Cuba to eradicate illiteracy by 1970 as part of an agrarian reform proposal central to Alliance for Progress discourse,[79] hence the embryonic Freire program could be seen officially as an essential ingredient to fulfillment of moderate government-endorsed plans for economic modernisation within the prevailing mode of production. These reforms were not the product of new demands; Brazilian political reformer A.P. Figueiredo had articulated their logic as early as 1847.[80]

The state was seen by all sectors as having overriding responsibility for primary, secondary and adult education, despite a history of contest between state and church. For much of the twentieth century the state and civil society had coexisted uneasily, civil society coming to expect of the state a significant degree of intervention in matters of national well-being. In this context the ready insertion of the left-catholic Freire by a supposedly left-catholic government into a state-run Agriculture Ministry literacy campaign seems unremarkable.

Here we simultaneously call into question the left credentials of the Christian Democrat [PDC] regime of Frei Montalva on several criteria: the well-known United States funding of his 1964 electoral campaign,[81] Vatican intervention on behalf of the PDC,[82] Frei's earlier flirtation with Mussolini,[83] repressive labour regulation, and the highly favourable arrangements extended to foreign multinationals for the "Chilenisation" of the country's copper resources, inter alia.[84]

Against this background, Freire entered the Ministries of Agriculture and Education in a conjoint strategy intended to reduce adult illiteracy by two-thirds by the next presidential election, a time frame hinting at an electoral sub-text as much as social motives. According at least to Waldemar Cortés, Freirian methodology only came to be known as "psycho-social" once fieldwork got underway and called forth literacy monitor preparation courses.[85] Prior literacy programs had used infant and infantile pedagogy, reinforcing the mirror negative of developmentalist ideology in the subject's construction of self: a necessarily inferior identity, child-like, a metaphor for underdevelopment and dependency.[86]

Freirian psycho-social methodology was introduced into the national literacy campaign from the time of Freire's team being established at the *Instituto de Desarrollo Agropecuario* [Institute for Agrarian Development (INDAP)], part of the Agriculture ministry, in 1965. As Gajardo notes, however, the popular education and popular culture movements had already moved beyond an earlier accommodation with the state to outright antagonism to the hegemony of the dominant classes, regarding education as an instrument of class struggle to be deployed in the creation of a hegemony favouring the popular classes.[87] Populist accounts of the vanguardist nature of Freire's work are seen from this perspective to be somewhat overstated.[88]

The overriding difficulty with the conscientizacion element as a methodology in adult education has been that in its foundational statements from the sixties it is vague, "naive" as Freire himself has since conceded. This has left open the door for any number of regimes of authoritarian as premised on the psycho-social method, Pinochet's Chile being the quintessential example.[89]

The tension between conservative Vatican doctrine and the nascent liberation theology movement in the Latin American church further sharpened differences within the Frei regime, the Christian left led by Jacques Choncol viewing advocacy of Freirian methodology as mandatory, especially in the wake of the Medellín General Conference of the Latin American Episcopate in 1968.

Theoretical and Methodological Comments

Though later state-produced literacy manuals of the Frei Montalva era substitute "coordinator" for "literacy teacher" and "participant" for "illiterate,"[90] Freire's 1965 text *Educación como Práctica de la Libertad* continuously uses the traditional term "illiterate" whilst lamenting the effects of traditional literacy primers which "cast the illiterate in the role of the object rather than the *Subject* of his learning."[91]

The mechanics of conscientisation as elaborated initially by Freire in 1965 cover five phases: vocabulary research among participants, generative word selection, codification [visual representation] of research, elaboration of agendas, and preparing cards with phonemic breakdown of generative words.[92] Care is taken with preparation of monitors to guard against the tendency to reproduce domesticating rather than liberatory pedagogy. Given the powerful traditions of socialist influence and political struggle in the state teaching service in Chile [noted earlier], Freire's perception of potentially non-dialogical 'banking' tendencies among his literacy teams is either profound or misplaced.

At the occidental level, the literature as to its validity is formidable; work dating from A.S. Neill, John & Evelyn Dewey, and more recently Ira Shor, Michael Apple and Linda Christian Smith document the verticalist, bureaucratic and anti-creative culture of Western schooling.[93] However, a palpable tension has existed in Chile for most of the twentieth century between the formal education process as a state reproductive apparatus and the unwillingness of radicalised teacher organisations to be uncritically complicit in those arrangements.[94]

The two great social actors of the post-colonial Latin American republics—the state and civil society—receive differential and inconclusive treatment in Freire's Chilean writings. Freirian pedagogy elaborated in Chile says little about state power, making vague reference to "human rights", social, political and economic forces [*Sobre la Acción Cultural*] or "revolutionary spirit", oppression, reaction and "closed society" [*Education as the Practice of Freedom*]. For a detailed analysis of Freire's construction of the state we must look to later writings, such as *Pedagogy of the Oppressed* [1970] or more convincingly *The Politics of Education* [1985] *and Learning to Question* {with Faúndez, 1989].

Complexities around the state and state power were shifting steadily throughout the sixties. Popular education had been a metaphor for state primary and secondary education for much of the preceding part of the twentieth century, a demand increasingly satisfied by the state albeit that oligarchic agendas tended to influence the operation of schooling—once won—in ways generally unfavourable to the popular classes.

As the oligarchy sought ways to mitigate the economic costs of modernisation, schooling as a huge budget item became vulnerable to attack. Coupled with elevated awareness of the political character of state schooling among the marginalised sectors of Chilean society, the emerging [or re-emerging] neoliberal view of state functions was matched by a renaissance of popular culture and re-constructed notion of popular education as that which served the popular interest, devoid of state influence.

Responding with characteristic generosity and incisiveness to these and related criticisms recently, Freire remarked that the theory of concientization had indeed been a weak point, particularly for its neglect of the "political character of education" and of "the problem of social classes and their struggle."[95]

To these concerns Marcela Gajardo—unacknowledged Chilean editor of several of Freire's major English works[96]—adds a comprehensive list questioning the type of practices which the methodology proposed to contribute to the liberation of the popular sectors:

> Among these, what was the relation between concientizing education and
> the different political and ideological projects of the social classes strug-
> gling for power; what was the relation between [Freirian] practices and
> those in which the popular movement and its base organisations were
> involved; what was the contribution of concientization to the constitution
> of class consciousness and the creation of a popular historical project; what
> was the relation between concientizacion and the political organisation of
> the popular sectors; and what was the function of the political parties,
> fronts and vanguards in this process of critical apprehension and trans-
> formation reality.[97]

Such a critique is not without prescience: Gajardo was a pivotal member of
one of the ICIRA teams with whom Freire worked. Recent qualifications of
that critique have not diminished the force of the above observations.[98]

Freire's departure for the United States in 1969 left only partial responses
to these issues, which were nevertheless more directly addressed in the
literacy program of the Allende administration from 1971. With that
government's brutal demise at the hands of the military in September, 1973
a new phase of popular organisation and popular education partially linked
to resolutions of such questions was begun.

The concept of "banking education," the accuracy of assertions as to
its international preponderance then and now, and Freire's exposition of
its theory and practice are well enough known. Most commonly associated with the English translation of *La Pedagogía del Oprimido [Pedagogy of
the Oppressed]*, an earlier formulation of the concept from sixties Chile appeared in *Sobre la Acción Cultural*.

> The educator's role in adult education requires: rigorous training ...
> permanent evaluation of the teacher's work, and constant [professional]
> guidance of the teacher, through which they feel secure in the realisation of
> their work.[99]

> Educators should not lose any opportunity to stimulate students to
> expound their observations, doubts and criticisms ... asking students to
> develop their observastions first on the blackboard and then on paper.[100]

The antithesis of banking education is of course liberatory education,
a set of dialectical practices which imply certain procedures to be adopted
by the educator consistent with the stages of concientization detailed earlier for literacy programs, varied but similar for post-literacy work. Their
objective is to lubricate the transformational process begun with the phases
of concientization described earlier. The teacher is central to this process.

Curiously then, in contrast to these observations from the mid-sixties,
Freire adopts a near counter-culture position on the teacher's role by the
time of his final year in Chile: Nobody educates anybody, nobody edu-

cates themself. Men educate themselves among themselves mediated by the world.[101]

Later, the primacy of the student over the teacher is reasserted [1981], and subsequently the educator is reinstated to primacy with the assertion that when an educator says he/she is equal to his/her student, either we have a demagogue or an incompetent. *If they were both equal, neither would recognise the other.*[102]

Material Gains, Interim Conclusions

Despite inconsistencies noted, an increasing division within the Frei regime over the direction and pace of the entire Agricultural Reform program, formidable advances were made which were significantly driven by Freire's energetic team, and would require state terrorism later to undo. In 1968 alone, 2000 Centres of Basic and Community Education [for adults] were established. In the period 1965-1968 ten thousand teachers were trained in the use of the Freirian psycho-social method, adopted as Frei Montalva's official adult education methodology.[103]

Nevertheless, that the incomplete project was sustainable until 1969 is of itself a tribute to the political dexterity and social commitment of the adult education teams at both the Education and Agriculture ministries. Indeed it seems to me that the durability and pragmatic responsiveness of Freire's Christian-Marxism was essential to the maintenance of a general progressive direction in what was an increasingly complex national project.

Contrary to the rather Freire-ocentric histories on this period, it is clear that as Freire himself acknowledges[104] a number of educators shared major responsibility for the design and implementation of the literacy program.[105] They were people such as: Marcela Gajardo who edited substantial Freirian works; Raúl Navarro with Professor Ormeño and others who organised short-notice campaign mode intensive training courses for adult educators at the *Instituto Pedagógico* of University of Chile; national program director Valdemar Cortés;[106] and literally thousands of enthusiastic literacy monitors operated in a pluralist political context increasingly destabilised by organised local reaction and those foreign forces with a growing sense of losing control in their own "backyard." As noted, the initial structural and policy support of the Frei Montalva government dissipated as class tensions sharpened and gave way to a regime increasingly subordinating its "revolution in liberty" to oligarchic re-ascendancy.

This said, we conclude with an interim acknowledgment that also ends an instructive piece by another eminent Latin American educator, namely Carlos Alberto Torres: "in pedagogy today, we can stay with Freire or against Freire, but not without Freire."[107]

Notes

1. Viviana Ramírez made helpful comments on an earlier draft; a fuller version appears as Chapter 4 in Austin, R. *A Critical History of Literacy Programs in Chile, 1964-1993* [forthcoming doctoral dissertation, University of Newcastle, 1995].

2. Tosh, J. *The Pursuit of History,* Longman, London 1993, pp. 206ff; Rubio, G. et al., *Historia Oral: Una Opción del Presente* CEAAL, Santiago de Chile, 1990, pp. 26-7.

3. Freire, P. In *Paulo Freire en Chile: Conversaciones, Conferncias y Entrevistas* Centro Canelo de Nos, San Bernardo, 1991, pp. 23-24.

4. See *Paulo Freire en los 90s: Diálogo con Francisco Vio Grossi, en Chile* Video y TV Canelo, San Bernardo, Chile 1991; and Weiler, K., "Freire and a Feminist Pedagogy of Difference" in *Harvard Educational Review* Vol. 61 No. 4, November 1991

5. Freire, P. In Gajardo, M. *La Concientización en América Latina: Una Revisión Crítica,* CREFAL, Michoacán, 1991; p. 15.

6. See Torres, C.A., *The Politics of Nonformal Education in Latin America,* Praeger, New York, 1990; Chapter 5.

7. See *Methods and Means Utilised in Cuba to Eliminate Illiteracy* [Unesco Report] Mined, Havana, 1971; MacDonald, T. *Making a New People: Education in Revolutionary Cuba* New Star, Vancouver 1985, especially Chapter 6; and *ibid.* Chapter 5.

8. See Cardenal, F. et al "Nicaragua 1980: The Battle of the ABCs" in *Harvard Educational Review* Vol. 51 No. 1, p. 4ff; Black, G. *Triumph of the People: The Sandinista Revolution in Nicaragua* Zed, London 1991, pp. 206, 255, 300, 311-16; and Torres, C.A. *op.cit.* Chapter 5.

9. UNESCO *ILY: Year of Opportunity* ILY Secretariat of Unesco, Paris, 1990; p. 8.

10. *Ibid.,* p. 8.

11. For useful discussion of UNESCO paradigms and problems, see Mackie, R. *Literacy and Revolution: the Pedagogy of Paulo Freire* Pluto, London, 1980; Chapter 3.

12. Anderson, B. *Imagined Communities* Verso, London, 1992; p. 7.

13. Barquera, H. *op.cit.* p. 16. One such campaign in Guatemala enrolled three thousand illiterate students, with 10% sitting the final exam and 3 passing.

14. *Ibid.,* p. 16.

15. Medina, G. *CREFAL: Presencia y acción en América Latina y el Caribe* CREFAL, Michoacán 1986, pp. 12-288.

16. La Belle, T. *Educación no formal y cambio social en América Latina* Nueva Visión, Ciudad México 1980, p. 146.

17. Barreiro, J. *Educación Popular y Cambio de Estructuras* Siglo XXI, México 1974, p. 72. For exposition of UNESCO's policy see UNESCO *Educación y Desarrollo en América Latina* Solar/Hachette, Buenos Aires 1967, especially pp. 61-3.

18. Gimeno, J. In UNESCO *op.cit.* p. 28.

19. See for instance Chilcote, R. *Theories of Development and Underdevelopment* Westview, Boulder 1984, Chapter 4.

20. Mackie, R. *op. cit.* p. 2.

21. Mackie, R. *op. cit.* pp. 99-101.

22. Loveman, B. *Chile: The Legacy of Hispanic Capitalism* Oxford, New York 1988; p. 279.

23. *Ibid.*, pp. 280-282.

24. The two quintessential manifestors here are the deliberations of the Second General Conference of Latin American Bishops at Medellin, 1968 [The "Medellin Conference"; see for instance Gunson, P. et al., *The Dictionary of Contemporary Politics of South America* Routledge, London, 1989, p. 15]; and that set out in Gutiérrez, G. *A Theology of Liberation: History, Politics and Salvation* Orbis, New York, 1988.

25. Freire, P. *Cultural Action for Freedom* Penguin, Ringwood, 1972; p. 29.

26. Aranowitz, A. In McLaren, P. And Leonard, P. [eds] *Paulo Freire: A Critical Encounter* Routledge, London 1993, p. 17.

27. Marx, K. Theses on Feuerbach: "The philosophers have only interpreted the world, in various ways; the point, however, is to change it." in *Marx Engels Selected Works* Vol. I Moscow, Progress 1973, p. 15 [original emphasis].

28. Cortés, V. et al *Manual del Método Psico-Social para la Enseñanza de Adultos* Santiago de Chile, Santillana 1966, p. 12.

29. Arévalo, S. et al *Sugerencias para la Alfabetización* Santiago de Chile, Quimantú 1971, p. 131.

30. Unnamed author *Manual del Método Psico-social para la Enseñanza de Adultos* Secretaria Nacional de la Mujer, Santiago de Chile, 1976; p. 58.

31. Ortiz, O. *Yo en la Familia* Mineduc, Santiago de Chile, 1980; pp. 35 & 50 respectively.

32. See for instance Labarca, A. *Feminismo Contemporáneo* Zig Zag, Santiago de Chile, 1947; Caffarena de Jiles, E. *¿Debe el marido alimentos a la mujer que vive fuera del hogar conyugal?* Universidad de Chile, Santiago de Chile, 1947; Donoso, M. *La Participación Política de la Mujer en Chile: Las Organizaciones de Mujeres* Fundación Friedrich Naumann, Buenos Aires 1987; Artígas, E.G. et al *Queremos Votar en las Próximas Elecciones: Historia del Movimiento Femenino Chileno 1913 - 1952* Fempress, Santiago de Chile, 1986; and Vitale, L. *La Mitad Invisible de la Historia* Sudamericana-Planeta, Buenos Aires 1987.

33. Weiler, K. *op.cit.* p. 453.

34. Infante, I. et al., *Escribe tu Palabra* [4 vols] Ministerio de Educación, Santiago de Chile, 1991.

35. See *ibid.* and Hooks, B. in McLaren, P. and Leonard, P. [eds.] *op. cit.* Chapter 7.

36. Author interview with parliamentarian Maria Antonieta Saa Díaz, Santiago de Chile, April 1995.

37. Silvert, K. et al., *Education, Class and Nation: the Experiences of Chile and Venezuela* Elsevier, New York 1976, p. 134.

38. Martner, C., "Contribuciones y Carencias del Discurso Educacional de la Izquierda Chilena, 1938 - 195,'" ECO occasional paper, Santiago de Chile 1986, p. 51.

39. On the act itself see Aylwin, M. et al., *Chile en el Siglo XX* Planeta, Santiago de Chile 1992, p. 77.

40. Cited in Lynch, J. *The Spanish-American Revolutions,1808-1826* Norton, New York 1973; p. 153.

41. See for instance Garretón, M. *The Chilean Political Process* Unwin Hyman, Boston 1989; p. 32.

42. *Informaciones Estadísticas de la Educación y Análisis Cuantitativo No. 25* UNESCO, Santiago de Chile 1982; the 1960 rate was 16.4% with the rural rate running at three times the urban rate, the official explanation for Frei's rural emphasis in literacy programs. See *Resúmen Nacional del Censo, 1960* INE, Santiago de Chile 1960.

43. Letelier, M.E. "Contribución de la Alfabetización en la Construcción de una Identidad Cultural: Taller de Acción Cultural de Chile," in Picón, C. *Alfabetizar para la Democracia* CEAAL/Año Internacional de la Alfabetización, Santiago de Chile, 1990; p. 27.

44. This was the so-called "War of the Pacific" fought ostensibly over a minuscule mining tax but, in reality, finally ceding the massive Peruvian nitrate deposits to Chile and severing crucial Bolivian access to the Pacific. See Loveman, B. *op.cit.* pp. 167-172.

45. See Bhola, H.S. *Campaigning for Literacy* UNESCO, Geneva 1982, p. 29; and Freire, P. *Cultural Action for Freedom* Penguin, Middlesex 1972; p. 23.

46. Freire, P. [ed. Gajardo, M] *Sobre la Acción Cultural* ICIRA, Santiago de Chile 1972; p. 28 [my translation].

47. Archives of the Biblioteca Heremóteca, Valparaiso.

48. See *Analfabetismo y Educación Popular en Chile: Conferencias Organizadas por 'El Mercurio' en julio de 1917* Imprenta Universitaria, Santiago de Chile, 1917.

49. Martner, C. *op.cit.* p. 67.

50. *Ibid.*, p. 73.

51. *Ibid.*, p. 51; my emphasis.

52. *Ibid.*, pp. 26-63.

53. The coalition of socialist and communist parties which became the electorally successful Unidad Popular in the 1970 presidential elections.

54. Stallings, B. *Class Conflict and Economic Development in Chile, 1958-1973* Stanford University Press, Stanford 1978; p. 98.

55. Cerro, Anaconda and Kennecott received double the book value of their copper mines, tax breaks and remained in administrative ascendancy; see *ibid.* p. 107.

56. The depth of occidentalisation of official Chilean educational discourse is manifest in an influential paper by José Joaquin Brunner and Nolfa Ibañez — *The Present and Future of our Education* — in the Conference Papers, 150th Anniversary Summer School, University of Chile; transcription by Ramírez, V. and this author, 1993. Brunner subsequently became a minister of state in the Frei Ruiz-Tagle government.

57. Author interview with Cortés, V. Santiago de Chile, January 1993. Cortés, as Head of Extraordinary Plans in the Ministry of Education, occupied a position especially created by Frei to direct the literacy campaign.

58. Wynia, G. *The Politics of Latin American Development* Cambridge U.P. New York, 1988; p. 98.

59. ICIRA was a joint Chilean Government/United Nations/FAO project

60. Author interview with Professor Rolando Pinto, Pontificia Universidad Católica de Chile, 21st April 1995

61. Cortés, W. et al., *Manual del Método Psico-Social ...*, p. 3.

62. *Manual de Alfabetización para Adultos* Santillana, Santiago de Chile, 1966; p. 2.

63. *Ibid.*, p. 10.

64. See for instance Giroux, H. "Literacy and the Politics of Difference" in Lankshear, C. et al., *Critical Literacy: Politics, Praxis and the Postmodern* SUNY Albany 1993, pp. 367ff; and Forgacs, D. et al. [eds] *Antonio Gramsci: Selections for Cultural Writings* Lawrence and Wishart, London 1985, pp. 164-171.

65. Freire, P. *Cultural Action for Freedom* Penguin, Victoria 1972, pp. 32-3.

66. Freire, P. *An Adult Literacy Process* [audiotape] Australian Council of Churches, Melbourne 1972; Section 8.

67. Fisher, J. *Out of the Shadows* Latin American Bureau, London 1993, pp. 17-44 & 177-200. Only since 1994 has the Chilean state through its Ministerio del *Servicio Nacional de la Mujer* seriously contemplated legislating for equal opportunity for women, encasing liberal women's movement discourse in a debate through conservative media around themes of employment and training for neoliberal economic goals. See María Josefina Bilbao Mendoza, Ministra Directora del Servicio Nacional de la Mujer "Sobre Igualdad de Opportunidades" in *El Mercurio* Santiago de Chile, 19 de abril, 1995, p. 2.

68. Author interview with Valdemar Cortés, Santiago de Chile, January 1993.

69. *Ibid.*

70. Gajardo, M. *op.cit.*, p. 82.

71. Stallings, B. *op.cit.*, p. 114.

72. Sigmund, P. *The Overthrow of Allende and the Politics of Chile, 1964-1976* University of Pittsburgh, 1977, p. 88.

73. Eduardo Carrasco, Chicago-trained director of INE 1987-1995 and hence a Pinochet *continuista*, agreed that Chilean census statistics are political fodder, and proffered the candid admission that there were problems with administration of the census questionnaire and with data obtained. Inter alia, the verbal-only inter-

view technique of census workers was agreed to be suspect in view of the factors impacting on admission of illiteracy, particularly among males [shame, machismo, feared loss of status]. The impact of high literacy results on potential government spending in the [adult] education sector was conceded. [author interview at INE, Santiago de Chile, April 1995].

74. Author interview with senior sociologist at INE, 19th April 1995.

This reflects historical continuity. In 1930 the census question on literacy was asked of over eight year olds: "Can you read?" with a second-chance question, "If not, do you go to school?" A similar 1940 census question was asked of seven year olds and above, although INE has accessible no records of it [author interview with senior INE sociologist, Santiago de Chile, april 1995].

75. *Manual del Empadronador: XVI Censo Nacional de Población y de Vivienda* Instituto Nacional de Estadisticas, Santiago de Chile 1992, p. 27.

76. A poignant example of such discourse appears in the Appendix to my forthcoming doctoral dissertation, an author interview with two senior Chilean adult educators, Eugenio Rodriguez and Raúl Navarro, Santiago de Chile, December 1992.

77. The intensity of Alliance for Progress and USAid activity throughout Latin America at the time is well documented; see for instance Marchetti, V. and Marks, J. *The CIA and the Cult of Intelligence* Jonathan Cape, London 1974; and Dunkerley, J. *Power in the Isthmus* Verso, London, 1988.

78. Chilcote, R. *op.cit.*, p. 64.

79. Cuba was ironically the only country to achieve the stated goal, and that some years in advance of 1970. See for instance *Report on the Method and Means Utilised in Cuba to Eliminate Illiteracy* UNESCO/Instituto Cubano del Libro, La Habana 1971; and MacDonald, T. *Making a New People: Education in Revolutionary Cuba* New Star, Vancouver, 1985, Chapter 6.

80. A.P. Figueiredo "The Need for Agrarian Reform in Brazil [1847]" in Smith, T.L. *Agrarian Reform in Latin America* Knopf, New York, 1966; p. 67.

81. Stallings, B. *op.cit.* p. 124.

82. Loveman, B. *op.cit.* pp. 277-9.

83. Stallings, B. *op.cit.* p. 94.

84. Sigmund, P. *op.cit.* p. 33.

85. Author interview with Valdemar Cortés, Santiago de Chile, January 1993

86. See for instance the analysis of Disney comics as vehicles of disempowerment in Dorfman, A. and Mattelart, A. *How to read Donald Duck: Imperialist Ideology in the Disney Comic* International General, New York 1991, pp. 98-99.

87. Gajardo, M. *op.cit.* p. 21.

88. Author interview with Valdemar Cortés, January 1993.

89. See for instance the dictatorship's *Manual del Método Psico-Social para la Enseñanza de Adultos: Adaptación preparada por la Secretaría Nacional de la Mujer* Santiago de Chile, 1976.

90. *Manual de Alfabetización para Adultos* Editorial Santillana, Santiago de Chile, 1966; p. 2.

91. Published in English as "Education as the Practice of Freedom" in Freire, P. *Education for Critical Consciousness* Sheed & WARD, London 1990; p. 49.

92. *Ibid.*, pp. 49-52.

93. See inter alia Neill's *Summerhill*, the Dewey's *Schools of Tomorrow*, Shor's *Culture Wars*, and Apple and Christian-Smith's *The Politics of the Textbook*.

94. See for instance Gysling, J. *Profesores: Un Análisis de su Identidad Social* CIDE, Santiago de Chile, 1992. The periodically fierce repression of teachers and their political representatives by inter alia the Ibañez administration [1946-52] and Pinochet dictatorship [1973-1989] is indicative of their historically progressive tendencies and ambivalent relationship to the state.

95. Freire, P. *The Politics of Liberation: Culture, Power and Liberation* Bergin & Garvey, New York 1985, p. 152.

96. In an interview with the author [Santiago Chile, April 19, 1994] Marcela Gajardo discounts this observation. Nevertheless, in view of concerns over the gender division of labour consistent with the philosophical premises of Freire's work in Chile, the issue seems to me important. Moreover, it is reflective of a historically patriarchal disposition inconsistent with liberation theology or pedagogy, which neither psycho-social methodology nor the subsequent *Unidad Popular* administration considered implicit in their programs. On the latter see Rosetti, J. "La Mujer y el Feminismo" in Jaquette, J. *The Women's Movement in Latin American Feminism and the Transition to Democracy* Unwin Hyman, Sydney 1989, p. 181.

97. Gajardo, M. *op.cit.* p. 45.

98. Author interview with Marcela Gajardo, Santiago de Chile, April 1994.

99. Freire, P. *Sobre la Acción Cultural* ICIRA, Santiago de Chile, 1970; p. 48.

100. *Ibid.*

101. Freire, P. quoted in Gajardo, M. *op.cit.* p. 57.

102. *Ibid.*, my emphasis.

103. *Ibid.*, p. 80.

104. See for instance his *Education as the Practice of Freedom* ICIRA, Santiago de Chile, 1971.

105. Torres, C. "From the Pedagogy of the Oppressed to A Luta Continua: The Political Pedagogy of Paulo Freire" in McLaren, P. and Leonard, P. *Paulo Freire: A Critical Encounter* Routledge, London 1993, p. 123.

106. See for instance his *Educación de Adultos* CAVE, Santiago de Chile, 1974

107. Torres, C. *op.cit.* p. 140.

12

Popular Education and the Reconstruction of El Salvador[1]

John L. Hammond

In 12 years of civil war, the Salvadoran government and the rebel Farabundo Martí National Liberation Front (FMLN) confronted each other not only on the field of battle but on the ideological and organizational fields as well. The FMLN and its allied community organizations created institutions to replace missing government services in the territory it controlled. Among other activities, they mounted education programs for guerrilla combatants and poor civilian communities. Community-based schools run by civilian community organizations offered what they called "popular education" and were among the most stable institutions in the conflictive zones.

These schools continue to operate today. As the controlled zones are reincorporated into national life, the schools' status and their relation to the country's official educational system must be worked out. The popular schools are a resource which the left hopes to use to consolidate its political position. Their status bears on relations not only between the left and the government but also within the left itself. The FMLN has now split, and the factions are seeking to transcend their past as military organizations and establish themselves as civilian, electoral parties, forging new kinds of links between leadership and base.[2]

Like its counterparts elsewhere in Latin America, the Salvadoran left and its allied popular organizations are trying to adapt themselves to the end of armed struggle. They are seeking new political forms which emphasize action in the sphere of culture, local organizing, and internal democracy over class issues, national-level power, and the top-down internal structure which is essential to waging an armed struggle.[3] Neither the focus on culture nor base-level action to build mass support is new to the Salvadoran left. But their integration into a strategy which accepts formal democracy and is centered on electoral politics does not come easily.

I will examine three issues which illustrate the relation of popular education to the government and the left: first, the evolving relation of the popular schools to the official educational system and the prospects for popular education to continue; second, the education of ex-combatants during the cease-fire period, a process of formal education but the result of popular education during the war; third, the government's EDUCO program, an attempt to coopt the participatory aspect of popular education in the service of neoliberalism and privatization of part of the national education system.

The place of popular education in the postwar period can be examined in two ways: first, as the expression of a particular political and methodological vision of education; second, as an object of bargaining in the political jockeying between left and right in El Salvador today—and, it must be added, not a major one. In this paper I will examine education from both points of view. Though the issues involving education are not the most important points of contention in the postwar settlement, the bargaining and struggle around them illustrate the interplay of opposition and accommodation to which the left is compelled because the war ended in a stalemate.

Educación popular means education of, by, and for the *pueblo* (people)—conducted by community members, usually with little education themselves, in areas where public schools were closed during the war or never existed. It occurs on three levels: elementary education for children; literacy and basic education for adults; and paraprofessional training in skills such as health work, teaching, and running cooperatives.

The ideological and methodological vision which popular education promotes is centered on the conception that education should be an instrument for social change, a means to achieve personal liberation and to create a new society. That vision distinguishes itself from the one which informs official education in four important respects.[4]

First, for popular educators, political content is an appropriate—even essential—element of education, and political commitment can motivate people to get educated. Promoters of formal education, in contrast, claim that it is politically neutral and provides purely technical skills. But popular educators argue that any educational process is necessarily political, and they criticize the official system for denying its political content while indoctrinating covertly.

Second, the teaching process encourages active participation and the development of critical consciousness over the rote learning and cultivated passivity which, they claim, are the pedagogical norm in El Salvador. The use of *concientización* (consciousness-raising) as a pedagogical tool is derived from the teaching methods of the Brazilian literacy pioneer Paulo Freire.[5]

Third, popular education rejects the technocratic assumptions, which govern official education, that the school is a differentiated institution, responsible primarily to itself, and that the proper role of the teacher is limited to the exercise of professional competence. Instead, schools should be responsible to the community and integrated into community life. Those who teach as volunteers are performing a social duty. Their political consciousness and dedication are regarded as more important qualifications than academic training and skills.

Finally, popular education aspires to offer universal access, on the assumption that everyone is not only entitled to education but capable of benefiting from it. The official Salvadoran system has never provided universal education—although that is its stated goal and mandate according to the Salvadoran constitution. As recently as 1990, estimates of the adult illiteracy rate ran as high as 50 percent, and in 1989, 19 percent of elementary school-age children had no access to school.[5] During the war, popular schools extended education widely in the conflictive zones, providing new schools where there had been none before, higher grade levels than official schools had offered before they were closed, and (though less systematically) adult education.

These were the principles which inspired popular education during twelve years of civil war. The war ended after the government of El Salvador and the FMLN signed an unprecedented peace settlement on January 16, 1992, in which neither side claimed victory. The government recognized the FMLN and accepted it as a legitimate political actor, and the two sides agreed to attempt to resolve their differences peacefully in an atmosphere of national reconciliation. But the settlement instead began a period of intense—though mostly nonviolent—conflict. The desire for reconciliation was tempered on both sides by jockeying for political advantage, and, even were good will guaranteed, mutual trust would not automatically ensue after two decades of conflict.

Reconciliation was meant not just to bring an end to the fighting but to initiate a process of reconstruction on the basis of *concertación* (usually translated as "consensus building," but in the present context, more appropriately "joint action") between the government, on the one hand, and the FMLN (still united at the time) and its institutions and supporters, on the other. The framework was provided by the National Reconstruction Plan proposed by the government in the weeks after the cease-fire took effect, to which the FMLN and allied organizations were to suggest amendments. *Concertación* was largely imposed on the Salvadoran government by the potential donors from the United States and Europe, working through the United Nations as mediator in the negotiations which ended the war.[7] They promised to finance the reconstruction plan on the condition that the FMLN and "civil society" (an umbrella term for popular organizations close to the FMLN) participate in formulating it and carrying it out. Those donors have given some aid directly to Salvadoran NGOs closely associated with the FMLN.[8]

The "civil society" whose participation was envisioned was exclusively on the insurgent side—reconstruction was not intended to affect areas outside of the formerly controlled and conflictive zones or within the political orbit of government supporters. The process of *concertación* would thus be inherently asymmetric: the government and its bureaucracies are bigger and more firmly established than the left parties and the popular organizations. Nevertheless, the promise raised expectations on the part of the FMLN and its sympathizers, especially those who had organized popular schools and other activities with a potential role in the development process, that their counterinstitutions would be accepted as part of the national system.

It may seem paradoxical to suggest that popular education might find a place within the official system, for popular education has always defined itself as deliberately, even militantly, outside of any formal system and *opposed* to formal education.[9] Yet there have been attempts to organize official school systems on popular education principles. The most notable experiments have occurred at the national level in societies where a revolutionary government has come to power and adopted a radical education program—as in China, Cuba, and Nicaragua.[10] In Nicaragua, as in El Salvador, popular education had been part of the revolutionary process, and it was adopted as the model for the transformation of the national education system.

In all these countries, new regimes expanded access to education (Cuba achieved virtually universal literacy) and invoked ideological motivations to encourage people to educate themselves. They found, however, that the large bureaucracy necessary to implement an educational project on a national scale was not entirely compatible with the spontaneity and localism inherent in the popular education model. To promote modernization and economic growth, moreover, each of them at certain times emphasized technical and specialized education for a relatively few over equal access for all.

Popular education has also been adopted at the city level. From 1989 to 1992 a leftist (Workers' Party) administration led the city government of

São Paulo, Brazil. Paulo Freire himself was named Secretary of Education. Among the initiatives he promoted for the public schools were reform of the elementary curriculum, a new form of school governance actively involving parents and community, and an innovative adult education program. Overall, his administration promoted close relations with urban-based social movements.[11] Nevertheless, reportedly frustrated by bureaucratic obstacles, Freire resigned his position in 1991 before the term of the mayor who appointed him had expired.

In all these cases, popular education was embraced by officials with formal power over the educational system. Salvadoran advocates of popular education have no such power. The war ended not in a revolutionary triumph but in a stalemate. The old regime, still in power, retained its authority over the national education system. *Concertación* means compromise between popular education and the official system, but the greater size, resources, and institutional legitimacy of the latter all demand most of the compromise from the side of popular education.

Promoters of popular education not only have no formal power to implement their own model within the official system; they have reason to seek accommodation. They want official recognition and the legitimation which the official system has. They also want certification for their pupils, recognition and salaries for their teachers, equipment and supplies for the schools.

That recognition will come, if at all, through the political process and will depend on the partisan strength of the left parties. But as they simultaneously seek short-run political power and long-run social transformation, they will find that the requirements of political advantage are not the same as the requirements for promoting social change, in education or elsewhere. The peace settlement and the pressure for *concertación* provided an opening to work for both at the same time, but educational reform has not had high priority. And if the popular schools achieve recognition they may find that they have to sacrifice their independent educational project. The period of reconstruction is thus a test of the effort to achieve official legitimacy for popular education while maintaining its political autonomy. But it is also a test of the place of education within the leftist political project.

Popular Education in the Controlled Zones

Popular education began in El Salvador about 1970 under the leadership of church workers inspired by liberation theology.[12] It was taken up by the political-military organizations which arose at the same time and which formed the FMLN in 1980. Those organizations rejected Che

Guevara's highly militaristic *foco* strategy, which most Latin American guerrilla organizations had adopted in the 1960s. They forged a new strategy (though with differences of emphasis among them) of cultivating support widely among the civilian population first.[13] Doing so entailed adopting a perspective close to that of the Christians inspired by liberation theology. Popular education became one of their organizing tools.

Repression mounted between 1977 and 1980, ending open organizing and driving the new political organizations and the grass-roots movements in rural and urban areas to clandestine organization and armed struggle.[14] But as the war dragged on, the FMLN recognized that a purely military victory was far away and called for a return to local organizing in the mid-1980s. In the midst of war, communities organized to restore disrupted services, especially education and health care.

Popular schools were created first in communities where they had been closed, and then in villages where they had never existed. While some popularly run schools predated this period, many more were founded. Classes were taught by community members, generally people who had only a few years of formal education at best, but who wanted to assure that their children got at least some education. The schools became a major focus of organizing and a basis of the guerrillas' claim to quasi-governmental legitimacy.[15]

These schools were—and continue to be—run by civilian community councils close to but formally independent of the FMLN. Activists and members are strongly encouraged to teach and to study, and the curriculum is suffused with political content. The schools' resources are meager and their teachers have a much lower level of training than teachers in official schools, but schools enjoy the active involvement of parents and community members who contribute their labor to make up for some of the material shortages. Community organizations and the FMLN itself put a high priority on education both to train people in various skills and to strengthen their political commitment.[16]

During the last years of the war, education projects increasingly received training and technical assistance from professionals in Salvadoran NGOs. Teachers who started out as volunteers began to receive small stipends paid by foreign donations. Though most of them had only a few years of formal schooling, they improved their knowledge and skills significantly through the experience and training they received as teachers. Those who had taught in refugee camps in Honduras received extensive teacher training from international volunteers;[17] Salvadoran NGOs and the Church offered some limited training to those working as popular teachers in El Salvador itself during the last years of the war.

Popular Education and the Peace Settlement

These schools have continued to operate since the end of the war. In 1994 they claimed 1,053 teachers and twenty thousand students.[18] Peace has returned to their communities, and some major problems have disappeared: classes are not interrupted by military operations, teachers are not detained, and books and supplies are not held up at roadblocks. But the end of the war adds new complications. The peace negotiations created expectations, so far unfulfilled, for a "peace dividend"—a budgetary reallocation which would favor education and other social projects—and for the incorporation of the popular schools into the official education system.

Popular teachers anticipated that peace would offer them the opportunity to upgrade their academic skills. Special classes for that purpose have begun. In some areas the teachers were admitted to the accelerated courses held for ex-combatants in 1992 (described below). Subsequently, all the popular teachers of Chalatenango attended a course which met for four days every two weeks for most of the academic year 1993 to prepare for exams at the sixth-, ninth-, and twelfth-grade levels. Few had completed ninth grade before the war, but some had studied as refugees in Honduras, and others had learned enough from the experience they had gained as teachers to be able to enter the high school classes. The course was organized by the Intersectoral Corporation for Economic Development and Social Progress (CIDEP), an NGO which promotes education, with European financing. The teachers were professionals, and they followed the official curriculum of the Ministry of Education. Similar courses were initiated in 1994 in other formerly controlled zones.

Teachers and organizers are determined to continue to run their schools on the principles of popular education. While they want to improve their skills, they are convinced that the form of education they have offered has been effective. Their own words make clear the strength of their belief in the value of what they have accomplished. Their conviction is all the stronger because their experience led them to recognize their previously unacknowledged abilities. Claudio, a 26-year-old popular teacher (and veteran of the guerrilla army) in Chalatenango, found that "this thing of popular education has been like a discovery that it's possible—that it's possible to teach with the little bit that you know."

It may be modesty—or even astonishment at the abilities they discover—which leads them to emphasize the "little bit" that they know, and to displace their pride in their own accomplishments to their students. Marta, who taught fourth grade (the highest grade offered) in a village in Morazán, when asked what happened to students who moved elsewhere and wanted to continue in another school, replied with evident delight:

They told me that they hadn't had any problem, and that they congratulated them when they saw how much they had learned from a popular
teacher. It made us very proud and encouraged us to continue, because
what we could give them was important, and now they're studying seventh and eighth grade. And it's a big surprise for me that, well, I got to
fourth grade, and I *taught* fourth grade. And they asked the pupils how
could it be that someone who had only been to fourth grade had taught
them.

They measure their success not only by the individual students they
have taught, but by having established schools even in tiny communities
where there had never been any government schools. According to Claudio
(quoted above),

> there are a bunch of villages and hamlets that are far from the towns,
> and the kids don't go to school because it's too far. They have to walk
> three or four hours, in the winter the rivers rise, there's no bridge, and
> the kids don't go because they're afraid of the currents.

> Here we have something like thirty schools in Chalatenango besides the
> schools in the main towns—there are schools in the villages and hamlets
> where there were never any schools. Now there are popular schools that
> teach up to fifth or sixth grade where before they didn't even have first
> grade. We want the government to recognize those schools and build
> buildings for them.

An important factor in their success has been the involvement of parents and community, who contribute their labor to build schoolhouses and
equipment and provide other important material assistance. According to
Isabel, a community education organizer in Chalatenango, "it couldn't have
worked all these years, even before the war, if the people hadn't been really involved."

Their involvement not only contributes essential material resources. It
makes them identify with the schools and overcomes the hostility which is
more typical of peasant communities: schools are often seen as alien institutions imposed from without. José Luís Guzmán, Director of the Institute
of Education of the Central American University, said that teachers from
outside the community are often not very effective. "That's something that
the national system could never solve: you study in a more or less elite
institution, then you go back to 'make the people develop.' You speak the
language of another paradigm."[19] Even when teachers themselves came
from poor families, their education drew peasants' attention to their own
inferiority and symbolized the social hierarchy which kept peasants oppressed.

Educating oneself and one's children, moreover, became a political obligation and an expression of one's integration into the community. Interviewed while the war was still going on, Julio Portillo, former secretary general of the National Association of Salvadoran Educators (ANDES), the national teachers' union, described the relationship:

> In those zones you can't be an illiterate and say you don't want education. You just can't, because if you say, "Look, I was born illiterate and I want to die illiterate," that's not allowed. ... Your refusal to learn becomes an obstacle which has negative effects for the whole community. Of course, no one is going to come with a club and beat you over the head. But if you say "no," someone is going to keep at you until they convince you, because the whole community needs for you to learn.[20]

Those who have promoted popular education for many years are convinced of its efficacy, but government education officials are not. They are bound to more traditional pedagogical principles; they are also bound to the governing party, and to acknowledge popular education would be to grant legitimacy to the practice of the FMLN and its allies in the popular organizations. Popular education is therefore an objection of contention in the postwar order, both for its educational merits and as a token of political advantage. The terms of this debate stand out in an examination of three issues: the future status of the popular schools, the education of demobilized combatants, and a government initiative to invoke popular education principles in the service of privatization of part of the public education system.

Incorporation of Popular Schools. Since the end of the war, the relation of the popular schools to the official education system has been contentious. Those who have conducted popular education want to maintain their control of the schools for several reasons: they want to continue to offer their brand of education, of whose efficacy they are convinced, and to put forward in the schools their alternative vision of a just society; they also want to consolidate their political position, and, not incidentally, provide employment for their personnel. They further argue that, having borne the burden of teaching during these years, they now deserve salaried positions, further training, and formal recognition of their status.

Despite their differences with the Ministry of Education, however, they want to be accepted into the official system. They are eager to continue their training. They want formally trained teachers to come to work with them even though new professional colleagues may raise questions about their capacity and responsibilities. But they do not want to be squeezed out. Chepe, a 24-year-old disabled veteran of the guerrilla army who is a popular teacher in Chalatenango, expressed these fears:

We can't lose everything we've fought for for 12 years. We don't want to give up these positions and have them put in teachers and tell us, "No, you people can study. We're going to take your places," and then when we finish studying find that there are no positions.

Even before the war ended, foreign government and nongovernment aid donors demanding *concertación* made clear that they would be offering reconstruction assistance not on the government's terms but only if the government reached some agreement with the FMLN and with popular organizations in the controlled zones. At the end of 1991, in anticipation of the peace settlement, Salvadoran NGOs and organizations involved in popular education—some primarily focused on education, some sectoral (peasants', women's, etc.) organizations which have education programs for their members, and others with professional staffs offering assistance to popular education—formed the *Concertación Educativa de El Salvador* (CEES). Its purpose was to coordinate efforts of NGOs and base organizations to influence the plans for education envisioned in the National Reconstruction Plan. Subsequently, as an umbrella group of organizations promoting popular education, the CEES sought to negotiate with the ministry for recognition.

At the beginning some organizations took a militant, rejectionist line and argued that negotiating with the ministry would mean selling out. But eventually they agreed on a platform of demands. Most importantly, they wanted the ministry to create a formal status for popular teachers, who would be hired to teach in public schools on the basis of their experience, though at a lower level than professional teachers. They also demanded certification of the grade levels completed by pupils in the popular schools and government funds to keep the school running. Negotiations on these issues have been going on between the organizers of popular education and the ministry for more than two years with few concrete results.

As of the end of 1993, the ministry had not adopted a general policy on the certification of pupils, although ministry supervisors or school principals in a few localities had agreed to examine them for certificates. In Chalatenango, a team of ministry teachers and popular teachers jointly composed exams for the various grade levels offered in the schools, and administered them to 1,844 pupils in 27 schools at the end of the 1992 academic year. Students who passed received official certificates.[21] In Morazán, a public school principal agreed to an informal arrangement to give certificates from his school to pupils in the popular schools. Several public schools have recognized the studies of individual students *de facto* by admitting them to the next grade level even though they have no certificates.

Beginning in 1992 the ministry agreed to meet with representatives of the CEES to discuss the demand for a formal status for popular teachers.

Initially, ministry officials said that teachers would have to have more formal education as a first condition. Even when equivalency courses were set up, however, the ministry continued to stall, arguing that it had made no commitments. In the campaign atmosphere before the national elections of March, 1994, accusations flew back and forth: right-wing politicians attacked the popular schools as centers of terrorism and weapons traffic, while the CEES repudiated the accusations and denounced the ministry for refusing to live up to its commitments. These negotiations continue sporadically into 1995 under the new government, but with few positive results.[22]

The ministry argued, among other things, that professional teachers, among whom unemployment is high, would oppose the employment of popular teachers with lower qualifications. But ANDES, the public school teachers' union, has embraced the popular teachers' proposal. (Like all Salvadoran unions, ANDES never acknowledged ties to the FMLN, but it has been a key component of the popular movement with a long history of leftist agitation.) The negotiating platform it adopted at its December 1992 convention included recognition of the popular teachers, and it became their interlocutor with the ministry, presenting the popular schools' platform in its own negotiations. According to Lisandro Navarrete, Education Secretary of ANDES, who has been involved in those negotiations, ANDES members see no threat from the acceptance of popular teachers because so few of them want jobs in the small, out-of-the-way villages where most of the popular schools are located.[23]

Deeper, unresolved issues about the popular schools underlie these immediate issues of certification and recognition of teachers: not only conflicting pedagogical principles but control of the educational system and competition for foreign donations. Official Salvadoran education is highly centralized under the Ministry of Education. While some compromise between adoption of official standards and local control must be found, those who have run the popular schools will struggle to keep as much control with the communities as possible. Further, they will do their best to maintain the contributions of material and moral support from community members.

Foreign funding is also an issue. Even before the war ended, major international donors, especially from the European Community, did not give all their development aid to government agencies but instead channeled a part through NGOs close to the FMLN. Organizations which have established schools, together with other service-providing organizations within the popular movement, compete for development aid with official agencies (and with each other).

So far, differences between the ministry and the communities have generally been fought out in negotiations rather than direct conflict. In a few cases the ministry has sent certified teachers to work alongside of popular teachers (as they did in some places during the last years of the war), and in other areas its attempts to intervene have been resisted.[24] But it has not attempted to assert control of the schools in formerly controlled areas to any significant degree.

Still, the relation of the popular schools to the formal system inevitably raises the question of the purposes and the constituencies the schools are to serve. Will they be coopted, or will they remain a focus of opposition? The ministry has shown little interest in incorporating them. Advocates of popular education themselves are pursuing incorporation at the same time as they defend their right to promote their own ideal of education, two objectives which appear to be contradictory.

It is striking, however, that the activists interviewed do not acknowledge the possible contradiction. They foresee major political battles with the ministry. In the face of ministry intransigence, Isabel, the Chalatenango organizer, talked of "direct action [*medidas de hecho*]. ... We've learned a lot of things here. We've learned that you can protest in the streets." She also insisted that while the government must take over responsibility for the schools, it must do so "without making us lose the experience we have gained." She saw that loss as a danger from outside rather than something that she and her fellow education workers themselves risked by pursuing accommodation. Activists apparently do not see incorporation as posing any threat of cooptation or dilution of their commitment to the principles of popular education.

Divergences Within the Left. The fate of the popular schools calls into question relations not only with the government, but also between the factions which formerly made up the FMLN, between the "core" and the "periphery" of the formerly controlled areas, and between professionals and community people working on education projects who have discovered with the advent of peace that their interests and concerns do not entirely coincide.

Factional differences among the FMLN's five parties did not take the form of competition over education but of independent action. Their failure to work in common revealed the tensions among them and foreshadowed the breakup of the FMLN in 1994. Each of the five parties jealously guarded its contacts with foreign sources of funding. Projects were negotiated separately by particular communities or by groups of neighboring communities under the hegemony of one organization.

The strength of popular education varies with the relative levels and geographical concentrations of strength of the political factions. Popular education was extensive only in the territory controlled by the two largest organizations, the FPL and the ERP: most extensive in the FPL's eastern Chalatenango, and second in the ERP's northern Morazán. Because the other three parties controlled much smaller areas, they did not sponsor popular schools as extensively.

Organizations close to the FPL and the ERP (the CCR and CIAZO, respectively) have taken leading roles in the negotiations with the ministry. The CCR (Coordinating Committee of Communities and Repopulations of Chalatenango), a regional affiliate of CRIPDES (Christian Committee for the Displaced), is based in the communities of Chalatenango which were resettied in the second half of the 1980s. It coordinates other community activities—notably health and assistance to agricultural production—as well as education. CIAZO (Inter-Organization [*Intergremial*] Literacy Committee of the Eastern Zone) is an organization staffed by professionals. It was founded to provide technical assistance to the adult literacy campaigns of popular organizations, but subsequently evolved to provide technical assistance to all educational efforts including, notably, the community-based schools.

The CEES claims to have battled *cinquismo* ("five-ism"), as the tendency to competition among the five parties was called, and with some justification. As of 1995, it still encompasses organizations close to each of the five former parties of the FMLN, as well as more independent education organizations. But the most tangible accomplishments, the agreements which have gotten certificates for pupils in some popular schools, have been made locally, benefiting the schools in communities tied to one or another party rather than the popular schools as a whole. These arrangements have been made locally simply because it has been possible to get results while the negotiations at the national level have remained stalled. But they reinforced the centrifugal tendencies within the FMLN and accentuated inequalities between the parties in the provision of education after the peace settlement.

They also reinforce another division, not so widely recognized, between what were the central areas of FPL and ERP control (eastern Chalatenango and northern Morazán, respectively) and the other areas where either of them was the dominant FMLN organization. Each of these parties and their allied NGOs and popular organizations have been strongest in their respective heartlands; so, too, have the popular schools. The heartlands have had the best training for teachers and the largest external donations to maintain the schools (and even in many cases to construct school buildings)—just as other projects there have benefited from more attention and support. They are now the places where teachers have received further training and equivalency classes as well. Both the present FMLN, in which the FPL is the largest force, and the PD, of which the ERP is the main component, hope to consolidate a future political base and proving ground for their political projects; it is likely that they see education and other projects in these areas as one of the means to that consolidation.

Differences of social status among FMLN militants and sympathizers also affect the popular schools. Schools bring popular teachers together with professionals who train them, and community people with the professional staffs of the NGOs. People of different social levels worked together effectively during the armed struggle, but the peace has made their differences more salient.

The income of community organizers working for popular organizations affords them a standard of living hardly higher than that of an average peasant in their communities, yet they perceive themselves to be doing the same work as NGO employees earning professional salaries. Professionals and local untrained teachers do not always have the same objectives for the popular schools: when professionals urge higher standards, popular teachers sometimes take their suggestions as covert criticisms, and insist on the value of the skills they have developed in practice:

> the way we peasants are, when we hear new words or meet well-educated people, we think the things we know aren't worth so much. Training has to reaffirm what we are doing and put it in a scientific context. We often think something up, and don't call it by the name that a formally educated person would use, but children have learned from us because we figure out how to reach them. (Isabel)

These divergences emerge when members of the two groups are together, as in training sessions and planning meetings. In 1992 educators from ANDES and the National University presented a proposal for postwar training of the teachers of Chalatenango, but people from the villages meeting with them found it insufficient. Justino, a CCR organizer who oversaw education in one of the four regions of eastern Chalatenango, exclaimed sarcastically, "we've had training when bombs were falling, and no one from the university was there!" Isabel, the CCR board member in charge of education, "begging Ernesto's pardon," compared the popular teachers' stipend of 150 colones a month (less than $20) to the salary of 5000 colones in the budget for the project director. Such comments are usually presented with good humor and cause no major rupture, but they do raise questions about the viability of class alliances within the left.

In summary, the situation of the popular schools remains unresolved. Decisions regarding them are subordinate to the political conflict between the government and the parties of the left. They continue to be important to the communities which support them, and they continue to educate those communities' children, but their longterm future depends on decisions which will be taken at the political level.

Reintegration of Ex-Combatants. Two other educational issues have arisen since the end of the war which are indirectly related to popular education. One is the education of veterans. Most of the combatants in the guerrilla army had little or no formal education, but throughout the war, they were taught informally by their fellow combatants.[25] The peace settlement brought the opportunity to consolidate what they had learned through popular education in the guerrilla army. Ex-combatants of the FMLN were concentrated in fifteen encampments for most of 1992 and were given classes. With financing from the United Nations Development Program, the National University hired teachers who taught 5,530 ex-combatants. They received classes daily at levels ranging from basic literacy to high school. Those who passed the final examination received official certificates.[26]

A principal purpose of these classes was to prepare candidates for the new National Civilian Police (PNC). The establishment of a new police force, removed from the control of the military hierarchy, is a central point of the peace settlement. It was created to replace the former National Police and National Guard, which have been disbanded.[27] Twenty percent of its recruits were to be excombatants of the FMLN, twenty percent demobilized soldiers, and the remaining 60 percent civilians (many of them recruited through popular organizations sympathetic to the FMLN). Candidates had to prove ninth-grade equivalency; most of the ex-combatants who applied had not completed that level of formal schooling before the war, but had earned certificates during the cease-fire following the basic education they had received while combatants.

Other ex-combatants pursued further study beyond the equivalency classes. In principle every demobilized member of both the government and the guerrilla armies was eligible to receive either farmland or a scholarship; while there were serious delays and deficiencies in the programs set up to provide them, some ex-combatants who received high-school diplomas during the cease-fire went on to university studies.

The educational program for the ex-combatants was put into place rapidly and effectively. It received high priority because the demobilization of the combatants and the formation of the PNC were key political tasks for the FMLN itself and could be presented to the international donor community as crucial to the success of the peace accords. The popular schools have not been so favored. Nothing gives them the same importance, so that while they have continued to operate, they did not enjoy the political attention that might get a response to their demands.

Government Privitization Initiative. The third important educational issue arises from a government initiative. The EDUCO program (Education with Community Participation) provides funds to local schools to enable them to expand. Funded by the World Bank, EDUCO authorizes the creation of local voluntary organizations to hire certified teachers and thus to offer more grades in a school.

Teachers work in an official school under the supervision of a principal, but they are hired by the local sponsoring organization rather than the Ministry of Education. They do not get civil servant status, and their salary, set by the local organization, is generally lower than that of official teachers. In 1993 some 2,500 teachers were working under the auspices of EDUCO.[28] In line with its broader neoliberal policy, the government has been trying to diffuse responsibility for education for several years. A previous initiative to turn local schools over to municipal authorities was defeated in 1990.

The EDUCO program is in part inspired by—and intended to compete with—popular education, as can be inferred from the claim that it will "deliver control of the local school to the organized community."[29] The principle of local control is double-edged. Those who run popular schools seek to maintain it; when the government promotes it in the context of neoliberalism and the push to privatization, however, its primary purpose is to contain government expenditures, and it can be expected to weaken the public school system.

Policy Implications

During the 1980s, government attention to and support for education were sacrificed to the war effort. Total real expenditures for education, which had doubled between 1970 and 1980, fell by 48 percent between 1980 and 1987, to almost the same level as in 1970.[30]

With the end of the war, public education attracted renewed attention and widespread perception of a profound crisis. In the three years after the war ended, two major studies examined education. In 1993 a national education sector assessment, funded by USAID, was performed by the Harvard Institute for International Development with the collaboration of the Ministry of Education, the School of Education of the Central American University, and the Business Foundation for Educational Development (FEPADE). Its 600-page final report was entitled *Education in El Salvador Facing the Twenty-First Century.* Six months after he took office in 1994, President Calderón Sol appointed a Commission on Education, Science, and Development which in June, 1995, completed a report, "Transformation of

Education for Peace and Development in El Salvador."[31] Though the two studies dealt with all levels of education, it is their findings regarding basic education, especially in rural areas, which are relevant to popular education. They identified similar problems and solutions.

The most glaring deficiency of official schooling in El Salvador is that primary education is still not realistically available to all school-age children. According to a 1991-92 national survey, 34 percent of children in rural areas between the ages of seven and 15 were not attending school (the corresponding figures were 8 percent in San Salvador and 12 percent in other urban areas).[32]

Both studies were critical of the teachers who staffed rural schools and identified their placement as a source of problems. Teachers do not want to teach in rural schools. Assigned by the central education bureaucracy without regard for where they live, most teachers do not live in the communities where they work, and they frequently miss school to meet bureaucratic obligations or because they prolong their weekend by traveling on Mondays and Fridays.[33]

Nonresident teachers do not identify with the communities in which they work. In much of rural El Salvador, peasants remain suspicious of education, which appears as an institution alien to rural communities and imposed from without. Parent participation in school activities is therefore low. Children adopt the same views, limiting their motivation to learn. Curriculum does not respond to local needs because it is set nationally by the ministry and formulated on the assumption that it can be determined on technical grounds without political implications. One collaborator of the national sector assessment (in an article published in his own name) claims that the rural schools offer "education for the community without the community."[34]

At the same time, the sector assessment recognizes the existence of a broad, diverse sector of nonformal education. "Nonformal education" is more inclusive than "popular education," also including classes offered by government agencies and nongovernmental organizations. The study presents the popular schools in the former conflictive zones favorably and calls (though not very prominently) for the incorporation of the popular teachers into the official system.[35]

The deficiencies identified in the two studies are widely recognized. They are reflected in the complaints about public education heard from the staff and parents of popular schools. Coming from inhabitants of the former conflictive zones, such complaints might be rejected as politically inspired, but parents and teachers in public schools raise the same issues. Focus groups of parents and teachers in a USAID-funded study also mentioned teachers' low commitment, their absenteeism, and the irrelevance of the curriculum to students' needs. Parents also complained that they were often required to contribute financially to the officially free schools.[36]

Popular education does not suffer from these problems, and aspects of its practice could profitably be incorporated into public education policy. After more than two decades' experience, popular education has demonstrated its ability to broaden access, to offer a curriculum which motivates students by its relevance to their needs, and to encourage community involvement.

Broadened Access. With very limited resources, popular education has been able to reach more communities and offer more grade levels in the areas where it is practiced than the official system did before the war, thanks to the assumption that everyone is capable of learning and many are capable of teaching. As long as the Ministry of Education is unable to create a school for every village and hamlet with a school-age population which warrants it, teachers with limited preparation but strong motivation could allow the system to offer at least basic education universally. The examinations given in the popular schools of Chalatenango in 1992 offer some evidence that popular teachers without advanced formal education can be reasonably effective: though not directly comparable to those offered in public schools, these exams nevertheless show that according to standards set by Ministry of Education officials, most students had mastered the material of the grades they had attended.

A Relevant Curriculum. One of the central tenets of popular education's ideology and methodology is that education for people in subaltern positions must teach them to contest their subalternity rather than reproduce it. To that end it incorporates political content into the education of people in subordinate positions. *Concientización* motivates children and helps them learn. The sense that education is empowering can make both children and their parents value it more highly. In the FMLN-controlled zones during the war, learning and contributing to the schools were seen as duties to the community but also as means of advancing oneself, because the new society which people aspired to create would demand higher levels of competence, but would also open up new opportunities.

Because the ministry views such a politicized curriculum as a thinly-veiled form of indoctrination, government-sponsored schools will never offer the political content which was part of education in FMLN-controlled territory during the war. Nevertheless, it may be possible to activate some of the same motivation by providing an education which pupils and their communities see as contributing both to social mobility for the pupils and to social transformation for the communities.

Community Participation. Another ideological/methodological lesson of popular education is the importance of integrating the school and the community. In the zones of popular education, direct involvement gives adults a strong proprietary interest in the schools, and makes them encourage their children more strongly. As we have seen, the government has tried to coopt such participation in the EDUCO program. Similar involvement could well create the same identification in other communities.

These are three ways in which the present practice of popular education might contribute to overcoming recognized deficiencies of official education. For its own part, the quality of popular education is limited by material shortages in plant, equipment and supplies and by its practitioners' lack of formal education and training. A government decision to support the schools might help to fill both these gaps.

But these lessons for educational policy threaten to get lost in politics. National education officials have shown no more than symbolic interest in learning any lessons from the popular education process. On its own side, popular education suffers from two handicaps: its advocates are pursuing the apparently contradictory objectives of promoting their own project and seeking the legitimation and material benefits of the official system, and the political movement which gave birth to popular education nevertheless accords it low priority. Whether popular education will be able to contribute to solving El Salvador's educational crisis will clearly depend less on its pedagogical value than on the outcomes of the political struggles around it.

Notes

1. An earlier version of this paper was presented at the Congress of the Latin American Studies Association, Atlanta, March 1994. My thanks Tim Crouse, Julia Kushner, and Salvadoran informants for current information, and to Bob Arnove and Laura Kramer for helpful comments.

2. The FMLN was founded in 1980 by five political-military organizations, the People's Revolutionary Army (ERP), the Popular Liberation Forces (FPL), the Communist Party (PCS), the Central American Revolutionary Workers' Party (PRTC), and the National Resistance (RN). In December, 1994, the ERP and the RN withdrew from the FMLN, and the following year they and another party merged into the new Democratic Party (PD). The remaining three organizations jointly retain the name FMLN, and they have taken steps to dissolve their separate identities and turn the FMLN into a unified party.

3. Jorge G. Castañeda, *Utopia Unarmed: The Latin American Left after the Cold War* (New York: Alfred A. Knopf, 1993); Carlos Vilas, "The Hour of Civil Society," *NACLA Report on the Americas* 27, No. 2 (September-October, 1993): 38-42.

4. I derive the following characterization of popular education from the literature based on experiences in other countries, cited below, and from my own study of popular education and guerrilla war in El Salvador. I conducted field work

in El Salvador between 1988 and 1993, observing popular education and interviewing 130 participants, including popular teachers, professional teachers who supervised and assisted them, political cadre, and newly literate adults. See John L. Hammond, "Popular Education in the Midst of Guerrilla War: An Interview with Julio Portillo," *Journal of Education*, 173 (1991), 91-106; Hammond, *Learning Together: Popular Education and Guerrilla War in El Salvador* (forthcoming).

When I attribute a quote to an informant identified by given name only, that name is a pseudonym. With their permission, some informants are identified by their real given name and surname.

5.　Paulo Freire, *Pedagogy of the Oppressed* (New York: Continuum, 1970); Freire, *Education for Critical Consciousness* (New York: Continuum, 1973); Freire, *The Politics of Education: Culture, Power and Liberation* (New York: Bergin and Garvey, 1985).

6.　"Education: The great challenge of national education," *Proceso* 568 (June 23, 1993), English edition distributed by Peacenet. Other estimates of illiteracy are lower, but this one is attributed to the Salvadoran Foundation for Economic and Social Development (FUSADES), an economic research institute close to the government.

7.　Jack Spence et al., *A Negotiated Revolution? A Two Year Progress Report on the Salvadoran Peace Accords* (Cambridge: Hemisphere Initiatives, 1994), 23-30.

8.　The division of labor among the types of organizations discussed in this paper is as follows (cf. Laura Macdonald, "A Mixed Blessing: The NGO Boom in Latin America," *NACLA Report on the Americas*, 28, No. 5 [March/April, 1995], 31-32): local projects, including popular schools, are run by community-based popular organizations. Some of these organizations are united in regionwide organizations closely tied to one of the five parties which formerly made up the FMLN, like the Coordinating Committee of Communities and Repopulations of Chalatenango (CCR) described below. Local projects receive technical assistance from Salvadoran NGOs, staffed by (mostly Salvadoran) professionals; each of the major NGOs supporting the popular schools is close to one of the five parties. These NGOs receive some funds from foreign donors, including governmental, intergovernmental, and nongovernmental (mainly church-related) organizations, and channel them to the community projects. Foreign funding increased as the peace settlement approached.

9.　Marcy Fink and Robert F. Arnove, "Issues and Tensions in Popular Education in Latin America," *International Journal of Educational Development*, Fall 1991; Carlos Alberto Torres, *The Politics of Nonformal Education in Latin America* (Westport: Praeger, 1990), especially pp. 18-19.

10.　Robert F. Arnove, *Education and Revolution in Nicaragua* (New York Praeger, 1986); Robert F. Arnove, *Education as Contested Terrain: Nicaragua, 1979-1993* (Boulder: Westview Press, 1995); Deborah Barndt, "Popular Education," in *Nicaragua: The First Five Years*, ed. Thomas W. Walker (New York: Praeger, 1985), 317-46; Martin Carnoy and Joel Samoff, *Education and Social Transition in the Third World* (Princeton: Princeton University Press, 1990); Richard R. Fagen, *The Transformation of Political Culture in Cuba* (Stanford: Stanford University Press, 1969); Thomas J. La Belle, *Nonformal Education in Latin America and the Caribbean: Stability, Reform, or Revolution?* (New York: Praeger Publishers, 1986), 221-50; Valerie Miller, *Between Struggle and Hope: The Nicaraguan Literacy Campaign* (Boulder: Westview, 1985); Torres, *The Politics of Nonformal Education,* 67-108.

11. Murray Cox, "Interview: Paulo Freire," *Omni,* 12 (April, 1990), 7494; Carlos Alberto Torres, "Democratic Socialism, Social Movements and Educational Policy in Brazil: The Work of Paulo Freire as Secretary of Education in the Municipality of São Paulo," *Comparative Education Review,* 38 (May, 1994), 181-214.

12. Philip Berryman, *The Religious Roots of Rebellion: Christians in Central American Revolutions* (Maryknoll: Orbis Books, 1984); Jorge Cáceres Prendes, "Political Radicalization and Popular Pastoral Practices in El Salvador, 1969-1985," in *The Progressive Church in Latin America,* ed. Scott Mainwaring and Alexander Wilde (Notre Dame: University of Notre Dame Press, 1989), pp. 103-48.

13. Norma Stoltz Chinchilla, "Class Struggle in Central America," *Latin American Perspectives* 7, No. 2 (Spring, 1980), 2-23; Jenny Pearce, *Promised Land: Peasant Rebellion in Chalatenango, El Salvador* (London: Latin. America Bureau, 1986) 122-34.

14. Robert Armstrong and Janet Shenk, *El Salvador: The Face of Revolution* (Boston: South End Press, 1982); Tommie Sue Montgomery, *Revolution in El Salvador: Origins and Evolution* (Boulder: Westview Press, 1982).

15. The exercise of local sovereignty by a revolutionary organization is discussed under the rubric of "dual power" by Leon Trotsky in *The History of the Russian Revolution* (London: Sphere Books, 1967), 1, 203, and under that of "guerrilla governments" by Timothy P. Wickham-Crowley in "The Rise (and Sometimes Fall) of Guerrilla Governments in Latin America," *Sociological Forum* 2, No. 3 (Summer, 1987), 473-99.

16. Hammond, "Popular Education in the Midst of Guerrilla War."

17. Beth Cagan and Steve Cagan, *This Promised Land, El Salvador: The Refugee Community of Colomoncagua and their Return to Morazán* (New Brunswick Rutgers University Press, 1991), 66; John L. Hammond, "War Uprooting and the Political Mobilization of Central American Refugees," *Journal of Refugee Studies,* 6, No. 2 (1993), 110.

18. "Propuesta de Programa de Becas para Nivelación y Formación Docente de los Educadores Populares de El Salvador," unpublished proposal presented by the Concertación Educativa de El Salvador to the Ministry of Education, January 1994.

19. Interview, July 1993. Guzman conducted a study of the popular schools of Chalatenango, cited below.

20. Interview, July, 1989, quoted in Hammond, "Popular Education in the Midst of Guerrilla War," 103.

21. José Luis Guzmán et al., Las Escuelas Populares de Chalatenango: Un Aporte para el Desarrollo de la Educación en las Zonas Rurales de El Salvador.

Unpublished paper (San Salvador: Universidad Centroamericana José Simeón Cañas, 1993), 38.

22. Kirio Waldo Salgado M., "Escuelas 'populares' ... terrorismo y tráfico de armas," *El Diario de Hoy*, January 20, 1994; CEES, *Comunicado de Prensa*, February, 1994; Companion Communities Development Alternatives, "Support for Popular Education Letter Drive," May 1995; personal communications.

23. Interview, August 1993.

24. El Rescate Human Rights Department, *El Salvador Chronology* No. 15 (February 15-19, 1993); El Rescate Human Rights Department, *El Salvador Chronology*, Vol. 8, No. 44 (May 24-28, 1993); distributed by Peacenet.

25. John L. Hammond, "Popular Education in the Salvadoran Guerrilla Army," *Human Organization*, 55 (1996), 436-45.

26. Alfredo Hernandez, "Combatientes del FMLN cambian fusil por la pluma," *El Universitario*, Epoca 12, No. 146, Segunda quincena de Julio, 1993, 2.

27. Spence et al., *A Negotiated Revolution?*, 9-13; Jack Spence et al., *The Salvadoran Peace Accords and Democratization: A Three Year Progress Report and Recommendations* (Cambridge: Hemisphere Initiatives, 1995), 5-6.

28. According to Rafael Antonio González, president of the EDUCO Teachers' Association, complaining of a three-month delay in payment of salaries. Fundación Flor de Izote/El Rescate, *Cronología de El Salvador*, Vol. 8, No. 88 (Septiembre 13-17, 1993), distributed by Peacenet.

29. Sandra Vásquez de Barraza, Henry Forero, Noel McGinn, Iván Nuñez y Carlos Varas, "Administración y descentralización del sector educación," in Fernando Reimers, ed., *La educación en El Salvador de cara al siglo XXI: Desafíos y oportunidades* (San Salvador: UCA Editores, 1995), 586.

30. Jorge A. Sanguinetty, *The Economics of Basic Education in El Salvador* (Washington: USAID, 1989), 3. To be sure, the imposition of austerity programs brought similar declines even without war in many countries of Latin America during the 1980s (Daniel Morales-Gómez and Carlos Alberto Torres, "Introduction: Education and Development in Latin America," in *Education, Policy, and Social Change: Experiences from Latin America*, edited by Daniel A. Morales-Gómez and Carlos Alberto Torres [Westport: Praeger, 1992], 14).

31. Reimers, op. cit.; Comisión de Educación, Ciencia y Desarrollo, "Transformación de la Educación para la Paz y el Desarrollo de El Salvador" (Supplement to *La Prensa Gráfica*, July 7, 1995).

32. Anthony Dewees, Elizabeth Evans, Carlos King, and Ernesto Schiefelbein, "Educación básica y parvularia," in Reimers, op. cit., 225.

33. Barraza et al., 584-90; Comisión de Educación, 22; Dewees et al., 240.

34. Luis Pérez Miguel, "La Escuela Rural. Educación para la comunidad sin la comunidad," *Realidad* 40 (Julio-Agosto, 1994), 617-52.

It is revealing that a USAID-financed program for curriculum reform and school upgrading is known as SABE. The acronym, although it spells the Spanish word for "he/she knows," is an abbreviation of the program's name in English: Strengthening Achievement in Basic Education (Dewees et al., 258).

35. Dewees et al., 259-61, 276; Mario Nóchez and Luis Pérez Miguel, "Educación No Formal," in Reimers, op. cit, 465-515.

36. Juarez and Associates, Inc., "The Quality of Education in El Salvador: A Report of Focus Group Results" (Washington: USAID, 1989).

About the Editors and Contributors

Robert Arnove, Professor, School of Education, Indiana University.

Robert Austin, Lecturer, Queensland University, Australia.

Marcelo Caruso, Instituto de Ciencias de la Educación, Facultad de Filosofía y Letras, Universidad de Buenos Aires, Argentina.

José Luis Coraggio, Professor, Universidad General Sarmiento, Province of Buenos Aires, Argentina.

Inés Dussel, Instituto de Ciencias de la Educación, Facultad de Filosofía y Letras, Universidad de Buenos Aires, Argentina.

Moacir Gadotti, Professor of philosophy of education, University of São Paulo, and Director, Paulo Freire Institute.

John L. Hammond, Professor of sociology, Hunter College and the Graduate Center, City University of New York.

Sheryl L. Lutjens, Associate Professor, Political Science Department, Northern Arizona University.

Marcela Mollis, Professor of history of education and comparative education, Universidad de Buenos Aires, Argentina.

Adriana Puiggrós, Professor of history of education, Facultad de Filosófia y Letras, Universidad de Buenos Aires, Argentina.

Ernesto Schiefelbein, Director, OREALC, Santiago de Chile, Chile.

Sylvia Schmelkes, Senior Professor-Researcher, Departmento de Investigaciones Educativas, Centro de Investigación y Estudios Avanzados, Instituto Politécnico Nacional, Mexico City, Mexico.

Daniel Schugurensky, Visiting Professor, Graduate School of Education & Information Studies, University of California, Los Angeles (UCLA).

Maria Teresa Tatto, Assistant Professor, School of Education, Michigan State University.

Carlos Alberto Torres, Professor of education, Graduate School of Education & Information Studies, and Director, Latin American Center, University of California, Los Angeles (UCLA).

Eduardo Velez, Senior Education Specialist, Africa Human Development, World Bank.

About the Book

This book offers a relevant sample of the current research on Latin American education in comparative perspective. In their introduction, Torres and Puiggrós, two of the most recognized researchers of Latin American education, draw from political sociology of education, theories of the state, history of education, and deconstructionist theories to focus on changes in state formation in the region and its implications for the constitution of the pedagogical subject in public schools. Throughout the different chapters, the contributors present and analyze the most relevant topics, research agendas, and some of the key theoretical and political problems of Latin American education.

Please remember that this is a library book,
and that it belongs only temporarily to each
person who uses it. Be considerate. Do
not write in this, or any, library book.

DATE DUE

JA 3 '03			

#47-0108 Peel Off Pressure Sensitive